HISTORICAL VIEWPOINTS

HISTORICAL VIEWPOINTS

NINTH EDITION

VOLUME ONE ■ TO 1877

EDITOR

John A. Garraty

Gouverneur Morris Professor of History
Columbia University

New York San Francisco Boston
London Toronto Sydney Tokyo Singapore Madrid
Mexico City Munich Paris Cape Town Hong Kong Montreal

Vice President and Publisher: Priscilla McGeehon
Acquisitions Editor: Ashley Dodge
Executive Marketing Manager: Sue Westmoreland
Project Coordination, Text Design, and Electronic Page Makeup: Nesbitt Graphics, Inc.
Cover Designer/Manager: Wendy Ann Fredericks
Cover Illustration: © Charles C. J. Hoffbauer/Super Stock
Photo Researcher: Photosearch, Inc.
Senior Manufacturing Buyer: Dennis J. Para
Printer and Binder: Hamilton Printing Co.
Cover Printer: Lehigh Press, Inc.

For permission to use copyrighted material, grateful acknowledgment is made to the copyright holders on ppp. 311–314, which are hereby made part of this copyright page.

Library of Congress Cataloging-in-Publication Data

Historical viewpoints / editor, John A. Garraty.—9th ed.
   p.   cm.
  Includes bibliographical references.
  Contents: v. 1. To 1877—v. 2. Since 1865.
  ISBN 0-321-10299-1 (v. 1)—ISBN 0-321-10211-8 (v. 2)
    1. United States—History.   I. Garraty, John Arthur, 1920–   II. American heritage.

E178.6 .H67 2003
973—dc21   2002069479

Please visit our website at http://www.ablongman.com

ISBN 0–321–10299–1

1 2 3 4 5 6 7 8 9 10—HT—05 04 03 02

To My Students, Past, Present, and Future

CONTENTS

INTRODUCTION

Thirteen Books You Must Read to Understand America

Arthur M. Schlesinger, Jr.

Arthur M. Schlesinger, Jr. won the Pulitzer Prize for *The Age of Jackson* (1945). In addition to serving as a special consultant to President John F. Kennedy, Schlesinger has written many important works of history, including his three-volume *Age of Roosevelt* (1957–1960), *A Thousand Days: John F. Kennedy in the White House* (1965), *The Imperial Presidency* (1973), *Robert Kennedy and His Times* (1978), *Disuniting of America* (1991), and, most recently, the first volume of his memoirs (2000).

When Drake McFeely of W. W. Norton proposed an updated and enlarged edition of my book *The Disuniting of America,* he thought it might be a good idea to add an all-American reading list. What are the dozen or so books, he wondered, that everyone should know in order to have a sense of the American experience? McFeely, as the son of the Pulitzer Prize–winning biographer of Ulysses S. Grant and Frederick Douglass, has a special interest in American history; and as the son of another eminent historian, I appreciated both the value and the challenge of his invitation.

A dozen books? A hundred—or a thousand—books would not do the job. All countries are hard to understand, and despite its brief history, the United States of America is harder to understand than most, because of its size in dreams, because of its obstreperousness, and because of its heterogeneity. Still, for all this, the United States has an unmistakable national identity. Here, in chronological order, are books that have described, defined, and enriched America's sense of itself. I am dismayed at all the significant works so brief a list must leave out, but I do think that these particular choices illuminate in a major way what Ralph Ellison called "the mystery of American identity": how we Americans are at once many and one.

THE FEDERALIST (1787–88) originated as an explanation and defense of the American Constitution. It survives as a brilliant exposition of the first principles of democratic government. Written mostly by **Alexander Hamilton** and **James Madison,** the eighty-five *Federalist* papers were published between October 1787 and May 1788 in New York City newspapers, were reprinted throughout the thirteen states, and were read avidly during the debates over the ratification of the Constitution— and have been read avidly ever since. Can one imagine any newspaper today, even the august *New York Times,* running a series of such length and weight?

WRITINGS, **Thomas Jefferson** (Library of America, 1984). Jefferson embodied much of American versatility within himself. He was an architect, an educator, an inventor, a paleontologist, an oenophile, a fiddler, an astute diplomat, a crafty politician, and a luminous prophet of liberty in words that light the human way through the centuries. President John F. Kennedy once called a dinner of Nobel Prize winners the most extraordinary collection of human knowledge ever to be gathered together at the White House "with the possible exception of when Thomas Jefferson dined alone."

But Jefferson was a man of contradictions: a champion of human freedom who did not, as George Washington had done, set his slaves free at his death; a champion of the free press who favored prosecuting editors for seditious libel; a champion of the strict construction of the Constitution who bent the sacred document for the sake of the Louisiana Purchase. Other early Presidents, observed Henry Adams, our most brilliant historian, could be painted with broad brushstrokes, but Jefferson "could be painted only touch by touch, with a fine pencil, and the perfection of the likeness depended upon the shifting and uncertain flicker of its semi-transparent shadows." That invaluable publishing project the Library of America brings together in a single volume Jefferson's most notable writings, including his *Autobiography,* his major addresses, and a selection of his letters.

DEMOCRACY IN AMERICA, Alexis de Tocqueville (two volumes, 1835, 1840). The concept of "national character" has been under a cloud in scholarly circles, but can anyone really deny that Englishmen tend to be different from Frenchmen, and Germans from Italians? And can anyone read this extraordinary book about a country of thirteen million people along the Atlantic seaboard without seeing how much of the description and analysis still applies to the nation of 265 million stretching from sea to sea?

When Tocqueville, a twenty-five-year-old French nobleman, arrived in the United States in 1831, he was more interested in democracy than he was in America—or rather he was interested in America as a test case of the "great democratic revolution" that, he felt, was "universal and irresistible" and destined to transform the world. The grand question was whether this revolution would lead to "democratic tyranny." Though concerned about the "tyranny of the majority," Tocqueville believed that the power of voluntary associations and intermediate institutions had put America on the road to democratic liberty. He traveled around the country from May 1831 to February 1832 (and never came back). But in those nine months he saw more deeply into American institutions and the American character than anyone before or since. More than a century and a half later, his great work still illuminates American society.

ESSAYS AND LECTURE, Ralph Waldo Emerson (Library of America, 1983). No one has expressed the American faith in the sovereignty of the individual more brilliantly, lyrically, and sardonically than Emerson. Born in 1803, trained for the Unitarian ministry, he left the pulpit for the lecture platform, from which he expounded his transcendentalist philosophy in crackling aphorisms.

Some critics have decried what they see as Emerson's shallow optimism, but underneath his alleged disregard of the problem of evil and his allegedly guileless faith in intuition lie shrewd, skeptical, hard-edged, almost ruthless Yankee insights into human nature. "For every benefit you receive," Emerson said, "a tax is levied." It is this tough side of Emerson that appealed in the nineteenth century to Hawthorne, Carlyle, and Nietzsche and that appeals to postmodernists today. The

Ralph Waldo Emerson was largely responsible for generating the transcendentalist movement and in a broader sense for fostering romantic thought in the United States.

Library of America volume contains his masterly study of national character *English Traits,* the penetrating biographical portraits in *Representative Men,* and his essays. For the tough-minded Emerson, read "History," "Self-Reliance," "Experience," and, in *The Conduct of Life,* "Power" and "Fate."

UNCLE TOM'S CABIN, Harriet Beecher Stowe (1852). She was forty years old, the wife of a professor of biblical literature, the mother of seven children, when her indignation over the forced return of slaves to bondage under the Fugitive Slave Act led her to write the most influential novel in American history. The book sold three hundred thousand copies in its first year—equivalent to a sale of three million copies in the 1990s. "So this is the little lady who made this big war," Lincoln is supposed to have said to her.

Uncle Tom's Cabin is remembered for its vivid depiction of the horrors of slavery—and often misremembered, because so many images derive from the stage versions rather than from the novel itself. *Uncle Tom's Cabin* is far more than the sentimental melodrama of "the Tom shows." It is a wonderfully shrewd and nuanced panorama of American life in the decade before the Civil War, rich in its variety of characters, settings, and perceptions. Mrs. Stowe may not in every respect meet contemporary standards of political correctness, but she was radical for her time in her insights and sympathies—one of the first, for example, to use the term *human rights.* Frederick Douglass called *Uncle Tom's Cabin* a book "plainly marked by the finger of God."

SPEECHES AND WRITINGS, **Abraham Lincoln** (two volumes, Library of America, 1989). The most miraculous of Presidents, he was the best writer and the most intense moralist, with the most disciplined intelligence and the greatest strength of purpose, and yet he sprang out of the bleakest and most unpromising of circumstances. Confronting the supreme test and tragedy of American nationhood, he saw the crisis in perspective—"with malice toward none, with charity for all"—but never let perspective sever the nerve of action.

His Gettysburg Address amended the work of the Founding Fathers by leaving no doubt that the United States was a single nation based on the proposition that all men are created equal. And his Second Inaugural affirmed human limitations by declaring that "the Almighty has His own purposes"—purposes that erring mortals could never ascertain. "Men are not flattered," he later wrote, "by being shown that there has been a difference of purpose between the Almighty and them. To deny it, however . . . is to deny that there is a God governing the world."

ADVENTURES OF HUCKLEBERRY FINN, **Mark Twain** (Samuel Langhorne Clemens) (1884). What piece of imaginative writing best expresses the spirit of America? A strong case can be made for Herman Melville's *Moby-Dick,* for Walt Whitman's *Leaves of Grass,* for Nathaniel Hawthorne's *The Scarlet Letter.* But in the end one is compelled to go for *Huck Finn.*

This is because of the mordant way Mark Twain depicts antebellum America and the corruptions encouraged by a system in which people owned other people as private property—the hypocrisy, the sanctimoniousness, the humbuggery, the murderous feuds, the lynch mobs, the overhanging climate of brutality and violence.

It is also because of the language; *Huck Finn* is the first purely American novel. In it Mark Twain shows how the colloquial idiom spoken by an uneducated boy can express the most subtle perceptions and exquisite appreciations. The book liberated American writers. "All modern American literature," Ernest Hemingway wrote in *The Green Hills of Africa,* "comes from one book by Mark Twain called *Huckleberry Finn.* . . . All American writing comes from that. There was nothing before. There has been nothing so good since."

And it is because the novel's climactic scene so wonderfully dramatizes the essential American struggle of the individual against absolutes. Huck, responding for a moment to conventional morality, decides that the "plain hand of Providence" requires him to tell Miss Watson where she can locate Jim, her runaway slave and Huck's companion on the Mississippi raft. Huck feels suddenly virtuous, "all washed clean of sin for the first time I had ever felt so in my life." He reflects on his narrow escape: "How near I come to being lost and going to hell."

Then Huck begins to remember Jim and the rush of the great river and the singing and the laughing and the comradeship. He takes up the letter to Miss Watson, the letter of betrayal, and holds it in his hand. "I was a-trembling because I'd got to decide, forever, betwixt two things, and I knowed it. I studied a minute, sort of holding my breath, and then says to myself; 'All right, then, I'll go to hell,'—and tore it up."

That, it may be said, is what America is all about. No wonder William Dean Howells called Mark Twain "the Lincoln of our literature."

THE AMERICAN COMMONWEALTH, **James Bryce** (two volumes, 1888). Bryce, a Scotsman born in Belfast in 1838, was one of those Victorian figures of fantastic energy, curiosity, versatility, and fluency, an expert in law, politics, diplomacy, history, literature, and mountaineering. He made his first visit to America in 1870 and, unlike Tocqueville, often came back, serving from 1907 to 1913 as British ambassador in Washington.

Bryce's mind was less probing and philosophical than Tocqueville's. His passion for facts has had the ironic effect of making *The American Commonwealth* more dated than *Democracy in America,* since facts in America change all the time. But Bryce was a canny observer of institutions, and his observations have great value for historians. He spent much more time than Tocqueville on the party system and on state and local government. His chapters on "Why Great Men Are Not Chosen President" and "Why the Best Men Do Not Go Into Politics" strike chords today. His analysis of the role of public opinion, "the great central point of the whole American polity," opened a new field of investigation. His aphorisms still reverberate: The Constitution "is the work of men who believed in original sin, and were resolved to leave open for transgressors no door which they could possibly shut." "The student of institutions, as well as the lawyer, is apt to overrate the effect of mechanical contrivances in politics." And, above all, "Perhaps no form of government needs great leaders so much as democracy."

WRITINGS, **William James** (two volumes, Library of America, 1987, 1992). The most American of philosophers, a wonderfully relaxed, humane, and engaging writer (his brother, Henry, people used to say, wrote novels like a psychologist, while William wrote psychology like a novelist), he moved on from psychology to philosophy. James's pragmatism, with its argument that the meaning of ideas lies in their practical consequences, could not have been more in the American vein.

So, too, was his argument for pluralism and an open universe against those who contend for a monist system and a closed universe. People, James wrote, can discover partial and limited truths, truths that work for them, but no one can discover absolute truths. He rejected the notion that the world can be understood from a single point of view, as he rejected the assumption that all virtuous principles are in the end reconcilable and "the great single-word answers to the world's riddle" and "the pretense of finality in truth." He had an exhilarating faith in the adventure of an unfinished universe.

THE EDUCATION OF HENRY ADAMS, **Henry Adams** (1918). Where William James saw the future as a great adventure, his friend and contemporary Henry Adams looked on it with foreboding. Oppressed by the exponential rate of scientific and technological change, Adams doubted that the human mind could keep abreast of the relentless transformations wrought by the increasing velocity of history.

The challenge, as Adams saw it, was to control the new energies created and unleashed by science and technology. This required education, and looking back at his own education, Adams believed that "in essentials like religion, ethics, philosophy; in history, literature, art; in the concepts of all science, except perhaps mathematics, the American boy of 1854 [when he went to Harvard, at the age of sixteen] stood nearer the year 1 than to the year 1900. The education he had received bore little relation to the education he needed."

The *Education* describes Adams's attempts to grapple with the emerging era. Along the way he distributes fascinating portraits of politicians and writers, fascinating accounts of historical episodes, fascinating reflections on the changing world. "The new Americans," he said, "must, whether they were fit or unfit, create a world of their own, a science, a society, a philosophy, a universe, where they had not yet created a road or even learned to dig their own iron." Could the new Americans rise to the challenge?

"Man has mounted science and is now run away with," he had written in 1862, when the *Monitor* and the *Merrimack* were foreshadowing new technologies in the instrumentation of war. "I firmly believe that before many centuries more, science will be the master of man. The engines he will have invented will be beyond his strength to control. Some day science shall have the existence of mankind in its power, and the human race shall commit suicide by blowing up the world."

THE AMERICAN LANGUAGE, H. L. Mencken (1936; supplements 1945, 1948). Mencken, of course (but why do I write "of course"? He is very likely a forgotten man today), was one of the literary heroes of the 1920s. He was a master of exuberant irreverence, and he presented a satirical take on America with swashbuckling vigor of style and a liberating polemical tone. But in the 1930s Mencken fell out of sync with the national mood. The great cultural heretic of the twenties, he was a libertarian, not a democrat, and suddenly confronted by the harsh political antagonisms of the thirties, he seemed sour and mean spirited.

But to his fans he redeemed himself by *The American Language*, his shrewd, copious, quite scholarly, highly entertaining account of the way a new language evolved out of the English spoken across the sea. This rich and readable book is a wonderful compendium of Americana. It shows, among other things, that assimilation, far from an unconditional surrender to Anglocentrism, has been a two-way street in which non-Anglo newcomers play an active part in transforming the English into the American language.

AN AMERICAN DILEMMA, Gunnar Myrdal (1944). Racism has been an organic element in American life from the start. Jefferson had mixed views on the subject of race; Tocqueville had prescient comments along with mistaken prophecies; Mark Twain was haunted by the enigma of race; for Lincoln it was a central issue. But most of the time the race question has been ignored or denied. It took a Swedish economist commissioned by an American foundation to undertake the first full-dress, comprehensive study of black-white relations. Heading a team that included such black scholars as Ralph Bunche and Kenneth B. Clark, Gunnar Myrdal produced *An American Dilemma* in 1944, eighty-one years after Lincoln's Emancipation Proclamation.

This powerful work was not only an analysis: It was a challenge. Written during the war against Hitler and his theory of a master race, it called on Americans to discard their own theories of racial superiority and live up to the promises of equality

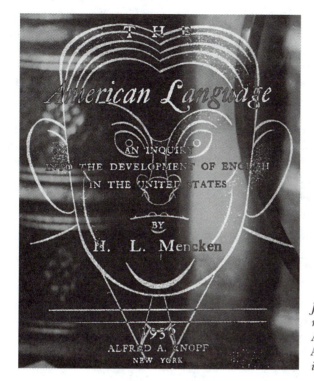

Journalist and critic H. L. Mencken made a lasting contribution to American scholarship with The American Language, *published in 1919.*

implicit in what Myrdal termed the American Creed. Myrdal was unduly optimistic in thinking that the American Creed by itself could overcome the pathologies of racism. But his work encouraged the activism of blacks, and it pricked the consciences of whites. And the account it offers of the conditions under which black Americans lived, worked, and died half a century ago provides a heartening measure of the changes that have taken place since its publication.

THE IRONY OF AMERICAN HISTORY, Reinhold Niebuhr (1952). The most influential American theologian of the century, Niebuhr approached American history from a neo-orthodox religious perspective—that is, from a tempered, nonfundamentalist belief in original sin (defined as the self-pride that mistakes the relative for the absolute), in the ambiguities of human nature, in divine judgment on human pretensions, and in the incompleteness of life within history. It is necessary, he wrote in this book, to understand "the limits of all human striving, the fragmentariness of all human wisdom, the precariousness of all historic configurations of power, and the mixture of good and evil in all human virtue."

Like William James, Niebuhr was a relativist and a pluralist who scorned monists and absolutists. Like Lincoln, he was especially critical of those whose vainglory leads them to suppose they grasp the purposes of the Almighty. By irony Niebuhr meant the situation that arises when the consequences of an action are contrary to the intentions of the actors because of weaknesses inherent in the actors themselves. This concept informed his reading of American history. Americans, Niebuhr felt, are too much inclined to believe in their own innocence and righteousness and too reluctant to recognize the self-regard in their own souls. He deplored the national inability "to comprehend the depth of evil to which individuals and communities may sink, particularly when they try to play the role of God to history."

Niebuhr's interpretation of the American past is wise and chastening, and it is deep in the American tradition. His conception of democracy is akin to that of the men who made the Constitution. "Man's capacity for justice makes democracy possible," he wrote in *The Children of Light and the Children of Darkness,* "but man's inclination to injustice makes democracy necessary."

HISTORICAL
VIEWPOINTS

1

A New World

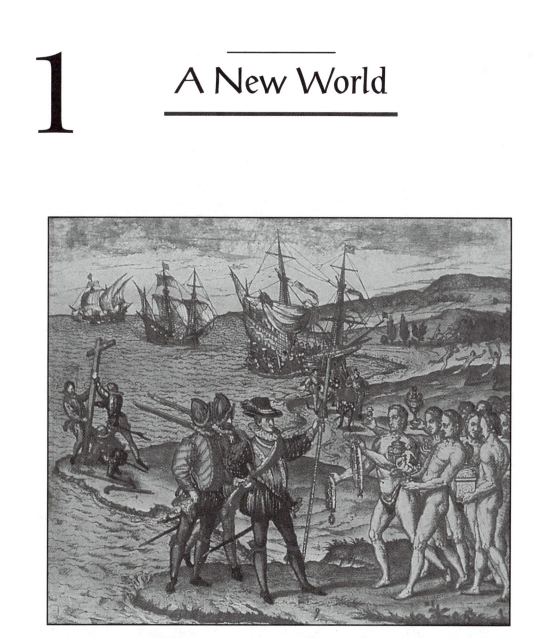

Columbus first landed on the Bahamian Island that he named San Salvador. He described the local natives as peaceful and generous, an image that changed rapidly as conquistadores swept over the native populace in their rush to tap into the riches of the Americas.

Mound Builders

Michael S. Durham

Unlike most of the articles in this collection, Michael S. Durham's "Mound Builders" is as much a voyage of discovery as it is a summary and analysis of its subject. Durham describes *how* he learned about the mysterious Indian civilization that had disappeared before Europeans settled in North America. He traces his personal journey of discovery, his gradual collection of facts, and his understanding of their meaning; the tale being as interesting as his portrait of the mound builders themselves.

Actually most conventional historians consult established authorities as well as engaging in original research, and like these historians, Durham has felt free to draw his own conclusions. He is also the author of *Ancient Native American Sites* (1994).

———————

Robert Maslowski and I made our way carefully across the tobacco field, trying not to disturb the neat rows of freshly plowed furrows. On the other side of the flat valley, a tractor moved slowly across the horizon "settin' tobacco," as they call planting seedlings in this part of West Virginia. Our destination was also far away: an oasis of greenery in the distance that was a prehistoric Indian mound.

Maslowski suddenly picked up something from a furrow and handed it to me. I could see it was a flint arrowpoint, less than two inches long, flatter on one side than the other, and unevenly shaped, but it wasn't until Bob said "Early Adena" that I realized I was holding a true prehistoric artifact in my hand, one that had been crafted by the Adena Indians hundreds of years before Christ and at least twenty centuries before Europeans set foot in this part of America.

Maslowski, an archeologist with the Army Corps of Engineers, explained that recently plowed fields were fertile grounds for finding prehistoric Indian artifacts. From time to time he would stop to pick up a fire-cracked rock, evidence of an ancient campsite, or to point out a grayish patch in the soil caused by the high ash content of prehistoric debris, probably mussel shells.

Our walk across the tobacco field came on the first day of a trip I took to the Indian mounds and other prehistoric earthworks of the upper Ohio River Valley, an area that includes sites on tributaries many miles away from the river itself. This part of the Ohio River has both heavy industry and great stretches of unspoiled scenery; it defines eastern and southern Ohio on one side and forms borders for western West Virginia and northern Kentucky on the other. An atlas published in 1814 shows how archeologically rich this region once was; dots on a map indicate large clusters of prehistoric sites, especially along rivers flowing into the Ohio, like the Muskingum, the Scioto, the Hocking, and the Great Miami. Most of these sites are gone, "plowed down," as they say, for agriculture or otherwise destroyed in the name of progress. But more survive here than in any other part of the country.

In the eighteenth and nineteenth centuries, the mounds were a source of wonder—and pride, in that they were thought to be much older than any man-made monument in Europe. Most Americans believed that they had been built by some prehistoric master race, the "ancient white aborigines of America," a people of skill and culture who came to be known as the Mound Builders. At the heart of the Mound Builder theory was the assumption that contemporary Indians lacked the intelligence, technical know-how, or energy to be Mound Builders—a theory bolstered by the fact that more modern Indians had no knowledge or collective memory of the mounds.

Ideas about where the ancient builders came from varied, ranging from Europe—Wales, Norway, Greece—to the Bible: the Lost Tribes of Israel or the sons of Shem. Ephraim Squier and Edwin Davis, authors of the important mid-nineteenth-century survey *Ancient Monuments of the Mississippi Valley,* thought the Mound Builders originally came from Mexico or Peru. Others claimed they were a superior indigenous race that had been driven south to Mexico by savage invaders.

There were dissenters from Mound Builder orthodoxy all along, enlightened souls who had no trouble believing that the mounds had been built by ancestors of modern Indians, and they grew in number as the nineteenth century wore on. Among them were Thomas Jefferson, who described excavating a mound in *Notes on the State of Virginia,* and the famous explorer John Wesley Powell, who dismissed the Mound Builder theory as a "romantic fallacy." In 1881, as the first head of the Bureau of Ethnology, Powell assigned the eminent archeologist Cyrus Thomas to survey prehistoric earthworks. Thomas and his crews excavated many mounds in the Ohio Valley, including the one toward which Maslowski and I were now heading. Thomas concluded in a 730-page report published in 1894 that there was "an unbroken chain connecting the moundbuilders and the historical Indians." Thomas's well-researched conclusions were supposed to put an end to the Mound Builder theory once and for all.

On my trip I would see more impressive mounds even close up, this one looked more like a natural feature that farmers had plowed around rather than over. And I would see more accessible ones, with parking lots and visitors' centers, paved paths, and steps to the summit. Here access was difficult, and the top could be reached only by bushwhacking up through locust trees and brambles. The view from the top was blocked by vegetation, but on the ground we could make out a rock-filled indentation in the earth that, Bob informed me, had been dug by the Cyrus Thomas expedition in 1890.

I was disappointed. I had enjoyed the walk across the field, but compared with the thrill of finding the arrowpoint, this hole in the ground that amounted to no more than a shallow pit was an anticlimax. Only later, in retrospect, did its significance come into focus. Cyrus Thomas's 1894 report was a milestone, "the birth of American archaelogy," Maslowski has written. By demolishing the myth of an ancient race of Mound Builders and determining that the mounds were constructed by American Indians, it put archeology on a scientific footing. This unimpressive hole in the ground was part of that process and therefore had a historical importance all its own. I understand that now, but at the time it was just a hole; I missed the point entirely.

"How much do you know about Woodland people?" Susan Yoho asked me. It was a question I was hoping to avoid. I knew that *Woodland* was a term that covered roughly three thousand years of human development before white men arrived in eastern America, but otherwise I had to admit that I knew very little prehistory (a curious term covering the centuries before man began writing down his story). And this despite some fancy schooling and a long association with publications in the American history field.

Yoho, who is curator of the Grave Creek Mound State Park in Moundsville, West Virginia, assured me I wasn't alone. "There is widespread ignorance about prehistoric sites," she said. "People still come here who think that the Grave Creek Mound is historic. When you tell them that it was built before the birth of Christ, they are astounded."

In historic times, after Moundsville was founded by white settlers, the local citizenry put the huge mound to a variety of uses, including building a racetrack around its base and a saloon on its pinnacle. ("After a long night of drinking that first step must have been a doozy," Yoho says.) When Yoho took over as curator in 1981, she ended the practice of draping the mound with lights at Christmas on the ground that "an Adena mound built several hundred years before the birth of Christ really had very little to do with Christmas." Yoho is not an archeologist, but, she warns, "like all amateurs, I have my own opinions."

Sixty-two feet high and two hundred and forty feet through at its base, Grave Creek Mound, built between 250 and 100 B.C., is one of the largest man-made earthworks in the world. It took people who had neither the horse nor the wheel the equivalent of three million basketloads of earth to build it. The Adena lived in this part of the country from roughly 1000 B.C. to A.D. 200; they came after the Late Archaic people and before the Hopewell (about 150 B.C. to A.D. 500), although as the dates show, there is considerable overlap between the Adena and the Hopewell cultures. The Adena lived throughout the southern half of Ohio and in adjacent parts of Indiana, Kentucky, West Virginia, and Pennsylvania. The Hopewell were concentrated in southwestern Ohio, at the hub of a trading network that extended from the Great Lakes to the Gulf of Mexico. The impact of their culture was felt throughout that vast territory.

The Adena were the region's first serious mound builders. They built them in stages, starting with a burial, sometimes in a log tomb like the one found at Grave Creek, which they then covered with earth. Then another burial and more earth, and so, depending on the number of burials, the mounds grew, sometimes to immense size.

The Hopewell had a different approach: their mounds were one-stage affairs. They first disposed of their dead in a charnel house, which, when filled with bodies, they covered with earth to construct a mound. Then they started all over again in another location. This is why Hopewell mounds are smaller than Adena mounds, the highest being barely half the size of the mound at Grave Creek.

What they lacked in size, the Hopewell mounds made up for in treasure. The burial goods found in them were far more abundant and finely crafted than the items buried with the Adena. Where an Adena mound might contain tools or simple neck ornaments called gorgets, Hopewell burials have yielded quantities of

The Great Serpent Mound, which is in the shape of a snake almost a quarter-mile long, is one of the most lasting legacies of the Adena and Hopewell cultures.

items crafted from mica or copper or gold or large numbers of precious freshwater pearls. Because they were in pristine condition when excavated, it appears that the Hopewell goods were produced solely for burials and went into the grave unused.

Both the Adena and the Hopewell mounds were for the elite only; archeology does not yet know, although it would dearly like to, where and how the common folk were laid to rest. There are many other unanswered questions. It isn't known if the Hopewell drove out the Adena or whether one culture simply melded into the other. Archeologists don't even know the bare outlines of the story: where the prehistoric people of the region came from, where they went, or what happened to them. (There were no Indians living in their region when white settlers arrived.) With the Adena and Hopewell, burial of the dead appears to have been an obsession amounting to a cult. But we don't know why they built mounds, or even what the people of those cultures called themselves. And because the Adena and Hopewell, like all of America's prehistoric peoples, had no written language, the answers to these questions may never be known.

The Grave Creek Mound was first excavated in 1838 by local amateurs, who dug two shafts, one vertical and one horizontal, into the earthwork and discovered two burial vaults, one above the other. The first excavation also produced the notorious Grave Creek Tablet, a "curious relic" that the early anthropologist Henry Rowe Schoolcraft saw "lying unprotected among broken implements of stone, pieces of antique pottery, and other like articles." The oval stone, which immediately became more famous than the mound itself, is less than two inches long and inscribed with more than twenty hieroglyphic characters.

The Grave Creek Tablet intrigued the experts and provided support for the argument that the mounds were built by a civilized race that had a written language. Schoolcraft speculated that four of the twenty-five characters were from an ancient Celtic alphabet; others saw evidence of Greek, Phoenician, and Canaanite letters.

Faith in the authenticity of the stone diminished as the century progressed, but there are still believers, Yoho told me. "Just the other day a man was in here telling me that he could prove the tablet was written in Welsh." The actual tablet is privately owned; only a replica is on display at the park's Delf Norona Museum and Cultural Centre. Yoho recognizes its worth—"historically it's one valuable little item"—and would like to obtain the original for the museum. But she is sorry that it deflects attention from the mound itself.

"You don't have to sensationalize the mound to make it interesting," she says. "The Adena and Hopewell led wonderful, peaceful, and complicated lives. To me that alone is sensational. There's no need here to look for the Loch Ness monster." . . .

Mounds are the stars of the prehistoric sites of the Ohio Valley. There are other ancient attractions—forts, quarries, a reconstructed village—but nothing with the visual impact of a mound. Some of them were in state or federal parks with trails and museums and other facilities, but they could be found almost anywhere, often in bizarre juxtaposition with the man-made environment. "They liked the same land we like," says N'omi Greber, a Hopewell expert at the Cleveland Museum of Natural History. "Land gets reused."

Most mounds that have been excavated have revealed burials—both skeletons and cremated remains—as well as tombs made of wood, graves lined with sheets of mica, and immense quantities of burial goods. These days it is also believed that mounds were used as astronomical observatories. "There is rarely just one reason for doing anything," says Robert Petersen, an archeologist at a large Hopewell complex in Chillicothe, Ohio. At Sunwatch, a prehistoric village reconstructed on its original site near Dayton, archeologists, guided by evidence found in the ground, have rebuilt a solar observatory.

Mounds located in old cemeteries—where the recently old and the really old come together—were particularly to my liking. In Marietta, Ohio, the Revolutionary War general Rufus Putnam is buried at the foot of Conus Mound, which is separated from the historic burial ground by a prehistoric moat. Putnam led the Ohio Company party that settled Marietta in 1788. These same settlers had the foresight to set aside the city's extensive prehistoric earthworks, which include the 680-foot Sacra Via, an elegant graded esplanade that leads from a large square mound, now a park, to the Muskingum River.

Although mounds were new to me, in the Ohio Valley they are part of local culture. Every town with a mound usually had a Mound Street or Mound Avenue, and of course, Moundsville, West Virginia, takes its name from the Grave Creek Mound. Police in Newark, Ohio, the site of a large Hopewell complex, have a likeness of a mound embroidered on their shoulder patches, and in Tiltonsville, a working community amid the steel mills on the upper Ohio River, the local Lions Club has taken on responsibility for maintaining the town's thirteen-foot-high Adena burial mound, which is located in one of the state's earliest cemeteries.

Not all mounds are original; a number have been rebuilt after being damaged by agriculture or commerce or even archeology. The thought that archeology could do harm surprised me when Martha Otto, curator of archeology at the Ohio Historical Society, first brought it up. "Any excavation is destructive," she said. "Any time you put a shovel in the ground, you are taking on a responsibility to observe carefully and to understand what you are looking at."

Mounds themselves, she explained, are no longer the central objects of archeological curiosity. Instead scientists are focusing on broader issues, like interaction between historic cultures, diet (corn was once considered responsible for Hopewell achievements; now "we think it is much less important"), the relationship of prehistoric peoples to the environment, and "how they changed that environment." For example, the prairies that European settlers found when they arrived were not virgin terrain; they had been enhanced by the slash-and-burn practices of the Late Woodland people (A.D. 900–1500). . . .

After several days of traveling in mound country, I started to see prehistoric earthworks everywhere. Every undulation in a cornfield, every knoll, hillock, or protuberance became evidence of an ancient culture. Most of these I passed by, but south of Newark I braked my car when I glimpsed what I was sure was a mound on a hillside. My guidebook confirmed that this time I was not imagining; this was an Adena burial mound, about fifteen feet high, situated between the Fairmount Presbyterian Church and a graveyard.

In the late-afternoon light it was a pleasant sight, the church nestled by the side of the mound; the mound, like the cemetery, neatly mowed, the graves lined in neat rows down the hillside, ancient man and modern man buried together. If it weren't for that damned light pole sticking like a periscope out of the top of the mound, the picture would have been perfect.

Brad Lepper took the small arrowpoint I had found in a tobacco field and turned it over in his hand. I was surprised when he pronounced it "Late Archaic." Maslowski had said it was early Adena, but Lepper assured me that the two periods overlapped. And I was slightly irked when he described it as "clunky." I had been carrying the artifact with me for several days, and it had become, in my eyes, an object of beauty.

Lepper was until recently the curator of the Newark Earthworks, east of Columbus, Ohio, which he calls "the largest complex of geometric earthworks in the world." Although the earthworks once covered four square miles, they are now broken up into two major sites and two smaller ones spread about the city. In their 1848 work *Ancient Monuments of the Mississippi Valley,* Squier and Davis wrote that the Newark earthworks "are so complicated that it is impossible to give anything like a comprehensible description of them." This is even more true now that the complex has been overrun by civilization. A canal, a railroad, a fairground, and a racetrack all preceded today's golf course.

The widespread damage done to the earthworks, Lepper says, misled both professionals and the public into assuming that "there is nothing left here." That is far from true, he insists. A recent cultural-resource survey turned up evidence of a pre-historic habitation site just outside the earthworks. "I am constantly surprised by back-yard finds. It proves that you can destroy a site but you can't obliterate all information."

The headquarters of the complex, which includes a museum, is located in the twenty-six acres known as the Great Circle Earthworks, enclosed by an earthen wall eight to fourteen feet high and twelve hundred feet in diameter. (An unusual moat running along the *inside* of the wall reflects "principles of military science now lost or inexplicable," a puzzled observer wrote in 1839.) Two smaller, nearby sites—the six-foot-high Owen Mound and the Wright Earthworks, a surviving section of a large enclosure—are also part of the complex.

The second major section, the 120-acre Octagon State Memorial, includes the large earthen octagon covering 50 acres that is now part of the groomed golf course of the Mound Builders Country Club, which has held a lease from the Ohio Historical Society since 1933. Some years before that it was the site of a National Guard camp whose members damaged an embankment while practicing gunnery.

I met Lepper at his cubbyhole of an office in the museum at the Mound Builders State Memorial, but we were soon trudging our way through a cornfield headed for a distant thicket of trees and the remains of a walled highway that, Lepper is convinced, the Hopewell built from Newark straight to Chillicothe some sixty miles to the southwest.

Lepper warned me not to expect too much, and he was right: the remnants of the road's walls were hardly more than brush-covered irregularities in the surface of the ground. But these irregularities were eloquent to Lepper. "This is the first evidence we have of a great road in the eastern Woodlands. Not only is it monumental in size, it's older than any other we know about."

A walled roadway from the Newark earthworks to a creek about two and a half miles away appears on early maps, like the one Squier and Davis published in 1848. In 1990 Lepper rediscovered an unpublished map from 1862 that took the road another three miles toward Chillicothe. When he first saw the map, Lepper says, "It was as if I had gotten into a time machine and been transported back to 1862." Beyond that, aerial photographs and physical evidence of the wall have convinced him of that thoroughfare's reality.

Building a straight road is not that difficult—"Three men holding sticks could do that," says Lepper—but the fact that this one appears to go straight to a destination sixty miles away is astonishing. If the road can be confirmed, it will throw new light on the Hopewell culture, says Bob Petersen, an archeologist at the Hopewell Culture National Historical Park, a burial-mound grouping in Chillicothe at the other end of the putative highway. "It will show a greater commitment of time and energy than we thought them capable of and greater engineering skills than we thought they had."

Lepper describes the Newark earthworks as "monumental architecture that we usually associate with kings and queens." But there is no evidence that the Hopewell had a nobility or that the common people were coerced to build the earthworks, so it is possible that the architecture is the result of a common goal and vision shared by the populace over a span of generations. This is a difficult concept for us to grasp today, Lepper says, "when we can't seem to sustain a national vision for more than the four or eight years of a Presidency."

"There seems to be a message here from the past. We can work together."

For nearly two centuries Chillicothe has been the pre-eminent place to go to see mounds; it has a number of its own, and it is at the geographic center of mound country. Most of the other sites I visited, even those in West Virginia, lie within a hundred miles of it.

Chillicothe also has a firm place in the history of American archeology. The names archeologists have given to two principal prehistoric cultures come from there: Hopewell from the farm of Capt. M. C. Hopewell, where three dozen mounds were found in and around a 110-acre enclosure, and Adena from the estate of the same name belonging to Thomas Worthington, Ohio's governor from 1814 to 1818. With the excavation of a large mound on Worthington's estate in 1901, the Adena and Hopewell began to emerge as clearly separate cultures.

Chillicothe was also home to the young newspaper editor Ephraim George Squier and his physician-collaborator Edwin Hamilton Davis, authors of that influential 1848 work *Ancient Monuments of the Mississippi Valley*. The team did extensive work right in their own back yard, at twenty-three Hopewell burial mounds grouped in thirteen walled acres that today form the largest concentration of mounds in the Ohio Valley. The National Park Service, owner of the site, recently renamed it the Hopewell Culture National Historical Park, but it is still usually called by its previous name, Mound City. Badly damaged when the U.S. Army put a World War I training camp there, the site was extensively rebuilt and restored after it became a national monument in 1923.

Death Mask Mound, the largest at the site, was the only mound untouched during the war. When excavated, it yielded up the remains of thirteen individuals and an unusual ceremonial headpiece—or death mask—made from fragments of human skull. A cutaway section of the Mica Grave Mound reveals the burial site of four cremations and provides a glimpse into how the mound was constructed: the burials, a layer of earth over the cremated remains, then a layer of sand covered by sheets of mica, and then more earth. And so the mound grew.

When Squier and Davis explored the site in the 1840s, they struck archeological pay dirt. A single mound, now called Mound of the Pipes, contained "Not far from two hundred pipes, carved in stone. . . . The bowls of most of the pipes are carved in miniature figures of animals, birds, reptiles, etc. All of them are executed with strict fidelity to nature and with exquisite skill." Earlier in my trip, during a stop at the Ohio Historical Society in Columbus, Martha Otto explained that it was public dismay over the loss of the pipes to the British Museum that had led to the founding of the society, then called the Ohio State Historical and Archaeological Society.

The entire thirteen-acre Mound City complex can be seen from a balcony at the visitors' center. As archeological sites go, it is not large. But as Bob Petersen told me, its twenty-three mounds, compared with the two or three found elsewhere, "clearly indicate that something special was going on here." From my vantage point on the balcony I could see what he meant. In the haze of a hot June morning the well-groomed mounds rising from the earth lay mystical and beckoning.

Before being excavated in the twenties, Seip Mound, fourteen miles southwest of Chillicothe, was—at 240 feet long, 160 feet wide, and 30 feet high—the second-largest Hopewell mound in existence. Standing on top of it, N'omi Greber pointed out the full extent of the walled enclosure, which once consisted of two connected circles and a large square. She guesses that the Hopewell built two large buildings, whose size can be determined from the size and depth of the postholes found on the site, then mounded them over with earth and added a wall around the complex. Seip is a place Greber knows well, having camped out there with students on field trips. At dusk, she says, Seip becomes "theatrical with the sun going down, the moon coming up, fireflies blinking, clouds hovering around the tops of the mountains. If you wanted a place for a ceremony, this would be it."

As at other sites, archeology has produced more questions than answers. How many people did it take to build the mound? How was it used? Where did the Hopewell people live? Who was buried in there? Where was everybody else buried?

Greber, a mathematician before she became an archeologist, admits she is not one given to speculation. (When I showed her my arrowpoint, she declined to classify it, but she did suggest that a slight curve on one edge might indicate that it was a small knife rather than part of an arrow.) Still, she is fairly sure that a mound like Seip could be built by two hundred to two hundred and fifty people—"not the thousands that people associate with the Egyptian pyramids."

"It is generally assumed that you need a strong leader to do all these things, but I don't think that is true," she continues. "I think they were very autonomous. They probably had important people, but not as the basis of the social organization. The Europeans came here and imposed the concept of chiefs on what they saw, because that is what they understood. But not all societies are like that. There are more possibilities of how people arrange themselves than we think." . . .

As I headed home, I thought about what Greber had said about how people "arranged themselves"—maybe in ways we know nothing about—and what Lepper had said about their ability to cooperate without compulsion and how this could be a "message from the past."

I had to admit that the message seemed faint, but then, to me, messages from the past often are. More to the point, I thought, was a story Susan Yoho told me about a farmer who went out daily to his fields to look for prehistoric artifacts. Every day his wife would say to him, "Honey, I don't know what you're looking for, but I hope you find it."

Well, I thought, I didn't know what I was looking for in the Ohio Valley, but I had found it aplenty. I had gotten in my mind a vivid picture of what a nineteenth-century traveler called "the great monuments and pyramids . . . of the ancient nations of N. America" and, in my pocket, an arrowpoint from a tobacco field in West Virginia that I at least found beautiful.

The Clash of Cultures: Indians, Europeans, and the Environment

William Cronon and Richard White

One of the most interesting and productive recent developments in the study of American history has been work dealing with the interrelations between people and their environment. In part, this work is a result of our current concern with pollution and the exhaustion of valuable natural resources, but it has also proved to be a valuable way of learning more about how people of past generations and different cultures dealt with nature and with one another. The following discussion between two leading American "environmental" historians makes clear how much light this approach throws on the culture of the American Indians and their relations with European colonists.

William Cronon of Yale University is the author of *Changes in the Land: Indians, Colonists and the Ecology of New England*. This book, which won the 1984 Parkman Prize, is a study of how Indians and European settlers shaped and were in turn influenced by the New England landscape. Richard White, a professor of history at the University of Utah, has published *Land Use, Environment, and Social Change* and *The Roots of Dependency*, an environmental history of three Indian tribes.

WILLIAM CRONON: If historians thought about the environment at all up until a few years ago, they thought of it in terms of an older school of American historians who are often called "environmental determinists." People like Frederick Jackson Turner argued that Europeans came to North America, settled on the frontier, and began to be changed by the environment.

RICHARD WHITE: In a delayed reaction to Turner, historians in the late 1960s and early 1970s reversed this. They began to emphasize a series of horror stories when they wrote about the environment. The standard metaphor of the time was "the rape of the earth," but what they were really describing was the way Americans moving west cut down the forests, ploughed the land, destroyed the grasslands, harnessed the rivers—how they in effect transformed the whole appearance of the North American landscape.

WILLIAM CRONON: Since then, I think, we've realized that both positions are true, but incomplete. The real problem is that human beings reshape the earth as they live upon it, but as they reshape it, the new form of the earth has an influence on the way those people can live. The two reshape each other. This is as true of Indians as it is of European settlers.

RICHARD WHITE: My first connections with Indians in the environment was very immediate. I became interested because of fishing-rights controversies in the Northwest, in which the Indians' leading opponents included several major environmental organizations. They argued that Indians were destroying the fisheries. What made this odd was that these same groups also held up Indians as sort of primal ecologists. I remember reading a Sierra Club book which claimed that Indians had moved over the face of the land and when they left you couldn't tell they'd ever been there. Actually, this idea demeans Indians. It makes them seem simply like an animal species, and thus deprives them of culture. It also demeans the environment by so simplifying it that all changes come to seem negative—as if somehow the ideal is never to have been here at all. It's a crude view of the environment, and it's a crude view of Indians.

WILLIAM CRONON: Fundamentally, it's an ahistorical view. It says not only that the land never changed—"wilderness" was always in this condition—but that the people who lived upon it had no history, and existed outside of time. They were "natural."

RICHARD WHITE: That word *natural* is the key. Many of these concepts of Indians are quite old, and they all picture Indians as people without culture. Depending on your view of human nature, there are two versions. If human beings are inherently evil in a Calvinistic sense, then you see Indians as inherently violent and cruel. They're identified with nature, but it's the nature of the howling wilderness, which is full of Indians. But if you believe in a beneficent nature, and a basically good human nature, then you see Indians as noble savages, people at one with their environment.

WILLIAM CRONON: To understand how Indians really did view and use their environment, we have to move beyond these notions of "noble savages" and "Indians as the original ecologists." We have to look instead at how they actually lived.

RICHARD WHITE: Well, take the case of fire. Fire transformed environments all over the continent. It was a basic tool used by Indians to reshape landscape, enabling them to clear forests to create grasslands for hunting and fields for planting. Hoe agriculture—as opposed to the plow agriculture of the Europeans—is another.

WILLIAM CRONON: There's also the Indians' use of "wild" animals—animals that were not domesticated, not owned in ways Europeans recognized. Virtually all North American Indians were intimately linked to the animals around them, but they had no cattle or pigs or horses.

RICHARD WHITE: What's hardest for us to understand, I think, is the Indians' different way of making sense of species and the natural world in general. I'm currently writing about the Indians of the Great Lakes region. Most of them thought of animals as a species of *persons*. Until you grasp that fact, you can't really understand the way they treated animals. This is easy to romanticize—it's easy to turn it into a "my brother the buffalo" sort of thing. But it wasn't. The Indians *killed* animals. They often overhunted animals. But when they overhunted, they did so within the context of a moral universe that both they and the animals inhabited. They conceived of animals as having, not rights—that's the wrong word—but *powers*. To kill an animal was to be involved in a social relationship with the animal. One thing that has impressed me about Indians I've known is their realization that this is a harsh planet, that they survive by the deaths of other creatures. There's no attempt to gloss over that or romanticize it.

WILLIAM CRONON: There's a kind of debt implied by killing animals.

RICHARD WHITE: Yes. You incur an obligation. And even more than the obligation is your sense that those animals have somehow surrendered themselves to you.

WILLIAM CRONON: There's a gift relationship implied. . . .

RICHARD WHITE: . . . which is also a *social* relationship. This is where it becomes almost impossible to compare Indian environmentalism and modern white environmentalism. You cannot take an American forester or an American wildlife manager and expect him to think that he has a special social relationship with the species he's working on.

WILLIAM CRONON: Or that he owes the forest some kind of gift in return for the gift of wood he's taking from it.

RICHARD WHITE: Exactly. And it seems to me hopeless to try to impose that attitude onto Western culture. We distort Indian reality when we say Indians were conservationists—that's not what conservation means. We don't give them full credit for their view, and so we falsify history.

Another thing that made Indians different from modern Euro-Americans was their commitment to producing for *security* rather than for maximum yield. Indians didn't try to maximize the production of any single commodity. Most tried to attain security by diversifying their diet, by following the seasonal cycles: they ate what was most abundant. What always confused Europeans was why Indians didn't simply concentrate on the most productive part of the cycle: agriculture, say. They could have grown more crops and neglected something else. But once you've done that, you lose a certain amount of security.

WILLIAM CRONON: I like to think of Indian communities having a whole series of ecological nets under them. When one net failed, there was always another underneath it. If the corn died, they could always hunt deer or gather wild roots. In hard times—during an extended drought, for instance—those nets became crucial.

All of this was linked to seasonal cycles. For me, one of the best ways of understanding the great diversity of environmental practices among Indian peoples is to think about the different ways they moved across the seasons of the year. Because the seasons of North America differ markedly between, say, the Eastern forests and the Great Plains and the Southwestern deserts, Indian groups devised quite different ways of life to match different natural cycles.

New England is the region I know best. For Indians there, spring started with hunting groups drawing together to plant their crops after having been relatively dispersed for the winter. While women planted beans, squash, and corn, men hunted the migrating fish and birds. They dispersed for summer hunting and gathering while the crops matured, and then reassembled in the fall. The corn was harvested and great celebrations took place. Then, once the harvest was done and the corn stored in the ground, people broke up their villages and fanned out in small bands for the fall hunt, when deer and other animals were at their fattest. The hunt went on until winter faded and the season of agriculture began again. What they had was agriculture during one part of the year, gathering going on continuously, and hunting concentrated in special seasons. That was typical not just of the Indians of New England but of eastern Indians in general.

RICHARD WHITE: For me the most dramatic example of seasonal changes among Indian peoples would be the horticulturists of the eastern Great Plains. The Pawnees are the example I know best. Depending on when you saw the Pawnees, you might not recognize them as the same people. If you came upon them in the spring or early fall, when they were planting or harvesting crops, you would have found a people living in large, semisubterranean earth lodges and surrounded by scattered fields of corn and beans and squash. They looked like horticultural people. If you encountered the Pawnees in early summer or late fall, you would have thought you were seeing Plains nomads—because then they followed the buffalo, and their whole economy revolved around the buffalo. They lived in tepees and were very similar, at least in outward appearance, to the Plains nomads who surrounded them.

For the Pawnees, these cycles of hunting and farming were intimately connected. One of my favorite examples is a conversation in the 1870s between the Pawnee Petalesharo and a Quaker Indian agent who was trying to explain to him why he should no longer hunt buffalo. Suddenly a cultural chasm opens between them, because Petalesharo is trying to explain that the corn will not grow without the buffalo hunt. Without buffalo to sacrifice at the ceremonies, corn will not come up and the Pawnee world will cease. You see them talking, but there's no communication.

WILLIAM CRONON: It's difficult for a modern American hearing this to see Petalesharo's point of view as anything other than alien and wrong. This notion of sacrificing buffalo so corn will grow is fundamental to his view of nature, even though it's utterly different from what *we* mean when we call him a conservationist.

RICHARD WHITE: And yet, if you want to understand people's actions historically, you have to take Petalesharo seriously.

WILLIAM CRONON: Environmental historians have not only been reconstructing the ways Indians used and thought about the land, they've also been analyzing how those things changed when the Europeans invaded. A key discovery of the last couple of decades has been our radically changed sense of how important European disease was in changing Indian lives.

RICHARD WHITE: It was appalling. Two worlds that had been largely isolated suddenly came into contact. The Europeans brought with them diseases the Indians had never experienced. The resulting death rates are almost impossible to imagine: 90 to 95 percent in some places.

WILLIAM CRONON: The ancestors of the Indians came to North America from ten to forty thousand years ago. They traveled through an Arctic environment in which many of the diseases common to temperate and tropical climates simply couldn't survive. They came in groups that were biologically too small to sustain those diseases. And they came without the domesticated animals with which we share several of our important illnesses. Those three circumstances meant that Indians shed many of the most common diseases of Europe and Asia. Measles, chicken pox, smallpox, and many of the venereal diseases vanished during migration. For over twenty thousand years, Indians lived without encountering these illnesses, and so lost the antibodies that would ordinarily have protected them.

RICHARD WHITE: Most historians would now agree that when the Europeans arrived, the Indian population of North America was between ten and twelve million (the old estimate was about one million). By the early twentieth century it had fallen to less than five hundred thousand. At the same time, Indian populations were also under stress from warfare. Their seasonal cycles were being broken up, and they were inadequately nourished as a result. All these things contributed to the tremendous mortality they suffered.

WILLIAM CRONON: Part of the problem was biological; part of it was cultural. If a disease arrived in mid-summer, it had quite different effects from one that arrived in the middle of the winter, when people's nutrition levels were low and they were more susceptible to disease. A disease that arrived in spring, when crops had to be planted, could disrupt the food supply for the entire year. Nutrition levels would be down for the whole subsequent year, and new diseases would find readier victims as a result.

RICHARD WHITE: The effects extended well beyond the original epidemic—a whole series of changes occurred. If Indian peoples in fact shaped the North American landscape, this enormous drop in their population changed the way the land looked. For example, as the Indians of the Southeast died in what had once been a densely populated region with a lot of farmland, cleared areas reverted to grassy woodland. Deer and other animal populations increased in response. When whites arrived, they saw the abundance of animals as somehow natural, but it was nothing of the sort.

Disease also dramatically altered relationships among Indian peoples. In the 1780s and 1790s the most powerful and prosperous peoples of the Great Plains margins were the Mandans, the Arikaras, the Hidatsas, the Pawnees, all of whom raised corn as part of their subsistence cycles. Nomadic, nonagricultural groups like the Sioux were small and poor. Smallpox changed all that. Those peoples living in large, populous farming villages were precisely those who suffered the greatest death rates. So the group that had once controlled the region went into decline, while another fairly marginal group rose to historical prominence.

WILLIAM CRONON: That's a perfect example of biological and cultural interaction, of how complex it is. A dense population is more susceptible to disease than a less dense one: that's a biological observation true of any animal species. But which Indian communities are dense and which are not, which ones are living in clustered settlements and which ones are scattered thinly on the ground—these aren't biological phenomena but *cultural* ones.

RICHARD WHITE: Perhaps the best example of this is the way different Plains Indians responded to the horse, which, along with disease, actually preceded the arrival of significant numbers of Europeans in the region. The older conception of what happened is that when the horse arrived, it transformed the world. That may have been true for the Sioux, but not for the Pawnees. The Sioux became horse nomads; the Pawnees didn't. They were not willing to give up the security of raising crops. For them, the horse provided an ability to hunt buffalo more efficiently, but they were not about to rely solely on buffalo. If the buffalo hunt failed, and they had neglected their crops, they would be in great trouble. As far as I know, there is no agricultural group, with the exception of the Crows and perhaps the Cheyennes, that *willingly* gave up agriculture to rely solely on the buffalo. The people like the Sioux who became Plains nomads had always been hunters and gatherers, and for them horses represented a *more* secure subsistence, not a less secure one.

WILLIAM CRONON: It's the ecological safety net again. People who practiced agriculture were reluctant to abandon it, because it was one of their strongest nets.

RICHARD WHITE: And they didn't. When given a choice, even under harsh circumstances, people tried to integrate the horse into their existing economy, not transform themselves.

The horse came to the Sioux at a time when they were in trouble. Their subsistence base had grown precarious: the buffalo and beavers they'd hunted farther east were declining, and the decline of the farming villages from disease meant the Sioux could no longer raid or trade with them for food. The horse was a godsend: buffalo hunting became more efficient, and the buffalo began to replace other food sources. Having adopted the horse, the Sioux moved farther out onto the Plains. By the time they had their famous conflicts with the United States in the 1860s and 1870s, they were the dominant people of the Great Plains. Their way of life was unimaginable without the horse and buffalo.

WILLIAM CRONON: The result was that the Sioux reduced the number of ecological nets that sustained their economy and way of life. And although the bison were present in enormous numbers when the Sioux began to adopt the horse, by the 1860s the bison were disappearing from the Plains; by the early eighties they were virtually gone. That meant the Sioux's main ecological net was gone, and there wasn't much left to replace it.

RICHARD WHITE: To destroy the buffalo was to destroy the Sioux. Of course, given time, they might have been able to replace the buffalo with cattle and become a pastoral people. That seems well within the realm of historical possibility. But they were never allowed that option.

WILLIAM CRONON: Disease and the horse are obviously important factors in Indian history. But there's a deeper theme underlying these things. All North American Indian peoples eventually found themselves in a relationship of dependency with the dominant Euro-American culture. At some point, in various ways, they ceased to be entirely autonomous peoples, controlling their own resources and their own political and cultural life. Is environmental history fundamental to explaining how this happened?

RICHARD WHITE: I think it's absolutely crucial. Compare the history of European settlement in North America with what happened in Asia and Africa. Colonialism in Asia and Africa was very important, but it was a passing phase. It has left a strong legacy, but Africa is nonetheless a continent inhabited by Africans, Asia a continent inhabited by Asians. American Indian peoples, on the other hand, are a small minority in North America. Part of what happened was simply the decline in population, but as we've said, that decline was not simple at all. To understand it, we have to understand environmental history.

Many Indians were never militarily conquered. They nonetheless became dependent on whites, partly because their subsistence economy was systemati-

The appearance of Europeans had a corrupting effect on tribes such as the Micmac Indians of eastern Canada. These Native Americans began killing animals not only for food but also to supply clothing for waiting markets in Europe.

cally undercut. Virtually every American Indian community eventually had to face the fact that it could no longer feed or shelter itself without outside aid. A key aspect of this was the arrival of a market economy in which certain resources came to be overexploited. The fur trade is the clearest example of this.

WILLIAM CRONON: No question. The traditional picture of the fur trade is that Europeans arrive, wave a few guns and kettles and blankets in the air, and Indians come rushing forward to trade. What do they have to trade? They have beaver pelts, deerskins, bison robes. As soon as the incentive is present, as soon as those European goods are there to be had, the Indians sweep across the continent, wipe out the furbearing animals, and destroy their own subsistence. That's the classic myth of the fur trade.

RICHARD WHITE: It simply didn't happen that way. European goods often penetrated Indian communities slowly; Indian technologies held on for a long time. Indians wanted European goods, but for reasons that could be very different from why *we* think they wanted them.

WILLIAM CRONON: One of my favorite examples is the kettle trade. Indians wanted kettles partly because you can put them on a fire and boil water and they won't break. That's nice. But many of those kettles didn't stay kettles for long.

They got cut up and turned into arrowheads that were then used in the hunt. Or they got turned into high-status jewelry. Indians valued kettles because they were such an extraordinarily flexible resource.

RICHARD WHITE: The numbers of kettles that have turned up in Indian graves proves that their value was not simply utilitarian.

WILLIAM CRONON: The basic facts of the fur trade are uncontestable. Europeans sought to acquire Indian furs, food, and land; Indians sought to acquire European textiles, alcohol, guns, and other metal goods. Indians began to hunt greater numbers of furbearing animals, until finally several species, especially the beaver, were eliminated. Those are the two end points of the fur-trade story. But understanding how to get from one to the other is very complicated. Why did Indians engage in the fur trade in the first place? That's the question.

RICHARD WHITE: We tend to assume that exchange is straightforward, that it's simply giving one thing in return for another. That is not how it appeared to Indian peoples.

WILLIAM CRONON: Think of the different ways goods are exchanged. One is how we usually perceive exchange today: we go into the local supermarket, lay down a dollar, and get a candy bar in return. Many Europeans in the fur trade thought that was what they were doing—giving a gun, or a blanket, or a kettle and receiving a number of furs in return. But for the Indians the exchange looked very different.

RICHARD WHITE: To see how Indians perceived this, consider two things we all know, but which we don't ordinarily label as "trade." One is gifts. There's no need to romanticize the giving of gifts. Contemporary Americans exchange gifts at Christmas or at weddings, and when those gifts are exchanged, as anybody who has received one knows, you incur an obligation. You often have relatives who never let you forget the gift they've given you, and what you owe in return. There's no *price* set on the exchange, it's a *gift,* but the obligation is very real. That's one way Indians saw exchange. To exchange goods that way, the two parties at least had to pretend to be friends.

At the other extreme, if friendship hadn't been established, goods could still change hands, but here the basis of exchange was often simple theft. If you had enemies, you could rob them. So if traders failed to establish some friendship, kinship, or alliance, Indians felt perfectly justified in attacking them and taking their goods. In the fur trade there was a fine line between people who sometimes traded with each other and sometimes stole from each other.

WILLIAM CRONON: To make that more concrete, when the Indian handed a beaver skin to the trader, who gave a gun in return, it wasn't simply two goods that were moving back and forth. There were *symbols* passing between them as well. The trader might not have been aware of all those symbols, but for the Indian the exchange represented a statement about their friendship. The Indian might expect to rely on the trader for military support, and to support him in return. Even promises about marriage, about linking two communities together, might be expressed as goods passed from hand to hand. It was almost as if a language was being spoken when goods were exchanged. It took a long time for the two sides to realize they weren't speaking the same language.

RICHARD WHITE: Right. But for Indians the basic meanings of exchange were clear. You gave generously to friends; you stole from enemies. Indians also recognized that not everybody could be classified simply as a friend or an enemy, and this middle ground is where trade took place.

But even in that middle ground, trade always began with an exchange of gifts. And to fail to be generous in your gifts, to push too hard on the price—Indians read that as hostility. When Europeans tried to explain the concept of a "market" to Indians, it bewildered them. The notion that demand for furs in London could affect how many blankets they would receive for a beaver skin in Canada was quite alien to them. How on earth could events taking place an ocean away have anything to do with the relationship between two people standing right here who were supposed to act as friends and brothers toward each other?

WILLIAM CRONON: So one thing Indian peoples had trouble comprehending at certain stages in this dialogue was the concept of *price:* the price of a good fluctuating because of its abundance in the market. Indian notions were much closer to the medieval "just price." This much gunpowder is always worth this many beaver skins. If somebody tells me they want twice as many skins for the same gunpowder I bought last year at half the price, suddenly they're being treacherous. They're beginning to act as an enemy.

RICHARD WHITE: Or in the words Algonquians often used, "This must mean my father doesn't love me any more." To Europeans that kind of language seems ludicrous. What in the world does love have to do with giving a beaver skin for gunpowder? But for Indians it's absolutely critical.

Of course, exchange became more commercial with time. Early in the fur trade, Indians had received European goods as gifts, because they were allies against other Indians or other Europeans. But increasingly they found that the only way to receive those goods was through direct economic exchange. Gift giving became less important, and trading goods for set prices became more important. As part of these commercial dealings, traders often advanced loans to Indians before they actually had furs to trade. By that mechanism, gifts were transformed into debts. Debts could in turn be used to coerce greater and greater hunting from Indians.

WILLIAM CRONON: As exchange became more commercial, the Indians' relationship to animals became more commercial as well. Hunting increased with the rise in trade, and animal populations declined in response. First the beaver, then the deer, then the bison disappeared from large stretches of North America. As that happened, Indians found themselves in the peculiar position of relying more and more on European goods but no longer having the furs they needed to acquire them. Worse, they could no longer even *make* those same goods as they once had, in the form of skin garments, wild meat, and so on. That's the trap they fell into.

RICHARD WHITE: And that becomes dependency. That's what Thomas Jefferson correctly and cynically realized when he argued that the best way for the United States to acquire Indian lands was to encourage trade and have government storehouses assume Indian debts. Indians would have no choice but to cede their lands to pay their debts, and they couldn't even renounce those debts because they now needed the resources the United States offered them in order to survive. Not all tribes became involved in this, but most who relied on the fur trade eventually did.

Of course, the effects go both ways. As whites eliminated Indians and Indian control, they were also, without realizing it, eliminating the forces that had shaped the landscape itself. The things they took as natural—why there were trees, why there weren't trees, the species of plants that grew there—were really the results of Indian practices. As whites changed the practices, those things vanished. Trees began to reinvade the grassland, and forests that had once been open became closed.

WILLIAM CRONON: Once the wild animals that had been part of the Indians' spiritual and ecological universe began to disappear, Europeans acquired the land and began to transform it to match their assumptions about what a "civilized" landscape should look like. With native animals disappearing, other animals could be brought in to use the same food supply that the deer, the moose, and the bison had previously used. And so the cow, the horse, the pig—the animals so central to European notions of what an animal universe looks like—began to move across the continent like a kind of animal frontier. In many instances the Indians turned to these domesticated European species to replace their own decreasing food supply and so adopted a more pastoral way of life. As they lost their lands, they were then stuck with the problem of feeding their animals as well as themselves.

RICHARD WHITE: The Navajos are a good example of this. We tend to forget that Indians don't simply vanish when we enter the twentieth century. The Navajos are perhaps the group who maintained control over their own lands for the longest time, but their control was increasingly subject to outside pressures. They very early adopted European sheep, which became more and more important to their economy, both because wild foods were eliminated and because the government strongly encouraged the Navajos to raise more sheep. They built up prosperous herds but were gradually forced to confine them to the reservation instead of the wider regions they had grazed before.

The result was a crisis on the Navajo reservation. The land began to erode. By the 1920s and 1930s the Navajos had far more sheep than could be sustained during dry years. And here's where one of the more interesting confrontations between Indians and conservationists took place. The government sought to reduce Navajo stock, but its own motives were mixed. There was a genuine fear for the Navajos, but the main concern had to do with Boulder Dam. Conservationists feared Lake Mead was going to silt up, and that the economic development of the Southwest would be badly inhibited.

What they didn't understand were the causes of erosion. They blamed it all on Navajo sheep, but it now appears that there was a natural gullying cycle going on in the Southwest. Anybody familiar with the Southwest knows that its terrain is shaped by more than sheep and horses, no matter how badly it is overgrazed. So the result of government conservation policy for the Navajos was deeply ironic. Having adjusted to the European presence, having prospered with their sheep, they found their herds being undercut by the government for the good of the larger economy. It's a classic case of Indians—as the poorest and least powerful people in a region—forced to bear the brunt of economic-development costs. So the Navajo economy was again transformed. As the Navajos became poorer and poorer, they grew more willing to lease out oil and allow strip mining on the reservation. They found themselves in the familiar situation of being forced to agree to practices that were harmful, even in their view, to the land. They had to do it in order to survive, but they were then attacked by white conservationists for abandoning their own values.

WILLIAM CRONON: A real no-win situation.

RICHARD WHITE: There are lessons in all this. We can't copy Indian ways of understanding nature, we're too different. But studying them throws our own assumptions into starker relief and suggests shortcomings in our relationships with nature that could cost us dearly in the long run.

WILLIAM CRONON: I think environmental history may be capable of transforming our perspective, not just on Indian history, but on all human history. The great arrogance of Western civilization in the industrial and postindustrial eras has been to imagine human beings existing somehow apart from the earth. Often the history of the industrial era has been written as if technology has liberated human beings so that the earth has become increasingly irrelevant to modern civilization—when in fact all history is a long-standing dialogue between human beings and the earth. It's as if people are constantly speaking to the earth, and the earth is speaking to them. That's a way of putting it that Indians would be far more capable of understanding than most modern Americans. But this dialogue, this conversation between earth and the inhabitants of earth, is fundamental to environmental history. With it we can try to draw together all these pieces—human population changes, cultural changes, economic changes, environmental changes—into a complicated but unified history of humanity upon the earth. That, in rather ambitious terms, is what environmental historians are seeking to do.

2 Colonial Life

Fox hunting was a passion that colonial gentry gladly indulged. This rendering of a hunting party is a detail from an overmantel painting of the late seventeenth century.

Spain in North America

Henry Wieneck

As Henry Wieneck points out in this essay, the history of the United States is too often examined from the perspective of the English settlers of seventeenth-century Virginia and New England. True, some recognition is usually given to the adventures of Columbus and the Spanish explorers who followed in his wake, but "our" history is usually said to have begun at Jamestown and Plymouth and marched steadily westward to the Pacific.

This view distorts what actually happened and obscures the tremendous importance of Spain and Spanish culture in the development of the nation. Long before the founding of Jamestown, there were Spaniards not only in Florida, California, and New Mexico, but also in what is now Georgia, Tennessee, and Virginia. Where these colonists lived, what they did there, and their ultimate contribution to American development is explained here by Wieneck, editor of the *Smithsonian Guide to Historic America*.

In 1833 Walt Whitman received an invitation to visit Santa Fe and deliver a poem at a celebration of the city's founding. The ailing sixty-four-year-old poet wrote back from his home in Camden, New Jersey, that he couldn't make the trip or write a poem for the occasion, but he sent along some remarks "off hand": "We Americans have yet to really learn our own antecedents, and sort them, to unify them. They will be found ampler than has been supposed, and in widely different sources. Thus far, impress'd by New England writers and schoolmasters, we tacitly abandon ourselves to the notion that our United States have been fashion'd from the British Islands only and essentially form a second England only—which is a very great mistake."

Whitman was concerned less with rearranging a view of the past than with creating a vision of the future. Although the United States was enjoying immense prosperity, the poet said that the country did not possess "a society worthy the name." The national character was yet to be established, he thought, but he knew that it would be a "composite" and that "Spanish character would supply some of its parts." "No stock shows a grander historic retrospect—grander in religiousness and loyalty or for patriotism, courage, decorum, gravity, and honor. . . . As to the Spanish stock of our Southwest it is certain to me that we do not begin to appreciate [its] splendor and sterling value. Who knows but that element, like the course of some subterranean river, dipping invisibly for a hundred or two years, is now to emerge in broadest flow and permanent action?"

But in fact, the Spanish achievement was far from subterranean. It merely seemed so from the Northeast. A great part of the West, from Texas to California, was profuse with the landmarks of Spanish achievement—towns and villages, ranches and churches, places where the Spanish language and culture were defining. The town where he was asked to speak, Santa Fe, was then and is now the oldest political capital in the United States, having been founded in 1609. And the city where Whitman had lived for many years, New York, had been home to a community of Sephardic Jews as early as 1654. Yet Whitman was correct in saying that the Spanish role in America's past was not fully appreciated and that the Spanish role in America's future would be critical. These points were raised more forcefully a decade ago when the Americas marked the five hundredth anniversary of their discovery by Columbus, on behalf of Spain.

What exactly is the Spanish legacy? What is the Spanish imprint on the United States? For most Americans the word *Spanish* immediately summons up the word *mission* and an image of whitewashed walls and ornate towers gleaming in the California sun. The missions are indeed the best-known Spanish legacy. In their time they influenced the spiritual and cultural life of millions, and they exert a broad influence on American architecture to this day. The oldest surviving documents written in the United States by Europeans are Spanish—parish registers from St. Augustine, Florida, which is the oldest surviving European settlement in the country. Millions of Americans live in places founded by the Spaniards, places such as San Antonio, El Paso, Santa Fe, San Diego, Los Angeles (actually founded by a party of blacks and Indians under Spanish auspices), and San Francisco. Many of these cities and towns continue to be largely Hispanic in population, culture, and language. The West was explored and settled by Spaniards. Ranching, which is regarded as a peculiarly American way of life, was invented by the Spaniards, and without the efforts of a man named Bernardo de Gálvez we might have lost the Revolutionary War.

But the Spanish legacy runs far deeper and influences us more today than a list of buildings and place names and heroes would suggest. We are still on a path that the Spaniards began to blaze five hundred years ago. They were the first pupils of the New World, the first to learn the lesson that these continents are the land of dreams. In their books we read the first descriptions of the sequoia, of hailstones that dent helmets, and the inextinguishable hope that the place of utter happiness is just over the horizon. The words *más allá* (farther on) appear like an incantation in their chronicles. *Not here? Very well. ¡Más allá!*

From the twentieth-century perspective the wanderings of the first Spanish explorers have a comical element—who would look for gold in Kansas? In some books you will find Francisco Vásquez de Coronado written down as a fool for doing exactly that (one prominent writer speaks of the "Coronado fiasco"). Then why, we might ask, have scores, even hundreds, of modern Americans, professionals and amateurs, expended fortunes in time, money, laborious study, and physical effort in trying to trace the exact path of this fool and find the merest scrap of material evidence of him? The answer is that we have learned, in large part from the efforts of the Spaniards, that the very act of seeking lies at the heart of the American character. We look for Coronado's path because he was a great, original American seeker. He went in search of wealth and found something better instead; he found the American West. Wallace Stegner writes, "America was discovered by accident and explored to a considerable extent by people trying to find a way to somewhere else": to India; to a Northwest Passage; to the land of El Dorado; to the fabled land of Queen Califía, for whom the Spaniards named California; or to the Seven Cities of Cíbola—Coronado's personal dream. With some three hundred men he searched through Arizona, New Mexico, Texas, Oklahoma, and into Kansas.

Do we still laugh that Coronado found Kansas instead of gold? In one of our own modern myths, Dorothy returns, transformed, to that very place, unburdened by the emeralds of Oz, but having learned about courage, love, and wisdom. The Spaniards were the first to learn about the transforming power of the New World, that this is a place of mirage and miracle and that the two are forever getting mixed up; that the land that refuses to yield up silver or gold dispenses, *más allá*, a Grand Canyon, maize, buffalo, and an Eden in the Rio Grande Valley—and, in time, the richest nation in history.

The Grand Canyon was discovered when Coronado sent a detachment under García López de Cárdenas to find the passes to the South Sea (the Pacific) that the Indians had told of. López went off, did not find the South Sea, but did find himself at the edge of a precipice the likes of which he had never seen before. He sent men down to the river at the bottom. It did not seem that far, judging by some rocks below that appeared to be a man's height. The scouts came back in a few hours; too far to the river—those rocks are higher than the tallest tower in Seville!

In Texas the chronicler Pedro de Castañeda found himself in the field of dreams; the earth there was so flat it seemed round "in the shape of a ball"; it was like standing at the top of the world: "wherever a man stands . . . he is surrounded by the sky at the distance of a crossbow shot." Farther on they found America's inland sea, the ocean of grass. Walking across it was like sailing in a boat with no rudder. It could swallow an army. In amazement Castañeda watched the grass spring up again after the column had passed. "Who could believe," he marveled, ". . . they left no more traces when they got through than if no one had passed over?" One man strolled into the grass and was never seen again; the search party itself was lost for days.

At home in Mexico Castañeda pondered the worth of the enterprise: "For although they did not obtain the riches of which they had been told, they found the means to discover them and the beginning of a good land to settle in and from which to proceed onward." *¡Más allá!*

Charles F. Lummis, the great collector and savior of Southwestern art and architecture, called the Spanish the "world-finders." A tremendous outpouring of Spanish exploration culminated in 1542, the year Coronado's expedition ended. Hernando de Soto's party was on its way to Mexico, having landed in Florida in 1539 and explored Georgia, the Carolinas, Tennessee, and Alabama, crossed the Mississippi (the first Europeans to do so), and pressed up the Arkansas River into Oklahoma. At sea Juan Rodríguez Cabrillo sailed from Mexico along the Baja Californian coast and discovered San Diego Bay and the Channel Islands. After Cabrillo's death his second-in-command continued up the Pacific coast to make the first European sighting of Oregon. Ruy López de Villalobos sailed across the Pacific to a group of islands he named the Philippines. Francisco de Orellana, having ascended and descended the Andes to reach the headwaters of the Amazon, emerged at the mouth of that river after two years.

It is interesting to compare this record with that of English wanderlust. Nearly two centuries later William Byrd, upon his return from a surveying trip along the Virginia-Carolina border, wrote that "our country has now been inhabited more than 130 years by the English, and still we hardly knew anything of the Appalachian Mountains, that are no where above 250 miles from the sea."

The period from Columbus's first landfall in 1492 to 1607, when the English made their settlement at Jamestown, has traditionally been a blank spot in American history books. Some texts state quite plainly that the history of the United States begins in 1607, making only the most cursory mention of the sixteenth century—the century when, in the words of the historian Bernard Bailyn, Spain created "the largest and most populous empire the western world had seen since the fall of Rome." The historian Howard Mumford Jones also compared Spain's sixteenth-century achievements to those of antiquity: "The Spaniards invented a system of colonial administration unparalleled since the days of ancient Rome; in religion they launched the most sweeping missionary movement since the Germanic tribes accepted Christianity. . . . As for culture, the Spaniards transplanted dynamic forms of Renaissance art, thought, and institutions to the Americas with amazing quickness." The Spanish established a college for the sons of Indian chiefs in Mexico in 1536, a university in Santo Domingo in 1538, the University of Mexico in 1553. Spaniards set up the first printing press in the New World in 1539, and, as Jones observed, "When in 1585 a forlorn little band of Englishmen were trying to stick it out on Roanoke Island, three hundred poets were competing for a prize in Mexico City."

The earliest naturalist of the New World was probably Gonzalo Fernández de Oviedo y Valdés, who first visited the Americas in 1514 and published a multivolume general and natural history between 1535 and 1557. Two centuries later Capt. Alejandro Malaspina led one of the most important West Coast explorations. In the early 1790s Malaspina's ships made their first landfall in Mulgrave Sound in Alaska, where Malaspina and his staff studied a glacier that was later named for the captain, traded with the Tlingits for artifacts (the Spaniards carefully noted the Tlingit names for the objects they collected), and carried out experiments with a pendulum, seeking to measure the intensity of gravity at that latitude as a way of computing the exact size of the earth. Heading south, a member of the expedition became the first botanist to discover and describe the sequoia. The paintings of birds and landscapes made on this visit are today the oldest surviving works of art made in California.

In California Malaspina received valuable assistance from Father Fermín Francisco de Lasuén, the founder of nine missions, who provided native guides to take the scientists into the field. The first European settlement in California had been established in 1769 at San Diego by Gaspar de Portolá, who blazed El Camino Real, today's Highway 101; discovered the La Brea tar pits (the Indians had long used their pitch to caulk their boats); and experienced an earthquake that knocked his men from their feet. With Portolá came Father Junípero Serra, who founded nine missions. Fathers Serra, Lasuén, and their successors established a total of twenty-one missions and baptized about 88,000 Indians in the course of nearly seven decades of evangelical work. The two great mission founders are buried at the jewel

Aerial view of the Castillo de San Marcos in St. Augustine, Florida's dominant colonial land-mark. Built in 1672, it is the oldest fort in the United States.

of the California missions, San Carlos Borromeo del Río Carmelo, in Carmel. The high architectural aspirations of the Franciscans there were carried out by Indian workers inexperienced at making such things as a Moorish dome. The result, with its irregular walls and heartfelt but misshapen dome, is a handmade frontier masterpiece of poignant beauty. When it was crumbling in the 1870s, Robert Louis Stevenson helped raise funds for a restoration with an angry article, saying, "The United States Mint can coin many millions more dollar pieces, but . . . when the Carmel church is in the dust, not all the wealth of the states and territories can replace what has been lost."

The greatest Spanish landmark on the East Coast is at St. Augustine, Florida: the Castillo de San Marcos. This fortress is the oldest in the United States, begun in 1672. But even before that, nine previous Spanish fortresses, made of wood, had stood on the site; the first one was put up more than half a century before the Pilgrims landed. But the fortress is only the most visible evidence of Florida's Spanish heritage. It is not widely known that Florida was once the site of a flourishing system of missions comparable to those in the Southwest and California. In the mid-1600s 70 Franciscans were ministering to 25,000 Indians at 38 missions in the Southeast.

Florida has been a part of the United States only since 1821; it was Spanish for three centuries. It is one of those parts of the country that were fought and argued over, quite bloodily, by Americans, Spanish, French, and English. . . .

Más allá. When the Mexican writer Carlos Fuentes received the Cervantes Prize for Literature in 1987, he gave an address saying, "The quixotic adventure has not yet ended in the New World." He spoke about the "debate with others, debate with ourselves" over the meaning of the five-hundredth anniversary "of a disquieting date—1492" and asked: "Who is the author of the New World? Columbus, who first set foot on it, or Vespucio, who first named it? The gods who fled or the gods who arrived? . . . What does America mean? To whom does this name belong? What does New World mean? . . . How does one baptize the river, mountain, jungle, seen for the first time? And, most importantly, what name do you give to the anonymous vast humanity—Indian and Creole, mestizo and Black—of the multiracial culture of the Americas? . . . Who is the author of the New World? All of us are, all of us who incessantly imagine it because we know that without our imagination, America, the generic name of new worlds, would cease to exist."

about fourteen thousand pounds, which he paid for in wampum and in bartered goods. They also bought thousands of skins of otter, muskrat, mink, fox, raccoon, wildcat, and moose. These skins were packed in hogsheads and carted down the river to his warehouse just below the rapids, in what is now Windsor Locks, where they were transferred to coastal vessels for shipment to Boston and thence by packet to London. There they were sold, partly for cash and partly in exchange for bright-colored cloth and coats, knives, awls, axes, and trinkets for their trading posts.

For years William Pynchon paid over half the taxes of Springfield and ruled his growing settlement with the aid of a "cabinet" consisting of his son and two sons-in-law. Eventually he had the temerity to write a theological treatise that was denounced by the clergy and publicly burned in Boston, whereupon he returned in 1652 to England, leaving his wilderness empire to his son, twenty-six-year-old John.

John Pynchon continued and extended the fur monopoly, establishing additional posts in the Connecticut and Housatonic valleys and building up extensive interests in the West Indies, where he traded with his own fleet of ships. In addition to his trading enterprises, he was an early and successful real estate operator. As settlers pushed into the fertile valley, he would buy tracts of land from the Indian sachems who were supplying him with furs, giving them credit at his trading posts to the extent of the price agreed upon, and sell the land to the colonists at the same price, having made his profit on the goods which the Indians took in payment. . . .

John Pynchon's account books were kept in fathoms and hands of wampum. (Fathoms he wrote *fadams*.) He computed ten hands of wampum as equal to a fathom of six feet, making his hands a little over seven inches instead of the usual four. The white wampum he valued at five shillings (in 1660) a fathom. At his death in 1702 he was worth about five thousand pounds, a vast estate for that place and time.

Amicable though the relations were between Indians and whites in the Connecticut Valley during the first quarter-century, the abyss that separated the two civilizations was too wide to be permanently bridged. In 1675 years of peace were shattered by King Philip's War when Indian treacheries and torturings led to reprisals. Perhaps the most chilling example is a terse note scribbled on the margin of a letter in which the captain of a troop of soldiers in Springfield forwarded to the governor in Boston information that had been extorted from a captured squaw. The note reads, "This aforesaid Indian was ordered to be tourne to peeces by dogs, and she was so dealt with."

From the beginning the Great and General Court set bounties on wolves, wildcats, and other predators. During the long terror of the French and Indian Wars in the first half of the eighteenth century, the largest bounty of all was set on Indians. Ten pounds was paid for each Indian scalp taken by a soldier or one hundred pounds if taken by a volunteer; later the amount was raised to forty pounds to soldiers and three hundred to volunteers for Indian braves and twenty pounds for squaws or children under twelve. Men of the Connecticut Valley ventured into the wilderness on scalping parties, and [Sylvester] Judd reports that the accounts of the treasurer for Hampshire County during 1757 and 1758 show that he paid bounties of fifteen hundred pounds for five scalps.

In order that money might not be wasted on nonessentials, the General Court passed a law in 1651 forbidding persons whose estate did not exceed two hundred pounds, and those dependent on them, to wear gold or silver lace, gold or silver buttons, bone lace above two shillings a yard, or silk scarves or hoods, under penalty of ten shillings for each offense. The first attempt to enforce this law in Hampshire County (Massachusetts) was made in 1673 when twenty-five wives and five maids were haled into court as "persons of small estate who used to wear silk contrary to law." Of the thirty only three were fined.

In 1676 there was a roundup of the younger set with thirty-eight wives and maids and thirty young men brought into court—the men, "some for wearing silk, and that in a flaunting manner, and others for long hair and other extravagancies." Only two of the sixty-eight were fined, which seems to have had a discouraging effect upon the officers of the law, as six years later, in a curious reversal, the officials of five towns were brought to court for *not* arresting such inhabitants of their towns as wore unsuitable and excessive apparel. The battle was over and the younger set had won, but for many years their elders continued to wag their heads over the degeneracy of the age.

Flaunters were bad enough, but witches were even more troublesome. The first was Mary Parsons of Springfield, who was indicted in 1651 for having been seduced by the Devil; for having used "divers" hellish practices on the persons of two children of the Springfield minister; and for having murdered her own child. At her trial in Boston (local courts could not try capital offenses) she pleaded not guilty to witchcraft and was acquitted but she was found guilty of murder and was condemned to death. Her husband, Hugh, was also indicted for witchcraft, largely on the word of his wife, who testified that "sometymes he hath puld of the Bed Clothes and left me naked abed. . . . Sometimes he hath thrown pease about the Howse and made me pick them up. . . . Oftentymes in his sleep he makes a gablings Noyse." Hugh was found guilty by the jury, but the verdict was overruled by the magistrates.

In 1674 another Mary Parsons, this one of Northampton, was accused of familiarity with the Devil and of having caused the death of Mary Bartlett. The accused was a respectable woman and the wife of one of Northampton's richest citizens, but according to Judd, she was proud and high-spirited to a point that had excited the ill will of her neighbors. At the preliminary hearing she vehemently asserted her innocence, whereupon the magistrate appointed a "jury of soberized, chaste women to make a diligent search upon the body of Mary Parsons, whether any marks of witchcraft might appear." Suspicious marks were discovered, and she was sent to Boston for trial but there found innocent and discharged. . . .

When the white men came to the valley, it was not, as supposed, covered with dense forests. The Indian custom of burning over the land each year to destroy the undergrowth and facilitate hunting had made it like a park where a deer could be seen at forty rods. Pine gradually took the place of oak for building, but all pine trees of two feet or more in diameter were reserved for the king's navy, a law that produced more discontent than logs. In Northampton, Massachusetts, for example, of 363 logs marked for the king, all but 37 were poached for private use.

During the seventeenth century wheat was the staple crop. Corn, peas, and oats, rye for bread, barley for malt, and flax for cloth were also raised. Horses, cattle, and sheep were pastured in the forest, and hogs and young stock ran wild. To help in sorting them out, each town was required by law to have its own brand mark. Cattle and horses were driven to pasture before the sun was an hour high by the town herdsmen and brought back "seasonably" at night. Sheep were watched by the town shepherd and "folded" at night in hurdles, or movable pens. Geese often wore a shingle with a hole bored in it about their necks to keep them from straying. They splashed and honked in the puddles of the common and slept at night before their owners' houses, being much esteemed as watchdogs. Four times a year the women of the village plucked them for feather beds, first pulling stockings over the heads of the geese to keep them from biting. Many families kept skeps (hives) of bees, and the only way they knew to get the honey was to kill the bees with brimstone.

In the seventeenth century horses were cheaply raised, little tended, and sold for as low as thirty shillings in barter or twenty in money. Fourteen hands was set by law as the proper height for a horse. They were used only under the saddle and could be hired for a penny and a half a mile or twopence if the horse carried double.

By 1655 cattle were being driven to Boston for market and sold for a penny a pound. When a farmer slaughtered, he "lent" his neighbors what meat he could not use before it spoiled and expected an equal return when they slaughtered. By 1700 milch cows were plentiful, and the tinkling of their bells as they browsed along the roads made a pleasant background to the sounds of the village.

For nearly a century all travel was on foot, by boat, or on horseback with goods and chattels fastened to the saddle and probably a batch of journeycake (later corrupted to *johnnycake*) in the saddlebag. Roads were merely paths through the woods. Indian paths were hardly more than a foot wide, and the first paths of the whites were scarcely wider. Not until the eighteenth century was there a cart road from Hadley to Boston. Before then produce was carried by canoe down the river to a point below the rapids and there transshipped to coastal vessels. Oxen were the beasts of burden, and oxcarts were used in farm work. The gradual increase in the use of horse carts and carriages, sleds and sleighs, and the subsequent opening up of highways, revolutionized travel and the conveyance of goods. . . .

By colony law of 1647, every town of fifty families was required to provide a school where children could learn to read and write, and towns of a hundred families had also to provide a grammar school with a master able to fit young men for college. The schools were supported in part by the town and in part by the parents of the pupils. Teachers were paid about thirty pounds a year, and to guard against truancy, parents were compelled to contribute their share whether or not their children attended school. Free schools were long a bone of contention, as the less well-to-do favored them, while the more well-to-do looked askance at the increased taxes this would entail. The former won but not until well into the eighteenth century.

Girls were commonly taught at home, as it was deemed improper for the sexes to mingle at school. As a result there were many private schools kept by "dames" in their own homes where girls were taught at minimum cost to read and sew. Writing was thought unnecessary for females in the seventeenth century, and not one in ten could sign her name.

By the standards of the times, ministers were well paid. The first minister of Hadley received an allotment of land and eighty pounds a year in produce, as well as free wood for his fireplace. (Since ministers sat at home to write sermons instead of working outdoors, they used prodigious amounts of firewood. The average Hadley family burned thirty cords a year but some ministers used up to seventy cords. A cord is a stack of wood four feet wide, four feet high, and eight feet long.) One shrewd minister of the eighteenth century stipulated a cost-of-living clause in his contract—that is, his salary should rise or fall as the prices of eight commodities of the period rose and fell.

In the old meetinghouses the allotting of places was done by a committee on the basis of the age, estate, and honors of each parishioner. Since prestige was involved, a man's standing in the community being publicly proclaimed by the seat given him, quarrels were common. Sermons in the unheated churches never diminished in length, even in zero weather, though they were sometimes hard to hear above the stamping of numbed feet. . . .

The standard dish of early New England was made of cornmeal and water and called hasty pudding or mush. On Saturday a huge batch was cooked to be eaten for breakfast and often for supper throughout the week. Pumpkins, another early favorite, were adopted from the Indians. They were pared and cut into circular slices through which poles were passed and on which they were then suspended from the kitchen ceiling to dry.

Salt pork was the principal meat dish. . . . Some pork was kept in brine, but most was salted in large pieces and hung in the great kitchen chimney to smoke. These smoked sides were called flitches of bacon.

Contrary to popular belief, baked beans were not eaten till the eighteenth century. Potatoes were first raised in the valley about 1750; tomatoes and rhubarb were unknown until well into the nineteenth century.

Candlewood (pine knots or silvers of pine) was commonly used for light in the seventeenth century as it was much easier to come by than candles, which country people made by spinning wicks of tow and dipping them in melted tallow.

The favorite drinks of the early settlers were beer and cider. Beer was the most popular, and almost every household made its own. Brew day was once a week, and into the kettle went not only malt and hops but also dried pumpkins, dried apple parings, and sometimes rye bran and birch twigs. After brewing, the beer was strained through a sieve, and from the emptyings (the settlings in the barrel) yeast was made. Of cider, the average country family drank four or five barrels a year, and innumerable apple trees were planted to supply this demand. At first the apples were pounded by hand in a trough, but cider mills came in around 1700. In winter, when milk was scarce, children were given cider sweetened with molasses and warmed in a pan.

Because the word *alehouse* had fallen into bad repute, inns or drinking places were called *ordinaries* and were strictly regulated. Indeed, governmental regulations today would have seemed puny to the Puritans, who believed that well-being could be assured by legislative enactment. The first ordinaries, for example, were not allowed to serve strong drinks, nor even cakes and buns except at weddings and funerals, nor to force meals costing twelve pennies or above on poor people.

This first law was soon repealed, but the strength of liquor continued to be regulated; four bushels of malt, for example, had to be used in making a sixty-three-gallon hogshead of beer under penalty of a stiff fine. Moreover, liquor could be sold only to "governors of families of sober carriage," as complaints were being made even then of drinking by wild youths. . . .

Clocks and watches were rare before the Revolution. A few country people had hourglasses or sundials, but for the most part, time was told by the sun or by a "noon mark," which many houses had on the bottom casing of a south window. The month of March, when most town meetings are still held, once marked the beginning of the new year. Some towns figured it as beginning March 1, but most towns began it on March 25 and called the days from January 1 to March 24, inclusive, mongrel time, to be written down thus: March 3, 167¾, the upper figure in the fraction denoting the year commencing March 25, the lower the year commencing January 1. This confusion continued until the calendar was reformed in 1752.

Country folk seldom used titles in the early days except for military officers. A few leading members of the community, including the minister, would be called Mister, but it would have been thought quite shocking to use it for a farmer or mechanic. Goodman and Goodwife (or Goody) were the titles for a yeoman (a farmer who owned or occupied land) and his wife. Until about 1720 both the wife and daughter of a Mister were called Mistress (abbreviated to Mrs.) and, for some time after that, Miss and Mrs. were used indiscriminately for married and unmarried females. Middle names came in during the eighteenth century; before then only one given name was used.

During its first half-century Hadley sometimes aided the aged and worthy poor by boarding them out around town; two weeks with one family, then moved on to the next. (A stay so brief might indicate that a fortnight was as long as any one family could tolerate them.) By the next century, when the number of paupers had increased, they were annually put up at vendue and knocked down to the lowest bidder; that is, each pauper was put on the block and auctioned off to the person who would keep him a year for the smallest sum.

The first minister of Hadley had three Negro slaves; a man, woman, and child, valued at sixty pounds. The peak year for slaves was 1754, when the number reached eighteen—a surprisingly large number for a New England village of about five hundred inhabitants. . . .

William Byrd II of Virginia

Marshall Fishwick

Whether William Byrd II was actually as unique a person as he seems can never be known, for it is only because of his marvelously candid diary that we know him as well as we do. Perhaps if others among the privileged but hard-working tobacco planters of eighteenth-century Virginia had left similar records, we would have had to conclude that Byrd was merely typical. In any case, Byrd the historical figure is important not because of his personal qualities, fascinating as these were, but because of what the story of his life tells us about the society of colonial Virginia.

If Byrd was, as Professor Marshall Fishwick, director of the American Studies Institute, Lincoln University, notes in the following essay, a "Renaissance man," he was one no doubt in part because the world he inhabited demanded versatility and rewarded achievement. His career helps explain the extraordinary self-confidence, imagination, and energy of several generations of Americans, not only his own but even more, those that immediately followed and, in the single case of his native Virginia, that produced Washington, Jefferson, Madison, Patrick Henry, and a host of others—the great Virginia leaders of the American Revolution.

He could never resist an old book, a young girl, or a fresh idea. He lived splendidly, planned extensively, and was perpetually in debt. Believing perhaps, like Leonardo, that future generations would be more willing to know him than was his own, he wrote his delicious, detailed diaries in code. Only now that they have been translated, and time has put his era in perspective, do we see what William Byrd of Westover was: one of the half-dozen leading wits and stylists of colonial America.

In the popular imagination, to be an American hero means to rise from rags to riches. William Byrd reversed the pattern, as he did so many other things: born to wealth, he never seemed able to hold on to it. His father, William Byrd I (1653–1704), was one of the most powerful and venerated men of his generation. Not only had he inherited valuable land on both sides of the James River, he had also won the hand of Mary Horsmanden, and a very dainty and wealthy hand it was, too. Some of the bold and red knight-errant blood of the Elizabethans flowed through the veins of William Byrd I. He had the same knack as did Captain John Smith (in whom that blood fairly bubbled) for getting in and out of scrapes. For example, William Byrd I joined Nathaniel Bacon in subduing the Indians, but stopped short of joining the rebellion against Governor William Berkeley, withdrawing in time to save his reputation and his neck. Later on he became receiver-general and auditor of Virginia, a member of the Council of State, and the colony's leading authority on Indians. The important 1685 treaty with the Iroquois bore his signature. Death cut short his brilliant career soon after his fiftieth birthday, and suddenly thrust his son and namesake into the center of the colonial stage. The boy, who had spent much of his time in England getting an education and, later, as an agent for Virginia, must now return to America and assume the duties of a man.

No one can read the story of young Will Byrd's early years, and his transformation, without thinking of Will Shakespeare's Prince Hal. If ever a young Virginian behaved scandalously in London, it was Will Byrd. "Never did the sun shine upon a Swain who had more combustible matter in his constitution," Byrd wrote of himself. Love broke out upon him "before my beard." Louis Wright, to whose editing of Byrd's diaries we are indebted for much of our knowledge of the man, says that he was notoriously promiscuous, frequenting the boudoirs of highborn and lowborn alike. Indeed, as his diary shows, he was not above taking to the grass with a *fille de joie* whom he might encounter on a London street.

Once, when he arrived for a rendezvous with a certain Mrs. A-l-n, the lady wasn't home, so he seduced the chambermaid. Just as he was coming down the steps Mrs. A-l-n came in the front door. Then Will Byrd and Mrs. A-l-n went back up the stairs together. Several hours later, he went home and ate a plum cake.

On his favorites he lavished neoclassic pseudonyms and some of the era's most sparkling prose. One such lady (called "Facetia" and believed to have been Lady Elizabeth Cromwell) was his preoccupation during 1703. When she left him to visit friends in Ireland, Will Byrd let her know she would be missed:

> The instant your coach drove away, madam, my heart felt as if it had been torn up by the very roots, and the rest of my body as if severed limb from limb. . . . Could I at that time have considered that the only pleasure I had in the world was leaving me, I had hung upon your coach and had been torn in pieces sooner than have suffered myself to be taken from you.

Having said all the proper things, he moved on to relate, in a later letter, some of the juicier bits of London gossip. Mrs. Brownlow had finally agreed to marry Lord Guilford—"and the gods alone can tell what will be produced by the conjunction of such fat and good humour!" The image is Falstaffian, as were many of Byrd's friends. But with news of his father's death he must, like Prince Hal, scorn his dissolute friends and assume new duties. With both Hal and Will the metamorphosis was difficult and partial, but nonetheless memorable.

The Virginia to which in 1705 William Byrd II returned—the oldest permanent English settlement in the New World and the first link in the chain that would one day be known as the British Empire—was a combination of elegance and crudity, enlightenment and superstition. While some of his Virginia neighbors discussed the most advanced political theories of Europe, others argued about how to dispose of a witch who was said to have crossed over to Currituck Sound in an eggshell. In 1706, the same year that Byrd was settling down in Virginia after his long stay in England, a Virginia court was instructing "as many Ansient and Knowing women as possible . . . to search her Carefully For teats spotts and marks about her body." When certain mysterious marks were indeed found, the obvious conclusion was drawn, and the poor woman languished in ye common gaol. Finally released, she lived to be eighty and died a natural death.

Other Virginia ladies faced problems (including, on occasions, Will Byrd) that were far older than the colony or the witch scare. A good example was Martha Burwell, a Williamsburg belle, who rejected the suit of Sir Francis Nicholson, the governor, so she might marry a man more to her liking. If she did so, swore the enraged Nicholson, he would cut the throat of the bridegroom, the clergyman, and the issuing justice. Unaware that females are members of the weaker sex, Martha refused to give in—even when Nicholson threw in half a dozen more throats, including those of her father and brothers. She married her true love. No throats were cut—but visitors to the Governor's palace in Williamsburg observed that His Excellency made "a Roaring Noise."

In those days Tidewater Virginia was governed by benevolent paternalists. The aristocrats intermarried, and the essential jobs—sheriff, vestryman, justice of the peace, colonel of militia—stayed in the family. The support of the gentry was the prerequisite to social and political advancement. Wealth, status, and privilege were the Tidewater trinity, and it was a case of three in one: wealth guaranteed status; status conveyed privilege; and privilege insured wealth.

Will Byrd both understood and mastered the world to which he had returned. He retained the seat in the House of Burgesses which he had won before going to England, and turned his attention to finding a suitable wife. Like many of his contemporaries, he confined "romantic love" to extracurricular affairs, and called on common sense to help him in matrimony. Both Washington and Jefferson married rich widows. Ambitious young men found they could love a rich girl more than a poor one, and the colonial newspapers reported their marriages with an honesty that bordered on impropriety. One reads, for example, that twenty-three-year-old William Carter married Madam Sarah Ellson, widow of eighty-five, "a sprightly old Tit, with three thousand pounds fortune."

Will Byrd's choice was the eligible but fiery Lucy Parke, daughter of the gallant rake Daniel Parke, who had fought with Marlborough on the Continent and brought the news of Blenheim to Queen Anne. Many a subsequent battle was fought between Lucy Parke and William Byrd after their marriage in 1706, though neither side was entirely vanquished. Byrd was quick to record his victories, such as the one noted in his diary for February 5, 1711: "My wife and I quarrelled about her pulling her brows. She threatened she would not go to Williamsburg if she might not pull them; I refused, however, and got the better of her and maintained my authority."

That Mrs. Byrd had as many good excuses for her fits of temper and violence as any other lady in Virginia seems plain—not only from her accusations, but from her husband's admissions. From his diary entry of November 2, 1709, for example, we get this graphic picture of life among the planters:

> In the evening I went to Dr. [Barrett's], where my wife came this afternoon. Here I found Mrs. Chiswell, my sister Custis, and other ladies. We sat and talked till about 11 o'clock and then retired to our chambers. I played at [r-m] with Mrs. Chiswell and kissed her on the bed till she was angry and my wife also was uneasy about it, and cried as soon as the company was gone. I neglected to say my prayers which I should not have done, because I ought to beg pardon for the lust I had for another man's wife. However I had good health, good thoughts, and good humor, thanks be to God Almighty.

As we read on, we begin to realize that we are confronting a Renaissance man in colonial America—a writer with the frankness of Montaigne and the zest of Rabelais. Philosopher, linguist, doctor, scientist, stylist, planter, churchman, William Byrd II saw and reported as much as any American who died before our Revolution.

Here was a man who, burdened for most of his life with the responsibility of thousands of acres and hundreds of slaves, never became narrow or provincial. Neither his mind, nor his tongue, nor his pen—the last possibly because he wrote the diaries in code—was restrained by his circumstances, and no one at home or abroad was immune from the barbs of his wit. When we read Byrd, we know just what Dean Swift meant when he said: "We call a spade a spade."

One of Byrd's most remarkable achievements, and one not nearly well enough known and appreciated, is his sketch of himself, attached to a letter dated February 21, 1722. For honesty and perception, and for the balance that the eighteenth century enthroned, it has few American counterparts.

Poor Inamorato [as Byrd calls himself] had too much mercury to fix to one thing. His Brain was too hot to jogg on eternally in the same dull road. He liv'd more by the lively moment of his Passions, than by the cold and unromantick dictates of Reason. . . . He pay'd his Court more to obscure merit, than to corrupt Greatness. He never cou'd flatter any body, no not himself, which were two invincible bars to all preferment. . . . His religion is more in substance than in form, and he is more forward to practice vertue than profess it. . . . He knows the World perfectly well, and thinks himself a citizen of it without the . . . distinctions of kindred sect or Country.

He goes on to explain why, for most of his life, he began his day by reading ancient classics, and frowned upon morning interruptions:

A constant hurry of visits & conversations gives a man a habit of inadvertency, which betrays him into faults without measure & without end. For this reason, he commonly reserv'd the morning to himself, and bestow'd the rest upon his business and his friends.

The reason for his own candor is clearly stated:

He Lov'd to undress wickedness of all its paint, and disguise, that he might loath its deformity.

The extent of his philosophizing and his admitted heresy is made clear by this remarkable passage:

He wishes every body so perfect, that he overlooks the impossibility of reaching it in this World. He wou'd have men Angells before their time, and wou'd bring down that perfection upon Earth which is the peculiar priviledge of Heaven.

Byrd left us a scattered and largely unavailable body of literature—*vers de société*, historical essays, character sketches, epitaphs, letters, poems, translations, and hu-

The front elevation of Westover as it appears today.

morous satires. Of this work Maude Woodfin, one of the few scholars to delve adequately into Byrd's work, wrote:

"There is a distinctly American quality in these writings of the latter half of Byrd's life, in direct contrast to the exclusively English quality in the writings of his earlier years. Further study and time will doubtless argue that his literary work in the Virginia period from 1726 on, with its colonial scene and theme, has greater literary merit than his work in the London period."

Byrd has a place in our architectural history as well. His manor house, Westover, is in many ways the finest Georgian mansion in the nation. Triumphant architectural solutions never came quickly or easily: only first-rate minds can conjure up first-rate houses. In the spring of 1709, we know from Byrd's diary, he had workmen constructing brick. Five years later, stonecutters from Williamsburg were erecting the library chimney. There were interruptions, delays, faulty shipments, workmen to be trained. But gradually a masterpiece—noble in symmetry, proportion, and balance—emerged.

Built on a little rise a hundred yards from the James River, Westover has not changed much over the generations. The north and south façades are as solid and rhythmical as a well-wrought fugue, and the beautiful doorways would have pleased

Palladio himself. Although the manor is derived from English standards (especially William Salmon's *Palladio Londinensis*), Westover makes such superb use of the local materials and landscape that some European critics have adjudged it esthetically more satisfying than most of the contemporary homes in England.

Like other buildings of the period, Westover was planned from the outside in. The main hallway, eighteen feet wide and off center, goes the full length of the house. The stairway has three runs and a balustrade of richly turned mahogany. The handsomely paneled walls of the downstairs rooms support gilded ceilings. Underneath the house is a complete series of rooms, converging at the subterranean passage leading to the river. Two underground chambers, which could be used as hiding places, are reached through a dry well. Since he liked nothing less than the idea of being dry, William Byrd kept both chambers stocked with claret and Madeira.

Westover takes its place in the succession of remarkable Virginia manors that remain one of the glories of the American past. It was completed probably by 1736, after Stratford Hall, with its masculine vigor, and Rosewell, with its mahogany balustrade from San Domingo. Westover would be followed by Brandon, with chaste cornices and fine simplicity; Gunston Hall, with cut-stone quoins and coziness; Sabine Hall, so reminiscent of Horace's villa at Tivoli; and Pacatone, with its wonderful entrance and its legendary ghosts.

These places were more than houses. They were little worlds in themselves, part of a universe that existed within the boundaries of Virginia. The planters lavished their energy and their lives on such worlds. They were proud of their crops, their horses, their libraries, their gardens. Byrd, for example, tells us about the iris, crocus, thyme, marjoram, phlox, larkspur, and jasmine in his formal two-acre garden.

At Westover one might find the Carters from Shirley, the Lees from Stratford, the Harrisons from Randolph, or the Spotswoods from Germanna. So might one encounter Byrd's brother-in-law, that ardent woman-hater, John Custis, from Arlington. Surely the ghost of William Byrd would not want any tale of Westover to omit a short tribute to Custis' irascible memory.

While other founding fathers left immortal lines about life and liberty to stir our blood, Custis left words to warm henpecked hearts. With his highhanded lady he got on monstrous poor.

After one argument Custis turned and drove his carriage into the Chesapeake Bay. When his wife asked where he was going, he shouted, "To Hell, Madam." "Drive on," she said imperiously. "Any place is better than Arlington!" So that he might have the last word, Custis composed his own epitaph, and made his son execute it on pain of being disinherited:

UNDER THIS MARBLE TOMB LIES THE BODY
  OF THE HON. JOHN CUSTIS, ESQ.,

AGE 71 YEARS, AND YET LIVED BUT SEVEN YEARS,
  WHICH WAS THE SPACE OF TIME HE KEPT
  A BACHELOR'S HOME AT ARLINGTON
  ON THE EASTERN SHORE OF VIRGINIA.

Still Custis came to Westover, like all others who could, to enjoy the fairs, balls, parlor games, barbecues—but above all, the conversation.

One should not conclude that entertaining friends was the main occupation of William Byrd. As soon as he awoke he read Latin, Greek, or Hebrew before breakfast. His favorite room was not the parlor but the library, in which were collected over 3,600 volumes dealing with philosophy, theology, drama, history, law, and science. Byrd's own writings prove his intimate knowledge of the great thinkers and writers of the past.

Of those works, none except his diary is as interesting as his *History of the Dividing Line*. On his fifty-third birthday, in 1727, Byrd was appointed one of the Virginia commissioners to survey the disputed Virginia-North Carolina boundary; the next spring saw the group ready to embark on their task. Byrd's *History*, which proves he was one of the day's ablest masters of English prose, is a thing of delight. For days comedy and tragedy alternated for supremacy. Indians stole their food. Bad weather and poor luck caused Byrd to swear like a trooper in His Majesty's Guards. To mend matters, Byrd's companions arranged a party around a cheerful bowl, and invited a country bumpkin to attend. She must have remembered the party for a long time: ". . . they examined all her hidden Charms and play'd a great many gay Pranks," noted Byrd, who seems to have disapproved of the whole affair. "The poor Damsel was disabled from making any resistance by the Lameness of her Hand."

Whenever matters got too bad, the party's chaplain "rubbed up" his aristocratic swamp-evaders with a seasonable sermon; and we must adjudge all the hardships a small price to pay for the *History*. This was followed by *A Journey to Eden*, which tells of Byrd's trip to survey twenty thousand acres of bottom land. On September 19, 1733, Byrd decided to stake out two large cities: "one at Shacco's, to be called Richmond, and the other at the point of the Appomattuck River, to be called Petersburg."

It is a generally accepted belief that only in politics did eighteenth-century America reach real distinction. But as we look more closely at our colonial literature and architecture, and apply our own criteria rather than those imposed upon us by the English, we find that this may not be so. How, for example, could we have underestimated William Byrd's importance all these years? There are several answers. He never pretended to be a serious writer (no gentleman of his time and place would), any more than Jefferson would have set himself up as a professional architect. But at least we have Jefferson's magnificent buildings to refute the notion that he was a mere dabbler, and for years we had little of Byrd's prose. Because he did "call a spade a spade," many of his contemporaries, and even more of their descendants, have not wanted his work and allusions made public. Byrd had been dead almost a century when Edmund Ruffin published fragments of his writings in the *Virginia Farmers' Register*. Only in our own generation have the diaries been deciphered: not until 1941 did a major publisher undertake to set part of them into print; not until 1958 did we have *The London Diary* (1717–21); not even now can we read all that Byrd left for us.

No amount of reappraisal can turn Byrd into a figure of the highest magnitude. What it might do is to reveal a man who for candor, self-analysis, and wit is unsurpassed—this in an age that produced Washington, Adams, Franklin, Henry, and

Jefferson. Could any other colonial American, for example, have written such a delightful and ribald satire on women as "The Female Creed," which has an eighteenth-century lady profess: "I believe in astrologers, coffee-casters, and Fortunetellers of every denomination, whether they profess to read the Ladys destiny in their faces, in their palms or like those of China in their fair posteriors."

Nor will one often encounter in a colonial writer the desire to exhume his father's corpse, and then to report: "He was so wasted there was not one thing to be distinguished. I ate fish for dinner."

When William Byrd II died in the summer of 1744, the pre-Revolutionary ethos and attitudes were dying too. They have not attracted historians and novelists as have the earlier adventurous days of settlement or the later days that tried men's souls. The period from 1700 to 1750 remains the forgotten one in American history and literature, despite much excellent but rather specialized work in it since 1930.

When we know more of that important and colorful half century, William Byrd's reputation will rise. In him we shall find the most complete expression of a man who lived with us but belongs to the world. In his work we shall see, more clearly than in that of his contemporaries, the emerging differences between England and the American colonies destined to grow into their own nationhood. Beside him, the so-called Connecticut Wits of the late eighteenth century seem to be lacking half their title. Compared to his prose, the tedious sermonizing of the Puritan and Anglican ministers seems like copybook work in an understaffed grammar school. Not that William Byrd was a saint, or a model husband—as he would have been the first to point out. But as with the saints, we admire him all the more because he tells us about his faults and lets us tabulate the virtues for ourselves. All told, we can say of him what Abraham Lincoln supposedly said when he saw Walt Whitman far down the corridors of a building: "There goes a man." William Byrd of Westover would have settled for this.

Witchcraft in Colonial New England

John Demos

The notorious Salem witchcraft trials of 1692 were one of the most shocking incidents in colonial history, but as Professor John Demos of Yale University explains in the following essay, they were by no means unique. Demos is not content, however, to describe other New England cases where persons were accused of being witches. Nor does he write off the phenomenon as an example of mass hysteria, ignorant prejudice, and the miscarriage of justice. If everyone believed that witches existed, he argues, some people surely believed (or feared) that they were themselves witches, and of these, some no doubt deliberately tried to practice witchcraft. Demos's tale is fascinating, and it shows how important it is for historians to immerse themselves in the times they study. To do their job properly, they must see that world as those who actually lived in it saw it and simultaneously maintain the perspective of their own time.

Professor Demos is the author of *A Little Commonwealth: Family Life in Plymouth Colony* and *Entertaining Satan: Witchcraft and the Culture of Early New England*.

The place is the fledgling community of Windsor, Connecticut: the time, an autumn day in the year 1651. A group of local militiamen has assembled for training exercises. They drill in their usual manner through the morning, then pause for rest and refreshment. Several of the younger recruits begin a moment's horseplay; one of these—a certain Thomas Allen—cocks his musket and inadvertently knocks it against a tree. The weapon fires, and a few yards away a bystander falls heavily to the ground. The unfortunate victim is an older man, also a trainee, Henry Stiles by name. Quickly, the group converges on Stiles, and bears him to the house of the local physician. But the bullet has fatally pierced his heart.

One month later the "particular court" of the Connecticut colony meets in regular session. On its agenda is an indictment of Thomas Allen: "that . . . [thou] didst suddenly, negligently, carelessly cock thy piece, and carry the piece . . . which piece being charged and going off in thine hand, slew thy neighbor, to the great dishonor of God, breach of the peace, and loss of a member of this commonwealth." Allen confesses the fact, and is found guilty of "homicide by misadventure." For his "sinful neglect and careless carriages" the court orders him to pay a fine of twenty pounds sterling. In addition he is bound to good behavior for the ensuing year, with the special proviso "that he shall not bear arms for the same term."

But this is not the end of the matter. Stiles's death remains a topic of local conversation, and three years later it yields a more drastic result. In November, 1654, the court meets in special session to try a case of witchcraft—against a woman,

Lydia Gilbert, also of Windsor: "Lydia Gilbert, thou art here indicted . . . that not having the fear of God before thine eyes, thou hast of late years or still dost give entertainment to Satan, the great enemy of God and mankind, and by his help hast killed the body of Henry Stiles, besides other witchcrafts, for which according to the law of God and the established law of this commonwealth thou deservest to die." The court, in effect, is considering a complicated question: did Lydia Gilbert's witchcraft *cause* Thomas Allen's gun to go off, so as to kill Henry Stiles? Evidence is taken on various points deemed relevant. Henry Stiles was a boarder in the Gilbert household for some while before his death. The arrangement was not a happy one; neighbors could recall the sounds of frequent quarreling. From time to time Stiles loaned money and property to his landlord, but this served only to heighten the tension. Goodwife Gilbert, in particular, violated her Christian obligation of charitable and peaceable behavior. A naturally assertive sort, she did not conceal her sense of grievance against Goodman Stiles. In fact, her local reputation has long encompassed some unfavorable elements: disapproval of her quick temper, envy of her success in besting personal antagonists, suspicion that she is not above invoking the "Devil's means." The jury weighs the evidence and reaches its verdict—guilty as charged. The magistrates hand down the prescribed sentence of death by hanging. A few days thereafter the sentence is carried out.

On the next succeeding Sabbath day, and with solemn forewarning, the pastor of the Windsor church climbs to the pulpit to deliver his sermon. Directly he faces the questions that are weighing heavily in the minds of his parishioners. Why has this terrible scourge of witchcraft been visited on their little community? What has created the opportunity which the Devil and his legions have so untimely seized? For what reason has God Almightly condoned such a tragic intrusion on the life of Windsor? The pastor's answer to these questions is neither surprising nor pleasant for his audience to hear, but it carries a purgative force. The Windsor townsfolk are themselves at least partially to blame. For too long they have strayed from the paths of virtue: overvaluing secular interests while neglecting religious ones, tippling in alehouses, "nightwalking," and—worst of all—engaging one another in repeated strife. In such circumstances the Devil always finds an opening; to such communities God brings retribution. Thus the recent witchcraft episode is a lesson to the people of Windsor, and a warning to mend their ways.

Lydia Gilbert was not the first witch to have lived at Windsor, nor would she be the last. For so-called Puritans, the happenstance of everyday life was part of a struggle of cosmic dimensions, a struggle in which witchcraft played a logical part. The ultimate triumph of Almighty God was assured. But in particular times and places Satan might achieve some temporary success—and claim important victims. Indeed he was continually adding earthly recruits to his nefarious cause. Tempted by bribes and blandishments, or frightened by threats of torture, weak-willed persons signed the "Devil's Book" and enrolled as witches. Thereafter they were armed with his power and obliged to do his bidding. God, meanwhile, opposed this onslaught of evil—and yet He also permitted it. For errant men and women there was no more effective means of "chastening."

In a sense, therefore, witchcraft was part of God's own intention. And the element of intention was absolutely central, in the minds of the human actors. When a man lay dead from a violent accident on a training field, his fellow townspeople would carefully investigate how events had proceeded to such an end. But they sought, in addition, to understand the *why* of it all—the motives, whether human or supernatural (or both), which lay behind the events. The same was true for other forms of everyday mischance. When cows took strangely ill, when a boat capsized in a sudden storm, when bread failed to rise in the oven or beer went bad in the barrel, there was cause for careful reflection. Witchcraft would not necessarily provide the best explanation, but it was always a possibility—and sometimes a most convenient one. To discover an unseen hand at work in one's life was to dispel mystery, to explain misfortune, to excuse incompetence. Belief in witchcraft was rooted in the practical experience no less than the theology of the time.

A single shocking episode—the Salem "hysteria" of 1692—has dominated the lore of this subject ever since. Yet the Salem trials were distinctive only in a quantitative sense—that is, in the sheer numbers of the accused. Between the late 1630s and 1700 dozens of New England towns supported proceedings against witchcraft; some did so on repeated occasions. The total of cases was over a hundred (and this includes only actual trials from which some record survives today). At least forty of the defendants were put to death; the rest were acquitted or convicted of a lesser charge. Numerous additional cases went unrecorded because they did not reach a court of law; nonetheless they generated much excitement—and distress. "Witches" were suspected, accused informally, and condemned in unofficial ways. Gossip and rumor about such people constituted a staple part of the local culture.

The typical witch was a woman of middle age. Like Lydia Gilbert, she was married, had children, and lived as a settled member of her community. (However, widows and childless women were also suspected, perhaps to an extent disproportionate to their numbers in the population at large.) Some of the accused were quite poor and a few were given to begging; but taken altogether they spanned the entire social spectrum. (One was the wife of a leading magistrate in the Massachusetts Bay Colony.) Most seemed conspicuous in their personal behavior: they were cantankerous, feisty, quick to take offense, and free in their expression of anger. As such they matched the prevalent stereotype of a witch, with its emphasis on strife and malice and vengeance. It was no accident, in a culture which valued "peaceableness" above all things, that suspected witches were persons much given to conflict. Like deviant figures everywhere, they served to mark the accepted boundaries between Good and Evil.

Their alleged victims, and actual accusers, are much harder to categorize. Children were sometimes centrally involved—notoriously so at Salem—but witchcraft evidence came from people of both sexes and all ages. The young had their "fits"; older witnesses had other things of which to complain. Illness, injury, and the loss of property loomed largest in such testimony; but there were reports, too, of strange sights and sounds, of portents and omens, of mutterings and cures—all attributable in some way to the supposed witch. The chances for conviction were greatest when the range of this evidence was wide and the sources numerous. In some cases whole neighborhoods joined the ranks of the accusers.

Usually a trial involved only a single witch, or perhaps two; the events at issue were purely local. A finding of guilt would remove the defendant forever from her community. An acquittal would send her back, but with a clear warning to watch her step. Either way tension was lowered.

Occasionally the situation became more complicated. In Connecticut, during the years from 1662 to 1665, the courts heard a long sequence of witchcraft cases—perhaps as many as a dozen. Some of the accused were eventually executed; others fled for their lives to neighboring colonies. Almost none of the legal evidence has survived; it is known, however, that Connecticut was then experiencing severe problems of religious factionalism. The witch trials may well have been a direct result.

The context for the other wide-scale outbreak is much clearer. Salem, in the closing decades of the seventeenth century, was a town notorious for internal contention. An old guard of village farmers was arrayed against newly prosperous merchants and townsmen. For years, indeed decades, local governance was disrupted: town meetings broke up with important issues unresolved, ministers came and left (out of favor with one side or the other), lawsuits filled the court dockets. Thus when the first sparks of witchcraft were fanned, in a small group of troubled girls, they acted like tinder on a dried-out woodpile. Suspicion led immediately to new suspicion, and accusation to accusation—with results that every schoolchild knows. Soon the conflagration burst the boundaries of Salem itself; eventually it claimed victims throughout eastern Massachusetts. By the time cooler heads prevailed—especially that of the new governor, Sir William Phips—twenty witches had been executed and dozens more were languishing in local jails.

But the Salem trials—to repeat—were highly unusual in their sheer scope: witch-hunting gone wild. In the more typical case, events moved slowly, even carefully, within a limited and intensely personal framework. This dimension of the witchcraft story also deserves close attention.

October, 1688. A cart stops by the roadside in the south part of Boston. A tall man alights and hurries along a pathway toward a small house. A door opens to admit him and quickly closes again. The visitor is Rev. Cotton Mather, a young but already eminent clergyman of the town. The house is occupied by the family of a mason named John Goodwin.

Immediately upon entering, Mather becomes witness to an extraordinary scene. On the parlor floor in front of him two small human forms are thrashing about. A girl of thirteen (named Martha) and a boy of eleven (John, Jr.) are caught in the throes of agonizing fits. Their bodies contort into strange, distended shapes. Their eyes bulge. Their mouths snap open and shut. They shriek uncontrollably. From time to time they affect the postures of animals, and crawl about the room, barking like dogs or bellowing like frightened cows. Their father and several neighbors look on in horror, and try by turns to prevent serious damage to persons or property.

Mather waits for a moment's lull; then he opens a Bible, kneels, and begins to pray. Immediately the children stop their ears and resume their shrieking. "*They* say we must not listen," cries the girl, while hurling herself toward the fireplace. Her father manages to block the way; briefly he catches her in an awkward embrace. But she reels off and falls heavily on her brother.

Soon it is time for supper. The children quiet temporarily, and come to the table with their elders. However, when food is offered them, their teeth are set as if to lock their mouths shut. Later there are new troubles. The children need assis-

These scenes of the work of witches, devils, and other supernatural beings appeared in a treatise entitled "Saducismus Triumphatus, or a Full and Plain Evidence concerning Witches and Apparitions," *published in London in 1726. The images reflect common beliefs about what such creatures might do.*

tance in preparing for bed, and they tear their nightclothes fearfully. At last they quiet and pass into a deep sleep.

Mather sits by the fireside and reviews the history of their affliction with the distraught parents. The family is a religious one, and until the preceding summer the children were unfailingly pious and well behaved. Martha's fits had begun first, John's soon thereafter; indeed, two still younger children in the family have also been affected from time to time. A physician had been summoned, but he could discover no "natural maladies" at work.

The parents recall an episode that had directly preceded the onset of Martha's fits. The girl was sent to retrieve some family linen from a laundress who lived nearby. Several items had disappeared, and Martha complained—intimating theft. The laundress angrily denied the charges, and was joined in this by her own mother, an Irishwoman named Glover. Goodwife Glover was already a feared presence in the neighborhood; her late husband, on his deathbed, had accused her of practicing witchcraft. Now she poured out her retaliative anger on young Martha Goodwin. The girl has not been the same since.

Late in the evening, having listened with care to the entire story, Mather prepares to leave. John Goodwin explains that several neighbors have been urging the use of "tricks"—countermagic—to end his children's difficulties. But Goodwin prefers a strategy based on orthodox Christian principles.

In this Cotton Mather is eager to cooperate. He returns to the Goodwin house each day for a week, and on one particular afternoon he is joined by his fellow clergymen from all parts of Boston. Eventually he invites Martha Goodwin into his own home for a period of intensive pastoral care. (Martha's younger brother is taken, at the same time, into the home of the minister at Watertown.) Their afflictions continue, though with lessened severity.

Meanwhile the courts intervene and Goodwife Glover is put on trial for her alleged crimes. She has difficulty answering the prosecutor's questions; she can speak only in her native tongue (Gaelic), so the proceedings must involve interpreters. Her house is searched, and "poppets" are discovered—small images, made of rags, believed to be instrumental in the perpetration of witchcraft. Eventually she confesses guilt and raves wildly in court about her dealings with the Devil. The judges appoint six physicians to assess her sanity; they find her compos mentis. The court orders her execution.

On her way to the gallows Goodwife Glover declares bitterly that the children will not be cured after her death, for "others had a hand in it as well." And in fact, the fits suffered by Martha and young John increase immediately thereafter. Winter begins, and suspicion shifts to another woman of the neighborhood. However, the new suspect dies suddenly, and under strange circumstances, before she can be brought to trial. At last the children show marked improvement, and by spring they are virtually their former selves. Meanwhile a relieved, and triumphant, Cotton Mather is spending long days in his study, completing a new book that will soon be published under the title *Memorable Providences, Relating to Witchcrafts and Possessions*. A central chapter deals at length with selected "examples," and includes the events in which Mather himself has so recently participated. The Goodwin children will be leading characters in a local best seller.

Goodwife Glover was relatively rare, among those accused of witchcraft in early New England, in confessing guilt. Only at Salem did any considerable number choose to convict themselves—and there, it seemed, confession was the strategy of choice if one wished to avoid the gallows. Were Goody Glover's admissions, in effect, forced out of her? Was she perhaps seriously deranged (the opinion of the court-appointed physicians notwithstanding)? Did she truly believe herself guilty? Had she, in fact, sought to invoke the power of the Devil, by stroking poppets with her spittle—or whatever?

We have no way now to answer such questions; the evidence comes to us entirely through persons who believed—and prosecuted—the case against her. It does seem likely, in a community where virtually everyone accepted the reality of witchcraft, that at least a few would have tried to practice it. In a sense, however, it no longer matters whether specific individuals were guilty as charged. What does matter is that many of them were believed guilty—and that this belief was itself efficacious. As anthropologists have observed in cultures around the world, people who regard themselves as objects of witchcraft are vulnerable to all manner of mischance. They blunder into "accidents," they lose their effectiveness in work and social relations, they occasionally sicken and die.

No less was true in early New England. The victims of witchcraft—whatever the variety of their particular afflictions—had this in common: they believed *beforehand* that they had been marked as targets for attack. Their fearful expectation became, at some point, incapacitating—and yielded its own directly feared result. Thus the idea of witchcraft served both as the *ad hoc* cause of the victim's troubles and as the *post hoc* explanation. The process was neatly circular, for each explanation created a further cause—which, in turn, required additional explanation. In the language of modern medicine, these episodes were "symptoms," and their basis was "psychogenic."

The seizures of the afflicted children were but the extreme end of the symptomatic continuum. When Martha Goodwin had been drawn into a bitter exchange with a suspected witch, she was left deeply unsettled. She feared retaliation; she wished to retaliate herself; she felt acutely uncomfortable with the anger she had already expressed. Henceforth an anguished "victim" of witchcraft, she was, in effect, punished for her own vengeful impulse. Yet, too, she *had* her revenge, for her accusations led straight to the trial and conviction of her antagonist. The same inner processes, and a similar blend of wish and fear, served to energize fits in victims of witchcraft all across New England.

But fits could be explained in other ways—hence the requirement that all such victims be examined by medical doctors. Only when natural causes had been ruled out was a diagnosis of witchcraft clearly justified. Normally, beyond this point, clergymen would assume control of the proceedings, for they were "healers of the soul" and experts in the struggle against Evil. Long sessions of prayer, earnest conversation with the afflicted, occasional periods of fasting and humiliation—these were the preferred methods of treatment.

At least they were the *Christian* methods. For—much to the chagrin of the clergy—there were other ways of combating witchcraft. From obscure sources in the folk culture of pre-Christian times the New Englanders had inherited a rich

lore of countermagic—including, for example, the tricks which John Goodwin refused to try. Thus a family might decide to lay branches of "sweet bays" under their
threshold. ("It would keep a witch from coming in.") Or a woman tending a sick
child would perform elaborate rituals of protection. ("She smote the back of her
hands together sundry times, and spat in the fire; then she . . . rubbed [herbs] in
her hand and strewed them about the hearth.") Or a man would hurl a pudding
into a fire in order to draw a suspect to the scene of his alleged crimes. ("To get hay
was no true cause of his coming thither, but rather the spirit that bewitched the
pudding brought him.") All this was of a piece with other strands of belief and
custom in seventeenth-century New England: fortunetelling, astrology, healing
charms, love potions and powders—to mention a few. Witchcraft, in short, belonged to a large and complex world of interest in the supernatural.

Beyond the tricks against witches, besides the efficacy of prayer, there was always legal recourse. Witchcraft was a capital crime in every one of the New England
colonies, and thus was a particularly solemn responsibility of the courts. Procedure
was scrupulously observed: indictment by a grand jury, depositions from qualified
witnesses, verdict by a jury of trials, sentencing by the magistrates. Some features of
witchcraft trials seem highly repugnant today—for example, the elaborate and intimate body searches of defendants suspected of having "witch's teats" (nipplelike
growths through which the witch or wizard was believed to give suck to Satan). But
in the context of the times, such procedures were not extraordinary. Contrary to
popular belief, physical torture was *not* used to obtain evidence. Testimony was
taken on both sides, and character references favorable to the defendant were not
uncommon. Guilt was never a foregone conclusion; most trials ended in acquittal.
Perhaps *because* the crime was a capital one, many juries seemed reluctant to convict. Some returned verdicts like the following: "[We find her] not legally guilty according to indictment, but [there is] just ground of vehement suspicion of her having had familiarity with the Devil."

At Salem, to be sure, such caution was thrown to the winds. The creation of
special courts, the admission of "spectral evidence" (supplied by "shapes" visible
only to the afflicted victims), the strong momentum favoring conviction—all this
marked a decided tilt in the legal process. But it brought, in time, its own reaction.
Magistrates, clergymen, and ordinary participants eventually would see the enor-
mity of what they had done at Salem in the name of law and religion. And they
would not make the same mistakes again.

Thus the eighteenth century, in New England, was essentially free of *legal* action against witchcraft. However, the belief which had sustained such action did not
evaporate so quickly.

Hampton, New Hampshire: March 26, 1769. The finest house in the town, a
mansion by any standard, is destroyed in a spectacular fire. The owner is General
Jonathan Moulton—scion of an old family, frequent town officer, commander of
the local forces in various Indian wars, businessman of extraordinary skill and energy. Yet despite these marks of eminence, Moulton is no favorite of his fellow
townsmen. To them he seems ruthless, crafty, altogether a "sharp dealer." Indeed,
the local gossips have long suggested that Moulton is in league with the Devil.
There is no easier way to explain, among other things, his truly prodigious wealth.

The ashes of Moulton's house are barely cold when a new story circulates in the town: the fire was set by the Devil, because the General had cheated him in a bargain. The details are told as follows. Moulton had pledged his soul to the Devil, in exchange for regular payments of gold and silver coins. The payments were delivered down his chimney and into his boot, which was hung there precisely for this purpose. The arrangement went smoothly for awhile, but then came a time when the boot took far more coins than usual. The Devil was perplexed, and decided to go down the chimney to see what was wrong. He found that the General had cut off the foot of the boot; the room was so full of money that there was scarcely air to breathe.

The fire—and this account of it—notwithstanding, Moulton quickly recoups. He builds a new mansion even more grand than the first one. His business enterprises yield ever greater profit. He serves with distinction in the Revolutionary War and also in the convention which draws up the constitution of the state of New Hampshire. Yet his local reputation shows little change with the passage of years. When he dies, in 1788, the news is carried to the haymakers on the Hampton marsh: "General Moulton is dead!" they call to one another in tones of evident satisfaction. And there is one final peculiarity about his passing. His body, prepared for burial, is suddenly missing from the coffin. The people of Hampton are not surprised. "The Devil," they whisper knowingly to one another, "has got his own at last."

Similar stories are preserved in the lore of many New England towns. Through them we can trace an enduring interest in the idea of witchcraft—and also an unmistakable change. The figure of the witch gradually lost its power to inspire fear. In many towns, for many generations, there were one or two persons suspected of practicing the black arts, but the effects of such practice were discounted. Witches were associated more and more with simple mischief—and less with death and destruction. There was even, as the Moulton story shows, an element of humor in the later lore of witchcraft.

In our own time the wheel has turned full circle. There are many new witches among us—self-proclaimed, and proud of the fact. They haunt our television talk-shows and write syndicated columns for our newspapers. Their witchcraft is entirely constructive—so they assure us—and we are all invited to join in their celebration of things occult. Meanwhile some of the old witches have been rehabilitated.

Hampton, New Hampshire: March 8, 1938. A town meeting considers the case of a certain Eunice Cole, whose witchcraft was locally notorious three centuries before. The following motion is made: "*Resolved,* that we, the citizens . . . of Hampton . . . do hereby declare that we believe that Eunice (Goody) Cole was unjustly accused of witchcraft and familiarity with the Devil in the seventeenth century, and we do hereby restore to the said Eunice (Goody) Cole her rightful place as a citizen of the town of Hampton." The resolution is passed unanimously. In fact, the legend of Goody Cole has become a cherished part of the local culture. A bronze urn in the town hall holds material purported to be her earthly remains. A stone memorial on the village green affirms her twentieth-century rehabilitation. There are exhibits on her life at the local historical society. There are even some *new* tales in which she plays a ghostly, though harmless part: an aged figure, in tattered shawl, seen walking late at night along a deserted road, or stopping in the early dawn to peer at gravestones by the edge of the green.

And now an author's postscript:

Hampton, New Hampshire: October, 1972. The living room in a comfortable house abutting the main street. A stranger has come there, to examine a venerable manuscript held in this family through many generations. Laboriously his eyes move across the page, straining to unravel the cramped and irregular script of a by-gone era. Two girls, aged nine or ten, arrive home from school; after a brief greeting they move off into an alcove and begin to play. Awash in the sounds of their game, the stranger looks up from his work and listens. "I'll be Goody Cole!" cries one of the girls. "Yes," responds the other, "and I'll be the one who gives you a whipping—you mean old witch!"

It is a long way from their time to ours, but at least a few of the early New England witches have made the whole journey.

The Middle Passage

Daniel P. Mannix and Malcolm Cowley

To Europeans like William Byrd, America offered an environment of unparalleled freedom and stimulation; for those of lesser fortune, as the historical record shows, it supplied only somewhat less opportunity for self-expression and improvement. But for Africans—roughly ten percent of all the colonists by the middle of the eighteenth century—America meant the crushing degradation of slavery. Until recently, without excusing or justifying slavery, most historians have tended not so much to ignore as to compartmentalize (one is almost tempted to say "segregate") the history of African Americans from the general stream of American development. When generalizing about American "free institutions," "opportunity," and "equality," the phrase "except for blacks" needs always to be added if the truth is to be told.

Historical arguments have developed about the condition of slaves in America, about the differences between the British American and Latin American slave systems, and about other aspects of the history of blacks in the New World. But there has been only unanimity among historians about the horrors associated with the capture of blacks in Africa and with the dread "middle passage" over which the slaves were shipped to the Americas. In this essay literary critic Malcolm Cowley and historian Daniel P. Mannix combine their talents to describe what it meant to be wrenched from one's home and native soil, herded in chains into the foul hold of a slave ship, and dispatched across the torrid mid-Atlantic into the hell of slavery.

Long before Europeans appeared on the African coast, the merchants of Timbuktu were exporting slaves to the Moorish kingdoms north of the Sahara. Even the transatlantic slave trade had a long history. There were Negroes in Santo Domingo as early as 1503, and the first twenty slaves were sold in Jamestown, Virginia, about the last week of August, 1619, only twelve years after the colony was founded. But the flush days of the trade were in the eighteenth century, when vast supplies of labor were needed for the sugar plantations in the West Indies and the tobacco and rice plantations on the mainland. From 1700 to 1807, when the trade was legally abolished by Great Britain and the United States, more than seventy thousand Negroes were carried across the Atlantic in any normal year. The trade was interrupted by wars, notably by the American Revolution, but the total New World importation for the century may have amounted to five million enslaved persons.

Most of the slaves were carried on shipboard at some point along the four thousand miles of West African coastline that extend in a dog's leg from the Sahara on the north to the southern desert. Known as the Guinea Coast, it was feared by eighteenth-century mariners, who died there by hundreds and thousands every year.

Contrary to popular opinion, very few of the slaves—possibly one or two out of a hundred—were free Africans kidnapped by Europeans. The slaving captains had, as a rule, no moral prejudice against manstealing, but they usually refrained from it on the ground of its being a dangerous business practice. A vessel suspected of manstealing might be "cut off" by the natives, its crew killed, and its cargo of slaves offered for sale to other vessels.

The vast majority of the Negroes brought to America had been enslaved and sold to the whites by other Africans. There were coastal tribes and states, like the Efik kingdom of Calabar, that based their whole economy on the slave trade. The slaves might be prisoners of war, they might have been kidnapped by gangs of black marauders, or they might have been sold with their whole families for such high crimes as adultery, impiety, or, as in one instance, stealing a tobacco pipe. Inter-tribal wars, the principal source of slaves, were in many cases no more than large-scale kidnapping expeditions. Often they were fomented by Europeans, who supplied both sides with muskets and gunpowder—so many muskets or so much powder for each slave that they promised to deliver on shipboard.

The ships were English, French, Dutch, Danish, Portuguese, or American. London, Bristol, and finally Liverpool were the great English slaving ports. By 1790 Liverpool had engrossed five eighths of the English trade and three sevenths of the slave trade of all Europe. Its French rival, Nantes, would soon be ruined by the Napoleonic wars. During the last years of legal slaving, Liverpool's only serious competitors were the Yankee captains of Newport and Bristol, Rhode Island.

Profits from a slaving voyage, which averaged nine or ten months, were reckoned at 30 percent, after deducting sales commissions, insurance premiums, and all other expenses. The Liverpool merchants became so rich from the slave trade that they invested heavily in mills, factories, mines, canals, and railways. That process was repeated in New England, and the slave trade provided much of the capital that was needed for the industrial revolution.

A slaving voyage was triangular. English textiles, notions, cutlery, and firearms were carried to the Guinea Coast, where they were exchanged for slaves. These were sold in America or the West Indies, and part of the proceeds was invested in colonial products, notably sugar and rice, which were carried back to England on the third leg of the voyage. If the vessel sailed from a New England port, its usual cargo was casks of rum from a Massachusetts distillery. The rum was exchanged in Africa for slaves—often at the rate of two hundred gallons per man—and the slaves were exchanged in the West Indies for molasses, which was carried back to New England to be distilled into rum. A slave ship or Guineaman was expected to show a profit for each leg of its triangular course. But the base of the triangle, the so-called Middle Passage from Africa to the New World with a black cargo, was the most profitable part of the voyage, at the highest cost in human suffering. Let us see what happened in the passage during the flush days of the slave trade.

As soon as an assortment of naked slaves was carried aboard a Guineaman, the men were shackled two by two, the right wrist and ankle of one to the left wrist and ankle of another; then they were sent below. The women—usually regarded as fair prey for the sailors—were allowed to wander by day almost anywhere on the vessel, though they spent the night between decks, in a space partitioned off from that of the men. All the slaves were forced to sleep without covering on bare wooden floors, which were often constructed of unplaned boards. In a stormy passage the skin over their elbows might be worn away to the bare bones.

William Bosman says, writing in 1701, "You would really wonder to see how these slaves live on board; for though their number sometimes amounts to six or seven hundred, yet by the careful management of our masters of ships"—the Dutch masters, in this case—"they are so regulated that it seems incredible: And in this particular our nation exceeds all other Europeans; for as the French, Portuguese and English slave-ships are always foul and stinking; on the contrary ours are for the most part clean and neat."

Slavers of every nation insisted that their own vessels were the best in the trade. Thus, James Barbot, Jr., who sailed on an English ship to the Congo in 1700, was highly critical of the Portuguese. He admits that they made a great point of baptizing the slaves before taking them on board, but then, "It is pitiful," he says, "to see how they crowd those poor wretches, six hundred and fifty or seven hundred in a ship, the men standing in the hold ty'd to stakes, the women between decks and those that are with child in the great cabin and the children in the steeridge which in that hot climate occasions an intolerable stench." Barbot adds, however, that the Portuguese provided the slaves with coarse thick mats, which were "softer for the poor wretches to lie upon than the bare decks . . . and it would be prudent to imitate the Portuguese in this point." The English, however, did not display that sort of prudence.

There were two schools of thought among the English slaving captains, the "loose-packers" and the "tight-packers." The former argued that by giving the slaves a little more room, better food, and a certain amount of liberty, they reduced the death rate and received a better price for each slave in the West Indies. The tight-packers answered that although the loss of life might be greater on each of their voyages, so too were the net receipts from a larger cargo. If many of the survivors were weak and emaciated, as was often the case, they could be fattened up in a West Indian slave yard before being offered for sale.

The argument between the two schools continued as long as the trade itself, but for many years after 1750 the tight-packers were in the ascendant. So great was the profit on each slave landed alive that hardly a captain refrained from loading his vessel to its utmost capacity. Says the Reverend John Newton, who was a slaving captain before he became a clergyman:

> The cargo of a vessel of a hundred tons or a little more is calculated to purchase from 220 to 250 slaves. Their lodging rooms below the deck which are three (for the men, the boys, and the women) besides a place for the sick, are sometimes more than five feet high and sometimes less; and this height is divided toward the middle for the slaves to lie in two rows, one above the other, on each side of the ship, close to each other like books upon a shelf. I have known them so close that the shelf would not easily contain one more.
>
> The poor creatures, thus cramped, are likewise in irons for the most part which makes it difficult for them to turn or move or attempt to rise or to lie down without hurting themselves or each other. Every morning, perhaps, more instances than one are found of the living and the dead fastened together.

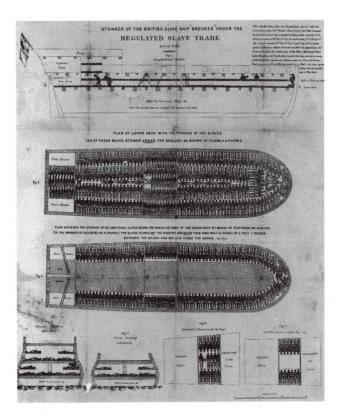

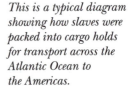

This is a typical diagram showing how slaves were packed into cargo holds for transport across the Atlantic Ocean to the Americas.

Newton was writing in 1788, shortly before a famous parliamentary investigation of the slave trade that lasted four years. One among hundreds of witnesses was Dr. Alexander Falconbridge, who had made four slaving voyages as a surgeon. Falconbridge testified that "he made the most of the room," in stowing the slaves, "and wedged them in. They had not so much room as a man in his coffin either in length or breadth. When he had to enter the slave deck, he took off his shoes to avoid crushing the slaves as he was forced to crawl over them." Falconbridge "had the marks on his feet where the slaves bit and pinched him."

Captain Parrey of the Royal Navy was sent to measure the slave ships at Liverpool and make a report to the House of Commons. That was also in 1788. Parrey discovered that the captains of many slavers possessed a chart showing the dimensions of the half deck, lower deck, hold, platforms, gunroom, orlop, and great cabin, in fact of every crevice into which slaves might be wedged. Miniature black figures were drawn on some of the charts to illustrate the most effective method of packing in the cargo.

On the *Brookes,* which Parrey considered to be typical, every man was allowed a space six feet long by sixteen inches wide (and usually about two feet seven inches high); every woman, a space five feet ten inches long by sixteen inches wide; every boy, five feet by fourteen inches; every girl, four feet six inches by twelve inches.

The *Brookes* was a vessel of 320 tons. By a new law passed in 1788 it was permitted to carry 454 slaves, and the chart, which later became famous, showed where 451 of them could be stowed away. Parrey failed to see how the captain could find room for three more. Nevertheless, Parliament was told by reliable witnesses, including Dr. Thomas Trotter, formerly surgeon of the *Brookes,* that before the new law she had carried 600 slaves on one voyage and 609 on another.

Taking on slaves was a process that might be completed in a month or two by vessels trading in Lower Guinea, east and south of the Niger delta. In Upper Guinea, west and north of the delta, the process was longer. It might last from six months to a year or more on the Gold Coast, which supplied the slaves most in demand by the English colonies. Meanwhile the captain was buying Negroes, sometimes one or two a day, sometimes a hundred or more in a single lot, while haggling over each purchase.

Those months when a slaver lay at anchor off the malarial coastline were the most dangerous part of her voyage. Not only was her crew exposed to African fevers and the revenge of angry natives; not only was there the chance of her being taken by pirates or by a hostile man-of-war; but there was also the constant threat of a slave mutiny. Captain Thomas Phillips says, in his account of a voyage made in 1693–94:

> When our slaves are aboard we shackle the men two and two, while we lie in port, and in sight of their own country, for 'tis then they attempt to make their escape, and mutiny; to prevent which we always keep centinels upon the hatchways, and have a chest full of small arms, ready loaden and prim'd, constantly lying at hand upon the quarter-deck, together with some granada shells; and two of our quarter-deck guns, pointing on the deck thence, and two more out of the steerage, the door of which is always kept shut, and well barr'd; they are fed twice a day, at 10 in the morning, and 4 in the evening, which is the time they are aptest to mutiny, being all upon the deck; therefore all that time, what of our men are not employ'd in distributing their victuals to them, and settling them, stand to their arms; and some with lighted matches at the great guns that yaun upon them, loaden with partridge, till they have done and gone down to their kennels between decks.

In spite of such precautions, mutinies were frequent on the Coast, and some of them were successful. Even a mutiny that failed might lead to heavy losses among the slaves and the sailors. Thus, we read in the Newport, Rhode Island, *Mercury* of November 18, 1765:

> By letters from Capt. Hopkins in a Brig belonging to Providence arrived here from Antigua from the Coast of Africa we learn That soon after he left the Coast, the number of his Men being reduced by Sickness, he was obliged to permit some of the Slaves to come upon Deck to assist the People: These Slaves contrived to release the others, and the whole rose upon the People, and endeavoured to get Possession of the Vessel; but was happily prevented by the Captain and his Men, who killed, wounded and forced overboard, Eighty of them, which obliged the rest to submit.

There are scores of similar items in the colonial newspapers.

William Richardson, a young sailor who shipped on an English Guineaman in 1790, tells of going to the help of a French vessel on which the slaves had risen while it was at anchor. The English seamen jumped into the boats and pulled hard for the Frenchman, but by the time they reached it there were "a hundred slaves in possession of the deck and others tumbling up from below." The slaves put up a desperate resistance. "I could not but admire," Richardson says, "the courage of a fine young black who, though his partner in irons lay dead at his feet, would not surrender but fought with his billet of wood until a ball finished his existence. The others fought as well as they could but what could they do against fire-arms?"

There are fairly detailed accounts of fifty-five mutinies on slavers from 1699 to 1845, not to mention passing references to more than a hundred others. The list of ships "cut off" by the natives—often in revenge for the kidnapping of free Africans—is almost as long. On the record it does not seem that Africans submitted tamely to being carried across the Atlantic like chained beasts. Edward Long, the Jamaica planter and historian, justified the cruel punishments inflicted on slaves by saying, "The many acts of violence they have committed by murdering whole crews and destroying ships when they had it in their power to do so have made these rigors wholly chargeable on their own bloody and malicious disposition which calls for the same confinement as if they were wolves or wild boars." For "wolves or wild boars" a modern reader might substitute "men who would rather die than be enslaved."

With the loading of the slaves, the captain, for his part, had finished what he regarded as the most difficult part of his voyage. Now he had to face only the ordinary perils of the sea, most of which were covered by his owners' insurance against fire, shipwreck, pirates and rovers, letters of mart and counter-mart, barratry, jettison, and foreign men-of-war. Among the risks not covered by insurance, the greatest was that of the cargo's being swept away by disease. The underwriters refused to issue such policies, arguing that they would expose the captain to an unholy temptation. If insured against disease among his slaves, he might take no precautions against it and might try to make his profit out of the insurance.

The more days at sea, the more deaths among his cargo, and so the captain tried to cut short the next leg of his voyage. If he had shipped his slaves at Bonny, Old Calabar, or any port to the southward, he might call at one of the Portuguese islands in the Gulf of Guinea for an additional supply of food and fresh water, usually enough, with what he had already, to last for three months. If he had traded to the northward, he made straight for the West Indies. Usually he had from four to five thousand nautical miles to sail—or even more, if the passage was from Angola to Virginia. The shortest passage—that from the Gambia River to Barbados—might be made in as little as three weeks, with favoring winds. If the course was much longer, and if the ship was becalmed in the doldrums or driven back by storms, the voyage might take more than three months, and slaves and sailors would be put on short rations long before the end of the Middle Passage.

On a canvas of heroic size, Thomas Stothard, Esquire, of the Royal Academy, depicted *The Voyage of the Sable Venus from Angola to the West Indies*. His painting is handsomely reproduced in the second volume of Bryan Edwards' *History of the British Colonies in the West Indies* (1793), where it appears beside a poem on the same allegorical subject by an unnamed Jamaican author, perhaps Edwards himself.

The joint message of the poem and the painting is simple to the point of coarseness: that slave women are preferable to English girls at night, being passionate and accessible; but the message is embellished with classical details, to show the painter's learning.

Meanwhile the *Sable Venus*, if she was a living woman carried from Angola to the West Indies, was roaming the deck of a ship that stank of excrement; as was said of any slaver, "You could smell it five miles down wind." She had been torn from her husband and her children, she had been branded on the left buttock, and she had been carried to the ship bound hand and foot, lying in the bilge at the bottom of a dugout canoe. Now she was the prey of the ship's officers.

Here is how she and her shipmates spent the day.

If the weather was clear, they were brought on deck at eight o'clock in the morning. The men were attached by their leg irons to the great chain that ran along the bulwarks on both sides of the ship; the women and half-grown boys were allowed to wander at will. About nine o'clock the slaves were served their first meal of the day. If they were from the Windward Coast—roughly, the shoreline of present-day Liberia and Sierra Leone—the fare was boiled rice, millet, or corn meal, sometimes cooked with a few lumps of salt beef abstracted from the sailors' rations. If they were from the Bight of Biafra, at the east end of the Gulf of Guinea, they were fed stewed yams, but the Congos and the Angolas preferred manioc or plantains. With the food they were all given half a pint of water, served out in a pannikin.

After the morning meal came a joyless ceremony called "dancing the slaves." "Those who were in irons," says Dr. Thomas Trotter, surgeon of the *Brookes* in 1783, "were ordered to stand up and make what motions they could, leaving a passage for such as were out of irons to dance around the deck." Dancing was prescribed as a therapeutic measure, a specific against suicidal melancholy, and also against scurvy—although in the latter case it was a useless torture for men with swollen limbs. While sailors paraded the deck, each with a cat-o'-nine-tails in his right hand, the men slaves "jumped in their irons" until their ankles were bleeding flesh. Music was provided by a slave thumping on a broken drum or an upturned kettle, or by an African banjo, if there was one aboard, or perhaps by a sailor with a bagpipe or a fiddle. Slaving captains sometimes advertised for "A person that can play on the Bagpipes, for a Guinea ship." The slaves were also told to sing. Said Dr. Claxton after his voyage in the *Young Hero*, "They sing, but not for their amusement. The captain ordered them to sing, and they sang songs of sorrow. Their sickness, fear of being beaten, their hunger, and the memory of their country, etc., are the usual subjects."

While some of the sailors were dancing the slaves, others were sent below to scrape and swab out the sleeping rooms. It was a sickening task, and it was not well performed unless the captain imposed an iron discipline. James Barbot, Sr., was proud of the discipline maintained on the *Albion-Frigate*. "We were very nice," he says, "in keeping the places where the slaves lay clean and neat, appointing some of the ship's crew to do that office constantly and thrice a week we perfumed betwixt decks with a quantity of good vinegar in pails, and red-hot iron bullets in them, to expel the bad air, after the place had been well washed and scrubbed with brooms." Captain Hugh Crow, the last legal English slaver, was famous for his housekeeping. "I always took great pains," he says, "to promote the health and comfort of all on board, by proper diet, regularity, exercise, and cleanliness, for I considered that on keeping the ship clean and orderly, which was always my hobby, the success of our voyage mainly depended." Certainly he lost fewer slaves in the Middle Passage than the other captains, some of whom had the filth in the hold cleaned out only once a week.

At three or four in the afternoon the slaves were fed their second meal, often a repetition of the first. Sometimes, instead of African food, they were given horse beans, the cheapest provender from Europe. The beans were boiled to a pulp, then covered with a mixture of palm oil, flour, water, and red pepper, which the sailors called "slabber sauce." Most of the slaves detested horse beans, especially if they were used to eating yams or manioc. Instead of eating the pulp, they would, unless carefully watched, pick it up by handfuls and throw it in each other's faces.

That second meal was the end of their day. As soon as it was finished they were sent below, under the guard of sailors charged with stowing them away on their bare floors and platforms. The tallest men were placed amidships, where the vessel was widest; the shorter ones were tumbled into the stern. Usually there was only room for them to sleep on their sides, "spoon fashion." Captain William Littleton told Parliament that slaves in the ships on which he sailed might lie on their backs if they wished—"though perhaps," he conceded, "it might be difficult all at the same time."

After stowing their cargo, the sailors climbed out of the hatchway, each clutching his cat-o'-nine-tails; then the hatchway gratings were closed and barred. Sometimes in the night, as the sailors lay on deck and tried to sleep, they heard from below "an howling melancholy noise, expressive of extreme anguish." When Dr. Trotter told his interpreter, a slave woman, to inquire about the cause of the noise, "she discovered it to be owing to their having dreamt they were in their own country, and finding themselves when awake, in the hold of a slave ship."

More often the noise heard by the sailors was that of quarreling among the slaves. The usual occasion for quarrels was their problem of reaching the latrines. These were inadequate in size and number, and hard to find in the darkness of the crowded hold, especially by men who were ironed together in pairs.

In squalls or rainy weather, the slaves were never brought on deck. They were served their two meals in the hold, where the air became too thick and poisonous to breathe. Dr. Falconbridge writes:

> For the purpose of admitting fresh air, most of the ships in the slave-trade are provided, between the decks, with five or six airports on each side of the ship, of about six inches in length and four in breadth; in addition to which, some few ships, but not one in twenty, have what they denominate wind-sails [funnels made of canvas and so placed as to direct a current of air into the hold]. But whenever the sea is rough and the rain heavy, it becomes necessary to shut these and every other conveyance by which the air is admitted. . . . The negroes' rooms very soon become intolerably hot. The confined air, rendered noxious by the effluvia exhaled from their bodies and by being repeatedly breathed, soon produces fevers and fluxes which generally carry off great numbers of them.

Dr. Trotter says that when tarpaulins were thrown over the gratings, the slaves would cry, "Kickeraboo, kickeraboo, we are dying, we are dying." Falconbridge gives one instance of their sufferings:

Some wet and blowing weather having occasioned the portholes to be shut and the grating to be covered, fluxes and fevers among the negroes ensued. While they were in this situation, I frequently went down among them till at length their rooms became so extremely hot as to be only bearable for a very short time. But the excessive heat was not the only thing that rendered their situation intolerable. The deck, that is, the floor of their rooms, was so covered with the blood and mucus which had proceeded from them in consequence of the flux, that it resembled a slaughter-house.

While the slaves were on deck they had to be watched at all times to keep them from committing suicide. Says Captain Phillips of the *Hannibal,* "We had about 12 negroes did wilfully drown themselves, and others starv'd themselves to death; for," he explained, "'tis their belief that when they die they return home to their own country and friends again."

This belief was reported from various regions, at various periods of the trade, but it seems to have been especially strong among the Ibos of eastern Nigeria. In 1788, nearly a hundred years after the *Hannibal's* voyage, Dr. Ecroide Claxton was the surgeon who attended a shipload of Ibos. Some, he testified,

wished to die on an idea that they should then get back to their own country. The captain in order to obviate this idea, thought of an expedient viz. to cut off the heads of those who died intimating to them that if determined to go, they must return without heads. The slaves were accordingly brought up to witness the operation. One of them by a violent exertion got loose and flying to the place where the nettings had been unloosed in order to empty the tubs, he darted overboard. The ship brought to, a man was placed in the main chains to catch him which he perceiving, made signs which words cannot express expressive of his happiness in escaping. He then went down and was seen no more.

Dr. Isaac Wilson, a surgeon in the Royal Navy, made a Guinea voyage on the *Elizabeth,* the captain of which, John Smith, . . . was said to be very humane. Nevertheless, Wilson was assigned the duty of flogging the slaves. "Even in the act of chastisement," Wilson says, "I have seen them look up at me with a smile, and, in their own language, say 'presently we shall be no more.'" One woman on the *Elizabeth* found some rope yarn, which she tied to the armorer's vise; she fastened the other end round her neck and was found dead in the morning.

On the *Brookes* when Thomas Trotter was her surgeon, there was a man who, after being accused of witchcraft, had been sold into slavery with all his family. During the first night on shipboard he tried to cut his throat. Dr. Trotter sewed up the wound, but on the following night the man not only tore out the stitches but tried to cut his throat on the other side. From the ragged edges of the wound and the blood on his fingers, he seemed to have used his nails as the only available instrument. His hands were then tied together, but he refused all food, and he died of hunger in eight or ten days.

Besides the propensity for suicide, another deadly scourge of the Guinea cargoes was a phenomenon called "fixed melancholy." Even slaves who were well fed, treated with kindness, and kept under relatively sanitary conditions would often die, one after another, for no apparent reason; they had simply lost the will to live.

Dr. Wilson believed that fixed melancholy was responsible for the loss of two thirds of the slaves who died on the *Elizabeth*. "No one who had it was ever cured," he says, "whereas those who had it not and yet were ill, recovered. The symptoms are a lowness of spirits and despondency. Hence they refuse food. This only increases the symptoms. The stomach afterwards got weak. Hence the belly ached, fluxes ensued, and they were carried off." But in spite of the real losses from despair, the high death rate on Guineamen was due to somatic more than to psychic afflictions.

Along with their human cargoes, crowded, filthy, undernourished, and terrified out of the wish to live, the ships also carried an invisible cargo of microbes, bacilli, spirochetes, viruses, and intestinal worms from one continent to another; the Middle Passage was a crossroad and market place of diseases. From Europe came smallpox, measles (somewhat less deadly to Africans than to American Indians), gonorrhea, and syphilis (which last Columbus' sailors had carried from America to Europe). The African diseases were yellow fever (to which the natives were resistant), dengue, blackwater fever, and malaria (which was not specifically African, but which most of the slaves carried in their blood streams). If anopheles mosquitoes were present, malaria spread from the slaves through any new territories to which they were carried. Other African diseases were amoebic and bacillary dysentery (known as "the bloody flux"), Guinea worms, hookworm (possibly African in origin, but soon endemic in the warmer parts of the New World), yaws, elephantiasis, and leprosy.

The particular affliction of the white sailors after escaping from the fevers of the Guinea Coast was scurvy, a deficiency disease to which they were exposed by their monotonous rations of salt beef and sea biscuits. The daily tot of lime juice (originally lemon juice) that prevented scurvy was almost never served on merchantmen during the days of the legal slave trade, and in fact was not prescribed in the Royal Navy until 1795. Although the slaves were also subject to scurvy, they fared better in this respect than the sailors, partly because they made only one leg of the triangular voyage and partly because their rough diet was sometimes richer in vitamins. But sailors and slaves alike were swept away by smallpox and "the bloody flux," and sometimes whole shiploads went blind from what seems to have been trachoma.

Smallpox was feared more than other diseases, since the surgeons had no way of curing it. One man with smallpox infected a whole vessel, unless—as sometimes happened—he was tossed overboard when the first scabs appeared. Captain Wilson of the *Briton* lost more than half his cargo of 375 slaves by not listening to his surgeon. It was the last slave on board who had the disease, say Henry Ellison, who made the voyage. "The doctor told Mr. Wilson it was the small-pox," Ellison continues. "He would not believe it, but said he would keep him, as he was a fine man. It soon broke out amongst the slaves. I have seen the platform one continued scab. We hauled up eight or ten slaves dead of a morning. The flesh and skin peeled off their wrists when taken hold of, being entirely mortified."

But dysentery, though not so much feared, probably caused more deaths in the aggregate. Ellison testified that he made two voyages on the *Nightingale*. On the first voyage the slaves were so crowded that thirty boys "messed and slept in the long boat all through the Middle Passage, there being no room below"; and still the vessel lost only five or six slaves in all, out of a cargo of 270. On the second voyage, however, the *Nightingale* buried "about 150, chiefly of fevers and flux. We had 250 when we left the coast."

The average mortality in the Middle Passage is impossible to state accurately from the surviving records. Some famous voyages were made without the loss of a single slave. On one group of nine voyages between 1766 and 1780, selected at random, the vessels carried 2,362 slaves and there were no epidemics of disease. The total loss of slaves was 154, or about six and one-half percent. That figure is to be compared with the losses on a list of twenty voyages compiled by Thomas Clarkson, the abolitionist, in which the vessels carried 7,904 slaves with a mortality of 2,053, or 26 percent. Balancing high and low figures together, the English Privy Council in 1789 arrived at an estimate of twelve and one-half percent for the average mortality among slaves in the Middle Passage. To this figure it added four and one-half percent for the deaths of slaves in harbors before they were sold, and thirty-three percent for deaths in the so-called "seasoning" or acclimatizing process, making a total of fifty percent. If these figures are correct, only one slave was added to the New World labor force for every two purchased on the Guinea Coast.

To keep the figures in perspective, it might be said that the mortality among slaves in the Middle Passage was possibly no greater than that of white indentured servants or even of free Irish, Scottish, and German immigrants in the North Atlantic crossing. On the better-commanded Guineamen it was probably less, and for a simple economic reason. There was no profit on a slaving voyage until the Negroes were landed alive and sold; therefore the better captains took care of their cargoes. It was different on the North Atlantic crossing, where even the hold and steerage passengers paid their fares before coming aboard, and where the captain cared little whether they lived or died.

After leaving the Portuguese island of São Tomé—if he had watered there—a slaving captain bore westward along the equator for a thousand miles, and then northwestward toward the Cape Verde Islands. This was the tedious part of the Middle Passage. "On leaving the Gulf of Guinea," says the author of a *Universal Geography* published in the early nineteenth century, ". . . that part of the ocean must be traversed, so fatal to navigators, where long calms detain the ships under a sky charged with electric clouds, pouring down by torrents of rain and of fire. This *sea of thunder*, being a focus of mortal diseases, is avoided as much as possible, both in approaching the coasts of Africa and those of America." It was not until reaching the latitude of the Cape Verde Islands that the vessel fell in with the northeast trades and was able to make a swift passage to the West Indies.

Dr. Claxton's ship, the *Young Hero*, was one of those delayed for weeks before reaching the trade winds. "We were so streightened for provisions," he testified, "that if we had been ten more days at sea, we must either have eaten the slaves that died, or have made the living slaves *walk the plank*," a term, he explained, that was widely used by Guinea captains. There are no authenticated records of cannibalism in the Middle Passage, but there are many accounts of slaves killed for various reasons. English captains believed that French vessels carried poison in their medicine chests, "with which they can destroy their negroes in a calm, contagious sickness, or short provisions." They told the story of a Frenchman from Brest who had a long passage and had to poison his slaves; only twenty of them reached Haiti out of five hundred. Even the cruelest English captains regarded this practice as Latin, depraved, and uncovered by their insurance policies. In an emergency they simply jettisoned part of their cargo.

Often a slave ship came to grief in the last few days of the Middle Passage. It might be taken by a French privateer out of Martinique, or it might disappear in a tropical hurricane, or it might be wrecked on a shoal almost in sight of its harbor. On a few ships there was an epidemic of suicide at the last moment.

These, however, were exceptional disasters, recounted as horror stories in the newspapers of the time. Usually the last two or three days of the passage were a comparatively happy period. All the slaves, or all but a few, might be released from their irons. When there was a remaining stock of provisions, the slaves were given bigger meals—to fatten them for market—and as much water as they could drink. Sometimes on the last day—if the ship was commanded by an easy-going captain— there was a sort of costume party on deck, with the women slaves dancing in the sailors' castoff clothing. Then the captain was rowed ashore, to arrange for the disposition of his cargo.

This was a problem solved in various fashions. In Virginia, if the vessel was small, it might sail up and down the tidal rivers, bartering slaves for tobacco at private wharves. There were also public auctions of newly imported slaves, usually at Hampton, Yorktown, or Bermuda Hundred. In South Carolina, which was the great mainland slave market, the cargo was usually consigned to a commission merchant, who disposed of the slaves at auction, then had the vessel loaded with rice or indigo for its voyage back to England.

In the smaller West Indian islands, the captain sometimes took charge of selling his own slaves. In this case he ferried them ashore, had them drawn up in a ragged line of march, and paraded them through town with bagpipes playing, before exposing them to buyers in the public square. In the larger islands, commission merchants took charge of the cargo, and the usual method of selling the slaves at retail was a combination of the "scramble"—to be described in a moment—with the vendue or public auction "by inch of candle."

First the captain, with the commission merchant at his side, went over the cargo and picked out the slaves who were maimed or diseased. These were carried to a tavern and auctioned off, with a lighted candle before the auctioneer; bids were received until an inch of candle had burned. The price of so-called "refuse" slaves sold at auction was usually less than half of that paid for a healthy Negro. "I was informed by a mulatto woman," Dr. Falconbridge says, "that she purchased a sick slave at Grenada, upon speculation, for the small sum of one dollar, as the poor wretch was apparently dying of the flux." There were some slaves so diseased and emaciated that they could not be sold for even a dollar, and these might be left to die on the wharves.

The healthy slaves remaining after the auction were sold by "scramble," that is, at standard prices for each man, each woman, each boy, and each girl in the cargo. The prices were agreed upon with the purchasers, who then scrambled for their pick of the slaves. During his four voyages Falconbridge was present at a number of scrambles. "In the *Emilia*," he says, at Jamaica, the ship was darkened with sails, and covered round. The men slaves were placed on the main deck, and the women on the quarter deck. The purchasers on shore were informed a gun would be fired when they were ready to open the sale. A great number of people came on board with tallies or cards in their hands, with their own names upon them, and rushed through the barricado door with the ferocity of brutes. Some had three or four handkerchiefs tied together, to encircle as many as they thought fit for their purposes.

For the slaves, many of whom believed that they were about to be eaten, it was the terrifying climax of a terrifying voyage.

The parliamentary investigations of 1788–1791 presented a complete picture of the Middle Passage, with testimony from everyone concerned except the slaves, and it horrified the English public. Powerful interests in Parliament, especially those representing the Liverpool merchants and the West Indian planters, prevented the passage of restrictive legislation at that time. But the Middle Passage was not forgotten, and in 1807 Parliament passed a law forbidding any slaver to sail from a British port after May 1 of that year. At about the same time, Congress prohibited the importation of slaves into American territory from and after January 1, 1808. All the countries of Europe followed the British and American example, if with some delay. During the next half century, however, reformers would learn that the trade was difficult to abolish in fact as well as in law, and that illegal slaving would continue as long as slavery itself was allowed to flourish.

———

3 The Birth of a Nation

Congress Voting Independence, *oil painting by Robert Edge Pine and Edward Savage, 1785. The committee appointed by Congress to draft a declaration of independence included (center, standing) John Adams, Roger Sherman, Robert Livingston, Thomas Jefferson, and (center foreground, seated) Benjamin Franklin. The committee members are shown submitting Jefferson's draft to the speaker.*

The Ordeal of Thomas Hutchinson

Bernard Bailyn

The furor that erupted in the colonies in 1765 when Great Britain attempted to collect new stamp taxes on legal documents, periodicals, and all sorts of printed matter has long interested historians because the Stamp Act was a major milestone along the road that led to the American Revolution. The sacking of the house of Lieutenant Governor Thomas Hutchinson of Massachusetts by a Boston mob was one of the most shocking examples of the violence that occurred at this time. It has often been said that Hutchinson was singled out because he was a vigorous supporter of the Stamp Act. Actually, as Bernard Bailyn of Harvard University points out in the following pages, Hutchinson considered the Stamp Act a mistake and had sought to prevent its passage by Parliament. Why, in spite of this, he was so cordially disliked by the people of Boston is the subject of this essay. Professor Bailyn is the author of a biography of Hutchinson and, among other books, *The Origins of American Politics* and *Pamphlets of the American Revolution*.

On the night of August 26, 1765, a mob, more violent than any yet seen in America, more violent indeed than any that would be seen in the entire course of the Revolution, attacked the Boston mansion of Thomas Hutchinson, chief justice and lieutenant governor of Massachusetts. Hardly giving Hutchinson and his family time to flee from the supper table into the streets, the rioters smashed in the doors with axes, swarmed through the rooms, ripped off wainscotting and hangings, splintered the furniture, beat down the inner walls, tore up the garden, and carried off into the night, besides £900 sterling in cash, all the plate, decorations, and clothes that had survived, and destroyed or scattered in the mud all of Hutchinson's books and papers, including the manuscript of Volume I of his *History of the Colony and Province of Massachusetts-Bay* and the collection of historical papers that he had been gathering for years as the basis for a public archive. The determination of the mob was as remarkable as its savagery: "they worked for three hours at the cupola before they could get it down," Governor Francis Bernard reported; only the heavy brickwork construction of the walls prevented their razing the building completely, "though they worked at it till daylight. The next day the streets were found scattered with money, plate, gold rings, etc. which had been dropped in carrying off." Hutchinson was convinced that he himself would have been killed if he had not given in to his daughter's frantic pleading and fled. He estimated the loss of property at £2,218 sterling.

People of all political persuasions, everywhere in the colonies, were shocked at such "savageness unknown in a civilized country." Hutchinson appeared in court the next day without his robes, and as the young lawyer Josiah Quincy, Jr., who would later pursue him like a fury, reported, the chief justice, "with tears starting from his eyes and a countenance which strongly told the inward anguish of his soul," addressed the court. He apologized for his appearance: he had no other clothes but what he wore, he said, and some of that was borrowed. His family was equally destitute, and their distress was "infinitely more insupportable than what I feel for myself."

> Sensible that I am innocent, that all the charges against me are false, I cannot help feeling—and though I am not obliged to give an answer to all the questions that may be put me by every lawless person, yet I call GOD to witness (and I would not for a thousand worlds call my *Maker* to witness to a falsehood)—I say, I call my *Maker* to witness that I never, in New England or Old, in Great Britain or America, neither directly nor indirectly, was aiding, assisting, or supporting, or in the least promoting or encouraging what is commonly called the STAMP ACT, but on the contrary, did all in my power, and strove as much as in me lay, to prevent it. This is not declared through timidity, for I have nothing to fear. They can only take away my life, which is of but little value when deprived of all its comforts, all that is dear to me, and nothing surrounding me but the most piercing distress. . . .

What had caused the riot? Resistance to the Stamp Act had generally been violent; and individuals, especially the would-be stamp distributors, had commonly been attacked. But no one in America had been as deliberately and savagely assaulted as Hutchinson, though he had not been appointed a stamp master and though, as he said, he had opposed the Stamp Act. What was the meaning and what would be the ultimate effect of the attack?

On July fourth, 1776, almost eleven stormy years after the sack of his mansion, Thomas Hutchinson, by now the exiled Loyalist governor of Massachusetts, was awarded an honorary doctorate of civil laws by Oxford University. "Probably no distinction which Hutchinson ever attained was more valued by him," his nineteenth-century biographer wrote; certainly none so fittingly symbolizes the tragedy of his life. For he was honored as an American—the most distinguished as well as the most loyal colonial-born official of his time. Provincial assemblyman, speaker of the Massachusetts House of Representatives, councillor, lieutenant governor, chief justice, governor, he had gone through the entire course of public offices and of official honors, and he was in addition America's most accomplished historian. But to the people who on the day of Hutchinson's award proclaimed their nation's independence, he was one of the most hated men on earth—more hated than Lord North, more hated than George III (both of whom, it was believed, he had secretly influenced). . . .

. . . The feeling was widespread among well-informed Americans that Thomas Hutchinson had betrayed his country; that for sordid, selfish reasons he had accepted and abetted—even stimulated—oppressive measures against the colonies; that he had supported them even in the face of a threat of armed resistance; and that in this sense his personal actions lay at the heart of the Revolution. So it was said, again and again. Was it true?

It is hard to imagine a man less disposed by background or heritage to betray his countrymen than Thomas Hutchinson. His family had helped to found New England, and they had prospered with its growth. Until Thomas only one of the family had been famous: the notorious seventeenth-century Anne, who had refused to adjust her singular convictions to the will of the community, for which she had been banished, to die in exile. But the family's main interest had never been hers. The Hutchinsons had been tradesmen in London before the Puritan migration; in New England they became merchants and remained merchants, with remarkable consistency, generation after generation. In the course of a century and a half they produced, in the stem line of the family, not a single physician, not a single lawyer, and not a single teacher or minister. The entire clan devoted itself to developing its property and the network of trade, based on kinship lines at every point, that Anne's brothers and nephews had created in the mid-seventeenth century. They prospered solidly but not greatly. Their enterprises were careful, not grand. They were accumulators, down-to-earth, unromantic middle-men, whose solid, petit bourgeois characteristics became steadily more concentrated in the passage of years until in Thomas, in the fifth generation, they reached an apparently absolute and perfect form.

He was born in Boston in 1711. His father, Colonel Thomas Hutchinson, had risen somewhat, though not greatly, beyond the level of his two prosperous merchant-shipowner relatives, Elisha and Eliakim. The colonel served on the provincial Council for over twenty years, donated the building for a Latin grammar school (which his son would attend), and improved into provincial magnificence the imposing town house bequeathed to him by a widowed aunt. The colonel's marriage fitted perfectly the pattern of his classically bourgeois existence. His wife, Sarah Foster, ten years his senior, was the daughter of John Foster, the Boston merchant to whom he had been apprenticed in trade, of status identical to the Hutchinson family's, who engaged in the same kinds of trade as they did and to whom, by force of the remarkable endogamy that characterizes the family history, Colonel Thomas became triply related by other marriages between the two families.

Colonel Thomas set the pattern for young Thomas' life. He was industrious, charitable, unaffected, unworldly, and clannish. A strait-laced, pious provincial, he read the Scriptures to his family mornings and evenings and devoted himself to trade and to the welfare of his kin and community. For over thirty years, his son later recorded, Colonel Thomas "kept a table on Saturdays with a salt fish or bacalao [codfish] dinner." To this unpretentious feast he regularly invited only four close friends, all of them merchants, two of them relatives; only "now and then," his son recalled, was a clergyman added to the group.

For young Thomas, the future governor, there was no break in the continuity of family and community life. He entered Harvard at the age of twelve, where he developed not so much the intellectual interests that later became important to him as his ability and resources in trade. At the time he entered college, he recalled a half century later, his father undertook his proper education by presenting him with "two or three quintals of fish." From this humble capital he managed to build, by "adventuring to sea" through his college years, a fund of £4–500 sterling, which, combined with an inheritance from his father, became a fortune, by provincial standards, by the time of the Revolution: in cash fifteen times his original capital, and in real estate eight houses, including the Boston mansion he had inherited, two wharves and a variety of lots and shop properties in Boston, and in suburban Milton a country house universally admired for its simple beauty and splendid setting and a hundred acres of choice land.

. . . At the age of twenty-six, Hutchinson entered politics. He was never thereafter out of it, and he maintained an altogether consistent policy in defense of what, until the great issues of the 1760s intervened, were widely considered to be the basic interests of the colony. As representative of Boston to the Massachusetts House from 1737 to 1749 (with the exception of a single year) and a councillor for the succeeding seventeen years, he distinguished himself by his effective defense of a hard-money policy and by his equally determined defense of the territorial integrity of Massachusetts and of its chartered rights. So convinced was the community of Hutchinson's "disinterestedness and integrity," Pownall reported in 1757, that even those who most sharply disagreed with him continued to respect him, even to revere him. In the end Hutchinson's views on the money question prevailed, in part because of the shrewd use that Massachusetts, led by Hutchinson, was able to make of the specie it received from the English government as repayment for its contribution to the war against France; and in part because when in 1741 the issue developed into a crisis that threatened violence, Governor Jonathan Belcher had seized the initiative and stamped out the incipient rebellion by force. There was no limit, Belcher wrote Hutchinson in a portentous letter of 1741, to what political fanatics would do; they would even defy Parliament, for the common people were told by their leaders that they were out of the reach of the government of England, and the Assembly was made to think they were as big as the Parliament of Great Britain. "They are grown so brassy . . . as to be now combining in a body to raise a rebellion. . . . I have this day sent the sheriff and his officers to apprehend some of the heads of the conspirators, so you see we are becoming ripe for a smarter sort of government."

In 1740 Hutchinson was sent by the colony to England to plead the case of certain Massachusetts landowners whose property had fallen to New Hampshire in a Crown ruling on the colony's boundary, and he negotiated repeatedly, almost annually, with the border Indians in the interest of his native colony, managed the province's lottery, supervised the financing of the Louisbourg expedition of 1745, dealt with other colonies on joint military efforts, and adjudicated boundary disputes with Connecticut and Rhode Island.

It is hard to see what more he could have done to serve his countrymen or how, as a leader of the establishment in trade and politics, he could have been more enlightened.

Yet in the end his services were forgotten and he was cursed as a traitor in the land of his birth—cursed not merely by the wild men, the alarmists, the political paranoids, and the professional agitators, but by some of the most stable, sensible people of the time, many of whom knew him personally. There was, they said, some deep flaw in his character, some perversion of personality, some profound "malignancy of heart," that had turned his patriotism into treason and led him to sacrifice the general good for the most sordid, selfish gain. . . .

Until 1757 Hutchinson had been one of those establishment figures who knew how to find their way successfully through the paths of factional intrigue. As a young man he had had Governor Belcher's favor, and in 1740 Hutchinson had gravitated to Belcher's successor, the ambitious and well-connected English lawyer William Shirley. For almost two decades thereafter Hutchinson had remained a leader of Governor Shirley's unusually stable political coalition.

Governor Thomas Pownall, who succeeded Shirley as governor in 1757, elevated Hutchinson to the lieutenant governorship, but he was a man with whom Hutchinson would struggle, directly or indirectly, for the rest of his life.

Pownall's administration was a brief interlude between the long, late-colonial era of William Shirley, which had nourished the young Thomas Hutchinson's success in trade and politics, and the disastrous decade of Sir Francis Bernard, in which Hutchinson's failure began; but though brief it was a critical interlude. For in these years Hutchinson's devotion to the welfare of the empire and his identification of America's well-being with the strength of Great Britain had become an intense commitment. At the same time his differences with the momentarily triumphant opposition forces, with which Pownall had allied himself, had become charged with more than ordinary political meaning. They were of course his rivals in quite traditional factional contests for the control of public offices. But beyond that he had been shocked by their pursuit of private gain at the expense of the general welfare, which he took to mean the welfare of the pan-Atlantic polity that had protected the infant colonies for a century and a half, and he distrusted the glib libertarianism by which they justified their resistance to appeals for wartime sacrifices.

The new governor, Francis Bernard, was the ideal type of the patronage appointee in the first British Empire. A well-educated barrister whose only administrative or political office in England had been the recordership of the town of Boston in Lincolnshire, he had practiced law until the financial needs of his ten children drove him to seek more lucrative employment in the colonies. Through the patronage of his wife's influential uncle, Viscount Barrington, he was appointed to the governorship of New Jersey in 1758 and then, feeling socially and culturally isolated there and seeking a better-paying position, managed to have himself transferred, at the age of fifty, to Massachusetts. He was a decent man who had simple, uncomplicated desires: peace and quiet, the respect of those he ruled, some comradeship in literary matters, appointments for his six sons, and a substantial income—from salary, from fees, and from lucrative investments. As far as he knew, the prospects in Massachusetts were excellent. "I am assured," he wrote shortly before he arrived in Boston, "that I may depend upon a quiet and easy administration." True, he had heard from Pownall the discouraging news (along with accounts of investment opportunities in northern New England land) that the total income of the Massachusetts governor, from salary and "all advantages and contingencies," was only £1,200 sterling; but he thought he could live more cheaply in Boston than in many other places, and in addition he would have far better opportunities for educating and providing jobs for his children there than he had had in Perth Amboy. Moreover, in Boston, "perhaps the most polished and scientific town in America," he was sure he would find the "refined conversation and the amusements that arise from letters, arts, and sciences . . . many very conversable men, tolerable music, and other amusements to which I had bid adieu not without regret." Finally, he had heard that the Massachusetts governor had (in the fortress to which he would repeatedly flee in the years to come) "a very pretty place to retire to, a pleasant apartment in Castle William, which stands in an island about three miles from the town at the entrance of the Bay."

He was thus a well-disposed and ordinary man, with ordinary desires, but he was no politician and he was innocent of the arts of governance. "Open in his behavior," Hutchinson wrote of him, "regardless of mere forms, and inattentive to the fashionable arts of engaging mankind," he was destined by his manner alone to offend the sensibilities of the proud Bostonians. But it was not simply a question of manner and sensibilities. He was determined to get every penny to which his office entitled him. It was this mainly that led him to his fatal decision to appoint Hutchinson to the vacant chief justiceship; and it was this—well before the Stamp Act raised fundamental questions of principle—that first pitched Hutchinson into open conflict with the opposition merchants and populist politicians.

Hutchinson had not sought the chief justiceship, which fell vacant when the incumbent, Stephen Sewall, died five weeks after Bernard arrived in Boston, nor had he attempted to solicit Bernard's patronage or to forge a political alliance with him. But if Hutchinson did not seek Bernard's support, Bernard had reason to seek his. Though the Assembly quickly granted the new governor a substantial salary and then went beyond that to give him the gift of Mount Desert Island, off the southeast coast of Maine, he quickly discovered the difficulty of maintaining the "quiet and easy" administration he had expected. The province, he found, was "divided into parties so nearly equal that it would have been madness for me to have put myself at the head of either of them." In this situation "management and intrigue," he wrote to Barrington, were required to preserve the force of government and at the same time convey at least "the appearance" of respect for the colonists' cherished liberties, "of which they formed high and sometimes unconstitutional ideas."

The appointment of the new chief justice was crucial to the success of this delicate balance. For it was the superior court in the end that would largely determine whether the interest of the state would be sustained in general, and in particular whether the trade regulations would be enforced and whether therefore the governor would receive his statutory third of the income from forfeited goods.

Bernard knew that Governor Shirley had promised the next court vacancy to the venerable Barnstable lawyer James Otis, Sr., then speaker of the House and, in Shirley's time, a political colleague of Hutchinson's. But word reached Bernard that Otis' appointment at this juncture would be inadvisable, perhaps because his brilliant but unstable son James, Jr., was leading the family into doubtful political alliances and was reluctant to use his office as deputy advocate-general of the vice-admiralty court to prosecute violations of the navigation laws. Hutchinson's commitment to maintaining close ties between England and America, on the other hand, was beyond question, as was his reputation with all parties for integrity, industry, judiciousness, and devotion to public service.

The day after Sewall died, "several gentlemen" (Bernard said they were "the best men in the government") told Hutchinson they were proposing him for the vacancy. He was pleasantly surprised, but he immediately expressed what he called "a diffidence of my own abilities," for he was no lawyer and he was not at all certain "that it would be advisable for me to undertake so great a trust." He repeated these same doubts "of my abilities to give the country satisfaction" when young James Otis called on him to seek his support for the elder Otis' appointment; and while he did not promise the Otises his help and said merely that the whole question was new to him and that he would have to think about it, he went out of his way to praise the elder Otis and to register his own lack of enthusiasm for the appointment. His passivity persisted even though most of the judiciary assured him of their support. When, after a month, Bernard finally broached the subject to him, explaining that "the major voices seemed to be in my favor," Hutchinson replied that while recognizing the importance of the position, he knew "the peculiar disadvantages I should be under" in following so distinguished a jurist as Sewall. And when some weeks later Bernard told him that he had definitely decided to appoint him and indicated that even if he refused he would not turn to Otis, Hutchinson "still expressed my doubts of the expedience of it. . . ."

Bernard was well aware of the problems: years later he would apologize to Lord Mansfield for having appointed a chief justice "not . . . bred to the law"; but he knew that the essential qualifications were as much political and intellectual as strictly legal, and he could count on Hutchinson's diligence in perfecting his knowledge of the law. So Hutchinson, still concerned about his lack of technical qualifications and having refused to solicit actively for the appointment but always eager for advancement, prestige, and a major public role, accepted. His appointment was announced on November 13, and on December 30, 1760, his commission was issued.

The general transformation of Hutchinson's reputation proceeded gradually in the months and years that followed his appointment to the chief justiceship, but John Adams and James Otis, Jr., who would ultimately shape opinion most powerfully, reached immediate conclusions. The 1760s were years in which the Massachusetts bar reached a high point of professionalization; its practitioners were exceptionally conscious of their craft and proud of their skills—and none more so than the twenty-five-year-old apprentice John Adams. Adams never forgot the outrage he felt at this elevation of a layman to the chief justiceship, so thwarting, insulting, and humiliating to his excruciatingly sensitive self-esteem. An appointment so unmerited, so perverse, and so unjust to those like himself who were sacrificing their lives to the law could only be the result of dangerous secret forces whose power would no doubt otherwise be felt and that would otherwise block the aspirations of powerless but honest and able new men.

Otis helped to substantiate these fears and to publicize this affront to the dignity of "old practitioners at the bar." Like Adams, Otis too registered shock that the new chief justice was "bred a merchant," but that was not the main burden of his response. Nor was it simply the rage of wounded pride at his family's humiliation . . . Hutchinson, Otis pointed out, was a dominant figure in the executive by virtue of being lieutenant governor, in the legislature as a councillor ("I have long thought it . . . a great grievance that the chief justice should have a seat in the Council and consequently so great a share of influence in making those very laws he is appointed to execute upon the lives and property of the people"), and in the judiciary as chief justice. "Mixed monarchy," Otis agreed, was, as everyone knew, the most perfect form of government, but—what everyone did not know—fundamental to it was the separation of legislative and executive powers, and without this, free government would dissolve. Montesquieu was right: "when the legislative and executive powers are united in the same person, or in the same body of magistrates (or nearly so) there can be no liberty because (just and great) apprehensions may arise lest the same monarch or senate (or junto) should enact *tyrannical* laws to execute them in a *tyrannical* manner." Within a few months of Hutchinson's appointment to the high bench Otis' attacks, cast in these terms and publicized again and again, became a blistering indictment.

The case of the writs of assistance—to support customs officers in searching for contraband—came before the superior court almost as soon as Hutchinson took his seat on the bench. The episode not only served to fuse Adams' resentment at unmerited professional advancement with Otis' fear of monopolized power, but it brought all of this into conjunction with the hostilities of a significant part of the merchant community for whom strict enforcement of trade regulations was a novel threat.

Hutchinson was especially well informed on the problems of these general search warrants, and he was much concerned to limit their use to the strict letter of the law as anyone in the colony. It had been he, in fact, in 1757, who had prevented the governor from issuing general warrants on his own authority, and as a result the power to grant these potentially dangerous instruments had been confined to the superior court acting as a court of exchequer. He knew of the warrants' unquestioned legality in England and of their common use there, and he knew, too, that they had been issued before in Massachusetts without provoking public controversy.

But if the positive law was clear (and the doubts it raised were quickly settled by queries to England), the higher law of "natural equity" was not, and it was to this that Otis, who formally represented the merchant opposition, in the end directed his plea. It was the moral basis of the law, not the literal provisions, that primarily concerned him. "This writ," he charged, in words that John Adams, an eager attendant at the trial, recorded on the spot, "is against the fundamental principles of law. The privilege of house. A man who is quiet is as secure in his house as a prince in his castle," and no act of Parliament can contravene this privilege. "An act [of Parliament] against the constitution is void, an act against natural equity is void. . . ." The executive courts must pass such acts into disuse—precedents to the contrary notwithstanding, Adams later recalled him saying, for "ALL PRECEDENTS ARE UNDER THE CONTROL OF THE PRINCIPLES OF THE LAW."

The *principles* of law? Who was to say what they were? Yet it was Otis' extravagant transjuridical claim that entered American awareness, not Hutchinson's scrupulous regard for the law as it existed. Fifty-six years later John Adams—as romantic in old age as he had been in youth—caught the inner, quasi-mythological meaning of the event in his famous description of the scene:

> near the fire were seated five judges, with Lieutenant Governor Hutchinson at their head as chief justice, all in their new fresh robes of scarlet English cloth, in their broad bands, and immense judicial wigs [and against them James Otis,] a flame of fire! With the promptitude of classical allusions, a depth of research . . . a profusion of legal authorities, a prophetic glare of his eyes into futurity, and a rapid torrent of

This portrait of Thomas Hutchinson, attributed to Edward Truman, is considered the only authentic portrait of Hutchinson in existence.

impetuous eloquence, he hurried away all before him. . . . Every man of an [immense] crowded audience appeared to me to go away, as I did, ready to take up arms against writs of assistance. . . . Then and there the child Independence was born.

Hutchinson had strongly disapproved of the Stamp Act from the time he first heard of it. . . . [He] had summarized his views in four forceful arguments against the projected stamp tax: first, that the Crown and Parliament had long ago conceded to the colonies the power to make their own laws and to tax themselves by their own representatives; second, that Americans were in no sense represented in Parliament and hence that the justification for parliamentary taxation based on presumptive representation was invalid; third, that the colonies owed no debt to the English government for their settlement and development—the colonies had been founded and sustained by private enterprise, at times in the face of state opposition; and finally, that economic arguments in favor of the act were fallacious, since England's natural profit from the colonies, which would be endangered by taxation, was greater than any prospective tax yield.

These were hardheaded arguments—all matters of historical fact of irrefutable logic. They contained no challenge to English authority as such and indulged in no speculative distinctions in Parliament's power. For Parliament's ultimate control, Hutchinson believed, was the price of American freedom, and that control must remain paramount, he concluded—in words that a decade later would toll through the continent, the death knell of his political ambition—even if it became necessary for that body to abridge "what are generally called natural-rights. . . . The rights of parts and individuals must be given up when the safety of the whole shall depend on it . . . it is no more than is reasonable . . . in return for the protection received against foreign enemies." It was better, he said, "to submit to some abridgment of our rights than to break off our connection."

The Massachusetts legislature undertook to prepare a petition to Parliament protesting the proposed stamp tax. The lead was taken by the "heads of the popular party" in the House, Hutchinson explained, who drafted a document that stated the colony's objections to the stamp duties in passionate and highly theoretical terms, grounded in principles of natural rights and in constitutional guarantees. The Council, over which Hutchinson as lieutenant governor presided, rejected this "informal and incautiously expressed" draft, and a joint committee of the two Houses was formed to frame an acceptable document. Hutchinson was chosen chairman of this committee, and he led it in rejecting two new versions, "both very exceptionable." "Ten days were spent in this manner," Hutchinson confided to Jackson, "which I thought time not ill spent as I had the more opportunity of showing them the imprudence of every measure which looked like opposition to the determinations of Parliament." He explained to them the folly of pressing principles merely because they seemed grand and glittering and somehow pure; he stated the need for calm and compromise; and he expounded the value of supporting existing structures because they were the basis of civil order. But the conferees resisted and in draft after draft confronted him with demands that the *theory* of the matter, the *principles* at stake, the commitments that were involved, should be clearly stated. But Hutchinson kept control, of himself and of the situations, and waited, patiently and skillfully, for precisely the right moment to resolve the controversy. He found it when his opponents were altogether "perplexed and tired" and about to resolve wearily on yet another unacceptable proposal; he then "drew a petition to the House of Commons, not just such as I would have chosen if I had been the sole judge but such as I thought the best I could hope for being accepted," and he pressed this version through. In this way the effort of the "popular party" to draw Massachusetts into "an ample and full declaration of the exclusive right of the people to tax themselves" had been defeated. The address as adopted, Hutchinson explained with some pride, assumed that American control of its own taxation was an indulgence which the colonists prayed the continuance of—"a matter of favor," he wrote in his *History,* "and not a claim of right."

Thus Hutchinson, and prudence, prevailed—but only briefly, and for the last time, and at great cost. Two developments quickly turned his victory into a dangerous defeat. Reports from the other colonies began to come in. Their petitions—especially New York's—appeared to be "so high," Hutchinson wrote, "that the heroes of liberty among us were ashamed of their own conduct," and they would have reversed their action if it had not been too late. Second, news soon arrived that the Stamp Act had in fact passed despite all the agitation against it in America and that in passing it Parliament had made no distinctions whatever among the various petitions filed against it; no purpose at all had been served by the prudence Hutchinson had imposed on the House. The reaction in Boston was immediate and severe. It was instantly concluded, he reported, "that if all the colonies had shown . . . firmness and asserted their rights, the act would never have passed," and therefore if some one person had deliberately destroyed that unanimity, his aim could only have been secretly to promote, not defeat, the Stamp Act, protestations to the contrary notwithstanding. And so it was that Hutchinson, as he later realized, because he had been "the promoter of the [Massachusetts petition], was charged with treachery and . . . [with] betraying his country."

So the charge originated; and it stuck, as passions rose in the months between the passage of the Stamp Act and the date of its legal inception, and seemed in fact more and more persuasive. Everything served to confirm the suspicions of Hutchinson's duplicity that had first been generated by his prudent refusal to defy Parliament's power in principle. When the stamp master for Massachusetts was announced, he proved to be none other than Hutchinson's brother-in-law, fellow councillor, and protégé, the colony's secretary, Andrew Oliver: by this appointment alone Hutchinson's secret motives seemed to be revealed. Vituperative squibs began to appear in the newspapers. Rumors (lies, Hutchinson said, that shocked him) circulated that he had written secretly to England to encourage the promoters of the act and that copies of those letters had been returned confidentially from London and were available in Boston to be read. Otis swore he knew for a fact that the whole idea of a stamp act had been hatched by Hutchinson and Bernard and that he could point to the very house in Boston—indeed, the very room—in which the act itself had been conceived. Hutchinson fought back. He explained his views again and again, but the only effect this had, he confessed, was to confirm "the groundless suspicions of my having promoted the act."

By the summer of 1765 suspicious episodes throughout the entire span of Hutchinson's long career were being recalled in public prints. He still commanded the respect of informed people; he was still a natural as well as a legal leader of his native society. Yet something crucial in all of his activities had been missing—some recognition that security is not all nor prudence necessarily the wisest guide to action, some understanding that in the end law, to be effective, must reflect human sensibilities, and authority must deserve the respect it would command. Gradually the law he represented had begun to seem arbitrary, his honors to seem undeserved, and the government he led to become distant and insensitive to the needs of the governed.

As his prominence had grown so too had his vulnerability. In the scorching heat of the Stamp Act resistance he became a marked man, and explanations were demanded. On August 14 crowds directed by well-known opposition leaders turned to Hutchinson for the first time, surrounding his mansion and demanding that he "declare to them I had never wrote to England in favor of the Stamp Act." Since, the leaders said, they respected Hutchinson's private character, they would accept his personal assurance that he did not favor the act. He knew he had nothing to hide, but should he concede to such intimidation? Was he responsible to a mob? Surely he was "not obliged to give an answer to all the questions that may be put me by every lawless person." Fortunately an unnamed "grave, elderly tradesman" who was a noted town-meeting speaker intervened and "challenged every one of them to say I had ever done them the least wrong [and] charged them with ingratitude in insulting a gentleman who had been serving his country all his days." Somehow the speaker convinced the crowd that Hutchinson was not likely to have done anything deliberately to hurt his country and got them to move off. The day closed for Hutchinson with a fervent prayer for "a greater share of fortitude and discretion here than I have ever yet been master of." Twelve days later the "hellish fury" of August 26 descended on him, his family, and his property in "the most barbarous outrage which ever was committed in America."

George Washington, Spymaster

Thomas Fleming

Nearly every American knows about Nathan Hale, the patriot who gave his life while collecting intelligence for his country, and of Benedict Arnold, the spy who committed treason against his country while betraying its secrets. During the late eighteenth century, however, spying provided more than an object lesson on patriotism; it was an essential component of warfare. All effective generals utilized spies to locate the enemy, assess its strengths and weaknesses, and determine its plans. As Thomas Fleming points out in this essay, George Washington was a good general partly because he was a diligent and wily spymaster. He recruited resourceful spies such as Lydia Darragh, an Irish-born Quaker midwife who warned the Continentals of a British attack on Valley Forge. His double agents—patriot spies posing as British spies—exaggerated the size and readiness of Washington's ragged force at Valley Forge. Late in the war, such agents also warned the British high command of an imminent (and nonexistent) attack on New York, allowing Washington to slip south to trap Cornwallis. Thomas Fleming, an accomplished historian and historical novelist, has written many books and novels. His most recent books include Duel: Alexander Hamilton, Aaron Burr and the Future of America (1999), The New Dealers' War: Franklin D. Roosevelt and the War Within World War II (2001), and Remember the Morning (1997), a novel.

George Washington a master of espionage? It is commonly understood that without the Commander in Chief's quick mind and cool judgment the American Revolution would have almost certainly expired in 1776. It is less well known that his brilliance extended to overseeing, directly and indirectly, extensive and very sophisticated intelligence activities against the British.

Washington had wanted to be a soldier almost from the cradle and seems to have acquired the ability to think in military terms virtually by instinct. In the chaos of mid-1776, with half his army deserting and the other half in a funk and all his generals rattled, he kept his head and reversed his strategy. The Americans had started with the idea that a general action, as an all-out battle was called, could end the conflict overnight, trusting that their superior numbers would overwhelm the presumably small army the British could afford to send to our shores. But the British sent a very big, well-trained army, which routed the Americans in the first several battles in New York. Washington sat down in his tent on Harlem Heights and informed the Continental Congress that he was going to fight an entirely different war. From now on, he wrote, he would "avoid a general action." Instead he would "protract the war."

In his 1975 study of Washington's generalship, *The Way of the Fox,* Lt. Col. Dave Richard Palmer has called this reversal "a masterpiece of strategic thought, a brilliant blueprint permitting a weak force to combat a powerful opponent." It soon became apparent that for the blueprint to be followed, Washington would have to know what the British were planning to do, and he would have to be able to prevent them from finding out what he was doing. In short, espionage was built into the system.

Washington had been acquainted with British colonial officials and generals and colonels since his early youth, and he knew how intricately espionage was woven into the entire British military and political enterprise. Any Englishman's mail could be opened and read if a secretary of state requested it. Throughout Europe every British embassy had its intelligence network.

Thus Washington was not entirely surprised to discover, shortly after he took command of the American army in 1775, that his surgeon general, Dr. Benjamin Church, was telling the British everything that went on in the American camp at Cambridge, Massachusetts. He *was* surprised to find out, not long after he had transferred his operations to New York in the spring of 1776, that one of his Life Guard, a soldier named Thomas Hickey, was rumored to be involved in a plot to kill him.

By that time Washington had pulled off his own opening gambit in a form of intelligence at which he soon displayed something close to genius: disinformation. Shortly after he took command in Cambridge, he asked someone how much powder the embryo American army had in reserve. Everyone thought it had three hundred barrels, but a check of the Cambridge magazine revealed most of that had been fired away at Bunker Hill. There were only thirty-six barrels—fewer than nine rounds per man. For half an hour, according to one witness, Washington was too stunned to speak. But he recovered and sent people into British-held Boston to spread the story that he had eighteen hundred barrels, and he spread the same rumor throughout the American camp.

In chaotic New York, grappling with a large and aggressive British army, deserting militia, and an inapplicable strategy, Washington temporarily lost control of the intelligence situation. That explains the dolorous failure of Capt. Nathan Hale's mission in September 1776. Hale, sent to gather information behind British lines, was doomed almost from the moment he volunteered. He had little or no contact with the American high command, no training as a spy, no disguise worthy of the name, and an amorphous mission: to find out whatever he could wherever he went.

There is little evidence that Washington was even aware of Hale's existence. He was involved in something far more serious: figuring out how to burn down New York City in order to deprive the British of their winter quarters, despite orders from the Continental Congress strictly forbidding him to harm the place. He looked the other way while members of Hale's regiment slipped into the city; they were experts at starting conflagrations thanks to a tour of duty on fire ships—vessels carrying explosives to burn enemy craft—on the Hudson.

On September 21 a third of New York went up in flames. The timing was disastrous for Hale, who was captured the very same day. Anyone with a Connecticut accent became highly suspect, and the British caught several incendiaries and hanged them on the spot. They gave Hale the same treatment: no trial, just a swift, humiliating death. Hale's friends were so mortified by his fate, which they considered shameful, that no one mentioned his now-famous farewell speech for another fifty years. Then an old man told his daughter about it, and Yale College, seeking Revolutionary War heroes among its graduates, quickly immortalized him.

Washington never said a word about Hale. His only intelligence comment at the time concerned New York. The fire had destroyed Trinity Church and about six hundred houses, causing no little discomfort for the British and the thousands of Loyalist refugees who had crowded into the city. In a letter, Washington remarked that "Providence, or some good honest fellow, has done more for us than we were disposed to do for ourselves."

One of Hale's best friends, Maj. Benjamin Tallmadge, never got over his death. He probably talked about it to Washington, who assured him that once they got the protracted war under control, all espionage would be handled from Army headquarters, and no spy's life would be wasted the way Hale's had been.

Surviving long enough to fight an extended conflict was no small matter. In the weeks after Hale's death, disaster after disaster befell the American army. Washington was forced to abandon first New York and then New Jersey. On the other side of the Delaware, with only the shadow of an army left to him, he issued orders in December 1776 to all his generals to find "some person who can be engaged to cross the river as a spy" and added that "expense must not be spared" in securing a volunteer.

He also rushed a letter to Robert Morris, the financier of the Revolution, asking for hard money to "pay a certain set of people who are of particular use to us." He meant spies, and he had no illusion that any spy would risk hanging for the paper money the Continental Congress was printing. Morris sent from Philadelphia two canvas bags filled with what hard cash he could scrape together on an hour's notice: 410 Spanish dollars, 2 English crowns, 10 shillings, and 2 sixpence.

The search soon turned up a former British soldier named John Honeyman, who was living in nearby Griggstown, New Jersey. On Washington's orders Honeyman rediscovered his loyalty to the king and began selling cattle to several British garrisons along the Delaware. He had no trouble gaining the confidence of Col. Johann Rall, who was in command of three German regiments in Trenton. Honeyman listened admiringly as Rall described his heroic role in the fighting around New York and agreed with him that the Americans were hopeless soldiers.

On December 22, 1776, having spent about a week in Trenton, Honeyman wandered into the countryside, supposedly in search of cattle, and got himself captured by an American patrol and hustled to Washington's headquarters. There he was publicly denounced by the Commander in Chief as a "notorious" turncoat. Washington insisted on interrogating him personally and said he would give the traitor a chance to save his skin if he recanted his loyalty to the Crown.

A half-hour later the general ordered his aides to throw Honeyman into the guardhouse. Tomorrow morning, he stated, the Tory would be hanged. That night Honeyman escaped from the guardhouse with a key supplied by Washington and dashed past American sentries, who fired on him. Sometime on December 24 he turned up in Trenton and told Colonel Rall the story of his narrow escape.

The German naturally wanted to know what Honeyman had seen in Washington's camp, and the spy assured him that the Americans were falling apart. They were half-naked and freezing, and they lacked the food and basic equipment, such as shoes, to make a winter march. Colonel Rall, delighted, prepared to celebrate

From his headquarters at Morristown, New Jersey, General George Washington planned and directed espionage activities during the Revolutionary War.

Christmas with no military worries to interrupt the feasting and drinking that were traditional in his country. He never dreamed that Honeyman had given Washington a professional soldier's detailed description of the routine of the Trenton garrison, the location of the picket guards, and everything else an assaulting force would need to know.

At dawn on December 26 Washington's ragged Continentals charged through swirling snow and sleet to kill the besotted Colonel Rall and capture most of his troops. New Jersey had been on the brink of surrender; now local patriots began shooting up British patrols, and the rest of the country, in the words of a Briton in Virginia, "went liberty mad again."

Washington set up a winter camp in Morristown and went to work organizing American intelligence. He made Tallmadge his second-in-command, though he was ostensibly still a major in the 2d Continental Dragoons. That regiment was stationed in outposts all around the perimeter of British-held New York, and Tallmadge visited these units regularly, supposedly to make sure that all was in order but actually working as a patient spider setting up spy networks inside the British lines. His methods, thanks to Washington's tutelage, could not have been more sophisticated. He equipped his spies with cipher codes, invisible ink, and aliases that concealed their real identities. The invisible ink, which the Americans called "the stain," had been invented by Dr. James Jay, a brother of the prominent patriot John Jay. . . .

Two of the most important American agents operating inside British-held New York were Robert Townsend, a Quaker merchant, and Abraham Woodhull, a Setauket, Long Island, farmer. Their code names were Culper Jr. and Culper Sr. As a cover, Townsend wrote violently Loyalist articles for the New York *Royal Gazette;* this enabled him to pick up information from British officers and their mistresses, and he sent it on to Woodhull via a courier named Austin Roe.

Woodhull would then have a coded signal hung on a Setauket clothesline that was visible through a spyglass to Americans on the Connecticut shore. A crew of oarsmen would row across Long Island Sound by night, collect Townsend's letters, and carry them to Tallmadge's dragoons, who would hurry them to Washington. The general applied a "sympathetic fluid" to reveal the secret messages written in Dr. Jay's "stain."

When the British occupied Philadelphia, in 1777, Washington salted the city with spies. His chief assistant there was Maj. John Clark, a cavalryman who became expert at passing false information about American strength at Valley Forge to a spy for the British commander General Howe. Washington laboriously wrote out muster reports of the Continental Army, making it four or five times its actual size; the British, recognizing the handwriting, accepted the information as fact and gave the spy who had obtained it a bonus. Washington must have enjoyed this disinformation game; at one point, describing a particularly successful deception, Clark wrote, "This will give you a laugh."

The most effective American spy in Philadelphia was Lydia Darragh, an Irish-born Quaker midwife and undertaker. The British requisitioned a room in her house to serve as a "council chamber" and discussed their war plans there. By lying with her ear to a crack in the floor in the room above, Mrs. Darragh could hear much of what they said. Her husband wrote the information in minute shorthand on scraps of paper that she hid in large cloth-covered buttons. Wearing these, her fourteen-year-old son would walk into the countryside to meet his brother, a lieutenant in the American army. He snipped off the buttons, and the intelligence was soon in Washington's hands.

Mrs. Darragh's biggest coup was getting word to Washington that the British were about to make a surprise attack on his ragged army as it marched to Valley

Forge in early December 1777. When the attack came, the Continentals were waiting with loaded muskets and cannon, and the king's forces withdrew.

The British returned to Philadelphia determined to find whoever had leaked their plan. Staff officers went to Mrs. Darragh's house and demanded to know exactly when everyone had gone to bed the previous night—except one person. "I won't ask you, Mrs. Darragh, because I know you retire each night exactly at nine," the chief interrogator said. Lydia Darragh smiled and said nothing. After the war she remarked that she was pleased that as a spy she had never had to tell a lie.

The British, of course, had a small army of spies working for them as well, and they constantly struggled to penetrate Washington's operations. Toward the end of 1779, one of their Philadelphia spies wrote to Maj. John André, the charming, witty, artistically talented director of British intelligence: "Do you wish to have a useful hand in their army and to pay what you find his services worth? The exchange is 44 to 1." The numbers refer to the vertiginous depreciation of the Continental dollar; British spies, too, wanted to be paid in hard money.

The Americans did their best to make trouble for André by spreading around Philadelphia and New York the rumor that he was given to molesting boys. It is not clear whether Washington was involved in these particular smears, and they hardly chime with André's reputation for charming women, notably a Philadelphia belle named Peggy Shippen, who eventually married Gen. Benedict Arnold.

In any event, André was very successful at keeping tabs on the Americans. Surviving letters from his spies show him obtaining good estimates of American army strength in 1779. At one point Gen. Philip Schuyler made a motion in the Continental Congress that it leave Philadelphia because "they could do no business that was not instantly communicated" to the British.

André's most successful agent was a woman named Ann Bates, a former schoolteacher who married a British soldier while the army was in Philadelphia. Disguised as a peddler, she wandered through the American camp, counted the cannon there, overheard conversations at Washington's headquarters, and accurately predicted the American attack on the British base in Newport, Rhode Island, in 1778.

The intelligence war reached a climax, or something very close to one, between 1779 and 1781. American morale was sinking with the Continental currency, and trusting anyone became harder and harder. Washington could never be sure when a spy had been "turned" by British hard money, and the British tried to accelerate the decline of the paper dollar by printing and circulating millions of counterfeit bills.

Soon an astonished American was writing, "An ordinary horse is worth twenty thousand dollars." In despair Congress stopped producing money; this brought the army's commissary department to a halt. The Continental desertion rate rose, with veterans and sergeants among the chief fugitives.

Washington struggled to keep the British at bay with more disinformation about his dwindling strength. His spies had achieved such professionalism that he had to appeal to Gov. William Livingston of New Jersey to spare three men arrested in Elizabethtown for carrying on an illegal correspondence with the enemy. That was exactly what they had been doing—as double agents feeding the British disinformation.

The three spies stood heroically silent. Washington told Livingston they were willing to "bear the suspicion of being thought inimical." But realism could not be carried too far; the Continental Army could not hang its own agents. Would the governor please do something? Livingston allowed the spies to escape, and intelligence documents show that three years later they were still at work.

By June 1780 agents had given the British high command accurate reports of the American army's weakness in its Morristown camp. The main force had diminished to four thousand men; because of a shortage of fodder, there were no horses, which meant the artillery was immobilized. The British had just captured Charleston, South Carolina, and its garrison of five thousand, demoralizing the South. They decided a strike at Washington's force could end the war, and they marshaled six thousand troops on Staten Island to deliver the blow.

A few hours before the attack, a furtive figure slipped ashore into New Jersey from Staten Island to warn the Continentals of the enemy buildup. He reached the officer in command in Elizabethtown, Col. Elias Dayton, and Dayton sent a rider off to Morristown with the news. Dayton and other members of the New Jersey Continental line, backed by local militia, were able to slow the British advance for the better part of a day, enabling Washington to get his army in motion and seize the high ground in the Short Hills, aborting the British plan.

It was a very close call. Without the warning from that spy, the British army would certainly have come over the Short Hills, overwhelmed Washington's four thousand men in Morristown, and captured their artillery. This probably would have ended the war.

After the royal army retreated to New York, word reached them that a French expeditionary force was landing in Newport, Rhode Island, to reinforce the struggling Americans. The British commander, Sir Henry Clinton, decided to attack before the French had a chance to recover from the rigors of the voyage and fortify.

This was the Culper network's greatest moment. Robert Townsend, alias Culper Jr., discovered the plan shortly after Clinton put six thousand men aboard transports and sailed them to Huntington Bay on the north shore of Long Island. They waited there while British frigates scouted Newport Harbor to assess the size of the French squadron.

Townsend's warning sent Washington's disinformation machine into overdrive. Within twenty-four hours a double agent was in New York, handing the British top-secret papers, supposedly dropped by a careless courier, detailing a Washington plan to attack the city with every Continental soldier and militiaman in the middle states.

The British sent horsemen racing off to urge Sir Henry Clinton in Huntington Bay to return to New York with his six thousand men. Clinton, already discouraged by the British admiral's lack of enthusiasm for his plan to take Newport, glumly agreed and sailed his soldiers back to their fortifications. There they waited for weeks for an assault that never materialized.

While Clinton was in Huntington Bay, he and two aides were made violently ill by tainted wine they drank with dinner aboard the flagship. He ordered the bottle seized and asked the physician general of the British army to examine the dregs in the glasses. The doctor said the wine was "strongly impregnated with arsenic." During the night the bottle mysteriously disappeared, and Clinton was never able to confirm the assassination attempt or find the perpetrator. This may have been Washington's way of getting even for the Hickey plot.

The main event in the later years of the intelligence war was the treason of Benedict Arnold in 1780. However, the American discovery of Arnold's plot to sell the fortress at West Point to the British for six thousand pounds—about half a million dollars in modern money—was mostly luck. There was little that Benjamin Tallmadge or his agents could claim to their credit except having passed along a hint of a plot involving an American general a few weeks before.

There is no doubt that West Point would have been handed over and Benedict Arnold and John André given knighthoods if three wandering militiamen in Westchester County had not stopped André on his return to New York with the incriminating plans in his boot. The motive of these soldiers was not patriotism but robbery; Westchester was known as "the neutral ground," and Loyalists and rebels alike wandered there in search of plunder.

Hanging John André was one of the most difficult things Washington had to do in the intelligence war. The major was the object of universal affection, and Alexander Hamilton and others on Washington's staff urged him to find a way to commute the sentence. Washington grimly replied that he would do so only if the British handed over Arnold. That of course did not happen, and André died on the gallows. In the next twelve months, Washington made repeated attempts to capture Arnold. He ordered an American sergeant named Champe to desert and volunteer to join an American legion that Arnold was trying to create. To give Champe a convincing sendoff, Washington ordered a half a dozen cavalrymen to pursue him, without telling them he was a fake deserter. Champe arrived in the British lines with bullets chasing him.

Washington would seem to have liked these little touches of realism. Unusually fearless himself, he had once said as a young man that whistling bullets had "a charming sound." One wonders if spies such as Honeyman and Champe agreed.

Soon Champe was a member of Arnold's staff, living in the former general's house on the Hudson River in New York. Through cooperating agents, Champe communicated a plan to knock Arnold unconscious when he went into his riverside garden to relieve himself one moonless night. A boatload of Americans would be waiting to carry him back to New Jersey and harsh justice.

On the appointed night the boat was there, and Arnold went to the garden as usual, but Champe was on a troopship in New York Harbor. Clinton had ordered two thousand men, including Arnold's American legion, south to raid Virginia. Champe had to watch for an opportunity and deserted back to the American side.

Arnold's defection badly upset American intelligence operations for months. He told the British what he knew of Washington's spies in New York, and they made several arrests. Townsend quit spying for six months, to the great distress of Washington and Tallmadge.

The intelligence war continued during the year remaining until Yorktown. Washington's reluctant decision to march south with the French army to try to trap a British army in that small Virginia tobacco port was accompanied by strenuous disinformation efforts intended to tie the British army to New York for as long as possible. In the line of march as the allied force moved south through New Jersey were some thirty large flatboats. British spies reported that the Americans were constructing large cooking ovens at several points near New York. Both seemed evidence of a plan to attack the city.

Benedict Arnold, now a British brigadier, begged Sir Henry Clinton to ignore this deception and give him six thousand men to attack the long, vulnerable American line of march. Clinton said no. He wanted to husband every available man in New York. By the time the British commander's Philadelphia spies told him where Washington was actually going, it was too late. The royal army under Charles Lord Cornwallis surrendered after three weeks of pounding by heavy guns, the blow that finally ended the protracted war.

Even after the fighting wound down, intelligence activity went on. In the fall of 1782, a year after Yorktown, a French officer stationed in Morristown wrote, "Not a day has passed since we have drawn near the enemy that we have not had some news of them from our spies in New York." For a final irony, the last British commander in America, Sir Guy Carleton, sent Washington a report from a British agent warning about a rebel plot to plunder New York and abuse Loyalists as the British army withdrew, and Washington sent in Major Tallmadge and a column of troops—not only to keep order but also to protect their agents, many of whom had earned enmity for appearing to be loyal to George III.

Among the American spies in New York was a huge Irish-American tailor named Hercules Mulligan who had sent Washington invaluable information. His greatest coup was a warning that the British planned to try to kidnap the American commander in 1780. Mulligan reported directly to Washington's aide Col. Alexander Hamilton.

Another of the deepest agents was James Rivington, editor of the unctuously loyal New York *Royal Gazette*. He is believed to have stolen the top-secret signals of the British fleet, which the Americans passed on to the French in 1781. The knowledge may have helped the latter win the crucial naval battle off the Virginia capes that September, sealing Cornwallis's fate at Yorktown.

The day after the British evacuated New York, Washington had breakfast with Hercules Mulligan—a way of announcing that he had been a patriot. He also paid a visit to James Rivington and apparently gave him a bag of gold coins. When he was composing his final expense account for submission to the Continental Congress with his resignation as Commander in Chief, Washington included from memory the contents of the bag of coins Robert Morris had rushed to him in late December 1776: 410 Spanish dollars, 2 English crowns, 10 shillings, and 2 sixpence. The circumstances under which he received it, Washington remarked, made it impossible for him ever to forget the exact amount of that crucial transfusion of hard money. It is another piece of evidence, barely needed at this point, that intelligence was a centerpiece of the strategy of protracted war—and that George Washington was a master of the game.

Women in the American Revolution

Mary Beth Norton

The liberating effects of the War of Independence on women were far smaller and less revolutionary than were the effects of the struggle on American men. The Declaration of Independence, it will be recalled, claimed that all men were created equal but said nothing about women. This did not mean that American women as a group were less patriotic than men or that their contributions to the war effort were unimportant or entirely in the conventional "female" mold typified by Betsy Ross's sewing of the flag. Hundreds of women got close to the fighting. They traveled with the army, doing most of the cooking and laundering and otherwise assisting the soldiers in the field. The famous "Molly Pitcher" really did help fire cannon at the Battle of Monmouth, but the soldiers gave her that nickname (her actual name was Mary Ludwig Hays) because of her labor of bringing pitchers of water for the wounded from a nearby well.

In this essay Mary Beth Norton, a professor at Cornell University, describes the wartime activities of an organization of patriotic Philadelphia women. Professor Norton is the author of *The British Americans* and of *Liberty's Daughters*, an account of how women were affected by the Revolution.

When news that the British had taken Charleston, South Carolina, reached Philadelphia in May of 1780, merchants and government officials reacted to the disaster by taking steps to support the inflated Pennsylvania currency and solicit funds to pay new army recruits. And in a totally unexpected move, the women of Philadelphia emerged from their usual domestic roles to announce their intention of founding the first large-scale women's association in American history. As the Pennsylvania Gazette put it delicately, the ladies adopted "public spirited measures."

Up until then, American women had not engaged in any organized support of the war effort. Now that the American soldiers were suffering a serious loss of morale in the aftermath of the fall of Charleston, the women proposed a nationwide female-conceived and -executed relief effort to aid the hard-pressed troops. The campaign began June 10, 1780, with the publication of a broadside, *The Sentiments of an American Woman*. It was composed by thirty-three-year-old Esther de Berdt Reed, who was to become president of the Ladies Association. The daughter of a prominent English supporter of America, Esther had lived in Pennsylvania only since her 1770 marriage to Joseph Reed, but she was nonetheless a staunch patriot. Her *Sentiments* asserted forcefully that American women were determined to do more than offer "barren wishes" for the success of the army: they wanted to be "really useful," like "those heroines of antiquity, who have rendered their sex illustrious."

Mrs. Reed built her case carefully. She began by reviewing the history of women's patriotic activity, referring alike to female monarchs, Roman matrons, and Old Testament women. Linking herself explicitly to such foremothers, she declared, "I glory in all which my sex has done great and commendable. I call to mind with enthusiasm and with admiration all those acts of courage, of constancy and patriotism, which history has transmitted to us." Mrs. Reed held up Joan of Arc as an especially appropriate model, for she had driven from France "the ancestors of these same British, whose odious yoke we have just shaken off, and whom it is necessary that we drive from this Continent."

Esther Reed went on to address the question of propriety. She admitted that some men might perhaps "disapprove" women's activity. But in the current dismal state of public affairs anyone who raised this objection would not be "a good citizen." Any man who truly understood the soldiers' needs could only "applaud our efforts for the relief of the armies which defend our lives, our possessions, our liberty." By thus hinting that critics of her scheme would be unpatriotic, Mrs. Reed cleverly defused possible traditionalist objections.

Finally, she outlined her plan. Female Americans should renounce "vain ornaments," donating the money they would no longer spend on elaborate clothing and hairstyles to the patriot troops as *the offering of the Ladies.*

Her appeal drew an immediate response. Three days after the publication of the broadside, thirty-six Philadelphia women met to decide how to carry out its suggestions. The results of their deliberations were printed as an appendix to *Sentiments* when it appeared in the June 21 issue of the *Pennsylvania Gazette.* Entitled "Ideas, relative to the manner of forwarding to the American Soldiers, the Presents of the American Women," the plan proposed nothing less than the mobilization of the entire female population. Contributions would be accepted from any woman, in any amount. A "Treasuress" appointed in each county would oversee the collection of money, keeping careful records of all sums received. Overseeing the work of each state's county treasuresses would be the wife of its governor, who would serve as "Treasuress-General." Ultimately, all contributions would be sent to Martha Washington to be used for the benefit of the troops. Only one restriction was placed on the contributions' use: "It is an extraordinary bounty intended to render the condition of the soldier more pleasant, and not to hold place of the things which they ought to receive from the Congress, or from the States."

The Philadelphians set to work collecting funds even before the publication of their "Ideas." Dividing the city into ten equal districts, they assigned between two and five women to each area. Traveling in pairs, the canvassers visited every house, requesting contributions from "each woman and girl without any distinction." Among the collectors in the fifth ward, Market to Chestnut Streets, were Sarah Franklin Bache, the daughter of Benjamin Franklin, and Anne Willing (Mrs. Tench) Francis; Julia Stockton (Mrs. Benjamin) Rush worked in district six; and in the eighth ward, Spruce to Pine Streets, the canvassers included Alice Lee Shippen, a member of the prominent Virginia family and wife of a Philadelphia physician; Mrs. Robert Morris; and Sally McKean, wife of the Pennsylvania chief justice. The fact that women of such social standing undertook the very unfeminine task of soliciting contributions not only from friends and neighbors but also from strangers, poor people, and servants supports the contention of one of the Philadelphians that they "considered it as a great honour" to be invited to serve as canvassers. In a letter to a friend in Annapolis, an anonymous participant declared that "those who were in the country returned without delay to the city to fulfil their duty. Others put off their departure; those whose state of health was the most delicate, found strength in their patriotism." When a nursing mother was reluctant to leave her baby, this witness recorded, a friend volunteered to nurse the child along with her own.

Accounts of the women's reception differ. The anonymous letter-writer claimed that "as the cause of their visit was known, they were received with all the respect due to so honourable a commission." She explained that no house was omitted, not even those inhabited by the pacific Quakers, and that even there the subscription met with success, for "nothing is more easy than to reconcile a beneficent scheme with a beneficent religion." But Anna Rawle—herself a Quaker—described the canvass of Quaker homes quite differently. "Of all absurdities the Ladies going about for money exceeded everything," she told her mother Rebecca Shoemaker, whose second husband, Samuel, was a loyalist exile. Sarah Bache had come to their door, Anna reported, but had turned away, saying that "she did not chuse to face Mrs. S. or her daughters." Anna characterized the collectors as "so extremely importunate that people were obliged to give them something to get rid of them." Even "the meanest ale house" did not escape their net, and men were harassed until they contributed in the name of their wives or sweethearts. "I fancy they raised a considerable sum by this extorted contribution," Anna concluded, but she felt the requests were "carried to such an excess of meaness as the nobleness of no cause whatsoever could excuse."

It is impossible to know whether the letter-writer's examples of women proudly giving to the cause or Anna Rawle's account of reluctant contributors dunned into paying up is more accurate. But by the time the Philadelphia canvass was completed in early July, more than $300,000 Continental dollars had been collected from over sixteen hundred people. Because of inflation, this amount when converted to specie equaled only about $7,500, but even that represented a considerable sum. In financial terms, the city canvass was a smashing success. And it was a success in other ways as well, for the Philadelphia women sought and achieved symbolic goals that went far beyond the collection of money. As the anonymous canvasser put it, the women hoped that the "general beneficent" subscription "will produce the happy effect of destroying *intestine discords,* even to the very last seeds." That hope was particularly appropriate for Philadelphia women, some of whom had become notorious during the British occupation in 1777–78 for consorting with enemy troops. The author of the 1780 letter alluded delicately to that conduct when she explained that the canvassers wanted to "give some of our female fellow citizens an opportunity of relinquishing former errors and of avowing a change of sentiments by their contributions to the general cause of liberty and their country."

The symbolism of the fund drive was national as well as local. The participant, who had so enthusiastically described the canvassing, stressed that through their gifts American women would "greatly promote the public cause, and blast the hopes of the enemies of this country" by demonstrating the people's unanimous support of the war. Others also viewed the women's efforts in this light: as early as June 27, a laudatory essay signed "Song of Debora" appeared in the *Pennsylvania Packet.* "It must strike the enemy as with an apoplexy, to be informed, that the women of America are attentive to the wants of the Soldiery," the author declared, arguing that "it is not the quantity of the money that may be collected, but the idea of favour and affection discovered in this exertion, that will principally give life to our cause, and restore our affairs." Urging others to copy the Philadelphians, she predicted that "the women will reinspire the war; and ensure, finally, victory and peace."

In July, newspapers throughout the country reprinted *Sentiments,* usually accompanied by the detailed collection plan, and editors occasionally added exhortations of their own to the women's call for action. The symbolic importance of the subscription was conveyed to the nation by a frequently reprinted "Letter from an Officer at Camp, dated June 29, 1780." The patriotism of Philadelphia women "is a subject of conversation with the army," the officer wrote. "We do not suppose that these contributions can be any stable support to the campaign for any length of time; but, as it is a mark of respect to the army, it has given particular satisfaction, and it may be a great temporary service," for the soldiers had felt themselves "neglected" and forgotten by their fellow citizens.

Successful as this publicity was in spreading the news of the Philadelphians' plan, Esther Reed and her fellow organizers did not rely solely upon print to involve other women in their association. The anonymous participant told her Annapolis friend that after they completed the city collections the women wrote circular letters to acquaintances in other counties and towns, "and we have it in charge to keep up this correspondence until the whole subscription shall be completed."

The women of Trenton, New Jersey, were the first to copy the Philadelphians' lead. In late June they began to organize their own subscription campaign, and on July 4 at a general meeting they outlined plans for a statewide association. When they announced their scheme in the newspapers, they published "Sentiments of a Lady in New Jersey" in deliberate imitation of the Philadelphians. "Let us animate one another to contribute from our purses in proportion to our circumstances towards the support and comfort of the brave men who are fighting and suffering for us on the field," the author urged her female compatriots. Although the final accounts of the New Jersey campaign have evidently failed to survive, in mid-July the secretary forwarded nearly $15,500 to George Washington as an initial contribution to the fund.

Maryland women also responded quickly to the Philadelphians' request. Mrs. Thomas Sim Lee, the wife of the governor, wrote to friends in each county to ask them to serve as treasuresses, and by July 14 the organization was actively soliciting money in Annapolis. In that city alone, even though many residents had left town for the summer, more than $16,000 in currency was collected, with additional sums in specie. Writing with particular reference to the Marylanders, the editor of the *Pennsylvania Packet* rhapsodized that "the women of every part of the globe are under obligations to those of America, for having shown that females are capable of the highest political virtue."

Only in one other state, Virginia, is there evidence of successful Ladies Association activity. Martha Wayles Jefferson, whose husband Thomas was then the governor, received a copy of the Philadelphians' plan directly from Martha Washington. Since she was in poor health. Mrs. Jefferson decided to encourage her friends to take part but not to assume an active role herself. Interestingly enough, the letter she wrote on August 8 to Eleanor Madison is the sole piece of her correspondence extant today. In it she asserted that "I undertake with chearfulness the duty of furnishing to my countrywomen an opportunity of proving that they also participate of those virtuous feelings" of patriotism. The following day an announcement of the campaign appeared in the *Virginia Gazette.* Only fragmentary records of the campaign have ever been located, but they indicate that county treasuresses gathered total currency contributions ranging from £1,560 (Albemarle) to $7,506 (Prince William).

The association's organizing efforts in other states seem to have failed not because of lack of will or interest but because of lack of financial resources. Hannah Lee Corbin, a Virginia widow, told her sister Alice Shippen that "the scheme of raising money for the Soldiers would be good—if we had it in our power to do it." But she was already "so heavily Laded" that she was having to sell her property just to obtain "common support." Catharine Littlefield (Mrs. Nathanael) Greene, replying to Esther Reed's circular letter, told a similar story. "The distressed exhausted State of this little Government [Rhode Island] prevents us from gratifying our warmest Inclinations," she declared, because one-fifth of its territory, including Newport, was still in British hands. "The Women of this State are animated with the liveliest Sentiments of Liberty" and wish to offer relief to "our brave and patient Soldiery," she exclaimed, "but alas! the peculiar circumstances of this State renders this impracticable."

Nevertheless, the women's association still collected substantial sums of money. Its organizers next had to decide how to disburse the funds in accordance with their original aim of presenting soldiers with "some extraordinary and unexpected relief . . . *the offering of the Ladies.*" Since Martha Washington had returned to Virginia by the time the collection was completed, the association's leaders agreed to leave the disposition of the funds to her husband. There was only one problem: George Washington had plans for the money that differed sharply from theirs. "Altho' the terms of the association seem in some measure to preclude the purchase of any article, which the public is bound to find," Washington told Joseph Reed in late June, "I would, nevertheless, recommend a provision of shirts in preference to any thing else." On July 31, Esther Reed responded to the general. Her much revised, amended, and overwritten draft, with all its tactful phrasing, suggests something of the consternation his proposal caused among the canvassers who had worked so hard and so long to collect the money.

Not only had she found it difficult to locate linen, she reported, she had also learned that Pennsylvania was planning to send two thousand shirts to its troops and that a large shipment of clothing had recently arrived from France, "These Circumstances together with an Idea which prevails that the Soldiers might not consider it in the Light," she began, then crossed out the words following "Soldiers," and continued, "Soldiers would not be so much gratified by bestowing an article to which they look upon themselves entitled from the public as in some other method which would convey more fully the Idea of a reward for past Services & an incitement to future Duty." There she ended the sentence, having been so involved in her intricate prose that she failed to realize she had composed a fragment without a verb. Undaunted, she forged breathlessly ahead. "Some who are of this Opinion propose turning the whole of the Money into hard Dollars & giving each Soldier 2 at his own disposal." Having made her point, Mrs. Reed attempted to soften the fact that she was daring to dispute the judgment of the Commander-in-Chief of the American army. "This method I hint only," she added, "but would not by any means wish to adopt that or any other without your full approbation." To further lessen her apostasy, she also assured Washington that if shirts were still needed after the "fresh supplies" had been distributed, some of the money could be applied to that use.

Washington's response was, as Mrs. Reed later told her husband, "a little formal as if he was hurt by our asking his Opinion a second time & our not following his Directions after desiring him to give them." In his letter, the general suggested that "a taste of hard money may be productive of much discontent as we have none but depreciated paper for their pay." He also predicted that some soldiers' taste for drink would lead them "into irregularities and disorders" and that therefore the proposed two-dollar bounty "will be the means of bringing punishment" on them. No, he insisted; if the ladies wanted to employ their "benevolent donation" well, the money should be used for shirts—which they should make to save the cost of hiring seamstresses. Faced with Washington's adamant stance, Esther Reed re-treated. "I shall now endeavour to get the Shirts made as soon as possible," she told her husband, and he agreed with her decision. "The General is so decided that you have no Choice left so that the sooner you finish the Business the better," he wrote on August 26, reminding her that "it will be necessary for you to render a publick Account of your Stewardship in this Business & tho you will receive no thanks if you do it well, you will bear much Blame should it be otherwise."

Unfortunately, however, Esther de Berdt Reed had no chance to "finish the Business" she had so ably begun; she died of dysentery the following month. The leadership of the association was assumed by Sarah Franklin Bache, with the assis-tance of four other women. They took control of the funds that had been in Mrs. Reed's possession, overseeing the purchase of linen and the shirtmaking process. By early December, when the Marquis de Chastellux visited Sarah Bache's home, more than two thousand shirts had been completed. He recorded that "on each shirt was the name of the married or unmarried lady who made it." Late that same month, the women gave the shirts to the Deputy Quartermaster General in Philadelphia, and Mrs. Bache told General Washington that "we wish them to be worn with as much pleasure as they were made."

In February, 1781, Washington offered profuse thanks to the members of the committee that had succeeded Esther Reed as leaders of the association. The orga-nization's contributions, he declared, entitled its participants "to an equal place with any who have preceded them in the walk of female patriotism. It embellishes the American character with a new trait; by proving that the love of country is blended with those softer domestic virtues, which have always been allowed to be more peculiarly *your own.*"

Washington's gratitude was genuine, and the army certainly needed the shirts, but the fact remains that the members of the association, who had embarked on a

Sarah Franklin Bache, the daughter of Benjamin Franklin, took over the leadership of the Ladies Association after Mrs. Reed died in 1780. This portrait by John Hoppner was painted a number of years later.

very unfeminine enterprise, were ultimately deflected into a traditional domestic role. The general's encomium made this explicit by its references to "female patriotism" and "those softer domestic virtues," which presumably included the ability to sew. Ironically and symbolically, the Philadelphia women of 1780, who had tried to chart an independent course for themselves and to establish an unprecedented nationwide female organization, ended up as what one amused historian has termed "General Washington's Sewing Circle."

The amusement has not been confined to subsequent generations, for male Revolutionary leaders too regarded the women's efforts with wry condescension. John Adams wrote to Benjamin Rush, "the Ladies having undertaken to support American Independence, settles the point." The women, on the other hand, saw nothing to smile at in the affair. Kitty Livingston, whose mother was a New Jersey canvasser, sent a copy of *The Sentiments of an American Woman* to her sister Sarah Jay, then in Spain. "I am prouder than ever of my charming countrywomen," Sarah told her husband John in forwarding the broadside to him. Abigail Adams had a similar reaction, one that stands in sharp contrast to her husband's. Mrs. Adams took the association as a sign that "virtue exists, and publick spirit lives—lives in the Bosoms of the Fair Daughters of America. . . ."

The anonymous Philadelphian who kept her Annapolis friend up-to-date on the ladies' organization was still more forthright: "Some persons have amused themselves with the importance which we have given it," she remarked, alluding to what must have been widespread condescension. "I confess we have made it a serious business, and with great reason; an object so interesting was certainly worthy an extraordinary attention." She and her fellow canvassers had "consecrated every moment we could spare from our domestic concerns, to the public good," enduring "with pleasure, the fatigues and inconveniences inseparable from such a task," because they could reflect proudly on the fact that "whilst our friends were exposed to the hardships and dangers of the fields of war for our protection, we were exerting at home our little labours to administer to their comfort and alleviate their toil."

The Most Successful Revolution

Irving Kristol

Responding to the celebration of the bicentennial of the Declaration of Independence, historians devoted much effort to reexamining the American Revolution. They attempted to explain why it occurred, how different social groups felt about it, and what its results and influences have been—in America and elsewhere in the world. As is usual with the study of complicated events, no general agreement has emerged from this research. Some historians of the Revolution, examining it "from the bottom up," have seen it as a radical effort of artisans and other ordinary people to reshape the society in which they lived. Other historians have viewed it as an ideological struggle led by people defending "the rights of Englishmen" against a clique of reactionary conspirators centered in London. Still others have adopted a more conservative approach. They stress the limited, essentially practical objectives of the revolutionary leaders. They say, in effect, "less was more" and they attribute the enduring achievements of the revolutionary era to the restraint and conservatism of the Founding Fathers of the nation. Irving Kristol, the author of the following essay, is a prominent member of this school.

Kristol, a leading American conservative critic and essayist, urges us to "ignore" Tom Paine's radical interpretation of the Revolution on the grounds that Paine "never really understood America." One need not agree with all of Kristol's arguments to profit from his approach. That there was a profoundly conservative side to the Revolution, that George Washington, for example, was basically different from revolutionaries such as Robespierre, Lenin, and Mao Tse-tung, are facts that must be accounted for in any well-rounded interpretation of the events of 1776. Kristol is editor of the journal *The Public Interest* and author of *On the Democratic Idea in America*, *America's Continuing Revolution*, and other works.

For several decades now there has been a noticeable loss of popular interest in the Revolution, both as a historic event and as a political symbol. The idea and very word, "revolution," are in good repute today; the American Revolution is not. We are willing enough, on occasion, to pick up an isolated phrase from the Declaration of Independence or a fine declamation from a Founding Father—Jefferson, usually—and use these to point up the shortcomings of American society as it now exists. Which is to say, we seem to be prompt to declare that the Revolution was a success only when it permits us to assert glibly that we have subsequently failed it. But this easy exercise in self-indictment, though useful in some respects, is on the whole a callow affair. It doesn't tell us, for instance, whether there is an important connection between that successful revolution and our subsequent delinquencies. It merely uses the Revolution for rhetorical-political purposes, making no serious effort at either understanding it or understanding ourselves. One even gets the impression that many of us regard ourselves as too sophisticated to take the Revolution seriously—that we see it as one of those naive events of our distant childhood which we have long since outgrown but which we are dutifully reminded of, at certain moments of commemoration, by insistent relatives less liberated from the past than we.

I think I can make this point most emphatically by asking the simple question: what ever happened to George Washington? He used to be a Very Important Person—indeed, *the* most important person in our history. Our history books used to describe him, quite simply, as the Father of his Country, and in the popular mind he was a larger-than-life figure to whom piety and reverence were naturally due. In the past fifty years, however, this figure has been radically diminished in size and virtually emptied of substance. In part, one supposes, this is because piety is a sentiment we seem less and less capable of, and most especially piety toward fathers. We are arrogant and condescending toward all ancestors because we are so convinced we understand them better than they understood themselves—whereas piety assumes that they still understand us better than we understand ourselves. And reverence, too, is a sentiment that we, in our presumption, find somewhat unnatural. Woodrow Wilson, like most Progressives of his time, complained about the "blind worship" of the Constitution by the American people; no such complaint is likely to be heard today. We debate whether or not we should obey the laws of the land, whereas for George Washington—and Lincoln, too, who in his lifetime reasserted this point most eloquently—obedience to law was not enough: they thought that Americans, as citizens of a self-governing polity, ought to have *reverence* for their laws. Behind this belief, of course, was the premise that the collective wisdom incarnated in our laws—and especially in the fundamental law of the Constitution—understood us better than any one of us could ever hope to understand it. Having separated ourselves from our historic traditions, and no longer recognizing the power inherent in tradition itself, we find this traditional point of view close to incomprehensible.

Equally incomprehensible to us is the idea that George Washington was the central figure in a real, honest-to-God revolution—the first significant revolution of the modern era and one that can lay claim to being the only truly successful revolution, on a large scale, in the past two centuries. In his own lifetime no one doubted that he was the central figure of that revolution; subsequent generations did not dispute the fact; our textbooks, until about a quarter of a century ago, took it for granted, albeit in an ever more routine and unconvincing way. We today, in contrast, find it hard to take George Washington seriously as a successful revolutionary. He just doesn't fit our conception of what a revolutionary leader is supposed to be like. It is a conception that easily encompasses Robespierre, Lenin, Mao Tse-tung, or Fidel Castro—but can one stretch it to include a gentleman like George Washington? And so we tend to escape from that dilemma by deciding that the American Revolution was not an authentic revolution at all, but rather some kind of pseudorevolution, which is why it could be led by so unrevolutionary a character as George Washington.

Hannah Arendt, in her very profound book *On Revolution*, has written: ". . . Revolutionary political thought in the nineteenth and twentieth centuries has proceeded as though there never had occurred a revolution in the New World and as though there never had been any American notions and experiences in the realm of politics and government worth thinking about." And it is certainly indisputable that the world, when it contemplates the events of 1776 and after, is inclined to see the American Revolution as a French Revolution that never quite came off— whereas the Founding Fathers thought they had cause to regard the French Revolution as an American Revolution that had failed. Indeed, the differing estimates of these two revolutions are definitive of one's political philosophy in the modern world: there are two conflicting conceptions of politics, in relation to the human condition, which are symbolized by these two revolutions. There is no question that the French Revolution is, in some crucial sense, the more "modern" of the two. There is a question, however, as to whether it is a good or bad thing to be modern in this sense. . . .

Every revolution unleashes tides of passion, and the American Revolution was no exception. But it *was* exceptional in the degree to which it was able to subordinate these passions to serious and nuanced thinking about fundamental problems of political philosophy. The pamphlets, sermons, and newspaper essays of the Revolutionary period—only now being reprinted and carefully studied—were extraordinarily academic, in the best sense of that term. Which is to say, they were learned and thoughtful and generally sober in tone. This was a revolution infused by *mind* to a degree never approximated since and perhaps never approximated before. By mind, not by dogma. The most fascinating aspect of the American Revolution is the severe way it kept questioning itself about the meaning of what it was doing. Enthusiasm there certainly was—a revolution is impossible without enthusiasm—but this enthusiasm was tempered by doubt, introspection, anxiety, skepticism. This may strike us as a very strange state of mind in which to make a revolution; and yet it is evidently the right state of mind for making a successful revolution. That we should have any difficulty in seeing this tells us something about the immaturity of our own political imagination—an immaturity not all incompatible with what we take to be sophistication.

One of our most prominent statesmen [recently] remarked to an informal group of political scientists that he had been reading *The Federalist Papers* and he was astonished to see how candidly our Founding Fathers could talk about the frailties of human nature and the necessity for a political system to take such frailties into account. It was not possible, he went on to observe, for anyone active in American politics today to speak publicly in this way: he would be accused of an imperfect democratic faith in the common man. Well, the Founding Fathers for the most part, and most of the time, subscribed to such an "imperfect" faith. They understood that republican self-government could not exist if humanity did not possess—at some moments, and to a fair degree—the traditional "republican virtues" of self-control, self-reliance, and a disinterested concern for the public good. They also understood that these virtues did not exist everywhere, at all times, and that there was no guarantee of their natural preponderance. As James Madison put it:

As there is a degree of depravity in mankind which requires a certain degree of circumspection and distrust; so there are other qualities in human nature which justify a certain portion of esteem and confidence. Republican government presupposes the existence of these qualities in a higher degree than any other form.

Despite the fact that Christian traditions are still strong in this country, it is hard to imagine any public figure casually admitting, as Madison did in his matter-of-fact way, that "there is a degree of depravity in mankind" which statesmen must take account of. We have become unaccustomed to such candid and unflattering talk about ourselves—which is, I suppose, only another way of saying that we now think democratic demagoguery to be the only proper rhetorical mode of address as between government and people in a republic. The idea, so familiar to the Puritans and still very much alive during our Revolutionary era, that a community of individual sinners could, under certain special conditions, constitute a good community—just as a congregation of individual sinners could constitute a good church—is no longer entirely comprehensible to us. We are therefore negligent about the complicated ways in which this transformation takes place and uncomprehending as to the constant, rigorous attentiveness necessary for it to take place at all. The Founders thought that self-government was a chancy and demanding enterprise and that successful government in a republic was a most difficult business. We, in contrast, believe that republican self-government is an easy affair, that it need only be instituted for it to work on its own, and that when such government falters, it must be as a consequence of personal incompetence or malfeasance by elected officials. Perhaps nothing reveals better than these different perspectives the intellectual distance we have travelled from the era of the Revolution. . . .

In what sense can the American Revolution be called a successful revolution? And if we agree that it was successful, why was it successful? . . . To begin at the beginning: the American Revolution was successful in that those who led it were able, in later years, to look back in tranquillity at what they had wrought and to say that it was good. This was a revolution that, unlike all subsequent revolutions, did not devour its children: the men who made the revolution were the men who went on to create the new political order, who then held the highest elective positions in this order, and who all died in bed. Not very romantic, perhaps; indeed positively prosaic; but it is this very prosaic quality of the American Revolution that testifies to its success. It is the pathos and poignancy of unsuccessful revolutions that excite the poetic temperament; statesmanship that successfully accomplishes its business is a subject more fit for prose. Alone among the revolutions of modernity the American Revolution did not give rise to the pathetic and poignant myth of "the revolution betrayed." It spawned no literature of disillusionment; it left behind no grand hopes frustrated, no grand expectations unsatisfied, no grand illusions shattered. Indeed, in one important respect the American Revolution was so successful as to be almost self-defeating: it turned the attention of thinking men away from politics, which now seemed utterly unproblematic, so that political theory lost its vigor, and even the political thought of the Founding Fathers was not seriously studied. The American political tradition became an inarticulate tradition: it worked so well we did not bother to inquire why it worked, and we are therefore intellectually disarmed before those moments when it suddenly seems not to be working so well after all.

The American Revolution was also successful in another important respect: it was a mild and relatively bloodless revolution. A war was fought, to be sure, and soldiers died in that war; but the rules of civilized warfare, as then established, were for the most part quite scrupulously observed by both sides—there was little of the butchery that we have come to accept as a natural concomitant of revolutionary warfare. More important, there was practically none of the off-battlefield savagery that we now assume to be inevitable in revolutions. There were no revolutionary tribunals dispensing "revolutionary justice"; there was no reign of terror; there were no bloodthirsty proclamations by the Continental Congress. Tories were dispossessed of their property, to be sure, and many were rudely hustled off into exile; but . . . not a single Tory was executed for harboring counter-revolutionary opinions. Nor, in the years after the Revolution, were Tories persecuted to any significant degree (at least by today's standards) or their children discriminated against at all. As Tocqueville later remarked, with only a little exaggeration, the Revolution "contracted no alliance with the turbulent passions of anarchy, but its course was marked, on the contrary, by a love of order and law."

A law-and-order revolution? What kind of revolution is that, we ask ourselves? To which many will reply that it could not have been much of a revolution, after all—at best a shadow of the real thing, which is always turbulent and bloody and shattering of body and soul. Well, the possibility we have to consider is that it was successful precisely because it wasn't that kind of revolution and that it is we rather than the American revolutionaries who have an erroneous conception of what a revolution is. . . .

One does not want to make the American Revolution a more prosaic affair than it was. This was a revolution—a real one—and it was infused with a spirit of excitement and innovation. After all, what the American Revolution was trying to do, once it got under way, was no small thing. It was nothing less than the establishment, for the first time since ancient Rome, of a large republican nation; and the idea of re-establishing under modern conditions the glory that had been Rome's could hardly fail to be intoxicating. This revolution did indeed have grand—even millennial—expectations as to the future role of this new nation in both the political imagination and the political history of the human race. But certain things have to be said about these large expectations if we are to see them in proper perspective.

The main thing to be said is that the millenarian tradition in America long antedates the Revolution and is not intertwined with the idea of revolution itself. It was the Pilgrim Fathers, not the Founding Fathers, who first announced that this was God's country, that the American people had a divine mission to accomplish, that this people had been "chosen" to create some kind of model community for the rest of mankind. This belief was already so firmly established by the time of the Revolution that it was part and parcel of our political orthodoxy, serving to legitimate an existing "American way of life" and most of the institutions associated with that way of life. . . .

To this traditional millenarianism the Revolution added the hope that the establishment of republican institutions would inaugurate a new and happier political era for all mankind. This hope was frequently expressed enthusiastically, in a kind of messianic rhetoric, but the men of the Revolution—most of them, most of the time—did not permit themselves to become bewitched by that rhetoric. Thus, though they certainly saw republicanism as the wave of the future, both Jefferson and Adams in the 1780's agreed that the French people were still too "depraved," as they so elegantly put it, to undertake an experiment in self-government. Self-government, as they understood it, presupposed a certain way of life, and this in turn presupposed certain qualities on the part of the citizenry—qualities then designated as republican virtues—that would make self-government possible.

Similarly, though one can find a great many publicists during the Revolution who insisted that, with the severance of ties from Britain, the colonies had reverted to a Lockean "state of nature" and were now free to make a new beginning for all mankind and to create a new political order that would mark a new stage in human history—though such assertions were popular enough, it would be a mistake to take them too seriously. The fact is that Americans had encountered their state of nature generations earlier and had made their social compact at that time. The primordial American social contract was signed and sealed on the *Mayflower*—literally signed and sealed. The subsequent presence of all those signatures appended to the Declaration of Independence, beginning with John Hancock, are but an echo of the original covenant.

To perceive the true purposes of the American Revolution it is wise to ignore some of the more grandiloquent declamations of the moment—Tom Paine, an English radical who never really understood America, is especially worth ignoring—and to look at the kinds of political activity the Revolution unleashed. This activity took the form of constitution making, above all. In the months and years immediately following the Declaration of Independence all of our states drew up constitutions. These constitutions are terribly interesting in three respects. First, they involved relatively few basic changes in existing political institutions and almost no change at all in legal, social, or economic institutions. Second, most of the changes that were instituted had the evident aim of *weakening* the power of government, especially of the executive; it was these changes—and especially the strict separation of powers—that dismayed Turgot, Condorcet, and the other French philosophers, who understood revolution as an expression of the people's will to power rather than as an attempt to circumscribe political authority. Third, in no case did any of these state constitutions tamper with the traditional system of local self-government; indeed they could not, since it was this traditional system of local self-government that created and legitimized the constitutional conventions themselves.

In short, the Revolution reshaped our political institutions in such a way as to make them more responsive to popular opinion and less capable of encroaching upon the personal liberties of the citizen—liberties that long antedated the new constitutions and that in no way could be regarded as the creation or consequence of revolution. Which is to say that the purpose of this revolution was to bring our political institutions into a more perfect correspondence with an actual American way of life that no one even dreamed of challenging. This restructuring, as we

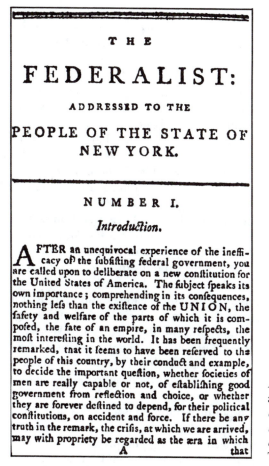

THE

FEDERALIST:

ADDRESSED TO THE

PEOPLE OF THE STATE OF NEW YORK.

NUMBER I.

Introduction.

AFTER an unequivocal experience of the ineffi-
cacy of the subsisting federal government, you
are called upon to deliberate on a new constitution for
the United States of America. The subject speaks its
own importance; comprehending in its consequences,
nothing less than the existence of the UNION, the
safety and welfare of the parts of which it is composed, the fate of an empire, in many respects, the
most interesting in the world. It has been frequently
remarked, that it seems to have been reserved to the
people of this country, by their conduct and example,
to decide the important question, whether societies of
men are really capable or not, of establishing good
government from reflection and choice, or whether
they are forever destined to depend, for their political
constitutions, on accident and force. If there be any
truth in the remark, the crisis, at which we are arrived,
may with propriety be regarded as the æra in which
A   that

A facsimile of the first page of The Federalist, Number 1 *(published in 1788)—a
compilation in book form of the papers published in a New York newspaper one year
earlier. These documents became known as*
The Federalist Papers.

should now call it, because it put the possibility of republican self-government once
again on the political agenda of Western civilization, was terribly exciting, to Europeans as well as Americans. But for the Americans involved in this historic task it
was also terribly frightening. It is fair to say that no other revolution in modern history made such relatively modest innovations with such an acute sense of anxiety.
The Founding Fathers were well aware that if republicanism over the centuries had
become such a rare form of government, there must be good reasons behind this
fact. Republican government, they realized, must be an exceedingly difficult
regime to maintain—it must have grave inherent problems. And so they were constantly scurrying to their libraries, ransacking classical and contemporary political
authors, trying to discover why republics fail, and endeavoring to construct a new
political science relevant to American conditions that would give this new republic
a fair chance of succeeding. That new political science was eventually to be embodied in *The Federalist Papers,* the only original work of political theory ever produced
by a revolution and composed by successful revolutionaries. . . .

The French Revolution promised not only a reformation of France's political institutions but far more than that. It promised, for instance—as practically all revolutions have promised since—the abolition of poverty. The American Revolution promised no such thing, in part because poverty was not such a troublesome issue in this country, but also, one is certain, because the leaders of this revolution understood what their contemporary Adam Smith understood and what we today have some difficulty in understanding: namely, that poverty is abolished by economic growth, not by economic redistribution—there is never enough to distribute—and that rebellions, by creating instability and uncertainty, have mischievous consequences for economic growth. Similarly, the French Revolution promised a condition of "happiness" to its citizens under the new regime, whereas the American Revolution promised merely to permit the individual to engage in the "pursuit of happiness." . . .

To the teeming masses of other nations the American political tradition says: to enjoy the fruits of self-government you must first cease being "masses" and become a "people," attached to a common way of life, sharing common values, and existing in a condition of mutual trust and sympathy as between individuals and even social classes. It is a distinctly odd kind of revolutionary message, by twentieth-century criteria—so odd that it seems not revolutionary at all, and yet so revolutionary that it seems utterly utopian. What the twentieth century wants to hear is the grand things that a new government will do for the people who put their trust in it. What the American political tradition says is that the major function of government is to supervise the orderly arrangement of society and that a free people does not make a covenant or social contract with its government, or with the leaders of any "movement," but among themselves.

In the end what informs the American political tradition is a proposition and a premise. The proposition is that the best national government is, to use a phrase the Founding Fathers were fond of, "mild government." The premise is that you can only achieve mild government if you have a solid bedrock of local self-government, so that the responsibilities of national government are limited in scope. And a corollary of this premise is that such a bedrock of local self-government can only be achieved by a people who—through the shaping influence of religion, education, and their own daily experience—are capable of governing themselves in those small and petty matters which are the stuff of local politics. . . .

Though we have been a representative democracy for two centuries now, we have never developed an adequate theory of representation. More precisely, we have developed two contradictory theories of representation, both of which can claim legitimacy within the American political tradition and both of which were enunciated—often by the same people—during the Revolution. The one sees the public official as a "common man" who has a mandate to reflect the opinions of the majority; the other sees the public official as a somewhat uncommon man—a more-than-common man, if you will—who because of his talents and character is able to take a larger view of the public interest than the voters who elected him or the voters who failed to defeat him. One might say that the first is a democratic view of the legislator, the second a republican view. The American political tradition has always had a kind of double vision on this whole problem, which in turn makes for a bewildering moral confusion. Half the time we regard our politicians as, in the nature of things, probably corrupt and certainly untrustworthy; the other half of the time we denounce them for failing to be models of integrity and rectitude. . . . But politicians are pretty much like the rest of us and tend to become the kinds of people they are expected to be. The absence of clear and distinct expectations has meant that public morality in this country has never been, and is not, anything we can be proud of.

In a way the ambiguity in our theory of representation points to a much deeper ambiguity in that system of self-government which emerged from the Revolution and the Constitutional Convention. That system has been perceptively titled, by Professor Martin Diamond, "a democratic republic." Now, we tend to think of these terms as near-synonyms, but in fact they differ significantly in their political connotations. . . . What is the difference between a democracy and a republic? In a democracy the will of the people is supreme. In a republic it is not the will of the people but the rational consensus of the people—a rational consensus that is implicit in the term "consent"—which governs the people. That is to say, in a democracy popular passion may rule—it need not, but it may; in a republic popular passion is regarded as unfit to rule, and precautions are taken to see that it is subdued rather than sovereign. In a democracy all politicians are, to some degree, demagogues: they appeal to people's prejudices and passions, they incite their expectations by making reckless promises, they endeavor to ingratiate themselves with the electorate in every possible way. In a republic there are not supposed to be such politicians, only statesmen—sober, unglamorous, thoughtful men who are engaged in a kind of perpetual conversation with the citizenry. In a republic a fair degree of equality and prosperity are important goals, but it is liberty that is given priority as the proper end of government. In a democracy these priorities are reversed: the status of men and women as consumers of economic goods is taken to be more significant than their status as participants in the creation of political goods. A republic is what we would call moralistic in its approach to both public and private affairs; a democracy is more easygoing, more permissive, as we now say, even more cynical.

The Founding Fathers perceived that their new nation was too large, too heterogeneous, too dynamic, too mobile for it to govern itself successfully along strict republican principles, and they had no desire at all to see it governed along strict democratic principles, since they did not have that much faith in the kinds of "common men" likely to be produced by such a nation. So they created a new form of popular government, to use one of their favorite terms, that incorporated both republican and democratic principles in a complicated and ingenious way. This system has lasted for two centuries, which means it has worked very well indeed. But in the course of that time we have progressively forgotten what kind of system it is and *why* it works as well as it does. Every now and then, for instance, we furiously debate the question of whether or not the Supreme Court is meeting its obligations as a democratic institution. The question reveals a startling ignorance of our political tradition. The Supreme Court is not—and was never supposed to be—a democratic institution; it is a republican institution that counterbalances the activities of our various democratic institutions. . . .

So it would seem that two hundred years after the American Revolution we are in a sense victims of its success. The political tradition out of which it issued, and the political order it helped to create, are imperfectly comprehended by us. What is worse, we are not fully aware of this imperfect comprehension and are frequently smug in our convenient misunderstandings. . . .

4 The Federalist Era

President Washington took the oath of office on the balcony of Federal Hall in New York City, where the new national government first met. The shield of the United States and thirteen stars emblazoned its cornice, while arrows (symbolizing war) and olive branches (symbolizing peace) appeared above the windows. (Museum of the City of New York)

Shays' Rebellion

Alden T. Vaughan

During the American Revolution a people rose against an oppressive government without losing their respect for government itself or for law. The American revolutionaries sought drastic change but pursued it, as Jefferson put it in the Declaration of Independence, with "a decent respect to the opinions of mankind." However, the dislocations that the Revolution produced were severe, and in the years after Yorktown the young nation had its full share of social and economic problems, some of which threatened to destroy the respect of the people for legally established authority. Whether this was truly a "critical period" has long been debated; the current opinion of historians seems to be that conditions, in the main, were not as bad as they have sometimes been pictured. But the new national government did lack many important powers, and many of the state governments displayed insufficient will and confidence and thus failed to assume responsibility for governing with the force and determination that critical times require.

In this essay Professor Alden T. Vaughan of Columbia University describes the difficulties that plagued Massachusetts in the 1780s and produced what is known as Shays' Rebellion. How the fundamental conservatism and respect for democratic values of the citizens of Massachusetts eventually resolved this conflict is the theme of his narrative, although he also weighs the influence of the affair on the Constitutional Convention at Philadelphia, which followed closely upon it.

October, 1786: "Are your people . . . mad?" thundered the usually calm George Washington to a Massachusetts correspondent. Recent events in the Bay State had convinced the General, who was living the life of a country squire at Mount Vernon, that the United States was "fast verging to anarchy and confusion!" Would the nation that had so recently humbled the British Empire now succumb to internal dissension and die in its infancy? To many Americans in the fall of 1786 it seemed quite possible, for while Washington was writing frantic notes to his friends, several thousand insurgents under the nominal leadership of a Revolutionary War veteran named Daniel Shays were closing courts with impunity, defying the state militia, and threatening to revamp the state government.

The uprising in Massachusetts was serious in itself, but more frightening was the prospect that it could spread to the other states. It had, in fact, already tainted Rhode Island, Vermont, and New Hampshire, and it showed some danger of infecting Connecticut and New York as well. By the spring of 1787, American spokesmen from Maine to Georgia were alarmed, Congress had been induced to raise troops for possible deployment against the rebels, and observers on both sides of the Atlantic voiced concern for the future of the nation. Even John Adams in London and Thomas Jefferson in Paris took time from their critical diplomatic duties to comment—the former, as might be expected, pessimistically; the latter with his usual optimism—on the causes and consequences of Shays' Rebellion. And well they might: the Massachusetts uprising of 1786–87 was to make a lasting contribution to the future of the United States by magnifying the demand for a stronger central government to replace the one created by the Articles of Confederation—a demand that reached fruition in the drafting and ratification of the Constitution in 1787–88. From the vantage point of the twentieth century, the rebellion of Daniel Shays stands—with the exception of the Civil War—as the nation's most famous and most important domestic revolt.

The root of the trouble in Massachusetts lay in the economic chaos that accompanied political independence. The successful war against Great Britain had left the thirteen former colonies free to rule themselves, but it had also left them without the commercial ties that had done so much to promote colonial prosperity. While American producers, merchants, and shippers scurried after new goods and new markets to replace the old, the ill effects of economic independence crept across the nation.

Of all the American states, perhaps none felt the postwar slump so grievously as did Massachusetts. Its $14 million debt was staggering, as was its shortage of specie. Bay Staters once again swapped wheat for shoes, and cordwood for help with the plowing. They suffered too from the ruinous inflation that afflicted the entire nation as the value of Continental currency fell in the three years after 1777 to a ridiculous low of four thousand dollars in paper money to one dollar in silver or gold. But in addition, Massachusetts caught the full brunt of England's decision—vengeful, the Americans considered it—to curtail trade between the United States and the British West Indies. To New Englanders, more than half of whom lived in Massachusetts, the new British policy threatened economic disaster. Gone was their dominance of the carrying trade, gone the booms in shipbuildings, in distilling, in food and lumber exporting, and in the slave trade. Gone too was New England's chief source of hard cash, for the West Indies had been the one place with which New England merchants enjoyed a favorable balance of trade.

Most residents of Massachusetts were probably unaware of the seriousness of their plight until it came close to home. By the early 1780s the signs were unmistakable. Men in debt—and debt was epidemic in the late seventies and eighties—saw their farms confiscated by the state and sold for as little as a third of what they considered to be the true value. Others, less fortunate, found themselves in the dark and filthy county jails, waiting helplessly for sympathetic friends or embarrassed relatives to bail them out of debtors' prison. As the economic crisis worsened, a gloomy pessimism spread among the farmers and tradesmen in the central and western parts of the state.

The economic problems of Massachusetts were difficult, but probably not insoluble. At least they could have been lessened by a wise and considerate state government. Unfortunately for the Bay Stater, good government was as scarce as good money in the early 1780's. After creating a fundamentally sound framework of government in the state constitution of 1780, the voters of Massachusetts failed to staff it with farsighted and dedicated servants of the people. "Thieves, knaves, and robbers," snorted one disgruntled citizen. With mounting grievances and apathetic legislators, the people increasingly took matters into their own hands.

As early as February, 1782, trouble broke out in Pittsfield in the Berkshires, and before the year was over, mob actions had disrupted the tranquillity of several other towns in the western part of the state. The immediate target of the Pittsfield agitators was the local court, which they temporarily closed by barring the door to members of the bench. A court that did not sit could not process foreclosures, pass judgments on debts, or confiscate property for defaulted taxes. In April, violence broke out at Northampton, where a former Connecticut clergyman named Samuel Ely— branded by one early historian as "a vehement, brazen-faced declaimer, abounding in hypocritical pretensions to piety, and an industrious sower of discord"—led the attack on the judges. Ely harangued a Northampton crowd to "go to the woodpile and get clubs enough, and knock their grey wigs off, and send them out of the world in an instant." Ely was promptly arrested and sentenced to six months in prison, but a mob soon freed him from the Springfield jail. The ex-parson found refuge in Vermont.

Instead of recognizing the validity of such protests, the Massachusetts legislature countered with a temporary suspension of habeas corpus and imposed new and higher court costs as well. And while the government did bend to the extent of authorizing certain foodstuffs and lumber to be used in lieu of money, the net effect of its measures was to rub salt into wounds already smarting. Currency remained dear, foreclosures mounted, the shadow of debtors' prison continued to cast a pall, and the state's legal system remained unduly complicated and expensive. Many citizens of western Massachusetts now began to question the benefits of independence; a few even concluded that the patriot leaders of 1776 had deluded them, and cheers for King George III were heard once again in towns that a few years before had cursed his name. And unrest continued to spread. In May, 1783, a mob tried to prevent the opening of the spring session of the Hampshire County Court at Springfield.

Perhaps the major outbreak of 1786 would have occurred a year or so sooner had it not been for a fortuitous combination of events that made the years 1784 and 1785 relatively easy to bear. In 1784 came news that a final peace had been signed with England; in 1785 Massachusetts farmers enjoyed their best harvest in several years, while the legislature, in one of its conciliatory if vagrant moods, refrained from levying a state tax. Although tempers continued to simmer, no serious outbreaks marred the period from early 1783 to midsummer 1786.

The episodes of 1782–83 and those that followed held a particular appeal for veterans of the Revolution. Even more than their civilian neighbors, the former soldiers nursed grievances that they could attribute to incompetent, if not dishonest, government. They had left their farms and shops to fight the hated redcoats, but they could not even depend on the paltry sums their services had earned for them. Inflation had made their Continental currency almost worthless, and now the government set up by the Articles of Confederation was delaying payment of overdue wages and retracting its promises of lifetime pensions to officers.

One lesson of the Revolution not lost on the Massachusetts veterans was that in times of necessity the people could reform an insensitive government by force of arms, and many of them still had in their possession the weapons they had used so effectively against the British and Hessian troops. Old habits and old weapons increasingly took on new meaning to the men of Massachusetts as the economic and political crisis of the 1780s deepened. The veterans of the Bay State knew where to find leadership, too, for among those hard-pressed by the economic problems of the decade were many who had served as officers during the War for Independence.

By 1786 several of these officers had emerged as acknowledged leaders in their own localities, although not until the final stages of the rebellion would any single commander claim the allegiance of more than a few hundred men at most.

In the eastern part of the state the most prominent leader was Captain Job Shattuck of Groton, a veteran of the French and Indian War as well as of the Revolution. Now in his fifties, Shattuck had been protesting vehemently, and sometimes violently, since 1781. His principal lieutenant in Middlesex County was Nathan Smith of Shirley, a tough veteran of both wartime and peacetime conflict—with a patch over one eye as testimony to his involvement in the latter. It was the burly Smith who on one occasion gave his hearers the unhappy choice of joining his band or being run out of town.

Farther west the rebels looked to other leaders. In Springfield and neighboring towns it was to Luke Day, said by some to be "the master spirit of the insurrection." A former brevet major in the Continental Army, Day seems to have had the inclination as well as the experience necessary to command a rebellion. In the dismal eighties he was often found grumbling his discontent in West Springfield's Old Stebbin's Tavern or drilling his followers on the town common.

But it was not upon Shattuck or Smith or Day that the final leadership devolved, with its mixed portions of glory and infamy, but on Captain Daniel Shays of Pelham. In some respects Shays was an improbable leader for a popular revolt, for he seems to have been a reluctant rebel in the first place; as late as the fall of 1786 he insisted: "I at their head! I am not." And even after he had assumed command of the bulk of the rebel army, he expressed eagerness to accept a pardon. But at the same time, Shays had attributes that made him a likely prospect for gaining the loyalty of the insurgents. Unlike the others, Shays presented a calm moderation that inspired confidence and respect. He also had a penchant for military courtesy and protocol, a quality that would have undoubtedly been repugnant to the veterans if overdone, but one that was essential if the "mobbers," as they were often called, were to acquire the discipline and organization necessary to resist the forces of government.

Daniel Shays also attracted confidence through his impressive Revolutionary War record. Joining the Continental Army at the outbreak of hostilities, he fought bravely at Bunker Hill (where his courage earned him a promotion to sergeant), served under Ethan Allen at Ticonderoga, helped thwart Gentleman Johnny Burgoyne at Saratoga, and stormed Stony Point with Mad Anthony Wayne. For recruiting a company of volunteers in Massachusetts Shays ultimately received a commission as their captain, a position he seems to have filled adequately if not outstandingly. And before leaving the service, Shays suffered at least one wound in battle.

Shays resigned from the army in 1780 and turned his hand to farming in the small town of Pelham, a few miles east of the Connecticut River. There his popularity, undoubtedly enhanced by his military reputation, won him election to various local offices. At the same time, Shays learned at first hand the problems that can be-set a returned veteran. He had already sold for cash the handsome ceremonial sword that the Marquis de Lafayette had presented to him in honor of the victory at Saratoga. On long winter evenings at Conkey's Tavern, Daniel Shays listened to his neighbors' tales of distress. In 1784 he was himself sued for a debt of twelve dollars; by 1786 he was deeply involved in the insurrection. Like so many other men in western and central Massachusetts, Shays had been maneuvered by events of the postwar period into actions that he would hardly have contemplated a few years earlier.

The relative calm that followed the outbreaks of 1782–83 was abruptly shat-tered in 1786. To make up for the low revenue of the previous year, the legislature in the spring of 1786 imposed unusually heavy poll and property taxes, amounting to one third of the total income of the people. In 1774 taxes had been fifteen cents per capita; in 1786 they leaped to $1.75—a hefty sum for heads of families in fron-tier areas where a skilled laborer earned thirty to fifty cents a day. Protested one poor cobbler, "The constable keeps at us for rates, rates, rates!" Besides, the new tax schedule was notorious for its inequity, placing heavy duties on land without re-gard to its value—a palpable discrimination against the poorer farmers. The new schedule also worked injury on the least affluent classes by seeking almost forty per-cent of its revenue through a head tax, asking equal amounts from pauper and merchant prince. As court and jail records poignantly testify, many people in the central and western parts of the state could not pay both the new taxes and their old debts. Worcester County, for example, had four thousand suits for debt in 1785–86 (double the total of the preceding two years), and the number of persons imprisoned for debt jumped from seven to seventy-two during that period. In 1786 debtors outnumbered all other criminals in Worcester County prisons 3 to 1.

The new taxes would probably have caused considerable anger by themselves, but when added to old grievances they were sure to bring trouble. During the sum-mer of 1786, conventions met in several western counties—in Worcester, in Hamp-shire, in Berkshire—and even as far east as Middlesex, only a few miles from Boston. From these quasi-legal meetings came resolutions to the Massachusetts leg-islature calling for a variety of reforms: reduction of court and lawyers' fees, reduc-tion of salaries for state officials, issuance of paper money, removal of the state cap-ital from Boston (where it was deemed too susceptible to the influence of eastern commercial interests), reduction of taxes, redistribution of the tax load, and many similar changes. A few protests called for still more drastic reforms, such as aboli-tion of the state senate and curtailment of the governor's appointive power, while some petitioners insisted on a state-wide convention to amend the constitution of 1780, now barely six years old. But on the whole the petitions demanded evolution, not revolution. This was a tempered and healthy challenge to an administration that had shown itself insensitive and incompetent.

In the protests about the government, two categories of citizens were singled out for criticism by the petitioners. First were the merchants and professional men, who enjoyed an unfair advantage within the tax system. Second were the lawyers, who seemed to be conspiring with judges and creditors to force the debtor still fur-ther into obligation. Perhaps not all lawyers were so harshly judged, but the con-demnation was certainly meant to apply to those whom John Adams called "the

This 1787 woodcut portrays Daniel Shays and Jacob [Job] Shattuck. Shays led a band of fellow farmers in revolt against a state government that was insensitive to rural needs. Their rebellion strengthened the demand for a strong new federal government.

dirty dabblers in the law," men who often created more litigation than they resolved. In contrast to the turbulent days before the Revolution, the new era in Massachusetts did not find lawyers in the vanguard of the movement for reform.

But in one respect, at least, the 1780s bore resemblance to the years before Lexington: peaceful protest soon gave way to more forceful action. In late August, following a Hampshire County convention at Hatfield, a mob of 1,500 men "armed with guns, swords, and other deadly weapons, and with drums beating and fifes playing" took command of the county courthouse at Northampton and forced the judges of the Court of Common Pleas and General Sessions of the Peace to adjourn sine die. During the next few months, similar conventions with similar results took place in Middlesex, Bristol, and Worcester counties. By early fall, mobs armed with muskets or hickory clubs and often sporting sprigs of hemlock in their hats as a sign of allegiance to the rebel cause moved at will through the interior counties.

The rebels did not go unopposed. In each county there were some citizens who looked askance at the growing anarchy and did their best to thwart it. In Worcester, seat of Worcester County, Judge Artemas Ward showed the mettle of those who would not succumb to mob rule. When on the fifth of September two hundred armed men blocked his path to the courthouse, the aging but still impressive ex-general defied the bayonets that pierced his judicial robes and for two hours lectured the crowd on the dangers of anarchy and the meaning of treason. A heavy downpour finally silenced the judge, though not until he had intoned a timely plea that "the sun never shine on rebellion in Massachusetts." But neither rain nor words had got the judge and his colleagues into the courthouse.

Elsewhere the story was much the same: a few citizens tried to stem the tide of rebellion but in the end were swept aside. At Great Barrington, in Berkshire County, a mob of 800 stopped the court, broke open the jail and released its prisoners, and abused the judges who protested. At Springfield, Daniel Shays and Luke Day made sure that the courthouse doors remained shut, while at Concord, less than twenty miles from Boston, Job Shattuck, aided by Nathan Smith and his brother Sylvanus, prevented the sitting of the Middlesex County court. Only at Taunton, in Bristol County, did a sizable mob meet its match. There Chief Justice (and former general) David Cobb was ready with a field piece, thirty volunteers, and a determination to "sit as a judge or die as a general." The Bristol court met as scheduled.

Governor James Bowdoin and the legislature responded to the latest outbreaks with a confusing mixture of sternness, concession, and indecision. In early September, the Governor issued his first proclamation, condemning the mobbers' flirtation with "riot, anarchy and confusion." In October the legislature suspended habeas corpus, but it also authorized some categories of goods as legal tender for specified kinds of public and private debts, and it offered full pardon to all rebels who would take an oath of allegiance before the end of the year. Yet the government failed to find solutions to the major complaints. No significant reforms were made in court procedures, the tax load was not reduced, officials' salaries were not lowered, the capital was not moved, and no curbs were placed on lawyers' machinations.

As mob violence continued through the fall of 1786, spokesmen in the Bay State and elsewhere voiced a growing fear that the anarchy of Massachusetts might infect the entire nation. Several months earlier John Jay had predicted a crisis— "something I cannot foresee or conjecture. I am uneasy and apprehensive; more so than during the war." Now Secretary of War Henry Knox, Massachusetts statesman Rufus King, and others began to have similar apprehensions. They wrote frantic letters to one another, asking for news and predicting disaster. Abigail Adams, then in London, bristled at the "ignorant and wrestless desperadoes," while reports of the uprising helped prod her husband John into writing his ponderous *Defence of the Constitutions*. Even General Washington lost his equanimity. "[For] God's sake, tell me," he wrote to his former aide-de-camp, David Humphreys, in October, "what is the cause of all these commotions? Do they proceed from licentiousness, British influence disseminated by the tories, or real grievances which admit of redress? If the latter, why were they delayed 'till the public mind had been so much agitated? If the former, why are not the powers of Government tried at once?"

Fearful that the powers of state government would not be sufficient to thwart the rebellion, Governor Bowdoin and Secretary of War Knox hatched a scheme for employing federal troops should the need arise. Knox discussed the matter with Congress: the outcome was a call for 1,340 volunteers for the federal army (which then numbered only 700), most of them to be raised in Massachusetts and Connecticut. The additional troops were ostensibly to be used against the Indians of the Northwest, but in secret session Congress acknowledged the possibility that they might be sent instead against the self-styled "regulators" in New England, and that they might be needed to protect the federal arsenal in Springfield—a likely target for the rebellious veterans. Meanwhile the Massachusetts Council authorized a state army of 4,400 men and four regiments of artillery, to be drawn largely from the militia of the eastern counties.

Command of the state forces fell to Major General Benjamin Lincoln, a battle-tested veteran of the Revolution, and a man of tact and humanity as well as martial vigor. But before taking the field, Lincoln served a brief stint as fundraiser for his own army, for the cost of a thirty-day campaign had been calculated at about

£5,000, or about $20,000, and the impoverished state treasury could offer nothing but promises of eventual reimbursement to any who would lend cash to the government. In less than twenty-four hours General Lincoln collected contributions from 130 of Boston's wealthy citizens, including £250 from Governor Bowdoin.

By the time Lincoln's army was equipped for action, the rebellion was over in eastern Massachusetts. It had never been strong there, but in November of 1786 a mob tried to halt the Middlesex County court. This time the militia was alert. After a brief skirmish in which Job Shattuck received a crippling wound, the Groton leader and two of his lieutenants were captured. While Shattuck languished in the Boston jail, his followers drifted west to join other rebel groups.

The situation now grew alarming in Worcester, where the Supreme Court was scheduled to meet on December 5; by late November, mobs of armed men drifting into town had closed the Court of Common Pleas and made it obvious that no court could meet without an army to back it up. Local officials looked on helplessly. Even bold Sheriff Greenleaf, who offered to help alleviate the high court costs by hanging every rebel free of charge, was powerless in the face of such numbers, and he became a laughingstock to boot when he strode away from the courthouse one day unaware that someone had adorned his hat with the symbolic hemlock tuft.

At first the rebels at Worcester suffered from lack of a universally recognized leader. Then in early December Daniel Shays rode in from Pelham, mounted on a white horse and followed by 350 men. He had not come to do battle if he could avoid it; to a friend he confided: "For God's sake, have matters settled peaceably: it was against my inclinations I undertook this business; importunity was used which I could not withstand, but I heartily wish it was well over." Still, as a showdown with the judges approached, Shays increasingly assumed the role of spokesman for the disparate forces. And it was just as well; with milling crowds of disgruntled veterans and a frightened and divided populace, violence might well have erupted. Instead, choosing wisdom as the better part of valor, the rebels put their energies into drafting a petition to the legislature for a redress of grievances and into several wordy defenses of their own actions. Violence was scrupulously avoided. And their immediate point, after all, had been won; the Worcester court gathered meekly in the Sun Tavern and adjourned until January 23. The insurgents then gave way before the more impressive force of winter blizzards and dispersed to the west. Friends of the rebels were not greatly heartened, however, for the basic grievances remained. Friends of the government rejoiced at the retreat of the rebels, and chanted:

> *Says sober Bill, "Well Shays has fled,*
> *And peace returns to bless our days!"*
> *"Indeed," cries Ned, "I always said*
> *He'd prove at last a fall-back Shays,*
> *And those turned over and undone*
> *Call him a worthless Shays, to run!"*

But Shays was only running to a new scene of action. The Hampshire County court, scheduled to meet in Springfield in late January, should be stopped. Besides, the federal arsenal in that town had the only cache of arms the rebels could hope to capture, and without weapons the rebellion must collapse.

General Lincoln was preparing to defend the January session of the Worcester court when news reached him of the crisis in Springfield. The arsenal there boasted a garrison of some 1,100 militia under General William Shepard, but surrounding the troops were three rebel forces: Daniel Shays commanded 1,200 men at Wilbraham, eight miles to the east; Eli Parson had 400 at Chicopee, three miles to the north; Luke Day led another 400 at West Springfield, just across the Connecticut River to the west. There was every reason to believe they could overwhelm Shepard's garrison if they were willing to risk some bloodshed. General Lincoln headed for Springfield on the double.

Had Shays and his cohorts carried out their original plan they would in all likelihood have had possession of the arsenal before Lincoln arrived with reinforcements. The attack had been set for January 25: Shays was to have led a frontal assault from the southeast while Day directed a flanking movement from the west. But at the last minute Day decided to wait until the twenty-sixth, and his note informing Shays of the change was intercepted by Shepard's men. When Shays moved forward on the afternoon of the twenty-fifth, Shepard confidently grouped his full strength against the lone attack. But not much strength was needed. Shepard fired only three cannon shots. When two warning volleys failed to turn back the rebels, Shepard aimed the third into their midst. Three insurgents fell dead in the snow, a fourth lay mortally wounded. The remainder fled in confusion. It was a shattered band that Shays succeeded in regrouping a few miles from the scene of conflict.

At this point General Lincoln arrived and took position between Day and Shays. Both rebel armies at once broke camp and headed for safer territory—Day's men so hastily that they left pork and beans baking in their ovens and discarded knapsacks strewn along their route. The main force, under Shays, beat a rapid retreat to the northeast, passing through Ludlow, South Hadley, Amherst, and Pelham. Lincoln followed in close pursuit, moving overland after Shays, while General Shepard marched up the frozen Connecticut River to prevent a reunion of the rebel army's eastern and western wings.

At Hadley, General Lincoln halted his pursuit long enough to discuss surrender proposals with Shays. The rebel leader was willing to negotiate, but his insistence on an unconditional pardon for himself and his men was more than General Lincoln was authorized to grant. With no agreement likely, Shays suddenly shifted his men to the relative security of Petersham, a center of regulator sentiment which lay in terrain easier to defend. It was midwinter—an unusually cold and stormy winter—and deep snow blanketed the Connecticut Valley. Perhaps the militia would not bother to follow.

But Shays reckoned without General Lincoln. Ever since 1780, when he had surrendered Charleston, South Carolina, and its garrison of 5,400 men to the British in the most costly American defeat of the Revolution, Benjamin Lincoln had had to endure charges of cowardice and indecision. Although he had been officially exonerated, a few critics persisted; in a vigorous suppression of the Shaysites General Lincoln could perhaps fully restore himself in the public's esteem. With superb stamina and determination, Lincoln marched his men the thirty miles from Hadley to Petersham through a blinding snowstorm on the night of Saturday, February 3, arriving at Petersham early the next morning. Taken completely by surprise, the insurgents were routed: some 150 were captured; the rest, including

Shays, escaped to the north. Lincoln then moved across the Connecticut River to disperse rebel nests in the Berkshires. By the end of February only scattered resistance remained. What the legislature had recently condemned as a "horrid and unnatural Rebellion and War . . . traiterously raised and levied against this Commonwealth" had come to an inglorious end.

While the militia crushed the remnants of rebellion, the state government drafted a series of regulations for punishing the insurgents. In mid-February, two weeks after Shays' dispersal at Petersham, it issued a stiff Disqualifying Act, offering pardons to privates and noncommissioned officers, but denying them for three years the right to vote, to serve on juries, and to be employed as school-teachers, innkeepers, or liquor retailers. Massachusetts citizens would thus be shielded from the baneful influence of the Shaysites. Not included in the partial amnesty were the insurgent officers, citizens of other states who had joined the Massachusetts uprising, former state officers or members of the state legislature who had aided the rebels, and persons who had attended regulator conventions. Men in those categories would be tried for treason.

The government's vindictive measures aroused widespread protest, not only from those who had sympathized with the rebel cause but from many of its active opponents as well. General Lincoln, among others, believed that such harsh reprisals would further alienate the discontented, and he observed to General Washington that the disfranchisement of so many people would wholly deprive some towns of their representation in the legislature. New outbreaks, he argued, would then occur in areas that had no other way to voice their grievances. In token concession to its critics, the legislature in March 1787, appointed a special commission of three men to determine the fate of rebels not covered by the Disqualifying Act. General Lincoln served on the commission, and under his moderating influence it eventually extended pardons to 790 persons. But in the meantime, county courts apprehended and tried whatever rebel leaders they could find. In Hampshire County, with Robert Treat Paine serving as prosecuting attorney, six men were sentenced to death and many others incurred fines or imprisonment. In Berkshire County eight men were sentenced to die for their part in the uprising.

Had the government of 1786–87 remained in office, more than a dozen lives would have been lost to the hangman, hundreds of other men would have suffered disqualifications, and the fundamental causes of Shays' Rebellion might have lingered on to trigger new outbreaks. But however strongly the regulators might complain of the legislative and judicial shortcomings of Massachusetts, they had cause to be thankful that its constitution required annual elections and that the franchise was broad enough to let popular sentiment determine the tenor of government. The result of the April election revealed the breadth and depth of the sympathy in which the regulators were held by the citizens and the extent of popular revulsion at the ineptitude of the government. In the gubernatorial contest, popular John Hancock, recently recovered from an illness that had caused him to resign the governorship early in 1785, overwhelmingly defeated Governor Bowdoin. Only 62 of the 222 members of the legislature and 11 members of the 24-man senate were returned to their seats. In some instances the voters chose men who had actively participated in the rebellion, including Josiah Whitney, who had recently served sixteen days in the Worcester jail.

Within the next few months the new legislature sharply mitigated both the causes of unrest and the punishments assigned to the rebels. It repealed the Disqualifying Act, reprieved all men under sentence of death—some on the very steps of the gallows—and by the following summer it had pardoned even Daniel Shays, though he and a few other leaders were still precluded from holding civil and military offices in the state. Equally important, it enacted long-range reforms—extending the law that permitted the use of certain personal and real property in payment of debts, imposing a lower and more equitable tax schedule, and releasing most debtors from prison.

Now in truth the rebellion was over. Peace, and soon prosperity, returned to the Massachusetts countryside. Differences of opinion still lingered, of course, as was made clear one Sunday when the church at Whately christened two infants—one named after Daniel Shays, the other after Benjamin Lincoln. But the Shaysites made no further trouble for Bay State authorities, and Daniel Shays, the reluctant leader, soon moved on to New York State, where he eked out a skimpy existence on his Revolutionary War pension until his death in 1825.

Americans of the 1780s drew various lessons from the affair in Massachusetts. Some, like Washington and Madison, appear to have misinterpreted the event and ascribed to the rebels a more drastic program than the majority of them had ever advocated. Others, like Mercy Warren, the lady historian, and Joseph Hawley, the Massachusetts patriot, detected the hand of Great Britain behind the uprising. Still others sensed that the true causes of Shays' Rebellion were local in origin and primarily the fault of the state government. Baron von Steuben had correctly surmised that "when a whole people complains . . . something must be wrong," while Thomas Jefferson, then American Minister to France, thought the rebellion of no dangerous importance and preferred to set it in a broader perspective than had most Americans. "We have had," wrote Jefferson, "13 states independent 11 years. There has been one rebellion. That comes to one rebellion in a century and a half for each state. What country before ever existed a century and a half without a rebellion? And what country can preserve its liberties if their rulers are not warned from time to time that the people preserve the spirit of resistance? . . . The tree of liberty must be refreshed from time to time with the blood of patriots and tyrants." But while observers were drawing these diverse conclusions from the episode in Massachusetts, an increasing number of Americans were concerned with how to make sure it would never happen again.

On May 25, 1787, less than four months after the rout at Petersham, the Constitutional Convention began its deliberations at Independence Hall, Philadelphia. Through a long hot summer the delegates proposed, argued, and compromised as they sought to construct a new and better form of government for the American nation. And among the knottiest problems they faced were several recently emphasized by Shays' Rebellion: problems of currency regulation, of debts and contracts, and of ways to thwart domestic insurrection. As the records of the federal Convention reveal, the recent uprising in Massachusetts lay heavily on the minds of the delegates. Although it is impossible to pinpoint the exact phrases in the final document that owed their wording to the fear of similar revolts, there is no doubt that the Constitution reflected the determination of the Founding Fathers to do all they could to prevent future rebellions and to make it easier for the new government to suppress them if they did occur. Significantly, the new polity forbade the states to issue paper money, strengthened the military powers of the executive branch, and authorized Congress to call up state militiamen to "suppress Insurrections" and enforce the laws of the land. Jefferson's first glimpse of the Constitution convinced him that "our Convention has been too much impressed by the insurrection of Massachusetts. . . ." Jefferson exaggerated, but it is clear that the movement for a stronger central government had gained immense momentum from the "horrid and unnatural Rebellion" of Daniel Shays.

By the summer of 1788 the requisite nine states had ratified the new Constitution, and in the following spring General Washington took the oath of office as President. In the prosperous and dynamic years that followed, the passions generated by the insurrection in Massachusetts were gradually extinguished. But the lesson and the impact of Shays' Rebellion are still with us. Because of it, important changes were made in the government of Massachusetts as well as in the government of the nation, changes that have stood the test of time. Perhaps this episode lends some ironic credence to Thomas Jefferson's suggestion that "the spirit of resistance to government is . . . valuable on certain occasions."

Adams and Jefferson: Intimate Enemies

Joseph J. Ellis

American democracy is sometimes equated with the "two-party system." This linkage is not unreasonable. If a minority is to function as an effective opposition, it must have an ongoing institutional structure: paid leaders to monitor government policies and actions; newspapers and magazines to disseminate the opposition viewpoint; and a fund-raising apparatus to maintain it all. The opposition must become, in other words, a political party. As historian Joseph Ellis observes, however, the Founding Fathers had not anticipated this development. They imagined that political disputes would be articulated spontaneously, according to ethical principles embodied in classical notions of right and wrong. The emergence of a two-party system was chiefly the work of Alexander Hamilton, a Federalist who favored a strong central government, and of Thomas Jefferson, a Democrat who opposed it. Ellis shows that Adams is an interesting figure because, though a member of the Federalists, he repudiated the notion that a president should also lead a political party. He thought of the president as a kind of "patriot king" who ruled on behalf of all. Adams was heroic, Ellis insists, but also slightly ridiculous, attempting to hold back the inevitable development of partisan political parties. Ellis's most recent books include *American Sphinx: The Character of Thomas Jefferson* (1997) and *Founding Brothers: The Revolutionary Generation* (2000).

During the first contested presidential election in American history, the voters were asked to choose between John Adams and Thomas Jefferson. In 2000, voters chose—though some may dispute it—George W. Bush over Al Gore. At first blush, the caustic observation of Henry Adams appears indisputable: The American Presidency stands as a glaring exception to Charles Darwin's theory of evolutionary progress.

But straightforward comparisons between now and then are notoriously treacherous ventures, in part because those statesmen who have been eulogized and capitalized as Founding Fathers enjoy privileged treatment in our memories, in part because the political culture of the early American Republic was a fluid and formative bundle of improvisations. Nothing remotely resembling modern parties yet existed. The method of choosing electors to that odd inspiration called the Electoral College varied from state to state. Voters did not choose between two party tickets; they voted for the two best men, and the runner-up became Vice President. Once elected, the President did not regard himself as the leader of a political party so much as the bipartisan spokesman for the public interest.

Perhaps the most historically significant development during the Adams Presidency was the emergence of party-based politics. This was the historical moment, in short, when the outlines of our modern system first began to congeal, the time when American politics began to move from then to now.

At the beginning of the story, however, no one envisioned the changes that were about to occur, and neither the institutions nor the vocabulary essential for making the transition were yet in place. In 1796 there were no political primaries, no party conventions with smoke-filled rooms. True enough, there were two identifiable political camps: the Federalists, who favored a more powerful central government and who had enjoyed the incalculable advantage of George Washington's presiding presence as the central figure symbolizing national authority for the first eight years of the government's existence, and the Republicans, the emerging opposition, who contested the authority of the federal government over domestic policy. But the chief qualification for the Presidency was less a matter of one's location within the political spectrum than a function of one's revolutionary status. Memories of the hard-won battle for American independence were still warm, which meant that prospective candidates needed to possess revolutionary credentials earned during the crucial years between 1776 and 1783. Only those leaders were eligible who had stepped forward at the national level to promote the great cause when its success was still perilous and problematic.

An exhaustive list of prospects would have included between 20 and 30 names, with Samuel Adams, Alexander Hamilton, Patrick Henry, and James Madison enjoying spirited support. But the four topping everyone's list would have been almost unanimous: George Washington, Benjamin Franklin, John Adams, and Thomas Jefferson. By 1796, of course, Washington had done his duty. Franklin was dead and gone. That left Adams and Jefferson as the obvious options. And by the spring of 1796 it had become a foregone conclusion that the choice was between them.

They were an incongruous pair, but everyone seemed to argue that history *had* made them into a pair. The incongruities leaped out for all to see; Adams the short, stout, candid-to-a-fault New Englander, Jefferson the tall, slender, elegantly elusive Virginian; Adams the highly combustible, ever-combative, mile-a-minute talker, whose favorite form of conversation was argument, Jefferson the always cool and self-contained enigma, who regarded argument as a violation of the natural harmonies he heard inside his own head. The list could go on: the Yankee and the Cavalier, the orator and the writer, the bulldog and the greyhound. Choosing between them seemed like choosing between the words and the music of the American Revolution.

As political rivals and personal friends, both men realized they were jockeying for position within the tremendous shadow of Washington, who was destiny's choice as the greatest American of the age and therefore inherently irreplaceable. Adams's strategy was to trade on the famous Adams-Jefferson friendship and to suggest a bipartisan administration. If no single leader could hope to fill the huge vacuum created by Washington's departure, perhaps the reconstituted team of Adams and Jefferson might enjoy at least a fighting chance of sustaining the legacy of national leadership that Washington had established. Adams began to float the idea in letters to mutual friends like Benjamin Rush that if elected President, he intended to include Vice President Jefferson as a full partner in his administration.

Much like Adams, Jefferson was also preoccupied with the long shadow of George Washington. As he confided to James Madison: "The President [Washington] is fortunate to get off just as the bubble is bursting, leaving others to hold the bag. Yet, as his departure will mark the moment when the difficulties begin to work, you will see, that they will be ascribed to the new administration. . . ." Jefferson was certain that "no man will ever bring out of that office the reputation which carries him into it." While strolling the grounds of Monticello with a French visitor, he expanded on his strategic sense of the intractable political realities: "In the present situation of the United States, divided as they are between two parties, which mutually accuse each other of perfidy and treason, . . . this exalted station [the Presidency] is surrounded with dangerous rocks; . . . and the most eminent abilities, will not be sufficient to steer clear of them all." If Adams was planning for a bipartisan victory in the election, Jefferson seemed to be hoping for a defeat.

Jefferson got his wish. In early February 1797, when the electoral votes were counted, they revealed that in a razor-thin victory, Adams had prevailed, 71–68. The question facing Jefferson now became painfully clear: As the newly elected Vice President, should he join hands with his old friend to establish a bipartisan executive team? As was his custom, Jefferson turned to his most trusted political confidant for advice, and James Madison provided a brutally realistic answer: "Considering the probability that Mr. A's course of administration may force an opposition to it from the Republican quarter, and the general uncertainty of the posture which our affairs may take, there may be real embarrassments from giving written possession to him, of the degree of compliment and confidence which your personal delicacy and friendship have suggested." In short, Jefferson must not permit himself to be drawn into the policymaking process of the Adams administration, lest it compromise his role as leader of the Republican opposition.

The decision played out in a dramatic face-to-face encounter. On March 6, 1797, Adams and Jefferson dined with Washington at the presidential mansion in Philadelphia. Adams learned that Jefferson was unwilling to join the cabinet; Jefferson learned that Adams had been battling with his Federalist advisers, who opposed a vigorous Jeffersonian presence in the administration. They left the dinner together and walked down Market Street to Fifth, two blocks from the very spot where Jefferson had drafted the words of the Declaration of Independence that Adams had so forcefully defended before the Continental Congress almost twenty-one years earlier. As Jefferson remembered it later, "We took leave, and he never after that said one word to me on the subject or ever consulted me as to any measure of the government."

A few days later, at his swearing-in ceremony as Vice President, Jefferson joked about his rusty recall of parliamentary procedure, a clear sign that he intended to spend his time in the harmless business of monitoring debates in the Senate. After Adams was sworn in as President on March 4, he reported to Abigail that Washington had murmured under his breath: "Ay! I am fairly out and you fairly in! See which of us will be happiest." Predictably, the sight of Washington leaving office attracted the bulk of the commentary in the press. Adams informed his beloved Abigail that it was like "the sun setting full-orbit, and another rising (though less splendidly)." Jefferson was on the road back to Monticello immediately after the inaugural ceremony, setting up the Republican government-in-exile, waiting for the inevitable catastrophes to befall the Presidency of his old friend. As for Adams himself, without Jefferson as a colleague, with a Federalist cabinet filled with men

One of the most flattering likenesses of John Adams is this portrait by John Trumbull done in 1793. Public criticism of Adams was high throughout his term of office.

loyal to Hamilton, he was left alone with Abigail, the only collaborator he could truly trust. In a number of letters, his call to her mixed abiding love with a sense of desperation: "I never wanted your advice and assistance more in my life," he pleaded; "The times are critical and dangerous and I must have you here to assist me. . . ."; "You must leave the farm to the mercy of the winds. I can do nothing without you." Adams intended to practice the old politics of trust while Jefferson began perfecting the new politics of partisanship.

Beyond the daunting task of following the greatest hero in American history, Adams faced a double dilemma. On the one hand, the country was already waging an undeclared war, called the Quasi-War, against French privateers in the Atlantic and Caribbean. Should the United States declare war on France or seek a diplomatic solution? Adams, like Washington, was committed to American neutrality at almost any cost, but he coupled this commitment with a buildup of the American Navy, which would enable the United States to fight a defensive war if negotiations with France broke down.

On the other hand, the ongoing debate between Federalists and Republicans had degenerated into unrelenting ideological warfare in which each side sincerely saw the other as traitor to the core principles of the American Revolution. The political consensus that had held together during Washington's first term and had then begun to fragment into Federalist and Republican camps over the Jay Treaty broke down completely in 1797. Jefferson spoke for many of the participants caught up in this intensely partisan and nearly scatological political culture when he described it as a fundamental loss of trust between former friends. "Men who have been intimate all their lives," he observed, "cross the street to avoid meeting, and turn their heads another way, lest they should be obliged to touch hats." He first used the phrase *a wall of separation*—which would later become famous as his description of the proper relation between church and state—to describe the political and ideological division between Federalists and Republicans.

The very idea of a legitimate opposition did not yet exist in the political culture of the 1790s, and the evolution of political parties was proceeding in an environment that continued to regard the term *party* as an epithet. In effect, the leadership of the revolutionary generation lacked a vocabulary adequate to describe the politics they were inventing. And the language they inherited framed the genuine political differences and divisions in personal terms that only exacerbated their nonnegotiable character. "You can witness for me," Adams wrote to his son John Quincy concerning Jefferson's opposition, "how loath I have been to give him up. It is with much reluctance that I am obliged to look upon him as a man whose mind is warped by prejudice, . . . however wise and scientific as a philosopher, as a politician he is a child and the dupe of party."

At the domestic level, then, Adams inherited a supercharged political atmosphere every bit as ominous and intractable as the tangle on the international scene. It was a truly unprecedented situation in several senses: His Vice President was in fact the leader of the opposition party; his cabinet was loyal to the memory of Washington, which several members regarded as embodied now in the person of Alexander Hamilton, who was officially retired from the government altogether; political parties were congealing into doctrinaire ideological camps, but neither side possessed the verbal or mental capacity to regard the other as anything but treasonable; and finally, the core conviction of the entire experiment in republican government—namely, that all domestic and foreign policies derived their authority from public opinion—conferred a novel level of influence on the press, which had yet to develop any established rules of conduct or standards for distinguishing rumors from reliable reporting. It was a recipe for political chaos that even the indomitable Washington would have been hard pressed to control.

What happened as a result was highly improvisational and deeply personal. Adams virtually ignored his cabinet, most of whom were more loyal to Hamilton anyway, and fell back on his family for advice, which in practice made Abigail his unofficial one-woman staff. Jefferson continued his partnership with Madison, the roles now reversed, with Jefferson assuming active command of the Republican opposition from the seat of government in Philadelphia and Madison dispensing his political wisdom from retirement at Montpelier. While the official center of the government remained in the executive and congressional offices at Philadelphia, the truly effective centers of power were located in two political partnerships based on personal trust. Having failed to revive the great collaboration of the revolutionary era, Adams and Jefferson went their separate ways with different intimates.

There was an almost tribal character to the Adams collaboration. Adams himself, while vastly experienced as a statesman and diplomat, had no experience whatsoever as an executive. He had never served as a governor like Jefferson or as a military commander like Washington. And he regarded the role of party leader of the

Federalists as not just unbecoming but utterly incompatible with his responsibilities as President, which were to transcend party squabbles in the Washington mode and reach decisions like a "patriot king" whose sole concern was the long-term public interest. As a result, the notion that he was supposed to manage the political factions in Congress or in his cabinet never even occurred to him. Instead, he would rely on his own judgment and on the advice of his family and trusted friends.

Abigail was his chief domestic minister-without-portfolio. In a very real sense, Adams did not have a domestic policy; indeed, he believed that paying any attention to the shifting currents of popular opinion and the raging party battles in the press violated his proper posture as President, which was to remain oblivious of such swings in the national mood. Abigail tended to reinforce this belief in executive independence. Jefferson, she explained, was like a willow who bent with every political breeze. Her husband, on the other hand, was like an oak: "He may be torn up by the roots, or break, but he will never bend."

Nevertheless, she followed the highly partisan exchanges in the Republican newspapers and provided her husband with regular reports on the machinations and accusations of the opposition. When an editorial in the pro-Republican *Aurora* described Adams as "old, querelous, Bald, blind, [and] crippled," Abigail joked that she alone possessed the intimate knowledge to testify about his physical condition. She relished reporting the Fourth of July toast: "John Adams. May he, like *Samson*, slay thousands of Frenchmen with the *jawbone* of Jefferson." She passed along gossip circulating in the streets of Philadelphia about plans to mount pro-French demonstrations, allegedly orchestrated by "the grandest of all grand Villains, that traitor to his country—the infernal Scoundrel Jefferson." She predicted that Jefferson and his Republican friends "will . . . take ultimately a station in the public's estimation like that of the Tories in our Revolution."

Although we can never know for sure, there is considerable evidence that Abigail played a decisive role in persuading Adams to support passage of those four pieces of legislation known collectively as the Alien and Sedition Acts. These infamous statutes, unquestionably the biggest blunder of the Adams Presidency, were designed to deport or disenfranchise foreign-born residents, mostly Frenchmen, who were disposed to support the Republican party, and to make it a crime to publish "any false, scandalous, and malicious writing or writings against the government of the United States. . . ." Adams went to his grave claiming that these laws never enjoyed his support, that he had signed them grudgingly and reluctantly.

All this was true enough, but sign them he did, despite his own reservations and against the advice of the moderate Federalists like John Marshall. Abigail, on the other hand, felt no compunctions. "Nothing will have an Effect until congress passes a Sedition Bill," she wrote her sister in the spring of 1798. "The wrath of the public ought to fall upon their [the Republican editors'] devoted Heads." In a later letter she went on to say, "In any other Country [Benjamin Franklin] Bache [editor of the *Aurora*] and all his papers would have been seazd. . . ." Her love for her husband, and her protective sense as chief guardian of his Presidency, pushed her beyond any doubts. She even urged that the Alien Act be used to remove Albert Gallatin, the Swiss-born leader of the Republican party in the House of Representatives. Gallatin, she observed, "that specious, subtle, spare Cassius, that imported foreigner," was guilty of treasonable behavior by delivering speeches or introducing amendments "that obstruct their cause and prevent their reaching their goals." Gallatin, along with all the henchmen in the Jefferson camp, should be regarded "as traitors to their country."

Ironically, the most significant—and in the long run the most successful—decision of the Adams Presidency occurred when Abigail was recovering from a bout with rheumatic fever back in Quincy. Federalists who opposed the policy attributed it to her absence. This was Adams's apparently impulsive decision, announced on February 18, 1799, to send another peace delegation to France. (The first delegation had failed when the French government brazenly demanded a bribe before negotiating.) Theodore Sedgwick, a Federalist leader in Congress, claimed to be "thunderstruck" and summed up the reaction of his Federalist colleagues: "Had the foulest heart and the ablest head in the world . . . have been permitted to select the most . . . ruinous measure, perhaps it would have been precisely the one which has been adopted." Timothy Pickering, the disloyal Secretary of State, whom Adams had come to despise, also described himself as thunderstruck and offered a perceptive reading of Adams's motives: ". . . it was done without any *consultation with any member of the government* and for a reason *truly remarkable—because he knew we should all be opposed to the measure.*"

The stories circulating in the Philadelphia press suggested that Adams had acted impulsively because his politically savvy wife had not been available to talk him out of it. (For the preceding two months Adams had in fact been complaining in public and private that he was no good as a "solitudionarian" and he "wanted my talkative wife.") Abigail had noted an editorial in *Porcupine's Gazette* regretting her absence. "I suppose," she wrote her husband, "they will want somebody to keep you warm." The announcement of the new peace initiative then gave added credibility to the charge that without Abigail, Adams had lost either his balance or his mind. Adams joked about these stories. "This ought to gratify your vanity," he wrote Abigail, "enough to cure you!" For her part, Abigail returned the joke but with a clear signal of support: "This was pretty saucy, but the old woman can tell them they are mistaken, for she considers the measure as master stroke of policy. . . ."

This has pretty much been the verdict of history, for the peace delegation Adams appointed eventually negotiated a diplomatic end to the Quasi-War. Adams's decision became the first substantive implementation of Washington's message in the Farewell Address, as well as a precedent for American isolation from European wars that would influence American foreign policy for more than a century. In the immediate context of the party wars then raging, however, Adams's unilateral action was politically suicidal. "He has sustained the whole force of an unpopular measure," Abigail observed, "which he knew would . . . shower down upon his head a torrent of invective." What she meant was that Adams had chosen to alienate himself from the mainstream of the Federalist party, which regarded his policy as pro-French, indeed just the kind of decision one might have expected from Jefferson and the Republicans. Federalist editorials in *Porcupine's Gazette* turned against him, suggesting that their erstwhile leader was mentally unbalanced. (Adams, feeling his oats, wrote Abigail that he might now use the Sedition Act to shut down the Federalist press.) He was the epitome of the President without a party.

It was the trademark Adams style, which might be described as enlightened perversity. He actually sought out occasions to display, often in conspicuous fash-

Thomas Jefferson described his election as president in 1800 as a "revolution." His goal was to reverse the centralizing policies of the Federalists.

ion, his capacity for self-sacrifice. If a decision was politically unpopular, well, that only confirmed that it must be right. He had defended the British troops accused of the Boston Massacre, insisted upon American independence in the Continental Congress a full year before it was fashionable, and argued for a more exalted conception of the Presidency despite charges of monarchical tendencies. It all was part of the Adams pattern, an iconoclastic and contrarian temperament that relished alienation. (John Quincy and then great-grandson Henry exhibited the same pattern over the next century, suggesting that the predilections resided in the bloodstream.) The political conditions confronting the Presidency in 1798 were tailor-made to call forth his vintage version of virtue.

All the domestic and international challenges facing the Adams Presidency looked entirely different to Jefferson and Madison. Once they decided to reject Adams's overture and set themselves up as the leaders of the Republican opposition, they closed ranks around their own heartfelt convictions and interpreted the foreign and domestic crises confronting Adams as heaven-sent opportunities to undermine the Federalist party, which they sincerely regarded as an organized conspiracy against the true meaning of the American Revolution. "As to do nothing, and to gain time, is everything with us," Jefferson wrote to Madison, the very intractability of the French question and "the sharp divisions within the Federalist camp" worked to their political advantage. For the Republican agenda to win, the Federalist agenda needed to fail. Although Adams never fitted comfortably into either party category and seemed determined to alienate himself from both sides, as the elected leader of the Federalists he became the chief target of their organized opposition.

Jefferson's nearly Herculean powers of self-denial helped keep the Republican cause pure, at least in the privacy of his own mind. In 1798 he commissioned James Callender, a notorious scandalmonger who had recently broken the story on Hamilton's adulterous affair with Maria Reynolds, to write a libelous attack on Adams. In *The Prospect Before Us,* Callender delivered the goods, describing Adams as "a hoary headed incendiary" who was equally determined on war with France and on declaring himself President-for-life—both suggestions were preposterous—with John Quincy lurking in the background as his biological successor to "the American throne." When confronted with the charge that despite his position as Vice President, he had paid Callender to write diatribes against the President, Jefferson claimed to know nothing about it. Callender subsequently published Jefferson's incriminating letters, proving his complicity, and the Vice President seemed genuinely surprised at the revelation, suggesting that for Jefferson the deepest secrets were not the ones he kept from his enemies but the ones he kept from himself.

By modern standards Jefferson's active role in promoting anti-Adams propaganda and his complicity in leaking information to pro-French enthusiasts like Bache were impeachable offenses that verged on treason. But, only ten years after the passage and ratification of the Constitution, what were treasonable or seditious acts remained blurry judgments without the historical sanction that only experience could provide. Lacking a consensus on what the American Revolution had intended and what the Constitution had settled, Federalists and Republicans alike were afloat in a sea of mutual accusations and partisan interpretations. The center could not hold because it did not exist.

There are only a few universal laws of political life, but one of them guided the Republicans during the last year of the Adams Presidency—namely, never interfere when your enemies are busily engaged in flagrant acts of self-destruction. As soon as the Federalists launched their prosecutions of Republican editors and writers under the Sedition Act—a total of 14 indictments were filed—it became clear that the prosecutions were generally regarded as persecutions. Most of the defendants became local heroes and public martyrs. Madison quickly concluded that "our public malady may work its own cure," meaning that the spectacle of Federalist lawyers descending upon the Republican opposition with such blatantly partisan accusations only served to create converts to the cause they were attempting to silence.

What Jefferson had described as "the reign of witches" even began to assume the shape of a political comedy in which the joke was on the Federalists. In New Jersey, for example, when a drunken Republican editor was charged with making a ribald reference to the President's posterior, Republican commentators argued that the jury could return a verdict of not guilty, on the ground that truth was a legitimate defense. (In the end, the editor pleaded guilty and paid a fine.) There was even more room for irony. It was while James Callender was serving his sentence for libel in a Richmond jail that he first heard rumors of Jefferson's sexual liaison with a mulatto slave named Sally Hemings. He subsequently published the story after deciding that Jefferson had failed to pay him adequately for his hatchet job on Adams.

But this delectable morsel of scandal, which was confirmed as correct beyond any reasonable doubt only by DNA studies done in 1998, did not arrive in time to help Adams in the presidential election of 1800. Indeed, Adams's string of bad luck or poor timing, call it what you will, persisted to the end. The peace delegation he dispatched to France so single-handedly negotiated a treaty ending the Quasi-War, but the good news arrived too late to influence the election.

Given this formidable array of bad luck, bad timing, and the highly focused political strategy of his Republican enemies, Adams did surprisingly well when all the votes were counted. He ran ahead of the Federalist candidates for Congress, who were swept from office in a Republican landslide. Outside of New York, he even won more electoral votes than he had in 1796. But thanks in great part to the deft political maneuverings of Aaron Burr, all twelve of New York's electoral votes went to Jefferson. As early as May of 1800, Abigail, the designated vote-counter on the Adams team, had predicted that "New York will be the balance in the scaile, scale scaill (is it right now? it does not look so)." Though she did not know how to spell *scale,* she knew where the election would be decided. In the final tally, her husband lost to the tandem of Jefferson and Burr, 73–65.

When Madison declared that the Republican cause was now "completely triumphant," he meant not only that they had won control of the Presidency and the Congress but also that the Federalist party was in complete disarray. Though pockets of Federalist power remained alive in New England for more than a decade, as a national movement it was a spent force. But no one quite knew what the Republican triumph meant in positive terms for the national government. It was clear, however, that a particular version of politics and above-the-fray political leadership embodied in the Washington and Adams administrations had been successfully opposed and decisively defeated. The Jefferson-Madison collaboration was the politics of the future. The Adams collaboration was the politics of the past.

What died was the presumption, so central to Adams's sense of politics and of himself, that there was a long-term collective interest for the American Republic that could be divorced from partisanship, indeed rendered immune to politics altogether, and that the duty of an American President was to divine that public interest while ignoring the partisan pleadings of particular constituencies. After 1800, what Adams had called the classical ideal of virtue was dead in American political culture, along with the kind of towering defiance that both Washington and Adams had harbored toward what might be called the morality of partisanship.

That defiance had always depended upon revolutionary credentials—those present at the creation of the American Republic could be trusted to act responsibly—and as the memory of the Revolution faded, so did the trust it conferred. The "people" had replaced the "public" as the sovereign source of political wisdom. No leader could credibly claim to be above the fray. As Jefferson had understood from the moment Washington stepped down, the American President must forever after be the head of a political party.

Neither member of the Adams team could ever comprehend this historical transition as anything other than an ominous symptom of moral degeneration. "Jefferson had a party," Adams observed caustically, "Hamilton had a party, but the commonwealth had none." If the Adams brand of statesmanship was now an anachronism—and it was—then he wanted the Adams Presidency to serve as a fitting monument to its passing. He could leave office in the knowledge that his discredited policies and singular style had actually worked. As he put it, he had "steered the vessell . . . into a peaceable and safe port."

The last major duty of the Adams collaboration was to supervise the transition of the federal government to its permanent location on the Potomac. Though the entire archive of the Executive branch required only seven packing cases, Abigail resented the physical burdens imposed by this final chore, as well as the cold and cavernous and still unfinished rooms of the presidential mansion. For several weeks it was not at all clear whether Jefferson would become the next occupant, because the final tally of the electoral vote had produced a tie between him and Burr. Rumors circulated that Adams intended to step down from office in order to permit Jefferson, still his Vice President, to succeed him. Adams let out the word that Jefferson was clearly the voters' choice and the superior man, that Burr was "like a balloon, filled with inflammable air." In the end the crisis passed when, on the thirty-sixth ballot, the House voted Jefferson into office.

Despite all the accumulated bitterness of the past eight years, and despite the political wounds Jefferson had inflicted over the past four years on the Adams Presidency, Abigail insisted that her husband invite their "former friend" for cake and tea before she departed for Quincy a few weeks before the inauguration ceremony. No record of the conversation exists, though Jefferson had already apprised Madison that he knew the Adamses well enough to expect "dispositions liberal and accommodating." On March 4, 1801, the day of his inauguration, however, Jefferson did not have Adams by his side as he rode down a stump-infested Pennsylvania Avenue to the yet unfinished Capitol. Rather than lend his presence to the occasion, Adams had taken the four-o'clock stage out of town that morning in order to rejoin Abigail. Apart from a brief note wishing him well, Adams did not exchange another word with Jefferson for twelve years.

Abigail managed to have the last word on the thoroughly modern and wholly partisan political world that Jefferson's Presidency inaugurated. In 1804, after he attempted to open a correspondence with her and, so he hoped, with her husband, Abigail cut him short with a one-sentence rejection: "Faithful are the wounds of a friend." It was a fitting epitaph for the Adams Presidency.

America, France, and Their Revolutions

Garry Wills

France and the United States have been allies in the two great world wars of this century and with minor exceptions have been on good terms with each other ever since the Civil War. However, for a much longer period (throughout the seventeenth century and for much of the eighteenth) America and France were frequently at war, deadly enemies, divided by religion, competition for land and other forms of wealth, and their respective ties to European power politics.

That long period of enmity ended in the last quarter of the eighteenth century, when the Americans and the French engineered their famous revolutions, both throwing off autocratic monarchs and establishing republics devoted to a common set of principles, what the Americans described as the right of all people to life, liberty, and the pursuit of happiness, the French as liberté, egalité, fraternité. These revolutions raised the hopes of oppressed people all over the world and inspired many similar revolts.

It seems safe to say that the common purposes of the two upheavals explain why relations between the two republics have been so harmonious in modern times. But the revolutionary era itself saw sharp fluctuations in the relationship of the two nations because, as Professor Garry Wills of Northwestern University explains in this article, the courses of the two revolutions differed greatly, despite their common objectives.

———

There were two great revolutions against European monarchs in the late eighteenth century. In the first, the French nation helped Americans achieve their independence from George III. Without that help our revolution could not have succeeded. Yet when the French rebelled against Louis XVI, Americans hailed their action, then hesitated over it, and finally recoiled from it, causing bitterness in France and among some Americans. Why had the "sister republics" not embraced each other when they had the opportunity? Instead of marching together, the revolutions, so similar in their ideals, roots, and principles, passed each other at shouting distance. What began in mutual encouragement ended in mutual misapprehension.

The root of the trouble lay in the equivocal nature of the aid France extended to America in the 1770s. The American Revolution wore two different faces in France, and each was one of the many faces of Benjamin Franklin. On the one hand, Louis XVI was using British colonists to discommode his rival, George III, and Franklin was the courtier who pointed out the advantages of such a course to Louis's ministers. A famous contemporary image of Franklin is the porcelain statuette group by Lemire, in which Franklin bows to the French king, who presents him with the Treaty of 1778, which allied us to France (a document that would be the subject of heated controversy just over a decade later).

In a 1786 French aquatint that proclaims Louis XVI as America's liberator, Washington's name is misspelled.

A more complex picture of the diplomatic forces at work is the allegorical print by Étienne Pallière, which shows Franklin helping unleash the French Hercules, who bashes with his club Britannia and her cowering lion. . . . (Although the Declaration of Independence had been specifically crafted to bring France into the conflict, Louis responded only after the first substantial defeat of an English army at Saratoga.)

But to the philosophies of the French Enlightenment, Franklin bore quite another face—himself a neoclassical god now, Prometheus, the tamer of lightning and the scourge of tyrants, the scientist and the philosopher of freedom.

Some of the officers who went to serve in the American Revolution—notably Lafayette, Rochambeau, Chastellux, and Admiral d'Estaing—were enlightened critics of their own government as well as supporters of American aspirations, but George Washington never forgot that the motive of King Louis in sending these auxiliaries was not any devotion to antimonarchical principle but a maneuver to regain some of the holdings in the New World he had lost to England after the Seven Years' War.

Washington alone took the measure of French aid in both its aspects. He was a champion of the Enlightenment in areas like his opposition to established churches, but he also had an eye to the practical conditions for exercising freedom. (In the current debates in Congress over Central America, he would definitely agree with those who think free elections mean little to people who cannot feed their own children.) He meant to keep America free from dependence on France as well as from submission to England.

When Lafayette, for example, tried to organize an army to recapture Canada, Washington expressed to Congress his vigorous objections. He wanted to use France, not be used by it. The independence of America could only be maintained by keeping it nonaligned between the great powers. The historian Edmund S. Morgan has convincingly traced Washington's neutrality policy back to the touchiness he felt about accepting French help from a king with his own designs in mind. Washington's caution was justified years later, at the end of the war over the American colonies, when it came out that Louis was negotiating with George III to grant Spain all American territory across the Alleghenies.

But this was a secret war of wills between Washington and King Louis that went on under a surface of amity. Washington did not even confide his misgivings to Lafayette, despite their friendship. After the war diplomatic relations between the two countries, though strained somewhat by French commercial losses in the war, were cordial as a result of Alexander Hamilton's efforts to repay on a regular basis the debts incurred to France. Meanwhile, the leading thinkers in the two countries seemed to form a single community of rational discourse. French visitors to America . . . found models for French social reform in American institutions. American visitors to France—Thomas Jefferson and [the poet] Joel Barlow—saw the stirrings of discontent with the established church and state as natural consequences of the example America had set in its state and federal constitutions. Thomas Paine, having argued for commonsense government in America, went to France to vindicate the rights of man. The French officers who had served with Washington were the only men at Louis XVI's court allowed to wear a foreign decoration—the Order of the Cincinnati eagle, designed by a Frenchman, Pierre Charles L'Enfant.

When the Bastille fell in 1789, Lafayette—recognizing the indebtedness of the French Revolution to Americans, who had shown the way—sent the key of that prison to Washington. Lafayette's face became the first of many that the French Revolution would turn toward America—and a more welcome appearance could not be wished. Jefferson, who had recently returned from France to become Secretary of State—Lafayette was at his farewell dinner in Paris—was actually more enthusiastic about the French Revolution than was France's minister to America, Jean Baptiste de Ternant. Jefferson thought the French experiment would not only confirm the American one but spread irresistibly to all the other enlightened parts of Europe. When the National Assembly in France, conscious of the model offered by the Declaration of Independence, issued a Declaration of the Rights of Man, it was designed to be adaptable to any country.

Hamilton, the Secretary of the Treasury, thought, like Jefferson, that French republicanism would spread to other countries—a prospect he feared as destabilizing. He reminded Washington that all treaties had been made with the regime of Louis XVI and that any new government in France would not have the same claim upon America as had the one that actually supplied help to America in its time of crisis. This was Hamilton's way of turning the revolutionary assistance France had given to America against that country's own revolutionary effort. The equivocal nature of Louis XVI's actions was coming back to haunt Franco-American relations.

Jefferson was not convinced. He argued heatedly in cabinet debate that treaties are made with the people who make up a nation and that any people can alter its form of government without forfeiting prior claims upon other nations. Washington agreed with Jefferson that treaty obligations must be met—that, for instance, payments on the war debt should be continued—but he was no more ready to commit America's fortunes to the giant republic of France than to the giant monarchy of France.

While the cabinet debate was going on in private, an international propaganda war broke out in 1790 over the future of the French Revolution. Thomas Paine was at the center of a triangular debate in England, France, and America. The mob's invasion of Versailles, menacing the queen—an attack repulsed by Lafayette—had ruffled the great [English] parliamentarian Edmund Burke's deep sense of historical decorum. Burke wrote his impassioned *Reflections on the Revolution in France* to defend ancient establishments. Paine responded from France with *The Rights of Man,* saying Burke "pities the plumage, but forgets the dying bird" of the French nation. Thomas Jefferson indiscreetly recommended Paine's book to its American publisher as an answer to "heresies" that had arisen in America over the French Revolution—an allusion to John Adams's *Discourses on Davila* (1790), in which Adams denounced French experiments with freedom. When Jefferson's letter was published, he had to apologize for this attack by one member of Washington's administration on the Vice-President of the United States.

There was great misunderstanding on all sides because events were moving rapidly in France, though reports of them came slowly to America. In 1792, when news arrived that France had declared war on the alliance of kings that was taking shape in response to the Revolution, Hamilton argued that America's guarantee of French rights in the West Indies was framed in case a *defensive* war should arise, and France had now taken the offensive. Jefferson replied that France was forced to take pre-emptive steps.

But Jefferson's words were being undermined without his knowledge. Lafayette, leading French troops (with Rochambeau) against the Austrians, concluded in 1792 that his home government had reeled out of control. He defected from the army and was soon writing Washington from an Austrian jail, posing delicate problems for the President, who wanted to help his old ally without committing America to either of the two sides Lafayette had already taken. The French Revolution no longer wore a face familiar from America's own fighting days.

. . . Jefferson had written to Lafayette, before his defection, that "we are not to expect to be translated from despotism to liberty in a feather-bed." After Lafayette's imprisonment Jefferson wrote to his former secretary, William Short: "My own affections have been deeply wounded by some of the martyrs to the cause, but rather than it should have failed, I would have seen half the earth desolated. Were there but an Adam & an Eve left in every country, & left free, it would be better than as it now is."

Jefferson did not know, when he wrote those words, that Louis XVI had been executed on January 21, 1793. Jefferson later wrote that he would have voted, if he were in the French government, for removing the king but not for killing him. That was also Thomas Paine's attitude at the time, and Paine was in a position to do something for the king. Ironically, he tried to arrange to have Louis conducted into exile in America, under the safe-conduct of the new minister about to depart for Philadelphia, Edmond Charles Edouard Genêt. Despite Paine's arguments, Citizen Louis Capet was condemned, and Americans began to realize that revolution meant one thing in a home country deposing its ruler and another in colonies seceding from an empire. There had been no regicide involved in the American Revolution—not even any executions of Loyalists. The death of the king raised the stakes of this second revolution, for its sympathizers as well as its participants.

"Republicans" in America had to rationalize the violence by a harsher definition of what revolution means. As French philosophes had used the American Revolution to change their society, so Jeffersonians out of government argued that the French Revolution, by its logic of antiaristocratic purity, showed that changes were still to be made in American society. If the French Revolution was different from the American, that only meant that the American Revolution should be made to resemble the French more closely. Democratic-Republican Societies were formed not only to support the French Revolution but to import some of its practices. Some Americans began to address each other as "Citizen" and to wear the liberty cap. Bostonians even decided that the proper term for a woman was "Citess."

The aim of all this activity was to push America into open support of France. To prevent this, Washington decided to proclaim the neutrality he had been observing all along. Jefferson argued that he had no power to do this—that only Congress can declare war and that the state of peace when no such declaration has occurred does not need to be proclaimed by the Executive, the department of government that lacks war powers. But Americans were organizing support for a foreign belligerent, and Washington wanted to prevent that. Jefferson at least succeeded in keeping the actual word *neutrality* out of the so-called neutrality proclamation of 1793.

At the very time Washington was proclaiming neutrality in Philadelphia, the new French minister arrived in Charleston. With him, the French Revolution acquired a particular face in America that would prove fatal to hopes for Franco-American unity—the face of Citizen Genêt. Genêt, a young aristocrat. . . , made it his open aim to rally the American citizenry against its own government's stated policy. This was a bracing prospect for people like James Madison, who deplored the President's neutrality in a letter to Jefferson: "The proclamation was in truth a most unfortunate error. It wounds the national honor, by seeming to disregard the stipulated duties to France. It wounds the popular feelings by a seeming indifference to the cause of liberty. . . . If France triumphs, the ill-fated proclamation will be a millstone which would sink any other character [but Washington's] and will force a struggle even on his."

Unfortunately for Genêt, he listened to similar talk from "true Americans," who felt that he must save the President from his own advisers. Hamilton had argued against receiving Genêt at all. Washington overruled him, but Genêt made matters sticky by not bothering to seek a diplomatic reception before he began rallying opinion and money for the French cause. He made a public tour that brought him in a leisurely fashion to the seat of government in Philadelphia.

Jefferson, for as long as he could, nurtured great hopes for the Genêt mission. He was glad to see Ternant, the royal minister, removed, since he thought that remnant of the old regime had been an obstacle to the natural sympathy that would be expressed between the two republics once they understood each other. Jefferson assured his friends that Genêt "offers everything and asks nothing." Genêt had brought with him a personal letter to Jefferson from his old friend Condorcet, which urged that "our republic, founded like yours on reason, on the rights of nature, on equality, ought to be your true ally . . . [that] we ought in some sort to form one people."

This was Jefferson's hope too, but Genêt took the idea of one people so literally that he . . . felt he could speak to all free men without regard for the ceremonies of established governments. He had replaced his own title with the universal "Citizen." He expected American officials to set aside their titles too.

When they did not, Genêt treated them as betrayers of their own revolution. He threatened to appeal over the head of Washington to the people the President claimed to represent. He even attacked Jefferson for the State Department's implementation of the neutrality policy. Jefferson, in his turn, came to realize that Genêt was doing far more damage to the French cause than Ternant ever had. By July 1793 he was writing Madison: "Never in my opinion was so calamitous an appointment made, as that of the present Minister of F[rance] here. Hot-headed, all imagination, no judgment, passionate, disrespectful and even indecent towards the P[resident] in his written as well as verbal communications, talking of appeals from him to Congress, from them to the people, urging the most unreasonable & groundless propositions, & in the most dictatorial style. . . . He renders my position immensely difficult."

Jefferson's only hope of preventing a public reaction against Genêt (and through him against France) was to keep the insulting record of his dealings from publication. But that was made impossible when Genêt went from propagandizing to active war making: he was in touch with Western leaders like George Rogers Clark, who wanted to seize Louisiana from the Spanish. Genêt, an adjutant general of the French army, offered the support of his nation to such a "filibustering" movement. This was all the more embarrassing for Jefferson since Genêt had extracted a letter of recommendation from him introducing Genêt's emissary in this matter to the governor of Kentucky. Genêt, at first a nuisance, had become a disaster.

Yet by the time his recall was demanded, Genêt had to request asylum in this country (where, indeed, he lived out the rest of his long life). During his absence the Jacobins had . . . instituted the Terror. Friends of America like d'Estaing were sent to the guillotine—to which Genêt would undoubtedly have been conducted had he returned to France. Paine, imprisoned by Robespierre, lived in the shadow of the guillotine until its blade fell on Robespierre himself. The Revolution was devouring its own.

America was now a "sister republic" to France only in its own bitter divisions. The ideal accepted by all sides at the beginning of the Washington administration had been a factionless society, in which partisan appeals were to be submitted to impartial consideration. Early divisions had occurred, in the cabinet and in Congress, over matters like the establishment of a federal banking system. But these had not become matters of widespread popular agitation until Genêt made his appeals to the people and Democratic-Republican Societies began staging rallies in imitation of the Parisian mobs. John Adams was no doubt exaggerating when he remembered, late in his life, a time "when ten thousand people in the streets of Philadelphia, day after day threatened to drag Washington out of his house." But there was tumult and disorder of the sort not seen since the demonstrations against George III.

When Washington criticized the Democratic-Republican Societies for introducing faction into American life, he was assailed for suppressing free speech. When Paine published his *Age of Reason* in 1794, it was made the occasion for attacks on the "atheism" of the French Revolution. Jefferson, suffering guilt by association with Paine, would be branded an atheist by his political enemies for the rest of his career. Not only were there public factions now, but one side saw behind the other a despotic foreign conspiracy and the other side saw an anarchic foreign atheism. Each looked through the other at a European specter. Monarchy had had its own odious image before 1789. But after 1794 even republicanism had a horrid aspect when one looked at a France reeling from the Terror.

John Adams's early prediction that force alone would put down the French disruption seemed confirmed by the ascent of Napoleon. The American statesman Stephen Higginson rightly assessed it as something that "drew a red-hot ploughshare through the history of America as well as through that of France. It not merely divided parties, but molded them; gave them their demarcations, their watchwords and their bitterness. The home issues were for a time subordinate, collateral; the real party lines were established on the other side of the Atlantic."

Despite the American Revolution's priority in time, the French Revolution became *the* revolution for all later ages. It is the model, the measure by which other uprisings are judged—the one used, retrospectively, to belittle or enlarge our own earlier rebellion. The Russian Revolution of 1917 was criticized according to its proximity to or departure from the French Revolution—not by its detractors and defenders only, but even by its participants, who were conscious, despite their emphasis on the future, that they were reenacting various stages of that primordial overturn and who looked among themselves for people to play the roles of Danton, Robespierre, and others.

The French Revolution ideologized the modern world. . . . It made the champions of unarticulated loyalties, people like Burke, paradoxically articulate a rationale for such loyalties, laying the basis for conservatism to this very day. Burke did not describe himself as a conservative, since the terms *liberal* and *conservative* were not yet in political use as polar terms. But the Revolution gave us the first lasting expression of such a polarity: the use of *left* and *right* in a political sense—taken from the pro-Revolutionary and anti-Revolutionary parties sitting to the left and right of the speaker in the National Constituent Assembly. . . .

Jefferson, looking back years later on the French Revolution, wrote Adams as one old man to another: "Your prophecies to Dr. Price proved truer than mine; and yet fell short of the fact, for instead of a million, the destruction of 8. or 10. millions of human beings has probably been the effect of these convulsions. I did not, in 89, believe they would have lasted so long nor have cost so much blood. But altho' your prophecy has proved true so far, I hope it does not preclude a better final result."

Jefferson sadly concluded that the French people were not yet "virtuous" enough to accept a sudden republicanism after so many years of superstition and despotism; this was the fear that made him want to limit immigration to America from lands where established churches had corrupted men's outlook. . . . For Jefferson, the past was destroying the Revolution. For Burke, the Revolution was destroying the past. Each was, in his own way, right.

The Electoral College

Frederic D. Schwarz

In the 2000 presidential election, Democrat Al Gore, Vice President, received 51 million votes, and Republican George W. Bush, governor of Texas, 50.5 million. Bush became president when the courts ruled that he had won Florida and its 25 "electoral" votes by several hundred popular votes. Thus Bush joined John Quincy Adams (1824), Rutherford B. Hayes (1877), and Benjamin Harrison (1888) as presidents who occupied the White House despite the awkward fact that more Americans voted for one of their opponents. After each of these elections, many Americans have questioned the fairness and wisdom of an electoral system where, as in Florida in 2000, the will of several hundred voters in a single state can trump that of hundreds of thousands elsewhere. In the essay that follows, Frederic D. Schwarz shows how the concept of the electoral college grew out of a complicated dispute between populous and sparsely populated states; the system has persisted, with only a handful of modifications, along with the tensions that generated the electoral college. But whatever its deficiencies, the electoral college seems here to stay.

So it has happened again. A close presidential election has led to recriminations, cries of fraud, and talk of tainted mandates. Just as predictably, the 2000 election has inspired calls to reform the Electoral College—predictably, that is, because such proposals have followed every close presidential contest since the beginning of the Republic. The only difference is that this time no one asked why there's such a long delay between election and inauguration.

The controversy goes back to America's first contested presidential election, in 1796, when John Adams edged Thomas Jefferson by three electoral votes. On January 6, 1797—a month before the votes would officially be counted, though the results had already been leaked—Rep. William L. Smith of South Carolina introduced the first constitutional amendment to reform the Electoral College. Between Smith's initial sally and 1889, the centennial of the Constitution's adoption, more than 160 such amendments were introduced in Congress. From 1889 through 1946 there were 109 proposed amendments, from 1947 to 1968 there were 265, and since then, virtually every session of Congress has seen its own batch of proposals. Still, the Electoral College simply refuses to die.

More constitutional amendments have been offered to reform our procedure for electing Presidents than for any other purpose. Statesmen from James Madison, Martin Van Buren, and Andrew Jackson to Lyndon Johnson, Richard Nixon, Gerald Ford, and Hillary Clinton have endorsed an overhaul of the process. Opinion polls consistently show a large, sometimes overwhelming margin in favor of reform. Nonetheless, with the exception of a small procedural change in 1804, the Electoral College functions under the same rules today as it did in the horse-and-buggy era of 1789, when it was adopted. What accounts for the remarkable resilience of such an unloved creation? And why can't we get rid of it?

In brief, the Electoral College works as follows: On Election Day, citizens in the 50 states and the District of Columbia go to the polls and vote for a presidential/vice-presidential ticket. Within each state, the candidate who wins the most votes gets to appoint a certain number of presidential electors, the number being equal to that state's total seats in the Senate and House of Representatives (the District of Columbia gets three). This winner-take-all feature, which has caused most of the trouble through the years, is not mandated by the Constitution, but it is virtually universal; only Maine and Nebraska have laws that provide for their electoral votes to be split. In fact, the Constitution permits states to choose their electors by any means they want, and in the early days many of them left the choice to their legislatures. Since the 1830s, however, winner-take-all popular elections have been all but obligatory.

On a specified date in December, the electors assemble in their states and go through the formality of casting their votes for the candidates from the party that appointed them. Each state reports its totals to Congress, and in early January the Vice President opens and counts the votes in the presence of both houses. Whichever candidates receive a majority of the electoral votes are declared President- and Vice President–elect.

If no candidate for President has a majority (this can happen if there is an exact tie or if more than two candidates receive votes), the House of Representatives chooses a President from among the top three electoral vote-getters. In this process, each state's congressmen combine to cast one vote, regardless of the state's size, and the House keeps on voting until someone receives a majority. Meanwhile, if no candidate for Vice President has a majority of the electoral votes, the Senate chooses between the top two electoral vote-getters. That's more important than it sounds, because if the House remains unable to make a choice from among its three candidates, the Vice President serves as President.

The first question that naturally arises when one is confronted with such a convoluted system is: Where did it come from? Most of us know that the Electoral College was adopted by the Constitutional Convention in 1787 as a compromise between large and small states. The large states wanted presidential voting to be based on population, as in the House of Representatives, while the small states wanted each state to have the same number of votes, as in the Senate (and the Constitutional Convention itself, for that matter). So they split the difference by giving each state a number of electors equal to its combined total of seats in both houses of Congress.

That was one reason for the Electoral College, but far from the only one. From the start, almost everyone favored some sort of indirect process for choosing a President. Although a few delegates suggested a direct popular election, the states had different qualifications for voting, and those with tight requirements—ownership of a certain amount of property, for example—worried that they would be short-changing themselves in a nationwide poll. In particular, the Southern states had a large group of residents who were automatically disqualified from voting: slaves.

(Something similar might be said about women, of course, but they were not concentrated in any one section.)

For purposes of allotting seats in the House of Representatives, the framers finessed this problem by counting each slave as three-fifths of a person. To retain the same measure of influence in a nationwide popular election, though, the South would have had to let its slaves vote. That, obviously, was out of the question. But with the Electoral College acting as an intermediary, the Southern states retained these "extra" votes based on their slave population. If not for the three-fifths rule, Adams would have defeated Jefferson in their 1800 election squeaker.

Slavery aside, there were other reasons the framers settled on an indirect scheme for choosing a President. Few of them thought the general public would be competent to make such a choice. George Mason of Virginia was particularly scathing in his denunciation of popular election. As summarized in Madison's notes, "He conceived it would be as unnatural to refer the choice of a proper character for chief Magistrate to the people, as it would, to refer a trial of colours to a blind man." This remark sounds supercilious until you read the next sentence: "The extent of the Country renders it impossible that the people can have the requisite capacity to judge of the respective pretensions of the Candidates."

In a country without nationwide media, where traveling 20 miles was an arduous undertaking, this concern made ample sense. Even nowadays, how many Americans can name the governors of more than two or three states besides their own? Or consider the most recent election. Without television, would you have known any more about the Vice President than you know about the Secretary of Commerce? The world of the average eighteenth-century American was parochial to an extent that is unimaginable in the information age. To most of the framers, a popular vote for President would have been about as useful as drawing names from a hat.

With this in mind, the framers thought of the Electoral College not as a formality to ratify the popular will, as it is now, but as an assembly of respected figures (not unlike themselves) who would exercise their judgment to bring forth deserving candidates for the nation's highest office. At one point, in fact, the Constitutional Convention considered a plan to have electors from across the country meet in a single place and hash things out as a body.

Also noteworthy is that in the original version of the Electoral College, electors did not specify one candidate for President and one for Vice President, as they do today. Instead, they put on their ballots two names for President, at least one of which had to be from outside their state. In this way, the framers thought, the electors could satisfy their local loyalties with one vote and use the other to recognize a man of national prominence. Under this system, if the first-place finisher was named on a majority of ballots, he would become President, and the second-place finisher—regardless of whether he was named on a majority of ballots—would become Vice President.

But that wasn't supposed to happen very often. The most important point to understand about the Electoral College is this: The Constitution's framers never actually expected it to choose the President. George Mason of Virginia thought the electors would give a majority to a single candidate only once in 20 times; later he amended this figure to 1 in 50. That's how rarely most of the framers thought anyone would be well known and well respected enough across the country.

Almost always, they expected, the Electoral College would serve as a nominating committee, winnowing a large body of candidates down to the top five vote-getters (reduced to three in 1804), from whom the House of Representatives would make the final choice. The framers, then, saw the Electoral College chiefly as a mechanism for bringing candidates to nationwide prominence. It sounds very cumbersome and inefficient until you look at how we do the same thing today.

This explains why the Constitutional Convention spent so much time debating which house of Congress would choose the President if no one had an Electoral College majority. Nowadays that's an afterthought, something that hasn't happened since 1824, but the framers expected it to be the normal course of events. After considerable discussion, the final choice was given to the House, rather than the presumably aristocratic Senate. To appease the small states, though, each state was given a single vote without regard to its size.

During the ratification debate, the Electoral College inspired remarkably little controversy. As Alexander Hamilton wrote in *The Federalist* No. 68, "The mode of appointment of the chief magistrate of the United States is almost the only part of the system [i.e., of the entire proposed Constitution], of any consequence, which has escaped without severe censure, or which has received the slightest mark of approbation from its opponents." Sure enough, the first two presidential elections went more or less as expected. Every elector used one of his votes for a figure of national prominence (in this case George Washington, though it was not expected that there would always be such an overwhelmingly obvious choice), and the second votes were scattered among a wide variety of local and national figures. In both elections, John Adams won the second-highest number of votes and thus the dubious honor of the Vice Presidency.

Even while Washington was in office, however, a change occurred that made a mockery of the framers' vision of disinterested wise men carefully weighing the merits of the nominees. This was the development of political parties. Madison, in his classic *Federalist* No. 10, had praised the Constitution's "tendency to break and control the violence of faction," predicting that in a country as large and diverse as the United States, nationwide factions, or parties, were unlikely to form. Yet all theory went out the window almost as soon as the First Congress assembled. What Madison and his fellow framers did not realize was that the very existence of a government makes people align themselves one way or another, pro or con, like iron filings under the influence of a magnet. Any time you have ins, you will also have outs, and parties will form spontaneously around these two poles.

In recognition of this reality, the Twelfth Amendment, ratified in 1804, imposed the only major change that the Electoral College has ever seen. By then the failure of the founders' vision was clear; in 1796 and 1800 electors had run as Adams men or Jefferson men, instead of standing on their own merits, as had been expected. Yet although the notion of a presidential/vice-presidential ticket had developed, electors still had to put two names on their ballots, both officially candidates for President.

In 1800 the duo of Jefferson and Aaron Burr won the election with 73 electoral votes against 65 for the Adams ticket. The trouble was that Jefferson and Burr each received exactly 73 votes, because every Jefferson elector had named both men on his ballot. The election went to the House of Representatives, where Jefferson's opponents managed to forestall a majority until they finally yielded on the thirty-sixth ballot. (In this case, the House was restricted to breaking the tie between Jefferson and Burr rather than choosing from the top five vote-getters, as it would have done if no one had gotten a majority.)

To avoid a repetition of such a fiasco, the Twelfth Amendment required electors to specify separate candidates for President and Vice President. (A similar plan had been the subject of Representative Smith's 1797 proposal.) Outside of this change, however, the rest of the Electoral College was left in place. Most Americans saw no need to open a can of worms by designing a new procedure from scratch.

After the excitement in 1800, the next five elections saw little controversy, with 1812 the only one that was at all close. Still, the inadequacies of the Electoral College—even in its new, improved form—were manifest. As Adams's old Federalist party dissolved and new factions started to crystallize, the 1824 election promised to be splintered, and some observers wondered if the Constitution's creaky old machinery would be up to the task. In 1823 Sen. Thomas Hart Benton of Missouri wrote: "Every reason which induced the convention to institute Electors has failed. They are no longer of any use, and may be dangerous to the liberties of the people." That same year, James Madison, the father of the Constitution, candidly admitted the failure of his beloved progeny and suggested dividing the states into districts and having each district choose its own elector.

In fact, the 1824 election worked closest to what the framers had in mind, and it was a God-awful mess. Four candidates—Andrew Jackson, John Quincy Adams, William Crawford, and Henry Clay—received electoral votes, with none having a majority. Three New York electors who were supposedly pledged to Clay voted for other candidates, while two Clay supporters in the Louisiana legislature were unable to vote for electors after falling from their carriage on the way to the capital. This combination of treachery and bad luck bumped Clay down to fourth place, eliminating him from the balloting in the House, of which he was the Speaker.

At this point the normally fastidious Adams, who had finished second to Jackson in the electoral vote, put aside his scruples and began making deals for all he was worth. Adams won the House vote on the first ballot by a bare majority and immediately made Clay—whose support had swung Kentucky's House delegation into the Adams column, though the citizens of that state had chosen Jackson—his Secretary of State. This led many to accuse the two men of a "corrupt bargain."

Jackson, it is often pointed out, won the most popular votes in this election. But 1824 was the first year popular votes were widely recorded, and the figures are of questionable accuracy. The reported turnout was a derisory 27 percent nationwide and less than 15 percent in some states where the race was one-sided. On top of that, in 6 of the 24 states, the legislature chose the electors, so there was no popular vote.

The 1824 election was the last gasp for legislative selection, though. In 1828 only South Carolina and tiny Delaware still used it, and by 1836 every state except

South Carolina (which would stubbornly retain legislative selection until the Civil War) had adopted the popular vote, winner-take-all method. Give or take a few small anomalies, then, the electoral system in place by the 1830s was identical to the one we are still using.

The dismay and outrage that have greeted the 2000 election were nothing compared with the public's reaction to the 1824 disaster. When the next Congress assembled, a flood of schemes was offered to reform America's procedure for electing a President. None of them got anywhere. And the pattern has repeated itself through the years: After a one-sided election, everyone shrugs off the Electoral College, and after a close election, everyone makes a fuss for a year or two, and then the issue fades away.

Through the years, numerous inadequacies of the Electoral College have come to the fore: potentially fractured multi-party elections (including 1912, 1924, 1948, and 1968); contested results (Hayes-Tilden in 1876 and Bush-Gore in 2000, plus a near-miss with Nixon-Kennedy in 1960); "minority" Presidents (1824, 1876, 1888, and 2000, with near-misses in 1960 and 1976); and "faithless" electors voting for candidates other than the ones they were chosen to vote for (as some Southern electors threatened to do in 1948 and 1960).

It's safe to say that if you were designing an election method from scratch, it wouldn't look like the Electoral College. Yet it's worth pointing out what's not wrong with our current system before we think about fixing what is. The famous 1876–77 Hayes-Tilden fiasco, for example, is not a good argument for abolition; it was the result of outright fraud and corruption, which could occur under any system. Indeed, the present Electoral College decreases the possibility for vote fraud (while admittedly increasing the payoff if it's successful) by restricting it to a few states where the vote is close. In a direct nationwide popular election, votes could be stolen anywhere, including in heavily Democratic or Republican states where no one would bother under the current rules. In this way, the Electoral College acts as a firewall to contain electoral tampering.

It is also often said that under the Electoral College a popular-vote winner can be an electoral-vote loser. But this "problem" dissolves upon closer examination. Popular-vote totals are not predetermined; if they were, there would be no use for campaign consultants and political donations. Rather, the popular vote is an artifact of the electoral system. With a winner-take-all Electoral College, candidates tailor their messages and direct their spending to swing states and ignore the others, even when there are lots of votes to be had.

In the recent election, for example, neither presidential candidate made more than a token effort in New York, which was known to be safely in Gore's pocket. To residents, it seemed as if neither man visited the state at all except to ask for money. Gore ended up receiving around 3.7 million votes to Bush's 2.2 million. Now suppose Bush had campaigned in New York enough to induce 170,000 of those Gore voters, or less than 5 percent, to switch. He would have made up the nationwide popular-vote gap right there. Instead, both candidates spent enormous amounts of time and money fighting over handfuls of uncommitted voters in Florida, Michigan, and a few other states. That's why in a close election, it doesn't make sense to compare nationwide popular-vote totals when popular votes don't determine the

Since its adoption in 1787 as a complete so-lution to the argument over presidential vot-ing between heavily populated and sparsely populated states, the Electoral College has been the subject of much debate over its pur-pose and usefulness. As yet, however, critics of the Electoral College have not agreed on a system to reform or replace it.

winner. You might just as well point out that the losing team in a baseball game got more hits.

As for faithless electors, not since the anomalous situation of 1824 have they made a difference in a presidential election. There is some reason to believe that if an elector broke his or her trust in a close race today, the switch would be ruled in-valid. In any case, this problem can easily be eliminated with state laws or an act of Congress. These laws could also be tailored to take account of what happens if a candidate dies before the Electoral College meets or if a third-party candidate wishes to give his or her votes to another candidate. Flexible electors can even sometimes be useful, as in the three-way 1912 race, when some Theodore Roosevelt electors said before the election that if Roosevelt could not win, they would switch their votes to William Howard Taft.

Nonetheless, the flaws of the Electoral College, however exaggerated they may be, are clear. It magnifies small margins in an arbitrary manner; it distorts the cam-paign process by giving tossup states excessive importance; it gives small states a dis-proportionate number of votes; and perhaps worst of all, many people don't have a clue about how it works.

Each of these except the last can be turned around and called an advantage by traditionalists: Magnified margins yield a "mandate" (though have you ever heard anyone who wasn't a journalist talk about presidential mandates?); the need to pander to a diverse set of constituencies makes candidates fashion platforms with broad appeal; and after all, small states deserve a break. Still, nobody really loves the Electoral College—until a specific alternative is proposed.

The lack of agreement among would-be reformers has allowed the Electoral College's vastly outnumbered supporters to defend it successfully against all attacks for nearly two centuries. Before the Civil War, slavery, called by its polite name of States' Rights, stymied electoral reform in the same way it stymied so many other things: The Southern states would not consider any reform that did not increase their region's importance in national elections, Oddly enough, by losing the war, the South got the influence it had always wanted.

From the end of Reconstruction into the 1940s, Democrats could count on a sure 100 to 120 electoral votes from the Solid South—the 11 states of the old Confederacy. Though the three-fifths rule was gone with the abolition of slavery, it had been replaced by something even worse, for while blacks were effectively disenfranchised in most of the South, their states now got full credit for their black populations in the House of Representatives and thus in the Electoral College. This allowed Southern whites not only to keep blacks from voting but in effect to vote for them. For most of a century after the 1870s, then, the Electoral College was a racket for the Democratic party.

Today the Solid South is a thing of the past. Nonetheless, since 1804 no electoral reform amendment has even made it through Congress. Why not? Who benefits from the Electoral College? Briefly put, two groups benefit: big states and small states. The winner-take-all feature favors the first of these groups, while the disproportionate allotment of electors favors the second.

With their tempting heaps of electoral votes, the big states attract by far the greatest bulk of the candidates' attention. If you consider having politicians descend upon your state a benefit, the winner-take-all feature is a big plus. In 1966, in fact, Delaware sued New York (which then had the most electoral votes) and other states in hopes of forcing them to abandon the winner-take-all policy. A dozen other states soon climbed on board. Although the suit, which was based on the novel theory that a provision of the Constitution can be unconstitutional, was summarily rejected by the Supreme Court, it revealed the frustration that the small fry have always felt. In response, the small states cling to their three or four electoral votes the way an infant clings to its blanket. Since no one pays any attention to them anyway, they feel entitled to an extra vote or two.

Partisan considerations persist as well, this time on the Republican side. Today a group of Plains and Mountain states (Kansas, Nebraska, the Dakotas, Montana, Wyoming, Idaho, and Utah) can be thought of as a Solid West, reliably delivering most or all of their 32 electoral votes (as of 2000) to the Republican ticket, though their combined population is about equal to that of Michigan, which has only 18. As we have recently seen, those few extra votes can make a big difference if the election is close; and if the election isn't close, any electoral system will do.

It's impossible to say definitively whether the big-state or small-state advantage predominates, though that hasn't stopped generations of political scientists from trying. But these two opposing factors explain how the 1970s notion of "urban liberal bias" and the 1980s notion of a "Republican electoral lock" can both be correct: The former results from winner-take-all, while the latter results from disproportionality.

Through all the analysis, reform proposals keep coming. They generally fall into three classes: a straightforward nationwide popular vote; election by districts, with the Electoral College retained but each congressional district choosing its own elector (and, in most such schemes, the statewide winner getting a bonus of two); and proportional representation, with electoral votes determined by each candidate's percentage of the popular vote in a given state. Any of these would probably be better than what we have now, but each one has imperfections. Since every change would hurt someone, the chances of getting through all the hoops needed to pass a constitutional amendment—a two-thirds vote in each house of Congress plus approval by three-quarters of the states—look dim.

Direct popular election? First of all, there's the question of what to do if no candidate receives a majority. Would there be a runoff, which would make the campaign season last even longer and might encourage third parties? Would the top vote-getter always be the winner—a system that could elect a candidate opposed by a majority of citizens? Would we mystify voters by asking for second and third choices?

Moreover, a nationwide election—something that has never taken place in America—would require a nationwide electoral board, with all the rules, forms, and inspectors that go along with it. Would states be allowed to set different times for opening and closing their polls? Would North Dakota be allowed to continue to have no form of voter registration, as it does now? Would a state seeking more influence be allowed to lower its voting age below 18? Then there is the potential discussed above for stolen or suppressed votes. Combine all these problems with the inevitable effect of concentrating candidates' time, resources, and money on populous areas, and the case for a small state to support direct election looks mighty shaky.

Election by districts sounds appealing, but it would replace 51 separate races with about 480. Swing states would lose their all-or-nothing leverage, so candidates might concentrate on major population centers even more than they do now. (Under the present system, each new election gives a different group of swing states their moment in the spotlight, whereas with any other system, the big states would always get the bulk of the attention.) The effects of gerrymandering would be amplified, and third-party candidates would find it easier to win a single district than an entire state. Also, the small-state advantage would remain (and in fact be reinforced, since in most cases—all the time for the three-vote minnows—they would continue to function as units) while the big-state advantage from winner-take-all would vanish. In fact, if the 1960 election had been contested by districts and the popular vote had been exactly the same (a questionable assumption, to be sure), Richard Nixon would have won.

Proportional division of electors would be even worse, combining all the disadvantages of a direct popular vote with none of the advantages. Under this method, if a state has 10 electoral votes and Candidate A wins 53.7 percent of the popular vote in that state, then Candidate A is credited with 5.37 electoral votes. In essence, proportional division amounts to a direct popular vote, except that the votes of small-state residents are given added weight. And that's the problem: By stripping the veil of illusion and ceremony and tradition from the Electoral College, this extra weighting makes the small-state advantage nakedly apparent, which infuriates one-person-one-vote fundamentalists.

But from the small-state point of view, proportional division would dilute the already tiny influence that goes with controlling three or four votes in a single lump. Also, there is a significant element of the public that views anything involving decimals as un-American—except baseball statistics, of course. Yet restricting the division of electors to whole numbers would be far more confusing, with different mathematical rules and minimum requirements in each state and often arbitrary results (if your state has four votes and the popular margin is 55–45, how do you divide them?). Proportional division would be fine for student-council elections at MIT, but to most American voters, it would amount to a mystifying black box.

To be fair, much worse ideas have been proposed. In the mist beyond proportional representation lies the wreckage of dozens of too-clever schemes, such as one cooked up in 1970 by Sen. Thomas Eagleton and Sen. Robert Dole (each of whom would within a few years take a personal interest in presidential elections). According to *The New Republic,* this plan provided that "a President would be elected if he (1) won a plurality of the national vote *and* (2) won *either* pluralities in more than 50 percent of the states and the District of Columbia, *or* pluralities in states with 50 percent of the voters in the election. . . ." And it went on from there.

In reviewing the history of the Electoral College, it quickly becomes clear how little anybody has to offer that is new. All the plausible reform ideas, and all the arguments for and against them, have been debated and rehashed for well over a century, in terms that have remained virtually unchanged. What has killed all the reform efforts has been the lack of a single alternative that all the reformers can agree on. As the politicians say, you can't beat somebody with nobody, and you can't beat one plan with three.

Moreover, the present system at least has the benefit of familiarity. Any change would be attended with an element of uncertainty, and politicians don't like that. Opinions differ widely about who would gain or lose from electoral reform, but too many states and interest groups *think* they would lose and too few are sure that they would gain. After all, as we have seen, the original Electoral College functioned nothing like what its designers had expected.

In the end, Americans are likely to do what they have always done about the Electoral College: nothing. Every reform or abolition scheme works to the disadvantage (or possible disadvantage) of some special interest, and when a good-government issue collides with special interests, you know who's going to win. Outside of academia and government, there is no obvious constituency for reform; since most people don't understand how the Electoral College works, most of them don't understand the case for changing it. The lack of exact numerical equality and other supposed biases have always bothered political scientists much more than the average citizen, who may endorse reform when questioned by a pollster but will hardly ever feel strongly about the issue.

So we're probably stuck with the Electoral College until the next close election, when reformers and abolitionists of various stripes will once again surge forth, only to end up annihilating each other. To break this pattern, someone will have to either find a novel and compelling set of arguments for reform and waste enormous amounts of political capital to pass a measure that arouses no public passion and has no clearcut beneficiary, or else devise a new scheme that is simple enough to be grasped by the average citizen yet has never been advanced before. Good luck.

Alexander Hamilton: The Founding Wizard

John Steele Gordon

In this essay John Steele Gordon describes the financial policies of Secretary of the Treasury Alexander Hamilton, the first and surely the most brilliant person to hold that office in American history. Gordon calls Hamilton a wizard and the term is scarcely an exaggeration. Hamilton's proposals for reordering the nation's finances were technically precise in every detail and at the same time designed to achieve a single overarching purpose.

Hamilton intended to strengthen the nation's position in the world by changing the very character of its economy. He was able, as Gordon shows, to accomplish this goal by a kind of conservative innovation. He worked in a formative period, a time when rules were being established, precedents set. This was a great advantage; it made what he did possible. But without his skill and vision, the result would not have been the same. Hamilton truly made history.

John Steele Gordon has written on a wide variety of topics in the field of economic and business history. His column, "The Business of America," is a regular feature in *American Heritage*.

Since the dawn of the Republic, whenever an American has expressed an unpopular opinion, he has had Jefferson, above all others, to thank for the certainty that no official retribution would come of it. Equally, whenever he has made a bank deposit or bought a U.S. Treasury bond, it has been because of Hamilton that he knew the value would still be there when he needed the money back. While this may seem a lesser accomplishment than Jefferson's, without it the American economy could not have flourished so abundantly and made the overwhelming majority of us so rich. Without Hamilton, Jefferson's freedom might easily have become "just another word for nothing left to lose."

Because of his singular success in establishing the financial foundations of the American economy, along with his contributions to the Constitution itself and to the *Federalist* papers, Hamilton has a claim to the title Founding Father that few can match.

With the exception of the United Kingdom and its unique unwritten constitution, the United States today has the oldest continuously constituted government on earth. It is hard for Americans even to imagine the situation that confronted the country on April 30, 1789, as George Washington was inaugurated as the nation's first President.

But in that April, as the new government came together in New York's City Hall, there was only the barest outline of how to proceed, provided by the seven thousand words of the Constitution that had been hammered out two years earlier. There was an enormous amount of work to be done. The new government had to prove itself and engender loyalty among its citizens, who overwhelmingly still regarded themselves as citizens of the individual states. The executive departments, virtually unmentioned in the Constitution, had to be created and their duties allocated.

Equally important, the country's disastrous financial situation had to be addressed at once. . . . It was the financial chaos caused by the expenses of the American Revolution, together with the incapacity of the government under the Articles of Confederation to deal with its debts or even to fund its current expenses, that finally impelled the creation of a strong federal government.

It is hard for us to imagine, but in 1789 the United States was little more, economically, than a very large banana republic. As early as 1779 the Continental Congress had issued fully two hundred million dollars in Continental currency to pay for the Revolution. This fiat money, along with that issued by the state governments, depreciated rapidly. In March 1780 Congress itself repudiated this debt, revaluing it to one-fortieth of its old value. Much of this paper remained in private hands, some held by speculators who hoped that it would one day be redeemed at more than they had paid for it. Meanwhile, "not worth a Continental" had become a stock phrase in this country.

In addition to the near-worthless currency, the United States had a large debt. It owed the French government and Dutch bankers $11,710,378. To its own citizens, the government owed $42,414,085. (In proportion to the government's revenues, that's equivalent to a foreign debt of $2.4 trillion and a domestic debt of $8.7 trillion today; the total national debt nowadays is roughly $3.0 trillion.) The interest on both debts was far in arrears.

Because the financial situation had been the most powerful impetus to the establishment of the new government, the most important of the new departments was certain to be the Treasury. It would soon have forty employees, to the State Department's mere five. The department would have to devise a system of taxation to fund the new government. A monetary and banking system would have to be developed to further the country's commerce and industry. The national debt needed to be refunded and rationalized. A customs service had to be organized and tariffs collected. The public credit had to be established so that the government could borrow as necessary.

All this was to be brilliantly accomplished in the first two years of the new government. It was, almost entirely, the work of the young first Secretary of the Treasury.

Alexander Hamilton was not like the other Founding Fathers. He was the only one of the major figures of the early Republic who was not born in what is now the United States. He was born on the British West Indian island of Nevis and came to manhood on what was then the Danish island of St. Croix, now part of the U.S. Virgin Islands. . . . Hamilton, still in his teens, left St. Croix in October 1772 [for New York], never to see the West Indies again.

As relations between Great Britain and its American colonies rapidly deteriorated, Hamilton threw in his lot with his new country. His immense talents and his capacity for work soon gave him a leading role in the Revolution and its aftermath. When Washington became President under the new Constitution, he asked Robert

Morris, the financier of the Revolution, to become Secretary of the Treasury, but Morris, intent on making money, turned him down. He recommended Hamilton instead. Washington was happy to appoint his former aide-de-camp, and Hamilton, in his early thirties, gladly gave up a lucrative law practice in New York to accept. . . .

. . . Far more than Jefferson, Washington, Adams, and Madison, Hamilton was a nationalist. His loyalty to America as a whole was unalloyed by any loyalty to a particular state.

Hamilton was also by far the most urban and the most commercial-minded of the men who made the country. He had grown up, almost literally, in a counting house and lived most of his life in what was already the most cosmopolitan and business-minded city in the country. He had founded the first American bank, the Bank of New York. Washington, Jefferson, Madison, and even Adams were far more tied to the land than was Hamilton. Jefferson, especially, longed to see America a country filled with self-sufficient yeoman farmers who shunned urban life. Hamilton, at home in the city and deeply learned in finance, saw far more clearly than Jefferson how the winds of economic change were blowing in the late eighteenth century.

He was always to be, to some extent, a social outsider. Today we tend to think of the American Revolution as having brought "democracy" to the thirteen colonies. In fact, it brought no such thing. The eighteenth century was an age of aristocracy, and the American colonies were no exceptions. Each colony had its oligarchy of rich, established families that dominated its economic and (under a royal governor) political affairs.

With the removal of royal control, these oligarchies inherited a near monopoly of political power in each colony. Although the population of the United States in 1787 and 1788 was almost 4,000,000, only 160,000—4 percent of the whole—voted for delegates to the state conventions to ratify the new Constitution, the most important political event of their lives. Even when only adult white males are considered, less than 25 percent voted. It was not for lack of interest. It was simply that the right to vote was limited to those who owned substantial property, in other words, the oligarchs.

The oligarchies often manipulated the legislatures to advance their own interests, such as suspending foreclosures for debt during the economically depressed 1780s. And taxes tended to be laid more heavily on those without the vote, such as small farmers and laborers. Oppressive taxes had led to Shays' Rebellion in Massachusetts in 1786 and 1787, which in turn was a powerful stimulant to calling the Constitutional Convention. It is no accident that that convention placed into the document it wrote a clause forbidding the states to impair the obligation of contracts. . . .

Hamilton has often been accused of seeking to establish an aristocratic form of government in this country. This is due partly to an inevitable contrast with Jefferson and his "democratic" political allies and partly to Hamilton's often-stated fear of "the mob." But it is not accurate. To be sure, he had envisioned a government wherein Washington would serve as a sort of uncrowned monarch and Hamilton would be his chief minister. (And Hamilton's political opponents were keenly aware that Sir Robert Walpole, half a century earlier, had transformed his office in the British government, that of first lord of the treasury, into the entirely new office of prime minister.) But for all his personal ambition, Hamilton in fact was a man of the extreme center, to use Stewart Alsop's marvelous phrase. He fully recognized how dangerous too much power in the hands of any one group could be. "Give all power to the many," Hamilton thought, and "they will oppress the few. Give all power to the few, they will oppress the many. Both therefore ought to have power, that each may defend itself against the other."

Here was the essence of Hamilton's political and economic philosophy. He believed, unashamedly, that people were driven by self-interest. . . . Control the channels in which people may pursue their interests, thought Hamilton, and you can direct their efforts in ways that are positive for society. As Forrest McDonald, one of the best of Hamilton's modern biographers, explains: "The rules determine the nature and outcome of the game. That was the heart of Hamiltonianism. . . .

Hamilton planned to use this philosophy to accomplish his goals of putting the country on a sound financial footing and binding its citizens to it. He would succeed so well that Hamilton, and very nearly Hamilton alone, laid the foundations upon which arose in the next hundred years the rich and powerful national economy we today take so much for granted. . . .

Hamilton's first major proposal was to refund the debt incurred by the old national government, and indeed, there was not much choice, since the new Constitution commanded that the federal government assume the debts of the old Confederation. The argument was over who should benefit from this refunding. Much of the debt had been issued to pay for requisitions from farmers and merchants. In the inflation caused by the war and the fiscal weakness of the Confederation, the bonds had depreciated greatly in value. Much of the debt had fallen into the hands of wealthy merchants in Boston and elsewhere who had bought it up at far below par (some for as little as 10 percent of its face value).

On January 14, 1790, Hamilton submitted his first "Report on the Public Credit," which called for redeeming the old national debt on generous terms and issuing new bonds to pay for it, backed by the revenue from the tariff. The plan became public knowledge in New York City immediately, but news of it spread only slowly, via horseback and sailing vessel, to the rest of the country. New York speculators moved at once to take advantage of the situation. They bought as many of the old bonds as they could, raising the price from 20 to 25 percent of par to about 40 to 45 percent.

There was an immediate outcry that these speculators should not be allowed to profit at the expense of those who had patriotically taken the bonds at par and then sold them for much less in despair or from necessity. James Jackson, a member of the House of Representatives from the sparsely settled frontier state of Georgia, was horrified by the avaricious city folk. "Since this report has been read in this House," he said in Congress, "a spirit of havoc, speculation, and ruin, has arisen, and been cherished by people who had an access to the information the report contained. . . . Three vessels, sir, have sailed within a fortnight from this port [New York], freighted for speculation; they are intended to purchase up the State and other securities in the hands of the uninformed, though honest citizens of North Carolina, South Carolina, and Georgia. My soul rises indignant."

Elias Boudinot of New Jersey, wealthy and heavily involved in speculation himself, demurred. "I . . . should be sorry," he said in reply, "if, on this occasion, the House should decide that speculations in the funds are violations of either the moral or political law. . . . [I agree] with [the] gentlemen, that the spirit of speculation had now risen to an alarming height; but the only way to prevent its future effect, is to give the public funds a degree of stability as soon as possible." This, undoubtedly, was Hamilton's view as well.

James Madison, as congressman from Virginia, led the attempt to undercut the speculators. He proposed that the current holders of the old bonds be paid only the present market value and that the original bondholders be paid the difference. There were two weighty objections to this plan.

The first was one of simple practicality. Identifying the original bondholders would have been a nightmare, in many cases entirely impossible. Fraud would have been rampant.

The second objection was one of justice. If an original bondholder had sold his bonds, "are we to disown the act of the party himself?" asked Boudinot. "Are we to say, we will not be bound by your transfer, we will not treat with your representative, but insist on resettlement with you alone?"

Further, to have accepted Madison's scheme would have greatly impaired any future free market in United States government securities and thus greatly restricted the ability of the new government to borrow in the future. The reason was simple. If the government of the moment could decide, on its own, to whom it owed past debts, any government in the future would have a precedent to do the same. Politics would control the situation, and politics is always uncertain. There is nothing that markets hate more than uncertainty, and they weigh the value of stocks and bonds accordingly.

Hamilton, deeply versed in the ways of getting and spending, was well aware of this truth. Madison, a land-owner and an intellectual, was not. Hamilton, in his report, had been adamant. "[Madison's plan] renders property in the funds less valuable, consequently induces lenders to demand a higher premium for what they lend, and produces every other inconvenience of a bad state of public credit." Hamilton was eager to establish the ability of the United States government to borrow when necessary. . . .

. . . One of the greatest problems of the American economy at the time was a lack of liquid capital, which is to say, capital available for investment. Hamilton wanted to create a well-funded national debt in order to create a larger and more flexible money supply. Banks holding government bonds could issue bank notes backed by them. He knew also that government bonds could serve as collateral for bank loans, multiplying the available capital, and that they would attract still more capital from Europe.

Hamilton's reasoning eventually prevailed over Madison's, although not without a great deal of rhetoric. . . .

The second major part of Hamilton's program was for the new federal government to assume the debts that the individual states had incurred during the Revolutionary War. Hamilton thought these debts amounted to 25 million dollars, but no one really knew for sure. It eventually turned out that only about 18 million dollars in state bonds remained in circulation.

Again, opinion was sharply divided. Those states, such as Virginia, that had redeemed most of their bonds were adamantly opposed to assumption. Needless to say, those states, like the New England ones, that had not were all in favor of it. So were financial speculators, hoping for a rise to par of bonds they had bought at deep discounts. But land speculators were opposed. Many states allowed public lands to be purchased with state bonds at face value. Any rise in price would increase the cost of land. . . .

In the middle of April 1790, the House voted down Hamilton's proposal 31 to 29. Four more times it was voted down, each time by so narrow a margin that Hamilton had hopes of making a deal. He had to do something, for he had tied the funding of the old national debt and the assumption of the state debts into one bill. Many thought that the state debt issue was, in the words of one of Hamilton's biographers, "a millstone about the neck of the whole system which must finally sink it."

Hamilton might have abandoned his effort to fund the state debts, but he had still one more reason for extinguishing as much state paper as possible and replacing it with federal bonds. The debts were largely held by the prosperous men of business, commerce, and agriculture—the oligarchs, in other words. These men's loyalties lay mainly with their respective states and cozy local societies. While they had largely supported the creation of the new Union, Hamilton had no reason to suppose that their support would not quickly fade away if their self-interest dictated it.

He was therefore eager to make it in the self-interest of these men to continue their support of the federal government. If they had a large share of their assets held in federal bonds, they would have powerful incentives for wishing the Union well. And so he was willing to throw a very large bargaining chip onto the table to save his funding and assumption scheme. The new federal government had come into existence in New York City, and Hamilton and nearly every other New Yorker were hoping that the city would become the permanent capital. Hamilton knew perfectly well that every state wanted the capital and that Jefferson and Madison especially wanted the capital located in the rural South, away from the commerce and corruption of the big cities.

Hamilton intercepted Jefferson outside President Washington's Broadway mansion one day and asked for help on getting his bill through Congress. Jefferson was opposed to the bill. Nonetheless, he offered to meet Hamilton the following night for dinner, with Madison in attendance. There a deal was made. Enough votes would be switched to assure passage of Hamilton's bill, in return for which Hamilton would see that the capital was located on the muddy and fever-ridden banks of the Potomac River. To assure Pennsylvania's cooperation, the temporary capital was to be moved to Philadelphia for ten years. . . .

The deal was made, and the bill was passed and then signed into law by President Washington. Hamilton was right that the bonds would find acceptance in the marketplace; the entire issue sold out in only a few weeks. The new government, with a monopoly on customs duties and possessing the power to tax, was simply a much better credit risk than the old government and the states had been.

When it became clear that the U.S. government would be able to pay the interest due on these bonds, they quickly became sought after in Europe, just as Hamilton had hoped. In the 1780s the United States had been a financial basket case. By

1794 it had a higher credit rating than any country in Europe, and some of its bonds were selling at 10 percent over par. . . .

The third major portion of Hamilton's program, after redeeming the old national debt and nationalizing the states' debts, was the creation of a central bank, modeled after the Bank of England. Hamilton saw it as an instrument of fiscal efficiency, economic regulation, and money creation. Jefferson saw it as another giveaway to the rich and as a potential instrument of tyranny. Furthermore, Jefferson and Madison thought it was patently unconstitutional for the federal government to establish a bank.

A central bank acts as a depository for government funds and a means of transferring them from one part of the country to another (no small consideration in Hamilton's day). It is also a source of loans to the government and to other banks, and it regulates the money supply.

The last was a great problem in the new Republic. Specie—gold and silver—was in critically short supply. Colonial coinage had been a hodgepodge of Spanish, Portuguese, and British coins. (Spanish dollars, the monetary unit upon which the dollar was originally based, were called pieces of eight because they comprised eight reals, or bits. This is why a quarter is still known as two bits and why the New York Stock Exchange to this day quotes fractional prices in eighths, not tenths, of a dollar.) . . .

Hamilton did not like the idea of the government itself issuing paper money because he thought that governments could not be trusted to exert self-discipline. Certainly the Continental Congress had shown none when it came to printing paper money. Hamilton thought that an independent central bank could supply not only a medium of exchange but the discipline needed to keep the money sound. If it issued notes that were redeemable in gold and silver on demand and accepted by the federal government in payment of taxes, those notes would circulate at par and relieve the desperate shortage of cash. Further, because the central bank could refuse the notes of state banks that got out of line—a position that would mean that no one else would take them either—it could supply discipline too. . . .

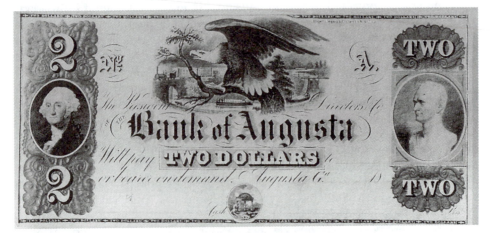

A classical bust of Hamilton adorns a two-dollar bank note from the 1840s or 1850s.

To make sure that the private owners of the bank did not pursue private interests at public expense, Hamilton wanted the bank's charter to require that its notes be redeemable in specie, that 20 percent of the seats on the board of directors be held by government appointees, and that the Secretary of the Treasury would have the right to inspect the books at any time.

There was little political discussion of the bank outside Congress, which passed Hamilton's bill, the House of Representatives splitting cleanly along sectional lines. Only one congressman from states north of Maryland voted against it, and only three from states south of Maryland voted for it.

Hamilton thought the bank was a *fait accompli*, but he had not reckoned on Thomas Jefferson and James Madison. Jefferson, the lover of rural virtues, had a deep, almost visceral hatred of banks, the epitome of all that was urban. "I have ever been the enemy of banks," he wrote years later to John Adams. "My zeal against those institutions was so warm and open at the establishment of the Bank of the U.S. that I was derided as a Maniac by the tribe of bank-mongers, who were seeking to filch from the public their swindling, and barren gains."

Jefferson and Madison, along with their fellow Virginian Edmund Randolph, the Attorney General, wrote opinions for President Washington that the bank bill was unconstitutional. Their arguments revolved around the so-called necessary and proper clause of the Constitution, giving Congress the power to pass laws "necessary and proper for carrying into execution the foregoing Powers."

The Constitution nowhere specifically authorizes the federal government to establish a central bank, they argued, and therefore, one could be created only if it were indispensably necessary to carry out the government's enumerated duties. A central bank was not *absolutely* necessary and therefore was absolutely unconstitutional. This line of reasoning is known as strict construction—although the phrase itself was not coined until the 1840s—and has been a powerful force in the American political firmament ever since.

President Washington recognized the utility of a central bank, but Jefferson and Randolph's arguments had much force for him. Also, it is possible that like most Southerners he was none too anxious for a central bank, useful or not. Further, he may have worried that if the bank were established in Philadelphia, the capital might never make its way to his beloved Potomac. He told Hamilton that he could not sign the bill unless Hamilton was able to overcome Jefferson's constitutional argument.

To counter Jefferson's doctrine of strict construction, Hamilton devised a counterdoctrine of implied powers. He said that if the federal government was to deal successfully with its enumerated duties, it must be supreme in deciding how best to perform those duties. "Little less than a prohibitory clause," he wrote to Washington, "can destroy the strong presumptions which result from the general aspect of the government. Nothing but demonstration should exclude the idea that the power exists." Further, he asserted that Congress had the right to decide what means were necessary and proper. "The national government like every other," he wrote, "must judge in the first instance of the proper exercise of its powers.". . .

Washington, his doubts quieted, signed the bill, and the bank soon came into existence. Its stock subscription was a resounding success, for investors expected it to be very profitable, and it was. It also functioned as Hamilton intended and did much to further the early development of the American economy. State banks multiplied under its control. There were only three states banks in 1790; there were twenty-nine a decade later.

Had Washington accepted Jefferson's argument, not Hamilton's, not only would the bank bill have been vetoed, but the development of American government would have been profoundly different. Indeed, it is hard to see how the Constitution could have long survived, at least without frequent amendment. Jefferson's doctrine of strict construction, rigorously applied, would have been a straitjacket, preventing the federal government from adapting to meet either the challenges or the opportunities that were to come in the future. Lincoln and Franklin Roosevelt would both push the Hamiltonian concept of implied powers very far in seeking to meet the immense national crises of the Civil War and the Great Depression. Even Jefferson, once in the White House, would come to realize that strict constructionism was a doctrine that appeals mainly to those in opposition, not to those who must actually exercise political power. He did not let the fact that the Constitution nowhere mentions the acquisition of territory from a foreign state stop him from snapping up the Louisiana Territory when the opportunity arose.

Jefferson's genius was philosophic, not political, in nature. He instinctively preferred abstractions to the practical, mundane, often messy aspects of actually governing. Hamilton was exactly the opposite. It was his passion to give the American nation a government that worked in the real world. With his contributions to the Constitution and to the *Federalist* papers, Hamilton gave the country a practical government for the time in which he lived. With his doctrine of implied powers, he made it into the dynamic instrument that has lasted through two centuries of tumult and change, amended only fourteen times since his death. . . .

———————

5 National Growing Pains

WE OWE ALLEGIANCE TO NO CROWN.

An early nineteenth-century allegory by John A. Woodside is symptomatic of the nationalistic fervor of the period. The triumphant seaman, his fetters broken, treads on England's crown and scepter.

Marbury v. Madison

John A. Garraty

One of the most remarkable aspects of the Constitution of the United States (and the secret of its longevity) is its flexibility. A form of government designed to deal with the problems of a handful of farmers, merchants, and craftsmen scattered along a thousand miles of coastline, separated from one another by acres of forest, and facing the trackless western wilderness has endured with a minimum of changes through nearly two centuries, in which the nation has occupied a continental domain and become an urban-industrial behemoth.

A major reason for the flexibility of the Constitution has been the system of judicial review, which exists in the document largely by implication but has nonetheless functioned with enormous effectiveness. The following essay deals with one of the great landmarks in the development of the power of the Supreme Court to interpret the meaning of the Constitution and thus to define the powers of both the federal government and the states. The case of Marbury v. Madison, like so many controversies that crucially affected the Constitution, was in itself of no importance. A minor federal official deprived of his office by a technicality was seeking redress from the Court. But in deciding his fate, the Court laid down a principle that altered the whole future of the country, shaping events that neither Marbury, nor Madison, nor the framers of the Constitution could possibly have anticipated.

It was the evening of March 3, 1801, his last day in office, and President John Adams was in a black and bitter mood. Assailed by his enemies, betrayed by some of his most trusted friends, he and his Federalist party had gone down to defeat the previous November before the forces of Thomas Jefferson. His world seemed to have crumbled about his doughty shoulders.

Conservatives of Adams' persuasion were deeply convinced that Thomas Jefferson was a dangerous radical. He would, they thought, in the name of individual liberty and states' rights, import the worst excesses of the French Revolution, undermine the very foundations of American society, and bring the proud edifice of the national government, so laboriously erected under Washington and Adams, tumbling to the ground. Jefferson was a "visionary," Chief Justice Oliver Ellsworth had said. With him as President, "there would be no national energy." Ardent believers in a powerful central government like Secretary of State John Marshall feared that Jefferson would "sap the fundamental principles of government." Others went so far as to call him a "howling atheist."

Adams himself was not quite so disturbed as some, but he was deeply troubled. "What course is it we steer?" he had written despairingly to an old friend after the election. "To what harbor are we bound?" Now on the morrow Jefferson was to be inaugurated, and Adams was so disgruntled that he was unwilling to remain for the ceremonies, the first to be held in the new capital on the Potomac. At the moment, however, John Adams was still President of the United States, and not yet ready to abandon what he called "all virtuous exertion" in the pursuit of his duty. Sitting at his desk in the damp, drafty, still-unfinished sandstone mansion soon to be known as "the White House," he was writing his name on official papers in his large, quavering hand.

The documents he was signing were mostly commissions formally appointing various staunch Federalists to positions in the national judiciary, but the President did not consider his actions routine. On the contrary: he believed he was saving the republic itself. Jefferson was to be President and his Democratic-Republicans would control the Congress, but the courts, thank goodness, would be beyond his control: as soon as the extent of Jefferson's triumph was known, Adams had determined to make the judiciary a stronghold of Federalism. Responding enthusiastically to his request for expansion of the courts, the lame-duck Congress had established sixteen new circuit judgeships (and a host of marshals, attorneys, and clerks as well). It had also given Adams blanket authority to create as many justices of the peace for the new District of Columbia as he saw fit, and—to postpone the evil day when Jefferson would be able to put one of his sympathizers on the Supreme Court—it provided that when the next vacancy occurred, it should not be filled, thus reducing the Court from six justices to five. (The Constitution says nothing about the number of justices on the Court; its size is left to Congress. Originally six, the membership was enlarged to seven in 1807. The justices first numbered nine in 1837. Briefly during the Civil War the bench held ten; the number was set at seven again in 1866 and in 1869 returned to nine, where it has remained.)

In this same period between the election and the inauguration of the new President, Chief Justice Ellsworth, who was old and feeble, had resigned, and Adams had replaced him with Secretary of State Marshall. John Marshall was primarily a soldier and politician; he knew relatively little of the law. But he had a powerful mind, and, as Adams reflected, his "reading of the science" was "fresh in his head." He was also but forty-five years of age, and vigorous. Clearly a long life lay ahead of him, and a more forceful opponent of Jeffersonian principles would have been hard to find.

Marshall had been confirmed by the Senate on January 27, and without resigning as Secretary of State he had begun at once to help Adams strengthen the judicial branch of the government. They had worked rapidly, for time was short. The new courts were authorized by Congress on February 13; within two weeks Adams had submitted a full slate of officials for confirmation by the Senate. The new justices of the peace for the District of Columbia were authorized on February 27; within three days Adams had submitted for confirmation the names of no less than forty-two justices for the sparsely populated region. The Federalist Senate had done its part nobly, pushing through the various confirmations with great dispatch. Now, in the lamplight of his last night in Washington, John Adams was affixing his signature to the commissions of these "midnight justices," as the last-minute appointees were to become derisively known.

Working with his customary puritanical diligence, Adams completed his work by nine o'clock, and when he went off to bed for the last time as President of the United States, it was presumably with a clear conscience. The papers were carried to the State Department, where Secretary Marshall was to affix the Great Seal of the United States to each, and see to it that the commissions were then dispatched to the new appointees. But Marshall, a Virginian with something of the southerner's easygoing carelessness about detail, failed to complete this routine task.

All the important new circuit judgeships were taken care of, and most of the other appointments as well. But in the bustle of last-minute arrangements, the commissions of the new justices of the peace for the District of Columbia went astray. As a result of this trivial slip-up, and entirely without anyone's having planned it, a fundamental principle of the Constitution—affecting the lives of countless millions of future Americans—was to be established. Because *Secretary of State* Marshall made his last mistake, *Chief Justice* Marshall was soon to make one of the first—and in some respects the greatest—of his decisions.

It is still not entirely clear what happened to the missing commissions on the night of March 3. To help with the rush of work, Adams had borrowed two State Department clerks, Jacob Wagner and Daniel Brent. Brent prepared a list of the forty-two new justices and gave it to another clerk, who filled in the blank commissions. As fast as batches of these were made ready, Brent took them to Adams' office, where he turned them over to William Smith Shaw, the President's private secretary. After they were signed, Brent brought them back to the State Department, where Marshall was supposed to affix the Great Seal. Evidently he did seal these documents, but he did not trouble to make sure that they were delivered to the appointees. As he later said: "I did not send out the commissions because I apprehended such . . . to be completed when signed & sealed." Actually, he admitted, he would have sent them out in any case "but for the extreme hurry of the time & the absence of Mr. Wagner who had been called on by the President to act as his private secretary."

March 4 dawned and Jefferson, who apparently had not yet digested the significance of Adams' partisan appointments, prepared to take the oath of office and deliver his inaugural address. His mood, as the brilliant speech indicated, was friendly and conciliatory. He even asked Chief Justice Marshall, who administered the inaugural oath, to stay on briefly as Secretary of State while the new administration was getting established. That morning it would still have been possible to deliver the commissions. As a matter of fact, a few actually were delivered, although quite by chance.

Marshall's brother James (whom Adams had just made circuit judge for the District of Columbia) was disturbed by rumors that there was going to be a riot in Alexandria in connection with the inaugural festivities. Feeling the need of some justices of the peace in case trouble developed, he went to the State Department and personally picked up a number of the undelivered commissions. He signed a receipt for them, but "finding that he could not conveniently carry the whole," he returned several, crossing out the names of these from the receipt. Among the ones returned were those appointing William Harper and Robert Townsend Hooe. By failing to deliver these commissions, Judge James M. Marshall unknowingly enabled Harper and Hooe, obscure men, to win for themselves a small claim to legal immortality.

The new President was eager to mollify the Federalists, but when he realized the extent to which Adams had packed the judiciary with his "most ardent political enemies," he was indignant. Adams' behavior, he said at the time, was an "outrage on decency," and some years later, when passions had cooled a little, he wrote sorrowfully: "I can say with truth that one act of Mr. Adams' life, and one only, ever gave me a moment's personal displeasure. I did consider his last appointments to office as personally unkind." When he discovered the justice-of-the-peace commissions in the State Department, he decided at once not to allow them to be delivered.

James Madison, the Secretary of State, was not yet in Washington. Jefferson called in his Attorney General, a Massachusetts lawyer named Levi Lincoln, whom he had designated Acting Secretary. Giving Lincoln a new list of justices of the peace, he told him to put them "into a general commission" and notify the men of their selection.

In truth, Jefferson acted with remarkable forbearance. He reduced the number of justices to thirty, fifteen for the federal District, fifteen for Alexandria County. But only seven of his appointees were his own men; the rest he chose from among the forty-two names originally submitted by Adams. Lincoln prepared two general commissions, one for each area, and notified the appointees. Then, almost certainly, he destroyed the original commissions signed by Adams.

For some time thereafter Jefferson did very little about the way Adams had packed the judiciary. Indeed, despite his much-criticized remark that office holders seldom die and never resign, he dismissed relatively few persons from the government service. For example, the State Department clerks, Wagner and Brent, were permitted to keep their jobs. The new President learned quickly how hard it was to institute basic changes in a going organization. "The great machine of society" could not easily be moved, he admitted, adding that it was impossible "to advance the notions of a whole people suddenly to ideal right." Soon some of his more impatient supporters, like John Randolph of Roanoke, were grumbling about the President's moderation.

But Jefferson was merely biding his time. Within a month of the inauguration he conferred with Madison at Monticello and made the basic decision to try to abolish the new system of circuit courts. Aside from removing the newly appointed marshals and attorneys, who served at the pleasure of the Chief Executive, little could be done until the new Congress met in December. Then, however, he struck. In his first annual message he urged the "contemplation" by Congress of the Judiciary Act of 1801. To direct the lawmakers' thinking, he submitted a statistical report showing how few cases the federal courts had been called upon to deal with since 1789. In January, 1802, a repeal bill was introduced; after long debate it passed early in March, thus abolishing the jobs of the new circuit judges.

Some of those deposed petitioned Congress for "relief," but their plea was coldly rejected. Since these men had been appointed for life, the Federalists claimed that the repeal act was unconstitutional, but to prevent the Supreme Court from quickly so declaring, Congress passed another bill abolishing the June term of the Court and setting the second Monday of February, 1803, for its next session. By that time, the Jeffersonians reasoned, the old system would be dead beyond resurrection.

This powerful assault on the courts thoroughly alarmed the conservative Federalists; to them the foundations of stable government seemed threatened if the "independence" of the judiciary could be thus destroyed. No one was more disturbed than the new Chief Justice, John Marshall, nor was anyone better equipped by temperament and intellect to resist it. Headstrong but shrewd, contemptuous of detail and of abstractions but a powerful logician, he detested Jefferson (to whom he was distantly related), and the President fully returned his dislike.

In the developing conflict Marshall operated at a disadvantage that in modern times a Chief Justice would not have to face. The Supreme Court had none of the prestige and little of the accepted authority it now possesses. Few cases had come before it, and few of these were of any great importance. Before appointing Marshall, Adams had offered the Chief Justiceship to John Jay, the first man to hold the post, as an appointee of President Washington. Jay had resigned from the Court in 1795 to become governor of New York. He refused the reappointment, saying that the Court lacked "energy, weight, and dignity." A prominent newspaper of the day referred to the Chief Justiceship, with considerable truth, as a "sinecure." One of the reasons Marshall had accepted the post was his belief that it would afford him ample leisure for writing the biography of his hero, George Washington. Indeed, in the grandiose plans for the new capital, no thought had been given to housing the Supreme Court, so that when Marshall took office in 1801 the justices had to meet in the office of the clerk of the Senate, a small room on the first floor of what is now the north wing of the Capitol.

Nevertheless, Marshall struck out at every opportunity against the power and authority of the new President; but the opportunities were pitifully few. In one case, he refused to allow a presidential message to be read into the record on the ground that this would bring the President into the Court, in violation of the principle of separation of powers. In another, he ruled that Jefferson's decision in a prize case involving an American privateer was illegal. But these were matters of small importance.

When he tried to move more boldly, his colleagues would not sustain him. He was ready to declare the judicial repeal act unconstitutional, but none of the deposed circuit court judges would bring a case to court. Marshall also tried to persuade his associates that it was unconstitutional for Supreme Court justices to ride the circuit, as they were forced again to do by the abolishment of the lower courts. But although they agreed with his legal reasoning, they refused to go along—because, they said, years of acquiescence in the practice lent sanction to the old law requiring it. Thus frustrated, Marshall was eager for any chance to attack his enemy, and when a case that was to be known as *Marbury* v. *Madison* came before the Court in December, 1801, he took it up with gusto.

William Marbury, a forty-one-year-old Washingtonian, was one of the justices of the peace for the District of Columbia whose commissions Jefferson had held up. Originally from Annapolis, he had moved to Washington to work as an aide to the first Secretary of the Navy, Benjamin Stoddert. It was probably his service to this staunch Federalist that earned him the appointment by Adams. Together with one Dennis Ramsay and Messrs. Harper and Hooe, whose commissions James Marshall had *almost* delivered, Marbury was asking the Court to issue an order (a writ of mandamus) requiring Secretary of State Madison to hand over their "missing" commissions. Marshall willingly assumed jurisdiction and issued an order calling upon Madison to show cause at the next term of the Supreme Court why such a writ should not be issued. Here clearly was an opportunity to get at the President through one of his chief agents, to assert the authority of the Court over the executive branch of the government.

This small controversy quickly became a matter of great moment both to the administration and to Marshall. The decision to do away with the June term of the Court was made in part to give Madison more time before having to deal with Marshall's order. The abolition of the circuit courts and the postponement of the next Supreme Court session to February, 1803, made Marshall even more determined to use the Marbury case to attack Jefferson. Of course Marshall was personally and embarrassingly involved in this case, since his carelessness was the cause of its very existence. He ought to have disqualified himself, but his fighting spirit was aroused, and he was in no mood to back out.

On the other hand, the Jeffersonians used every conceivable means to obstruct judicial investigation of executive affairs. Madison ignored Marshall's order. When Marbury and Ramsay called on the Secretary to inquire whether their commissions had been duly signed (Hooe and Harper could count on the testimony of James Marshall to prove that theirs had been attended to), Madison gave them no satisfactory answer. When they asked to *see* the documents, Madison referred them to the clerk, Jacob Wagner. He, in turn, would only say that the commissions were not then in the State Department files.

Unless the plaintiffs could prove that Adams had appointed them, their case would collapse. Frustrated at the State Department, they turned to the Senate for help. A friendly senator introduced a motion calling upon the Secretary of the Senate to produce the record of the action in executive session on their nominations. But the motion was defeated, after an angry debate, on January 31, 1803. Thus, tempers were hot when the Court finally met on February 9 to deal with the case.

In addition to Marshall, only Justices Bushrod Washington (a nephew of the first President) and Samuel Chase were on the bench, and the Chief Justice dominated the proceedings. The almost childishly obstructive tactics of administration witnesses were no match for his fair but forthright management of the hearing. The plaintiffs' lawyer was Charles Lee, an able advocate and brother of "Light-Horse Harry" Lee; he had served as Attorney General under both Washington and Adams. He was a close friend of Marshall, and his dislike of Jefferson had been magnified by the repeal of the Judiciary Act of 1801, for he was another of the circuit court judges whose "midnight" appointments repeal had cancelled.

Lee's task was to prove that the commissions had been completed by Adams and Marshall, and to demonstrate that the Court had authority to compel Madison to issue them. He summoned Wagner and Brent, and when they objected to being sworn because "they were clerks in the Department of State, and not bound to disclose any facts relating to the business or transactions in the office," Lee argued that in addition to their "confidential" duties as agents of the President, the Secretary and his deputies had duties "of a public nature" delegated to them by Congress. They must testify about these public matters just as, in a suit involving property, a clerk in the land office could be compelled to state whether or not a particular land patent was on file.

Marshall agreed, and ordered the clerks to testify. They then disclosed many of the details of what had gone on in the presidential mansion and in the State

Department on the evening of March 3, 1801, but they claimed to be unsure of what had become of the plaintiffs' commissions.

Next Lee called Attorney General Levi Lincoln. He too objected strenuously to testifying. He demanded that Lee submit his questions in writing so that he might consider carefully his obligations both to the Court and to the President before making up his mind. He also suggested that it might be necessary for him to exercise his constitutional right (under the Fifth Amendment) to refuse to give evidence that might, as he put it, "criminate" him. Lee then wrote out four questions. After studying them, Lincoln asked to be excused from answering, but the justices ruled against him. Still hesitant, the Attorney General asked for time to consider his position further, and Marshall agreed to an overnight adjournment.

The next day, the tenth of February, Lincoln offered to answer all Lee's questions but the last: What had he done with the commissions? He had seen "a considerable number of commissions" signed and sealed, but could not remember—he claimed—whether the plaintiffs' were among them. He did not know if Madison had ever seen these documents, but was certain that *he* had not given them to the Secretary. On the basis of this last statement, Marshall ruled that the embarrassing question as to what Lincoln had done with the commissions was irrelevant; he excused Lincoln from answering it.

Despite these reluctant witnesses, Lee was able to show conclusively through affidavits submitted by another clerk and by James Marshall that the commissions had been signed and sealed. In his closing argument he stressed the significance of the case as a test of the principle of judicial independence. "The emoluments or the dignity of the office," he said, "are no objects with the applicants." This was undoubtedly true; the positions were unimportant, and two years of the five-year terms had already expired. As Jefferson later pointed out, the controversy itself had become "a moot case" by 1803. But Marshall saw it as a last-ditch fight against an administration campaign to make lackeys of all federal judges, while Jefferson looked at it as an attempt by the Federalist-dominated judiciary to usurp the power of the executive.

In this controversy over principle, Marshall and the Federalists were of necessity the aggressors. The administration boycotted the hearings. After Lee's summation, no government spokesman came forward to argue the other side, Attorney General Lincoln coldly announcing that he "had received no instructions to appear." With his control over Congress, Jefferson was content to wait for Marshall to act. If he overreached himself, the Chief Justice could be impeached. If he backed down, the already trifling prestige of his Court would be further reduced.

Marshall had acted throughout with characteristic boldness; quite possibly it was he who had persuaded the four aggrieved justices of the peace to press their suit in the first place. But now his combative temperament seemed to have driven him too far. As he considered the Marbury case after the close of the hearings, he must have realized this himself, for he was indeed in a fearful predicament. However sound his logic and just his cause, he was on very dangerous ground. Both political partisanship and his sense of justice prompted him to issue the writ sought by Marbury and his fellows, but what effect would the mandamus produce? Madison almost certainly would ignore it, and Jefferson would back him up. No power but

John Marshall, *by Chester Harding.*

public opinion could make the executive department obey an order of the Court. Since Jefferson was riding the crest of a wave of popularity, to issue the writ would be a futile act of defiance; it might even trigger impeachment proceedings against Marshall that, if successful, would destroy him and reduce the Court to servility.

Yet what was the alternative? To find against the petitioners would be to abandon all principle and surrender abjectly to Jefferson. This a man of Marshall's character could simply not consider. Either horn of the dilemma threatened utter disaster; that it was disaster essentially of his own making could only make the Chief Justice's discomfiture the more complete.

But at some point between the close of the hearings on February 14 and the announcement of his decision on the twenty-fourth, Marshall found a way out. It was an inspired solution, surely the cleverest of his long career. It provided a perfect escape from the dilemma, which probably explains why he was able to persuade the associate justices to agree to it despite the fact that it was based on the most questionable legal logic. The issue, Marshall saw, involved a conflict between the Court and the President, the problem being how to check the President without exposing the Court to his might. Marshall's solution was to state vigorously the justice of the plaintiffs' cause and to condemn the action of the Chief Executive, but to deny the Court's power to provide the plaintiffs with relief.

Marbury and his associates were legally entitled to their commissions, Marshall announced. In withholding them Madison was acting "in plain violation" of the law of the land. But the Supreme Court could not issue a writ of mandamus, because the provision of the Judiciary Act of 1789 authorizing the Court to issue such writs was unconstitutional. In other words, Congress did not have the legal right to give that power to the Court.

So far as it concerned the Judiciary Act, modern commentators agree that Marshall's decision was based on a very weak legal argument. Section 13 of the Act of 1789 stated that the Supreme Court could issue the writ to "persons holding office under the authority of the United States." This law had been framed by experts thoroughly familiar with the Constitution, including William Paterson, one of Marshall's associate justices. The Court had issued the writ in earlier cases without questioning Section 13 for a moment. But Marshall now claimed that the Court could not issue a mandamus except in cases that came to it *on appeal* from a lower court, since the Constitution, he said, granted original jurisdiction to the Court only in certain specified cases—those "affecting ambassadors, other public ministers and consuls, and those in which a state shall be a party." The Marbury case had *originated* in the Supreme Court; since it did not involve a diplomat or a state, any law that gave the Court the right to decide it was unauthorized.

This was shaky reasoning because the Constitution does not necessarily *limit* the Supreme Court's original jurisdiction to the cases it specifies. And even accepting Marshall's narrow view of the constitutional provision, his decision had a major weakness. As the Court's principal chronicler, Charles Warren, has written, "It seems plain, at the present time, that it would have been possible for Marshall, if he had been so inclined, to have construed the language of [Section 13 of the Act of 1789] which authorized writs of mandamus, in such a manner as to have enabled him to escape the necessity of declaring the section unconstitutional."

Marshall was on more solid ground when he went on to argue cogently the theory that "the constitution controls any legislative act repugnant to it," which he called "one of the fundamental principles of our society." The Constitution is "the *supreme* law of the land," he emphasized. Since it is the "duty of the judicial department to say what the law is," the Supreme Court must overturn any law of Congress that violates the Constitution. "A law repugnant to the Constitution," he concluded flatly, "is void." By this reasoning, Section 13 of the Act of 1789 simply ceased to exist, and without it the Court could not issue the writ of mandamus. By thus denying himself authority, Marshall found the means to flay his enemies without exposing himself to their wrath.

Although this was the first time the Court had declared an act of Congress unconstitutional, its right to do so had not been seriously challenged by most authorities. Even Jefferson accepted the principle, claiming only that the executive as well as the judiciary could decide questions of constitutionality. Jefferson was furious over what he called the "twistifications" of Marshall's gratuitous opinion in *Marbury* v. *Madison,* but his anger was directed at the Chief Justice's stinging criticisms of his behavior, not at the constitutional doctrine Marshall had enunciated.

Even in 1803, the idea of judicial review, which Professor E. S. Corwin has called "the most distinctive feature of the American constitutional system," had had a long history in America. The concept of natural law (the belief that certain principles of right and justice transcend the laws of mere men) was thoroughly established in American thinking. It is seen, for example, in Jefferson's statement in the immortal Declaration that men "are endowed by their Creator" with "unalienable" rights. Although not a direct precedent for Marshall's decision, the colonial practice of "disallowance," whereby various laws had been ruled void on the ground that local legislatures had exceeded their powers in passing them, illustrates the American belief that there is a limit to legislative power and that courts may say when it has been overstepped.

More specifically, Lord Coke, England's chief justice under James I, had declared early in the seventeenth century that "the common law will controul acts of Parliament." One of the American Revolution's chief statesmen and legal apologists, James Otis, had drawn upon this argument a century and a half later in his famous denunciation of the Writs of Assistance. And in the 1780s, courts in New Jersey, New York, Rhode Island, and North Carolina had exercised judicial review over the acts of local legislatures. The debates at the Constitutional Convention and some of the Federalist Papers (especially No. 78) indicated that most of the Founding Fathers accepted the idea of judicial review as already established. The Supreme Court, in fact, had considered the constitutionality of a law of Congress before—when it upheld a federal tax law in 1796—and it had encountered little questioning of its right to do so. All these precedents—when taken together with the fact that the section of the Act of 1789 nullified by Marshall's decision was of minor importance—explain why no one paid much attention to this part of the decision.

Thus the "Case of the Missing Commissions" passed into history, seemingly a fracas of but slight significance. When it was over, Marbury and his colleagues returned to the obscurity whence they had arisen.* In the partisan struggle for power between Marshall and Jefferson, the incident was of secondary importance. The real showdown came later—in the impeachment proceedings against Justice Chase and the treason trial of Aaron Burr. In the long run, Marshall won his fight to preserve the independence and integrity of the federal judiciary, but generally speaking, the courts have not been able to exert as much influence over the appointive and dismissal powers of the President as Marshall had hoped to win for them in *Marbury* v. *Madison*. Even the enunciation of the Supreme Court's power to void acts of Congress wrought no immediate change in American life. Indeed, it was more than half a century before another was overturned.

Nevertheless, this trivial squabble over a few petty political plums was of vital importance for later American history. For with the expansion of the federal government into new areas of activity in more recent times, the power of the Supreme Court to nullify acts of Congress has been repeatedly employed, with profound effects. At various times legislation concerning the income tax, child labor, wages and hours, and many other aspects of our social, economic, and political life have been thrown out by the Court, and always, in the last analysis, its right to do so has depended upon the decision John Marshall handed down to escape from a dilemma of his own making.

---

*What happened to Marbury? According to his descendants, he became president of a Georgetown bank in 1814, reared a family, and died, uncommissioned, in 1835.

Jefferson, Adams, and the American Dialogue

Joseph J. Ellis

The long careers of John Adams and Thomas Jefferson were closely intertwined on many occasions. Both were on the committee that drafted the Declaration of Independence. Both later were Vice Presidents and Presidents of the United States. But although they were both ardent patriots and agreed on many issues, they differed greatly in personality and in their political styles. By the 1790s, they had become bitter enemies. In retirement, however, they made peace and then exchanged a remarkable series of kindly letters. The following article is based on this correspondence.

The author, Joseph J. Ellis, has written extensively on both men, most notably in *The Thought and Character of John Adams* (1993) and *American Sphinx: The Character of Thomas Jefferson* (1997). He obviously admires both of his subjects, but it should not be difficult to figure out who his particular favorite is.

To most of their contemporaries they were America's odd couple. John Adams was short, plump, passionate to the point of frenzy. Thomas Jefferson was tall, lean, serenely enigmatic. True, they had served together in the Continental Congress during the blossom days of the American Revolution. But throughout the remainder of their distinguished public careers, as Adams himself acknowledged, they had "look'd at the world through different ends of the telescope."

Adams had remained a loyal Federalist, serving as Vice President under George Washington for eight years, then a single term as President. Jefferson had broken with the Federalists after a term as Secretary of State, then opposed Adams for the Presidency, losing narrowly in 1796 and then winning the bitterly contested election of 1800. In the fierce and sometimes scatological political squabbles of the 1790s, the two men found themselves on opposite sides time and time again. Whether it was Hamilton's finance program, America's posture toward the French Revolution, the Jay Treaty with Britain, or the proper relationship between federal and state governments, Adams and Jefferson could be counted on to disagree. Their political convictions, like their personal styles and physical appearances, seemed always to fall on different sides of the American political equation.

Nevertheless, there remained an abiding affinity between the two men, a mysterious personal chemistry that seemed to defy logic. Although Adams had been heard to denounce Jefferson in 1797 as "a mind soured . . . and eaten to a honeycomb with ambition," Abigail Adams told friends that Jefferson was "the only person with whom my companion could associate with perfect freedom and reserve."

During the eight years of Jefferson's Presidency, Adams spent his retirement at Quincy, Massachusetts, reliving the old political battles in his memory and rocking back and forth between resentment against and affection for his successor. Jefferson was a "shadow man," he told friends; his character was "like the great rivers, whose bottoms we cannot see and make no noise." Yes, he and Jefferson had once been close friends, but then Jefferson had "supported and salaried almost every villain he could find who had been an enemy to me." When Benjamin Rush, the Philadelphia physician and Revolutionary gadfly, wrote to say that he had just woken from a dream in which the Sage of Monticello and the Sage of Quincy were reunited, Adams told him to "take a Nap and dream for my instruction and Edification the character of Jefferson and his administration," a dream that he predicted would be an unrelieved nightmare.

But chinks in the Adams armor began to open up in 1809. No, he harbored "no Resentment or Animosity against the Gentleman. . . ." How could he hold a grudge against Jefferson, adding jokingly that Jefferson was "always but a Boy to me. . . . I am bold to say that I was his Preceptor on Politicks and taught him every thing that has been good and solid in his whole Political Conduct." How could one resent a disciple? And what was it that had caused a break between them? As far as he could remember, "the only Flit between Jefferson and me . . . was occasioned by a Motion for Congress to sit on Saturday." Or was the source of the trouble an argument about hairstyles, he preferring them curled and Jefferson straight? Or was it the other way around? In this jocular mood Adams let it be known that he was open to an entreaty.

In 1811 Adams was visited at Quincy by Edward Coles, a Virginian close to Jefferson. In the course of the conversation Adams claimed that his long-standing political disagreements with Jefferson had never destroyed his affection for the man. "I always loved Jefferson," he told Coles, "and still love him." When news of this exchange reached Monticello, as Adams knew it would, Jefferson responded heartily, if a bit less affectionately. "This is enough for me," he wrote Benjamin Rush, adding that he "knew him [Adams] to be always an honest man, often a great one, but sometimes incorrect and precipitate in his judgments." The major caveat, however, came at the end, when Jefferson told Rush that he had always defended Adams's character to others, "with the single exception as to his political opinions." This was like claiming that the pope was usually reliable, except when he declared himself on matters of faith and morals. That was how it stood at the close of the year, the two former friends sniffing around the edges of a possible reconciliation like wary old dogs.

In the end it was Adams who made the move. The first letter went out from Quincy to Monticello on January 1, 1812, timing that suggests Adams had decided to revive the relationship as one of his resolutions for the new year. It was a short and cordial note, relaying family news and referring to "two pieces of Homespun" that he had sent along as a gift by separate packet.

There was a discernible awkwardness as well as a slight stumble at the start of the correspondence. Jefferson presumed, quite plausibly, that the "two pieces of Homespun" Adams was sending referred to domestically produced clothing, a nice symbol of the ongoing American embargo of European goods that also recalled the colonial response to British taxation policies in the 1760s, a fitting reminder of the good old days when Adams and Jefferson first joined the movement for American independence. And so Jefferson responded with a lengthy letter on domestic manufacturing, only to discover afterward that Adams had intended the homespun reference as a metaphor. His gift turned out to be a copy of his son John Quincy Adams's two-volume work *Lectures on Rhetoric and Oratory*. The exchange had begun on the same note that the friendship had foundered on, an elemental misunderstanding.

It quickly recovered, as both men demonstrated that they required no instruction in rhetoric from John Quincy or anyone else. "And so we have gone on," wrote Jefferson in his lyrical style, "and so we shall go on, puzzled and prospering beyond example in the history of man." The "puzzled and prospering" phrase was pure Jefferson, a melodic and alliterative choice of words conveying the paradoxical character of America's march toward its destiny. Not to be outdone, Adams shot back with an alliteration of his own. "Whatever a peevish Patriarch might say, I have never seen the day in which I could say I had no Pleasure; or that I have had more Pain than Pleasure."

Beyond their calculated eloquence, the early letters are careful, diplomatic, eager to avoid the political controversies. "But whither is senile garrulity leading me?" asked Jefferson rhetorically. "Into politics, of which I have taken leave. I think little of them, and say less. I have given up newspapers in exchange for Tacitus and Thucydides, for Newton and Euclid; and I find myself much the happier." Quite conscious of Adams's irritability and volcanic temperament, Jefferson felt compelled to wonder whether "in the race of life, you do not keep, in its physical decline, the same distance ahead of me which you have done in political honors and achievements." This gracious gesture prompted a gracious response from Quincy. Jefferson had taken the lead on all counts, Adams acknowledged; Adams was leading only in the sense that he would be first to the grave.

Later Adams took refuge in one of the recurrent motifs that both men used as a safe haven throughout the correspondence—the dwindling list of survivors of the Declaration of Independence: "I may rationally hope to be the first to depart; and as you are the youngest and the most energetic in mind and body, you may therefore rationally hope to be the last to take your flight." Like the last person to retire from the hearth in the evening, Adams noted, Jefferson would be the final one "to set up and rake the ashes over the coals. . . ."

But if Jefferson thought the reference to Thucydides and Tacitus would keep the dialogue a safe distance from politics, Adams reminded him that even the classics, especially those particular authors, spoke directly to his own pessimism. "I have read Thucydides and Tacitus so often, and at such distant Periods of my Life," he recalled, "that while elegant, profound and enchanting is their Style, I am weary of them"; their descriptions of Athens and Greece in decline he found reminiscent of "my own Times and my own Life." Then he apologized for this outbreak of self-pity, joking that "My Senectutal Loquacity has more than retaliated your 'Senile Garrulity.'"

A mutual sense of the fragility of their newly recovered friendship explains in part the initial politeness and obvious care with which each man composed his thoughts and arranged his words. Their trust was newly won and incomplete—nor, for that matter, would it ever be total. For example, when Adams asked Jefferson to assist in obtaining a judgeship for Samuel Malcolm, the former private secretary to Adams, Jefferson promised he would try—and then wrote President Madison to say Malcolm was "a strong federalist" and therefore an inappropriate choice. Later he wrote Adams to express regret at failing to place Malcolm, claiming his request to the President had arrived too late.

Adams was guilty of similar acts of duplicity. In 1819 he reported reading a copy of the Mecklenburg Declaration of Independence, a document purportedly drafted by a group of citizens in North Carolina in May of 1775 and containing language similar to Jefferson's later version of the Declaration. Jefferson responded immediately, contesting the authenticity of the document, which seemed to cast doubts on the originality of his own famous draft. Adams promptly reassured Jefferson that he believed "the Mecklenburg Resolutions are a fiction" and that it had always seemed "utterly incredible that they should be genuine." Meanwhile, however, he was telling other friends just the opposite. "I could as soon believe that the dozen flowers of Hydrangia now before my Eyes were the work of chance," he snickered, "as that the Mecklenburg Resolutions and Mr. Jefferson's declaration were not derived one from the other."

The special character of the correspondence—the sheer literary quality, the classical references and proses, letters that take on the tone of treatises—followed naturally from the realization that these private letters would have a public audience.

Adams said as much to Jefferson, envisioning the day when "your letters will all be published in volumes . . . which will be read with delight in future ages." The Adams obsession with posterity's judgment, of course, was notorious. Jefferson's concern was equally powerful but more disguised and controlled. It seems fair to conclude that both men sat down to write with one eye on the paper and the other on posterity.

Adams set the pattern and the pace, writing two letters for every one of Jefferson's, determining the intellectual agenda of the correspondence so that it accorded with his most passionate preoccupations. "Answer my letters at your Leisure," he advised Jefferson as it became clear that the stream of words from Quincy was threatening to flood Monticello. "Give yourself no concern," Adams added, explaining that the correspondence had become for him "a refuge and protection against Ennui." Jefferson apologized for his failure to keep up, claiming that he received more than twelve hundred letters each year, all of which required answers. Adams replied that he received far fewer but chose not to answer most so that he could focus his allegedly waning energies on Jefferson, whom he called the only person "on this side of Monticello, who can give me any Information upon Subjects that I am now *analysing* and *investigating:* if I may be permitted to Use the pompous Words now in fashion." Adams assured Jefferson that he was writing only "a hundredth part of what I wish to say to you." And after all, he pleaded to his famous friend, "You and I ought not to die, before We have explained ourselves to each other."

Even hostile voices from the past could not shake the two men's resolve to go to their graves as friends. In 1823 several of Adams's old letters to William Cunningham, a casual friend, were published by Cunningham's son as part of a campaign to vilify the Adams family and thereby undercut John Quincy's presidential prospects.

John Adams, by Charles-Balthazar-Julien Fevret de Saint-Memin.

These frank and intemperate letters dated from the early years of Adams's retirement, when he was still reeling from his defeat in the presidential election of 1800 and full of anger at Jefferson. Adams was worried that his old resentments had come back to haunt his newfound serenity with Jefferson. But the response from Monticello was a model of gracious charity: "Be assured, my dear Sir, that I am incapable of receiving the slightest impression from the effort now made to plant thorns on the pillow of age, worth, and wisdom and to sow tares between friends who have been such for nearly half a century. Beseeching you then not to suffer your mind to be disquieted by this wicked attempt to poison its peace, and praying you to throw it by. . . ."

Adams demanded that the letter be read aloud at the Quincy breakfast table, calling it "the best letter that ever was written . . . just such a letter as I expected, only . . . infinitely better expressed." The whole Cunningham episode merely solidified their friendship, he observed triumphantly, by exposing that "the peevish and fretful effusions of politicians . . . are not worth remembering, much less of laying to heart." He concluded his response to Jefferson with a "salute [to] your fire-side with cordial esteem and affection" and signed it "J. A. In the 89 years of his age still too fat to last much longer."

But one significant subject defied even the seasoned serenity of their latter years. Adams had alluded to slavery in 1816, when he confided to Jefferson that "there will be greater difficulties to preserve our Union, than You and I, our Fathers Brothers Friends Disciples and Sons have had to form it." Then, in 1819, while Congress was debating the extension of slavery into the newly recognized Territory of Missouri, Adams felt bold enough to broach the subject directly: "The

Missouri question I hope will follow the other Waves under the Ship and do no harm," he wrote, adding that he realized it was "high treason to express a doubt of the perpetual duration of our vast American Empire." But the sectional conflict over slavery had the potential to "rend this mighty Fabric in twain . . . [and] produce as many Nations in North America as there are in Europe." Finally, in 1821, after the Missouri Compromise allowed for slavery in the Western territories, Adams offered his most candid assessment of the national dilemma: "Slavery in this Country I have seen hanging over it like a black cloud for half a century. . . . I might probably say I had seen Armies of Negroes marching and countermarching in the ari, shining in Armour." Then he reiterated his long-standing position. "I have been so terrified with the Phenomenon," he explained to Jefferson, "that I constantly said in former times to the Southern Gentlemen, I cannot comprehend the object; I must leave it to you. I will vote for forcing no measure against your judgments." Jefferson never responded to Adams's comments, never once mentioned slavery in his letters to Quincy.

Silence had, in fact, become Jefferson's official position on the subject. After making several bold proposals for the end of the slave trade and the gradual abolition of slavery early in his career, he had remained mute since the 1780s. "I have most carefully avoided every public act or manifestation on that subject," he wrote to George Logan in 1805, promising that "should an occasion ever occur in which I can interpose with decisive effect, I shall certainly know & do my duty with promptitude and zeal." In the meantime, he observed, "it would only be disarming myself of influence to be taking small means."

But the propitious moment never arrived. In 1814 Edward Coles, the staunch Jeffersonian and fellow slaveowner who endorsed emancipation, begged the Sage of Monticello to break his silence, claiming that "this difficult task could be more successfully performed by the reverend father of our political and Social blessings than by any other succeeding Statesman." By then, however, Jefferson pleaded age. "No, I have outlived the generation with which mutual labors and perils begat mutual confidence and influence," he explained. Ending slavery was a glorious cause, he acknowledged, but had been passed on to "those who can follow it up, and bear it through to its consummation."

As much as he insisted that American society should not be divided into classes, Jefferson thought that American history should be separated into generations. In other contexts his belief that there were discrete generational units that came into the world and went out together had extremely radical implications, for it led him to the conclusion that one generation could not make laws for the next. "No society can make a perpetual constitution, or even a perpetual law," he had claimed, because to do so would defy the Jeffersonian principle that "the earth always belongs to the living generation." Or as he put it to Adams, "When we have lived our generation out, we should not wish to encroach upon another."

On the issue of slavery, however, Jefferson's belief in the generational sovereignty served the conservative purpose of justifying, indeed requiring, silence and passivity from the Revolutionary generation on the most ominous problem facing the new nation. "Nothing is more certainly written in the book of fate than that these people [i.e., slaves] are to be free," he announced in his autobiography, written in 1821. But it was equally obvious that emancipation would require a revolution in public opinion that Jefferson felt was a long way off, the work of the next generation or perhaps an even more distant cohort of American leaders several ages away.

Adams agreed with Jefferson that slavery constituted the most nearly intractable problem faced by the Revolutionary generation. "The Subject is vast and ominous," he noted in 1817. "More than fifty years has it attracted my thoughts and given me much anxiety. A Folio Volume would not contain my Lucubrations on this Subject. And at the End of it, I should leave my reader and myself as much at a loss, what to do with it, as at the Beginning." However, Adams did not agree with—for that matter, he did not comprehend at all—Jefferson's belief in generational sovereignty. For Adams, history was not a dead burden of accumulated weight that each generation was free to toss aside; it was a motley combination of mishaps and successes, ignorance and wisdom, from which future leaders should learn. The problem with slavery, Adams acknowledged, was that it constituted the one subject on which he, Jefferson, and the rather remarkable generation of leaders they symbolized had little wisdom to offer.

Just what Adams thought that limited wisdom was became clear in the national debate over the extension of slavery into Missouri, which prompted different reactions from the two patriarchs that were so loaded with emotion and implication that each man chose to avoid mentioning his thoughts to the other. Adams saw the issue as clear-cut. "Negro slavery is an evil of Colossal magnitude," he wrote to William Tudor, "and I am therefore utterly averse to the admission of Slavery into the Missouri Territory." He thought that the constitutional question—whether the federal or the state legislature had the power to make the decision—was of merely secondary importance. He hoped that "the Legislature of Missouri, or the [Territorial] Convention, may have the Wisdom to prohibit Slavery of their own accord," but whether or not they did, the federal government had established its right to rule for the territories when it approved the Louisiana Purchase. "I think the Southern gentlemen who thought it [the Louisiana Purchase] constitutional," he explained to his daughter-in-law, "ought not to think it unconstitutional in Congress to restrain the extension of Slavery in that territory." The primary issue for Adams was the moral imperative against slavery and, even more telling, his clear sense that the Revolutionary generation had never intended that the evil institution spread beyond the South. (This was eventually the position that Lincoln took in the 1850s.) In 1820 Adams was alerting several of his correspondents, though not Jefferson, that "we must settle the question of slavery's extension now, otherwise it will stamp our National Character and lay a Foundation for Calamities, if not disunion."

Jefferson seemed to resent the very existence of the debate, as if the eloquent silence he had maintained on the unmentionable subject should become national policy. Although he supported what he called the rights of slaveholders to live in Missouri, his major concern was federal power—the issue Adams considered secondary—which he began to describe as an encroachment on Southern rights reminiscent of British intrusions in the pre-Revolutionary years. "In the gloomiest moments of the Revolutionary War," he wrote in 1820, "I never had any apprehensions equal to what I feel from this source." His pronouncements became more pessimistic and morbid, outdoing even Adams at his most apocalyptic. "I regret that I am now to die in the belief that the . . . sacrifice of themselves by the generation of 1776, to acquire self-government and happiness," he warned, "is to be thrown away by the unwise and unworthy passions of their sons, and that my only consolation is to be that I live not to weep over it." Even his beloved University of Virginia, which he had conceived as a bastion of Southern ways to protect Virginia's rising generation against the seductive infidelities of Harvard and Yale, was plagued by a spate of disciplinary problems involving drunken and violent students.

"I look back with rapture to those golden days," Adams wrote to him in 1825, "when Virginia and Massachusetts lived and acted together like a band of brothers. . . ." But the golden age Adams referred to was gone for Jefferson, blasted into oblivion by sectional politics and what seemed to him a Northern conspiracy to make the unmentionable subject of slavery the dominant topic of the new age. Although Jefferson surely knew that Adams was one of the conspirators, just as he knew that John Quincy embodied the Federalist persuasion that so threatened the survival of the States' Rights, he sustained his commitment to the correspondence to the end, avoiding the troublesome topics, concealing his mounting bitterness and despair, maintaining pretenses. The friendship symbolized by the correspondence would thus serve as a testimony to posterity about the way it had once been within the generation that he and Adams symbolized.

Adams never knew the depth of the tragedy Jefferson felt or the irony of their shifting circumstances. From 1820 onward Jefferson—America's most attractive apostle of optimism—was trapped in a spiraling despondency. He had lost the faith that his very name was destined to epitomize and became an example of the paranoia and pessimism that Adams had recently overcome. He was racked by rheumatism and the painful intestinal disorder that would eventually kill him, and his physical condition deteriorated more rapidly than that of his older friend at Quincy. Jefferson's personal debts continued to mount, for he had never mastered the reconciliation of his expensive tastes with the financial facts of his household economy. His addiction to French wine, like his affinity for French ideas, never came to grips with the more mundane realities. Infirm, insolvent, and depressed that the future he had always trusted had somehow taken a wrong turn, Jefferson lived out his last days amidst two hundred slaves he could not free without encumbering his heirs with even greater debts, without his magnificent library, which he had been forced to sell for cash, on the deteriorating grounds of the once-proud Monticello, which was decaying at the same rapid pace as his own democratic hopes.

As the fiftieth anniversary of the Declaration of Independence approached, Adams and Jefferson were deluged with requests to attend official celebrations of the national birthday. Both men responded by pleading old age and ill health, offering regrets, then providing self-consciously eloquent testimonials that they knew would be read out loud to the assembled guests. It was an ironic opportunity for Adams, who had spent much of his retirement criticizing the historical significance of the Declaration as anything more than an ornamental epilogue to the real story of the American Revolution. But the annual celebration on July 4 was now too well established to make his criticism sound like anything more than small-minded carping.

Although he received requests to participate in what was being called the "Jubilee of Independence" from as far away as Washington, Philadelphia, and New York, his most resonant reply went to the organizers of the Quincy celebration. After lamenting that his physical condition precluded attendance, Adams defied the customary sentiments and solemnities by declaring, in effect, that the ultimate meaning of the American Revolution was still problematic. He acknowledged that the Revolutionary era had been a "memorable epoch in the annals of the human race," but he insisted that the jury was still out on its significance. He warned that America was "destined in future history to form the brightest or the blackest page, according to the use or the abuse of the political institutions by which they shall in time come to be shaped by the *human mind.*"

Posterity, in short, would not only judge but would play an active role in shaping the outcome. This was a disconcerting message for patriotic celebrants gathered to dispense praise rather than accept a challenge.

Meanwhile, down at Monticello the other great patriarch was receiving the same kinds of requests. Jefferson was also too old and infirm to leave his mountaintop, but he, more than Adams, sensed that this might be the last occasion to register his personal stamp on the public understanding of just what the American Revolution had meant. His most eloquent reply was sent to the committee responsible for the Independence Day ceremonies in Washington. Although his intestinal disorder had become nearly incapacitating, and despite the pessimism that had overtaken him, Jefferson worked over the draft of his reply with great care, correcting and revising with the same attention to detail that he had brought to the original draft of the Declaration, producing one of his most inspired and inspiring renditions of the Jeffersonian message.

After gracefully excusing himself from the ceremonies at the nation's capitol, he regretted his absence from "the small band, the remnant of that host of worthies who joined with us on that day, in the bold and doubtful election . . . between submission and the sword"; then he offered his distilled understanding of just what the band of worthies had done: "May it be to the world, what I believe it will be, (to some parts sooner, to others late, but finally to all,) the signal of arousing men to burst the chains under which monkish ignorance and superstition had persuaded them to bind themselves, and to assume the blessings of security and of self-government. . . . All eyes are opened or opening to the rights of man. The general spread of the light of science has already laid open to every view the palpable truth, that the mass of mankind has not been born with saddles on their backs, nor a favored few, booted and spurred, ready to ride them legitimately, by the grace of God. These are grounds of hope for others; for ourselves, let the annual return of this day forever refresh our recollections of these rights, and an undiminished devotion to them."

Both the language and the theme were vintage Jefferson and were immediately recognized as such when read aloud before the distinguished gathering in Washington on the Fourth. The fresh, vigorous statement contrasted sharply with

*Thomas Jefferson, by Charles-Balthazar-Julien
Fevret de Saint-Memin.*

Adams's more cautious message. For Jefferson the American Revolution was the
opening shot in a global struggle for liberation from all forms of oppression, a
struggle whose final victory was foreordained. Jefferson's formulation held that
something wonderful and elemental had *already happened,* that the individual energies released by America into the world during the preceding fifty years would run
their predestined course regardless of human foibles. Now that the American Revolution had propelled the country into its role as the global model for what he called
"self government," the fate of the American political experiment was no longer in
doubt or even in human hands.

The Adams formulation suggested exactly the opposite. He emphasized the
precarious and fragile character of the American experiment in republican government, challenging subsequent generations of Americans to meet the inevitable
threats to national survival with the same realistic rationality that his and Jefferson's
generation had managed to muster at the very beginning. The destiny of the new
nation was contingent upon wise and skillful leadership if it hoped to avoid the
same fate of all other republics.

Whatever superiority Adams's version may have had as an accurate expression
of his generation's best wisdom about America's prospects, the rhetorical superiority of Jefferson's was obvious. Anyone poised to assess their relative appeal to posterity would have been forced to conclude that Adams's chances were just as problematic as his diagnosis of America's future.

But before the historic reputations of the two patriarchs could diverge, their
lives were joined one final time. On the evening of July 3 Jefferson, whose health
had been declining since February, fell into unconsciousness. He awoke momentarily that night and uttered his last discernible words: "Is it the Fourth?" As midnight approached, his family, which had gathered around his bedside for the

deathwatch, offered a prayer for "a few minutes of prolonged life." As if in response, life lingered in him until the next morning, and he died at twenty minutes
past noon on July 4.

Meanwhile, Adams rose at his customarily early hour, wishing to keep his routine despite the special distinction of the day, and asked to be placed in his favorite
reading chair in the study. Around midmorning, however, he began to falter, and
family members moved him back to his bedroom. He lapsed into unconsciousness
at almost the exact moment that Jefferson died. The end then came quickly, at
about five-thirty in the afternoon of July 4. He awakened for a brief moment, indicated his awareness that death was near, and, with obvious effort, spoke his last
words: "Thomas Jefferson survives."

News of the nearly simultaneous death of America's two most eminent statesmen seeped out to the world over the next few weeks, and nearly every commenta-
tor described it as an act of divine providence. Amid all the plans for memorial services honoring the paired patriarchs, one of the few sour notes came from Horace
Binney, the old Philadelphia Federalist, who despised Jefferson and recalled the
long-standing political differences between the two men. "The most extraordinary
feature of their history is that of a joint or consociated celebration," Binney noted.
"Their tempers and dispositions toward one another would at one time have made
a very tolerable salad . . . [and] it never entered into my conception . . . to admit
one and the same apotheosis."

Actually the notion that Adams and Jefferson represented opposing impulses
in the life of the early Republic that blended together like the oil and vinegar of "a
very tolerable salad" was one of the dominant themes in the eulogies. Adams was
"the bold and eloquent debater . . . big with the fate of empires" while Jefferson was
the skilled writer who "embodied the principles of liberty in the language of inspiration." Adams represented the vigorous values of Rome; Jefferson the deep sereni-
ties of Greece. Adams was a noble descendant of the original Puritan settlers of
New England; Jefferson could trace his ancestry back to the Cavalier dynasty of Virginia. The correspondence between the Sage of Quincy and the Sage of Monticello—and these titles were now recognized as semiofficial designations—even revealed compensating differences between the writing styles of the two patriarchs;
Adams's prose was "plain, nervous and emphatic, and striking with a kind of epi-
grammatic force," while Jefferson was "light and flowing with easy and careless
melody." In short, Adams and Jefferson represented a kind of matched pair of
minds and dispositions that allowed the infant Republic to meet diverse challenges
because "whatsoever quality appeared deficient in the one, was to be found in the
character or talents of the other." Finally, an important emphasis for several of the
eulogists was the claim that both the New Englander and the Virginian embraced a
truly national vision and that "the two great chieftains of the North and South"
thereby served as telling symbols of the need to defy sectional divisions.

One could already detect the sectional bias that their lives evidently warned
against in some of the funeral orations. The eulogist in Charleston, South Carolina,
ignored Adams completely, while New England's memorialists accorded him decisive primacy as the one true father of the Revolution. Nevertheless, taken together,

the testimonials delivered throughout the summer and fall of 1826 reflected a clear consensus that the two recently departed sages had made roughly equal contributions to the shaping of American history and deserved to be remembered as they had lived—even more remarkably as they had died—as equal partners in the grand, unfolding saga of America's experiment with republicanism. There would be other heroes, of course, and Daniel Webster's bombastic testimonial before Bostonians at Faneuil Hall suggested that he had hopes of being one of them. But nothing quite like this brilliant pair of compatible opposites was likely ever again to appear on the national scene.

Adams and Jefferson became the supreme embodiment of the American dialogue: Adams was the words and Jefferson the music of the ongoing pageant begun in 1776; Adams the "is," Jefferson the "ought" of American politics. Not only were the respective reputations of Monticello and Quincy able to bask in the reflected glory of the other, but their differences defined the proper limits of posterity's debate over the original intentions of the founding generation.

Andrew Jackson and the Annexation of Texas

Robert V. Remini

Andrew Jackson is generally considered one of our great presidents, though, for reasons this essay makes abundantly clear, he was also one of our most controversial chief executives. Whether some of his more belligerent and indeed irrational statements were contrived rather than heartfelt is a matter of debate among historians, but there is no doubt that he was an extremely colorful person and as shrewd a politician as ever lived.

The desire to see Texas added to the United States was one of the major fixations of Jackson's remarkable career. How he pursued that objective, relentlessly and with every political weapon he could command, during and after his two terms as president, is the subject of this article. The author, Robert V. Remini of the University of Illinois at Chicago, is the leading contemporary authority on Jackson; his three-volume biography of Old Hickory won both an American Book Award and a Pulitzer Prize.

From the moment he entered the White House in March 1829, Andrew Jackson of Tennessee turned a cold and calculating eye on Texas. Sitting in his study on the second floor of the mansion, maps strewn around the room, the white-haired, sharp-featured, cadaverous President breathed a passion for Texas that was soon shared by other Americans.

Old Hickory always believed—or so he said—that Texas had been acquired by the United States as part of the Louisiana Purchase in 1803 and then had been recklessly thrown away when "that old scamp J. Q. Adams" negotiated the Florida treaty with Spain in 1819 and agreed to the Sabine River as the western boundary of the country. The claim was questionable at the very least, but many Southerners, outraged by Northern reaction to the slavery issue during the debates over the admission of Missouri and chagrined over the institution's prohibition in the Louisiana Territory north of 36° 30', decided to press it anyway.

The loss of Texas by virtue of the Florida treaty dismayed some Americans. It infuriated Jackson. "How infatuated must have been our councils who gave up the rich country of Texas," he wrote. Such action, in his mind, verged on treason. And why had it happened? "It surely must have been with the view to keep the political ascendence in the North, and east," he fumed, "& cripple the rising greatness of the West." No matter. He would attend to it at the first opportunity. And indeed he did—or tried to. "I have long since been aware of the importance of Texas to the United States," he wrote a friend just a few months after taking office as President, "and of the real necessity of extending our boundary west of the Sabine. . . . I shall keep my eye on this object & the first propitious moment make the attempt to regain the Territory as far south & west as the great Desert."

All his attempts at acquiring Texas proved feeble, however, mostly because he had assigned a freewheeling, fast-talking, double-dealing incompetent to represent the United States in Mexico. Col. Anthony Butler made numerous "diplomatic" efforts to purchase Texas from Mexico, and when those failed, he turned to bribery. "I have just had a very singular conversation with a Mexican," he wrote Jackson in October of 1833, and this Mexican "has much influence with the Presidt. Genl. St. Anna." The Mexican had bluntly asked Butler, "Have you command of Money?"

"Yes, I have money," Butler responded.

The price would be high, said the Mexican, in excess of half a million dollars. The Mexican himself required two or three hundred thousand, and Butler allowed that "there are others amongst whom it may become necessary to distribute 3 or 4 Hundred thousand more."

"Can you command that Sum?" the Mexican demanded.

"Yes," Butler assured him.

He was wrong. "I have read your confidential letter with care, and astonishment," a furious Jackson replied, ". . . astonishment that you would entrust such a letter, without being in cypher, to the mail." Moreover, wrote Jackson, he was astounded by Butler's presumption that "my instructions authorized you to apply to corruption, when nothing could be farther from my intention than to convey such an idea."

At length Jackson had to recall Butler. The President was discouraged not only by the diplomatic failure and the shady operations of his minister but also by the resistance of the Mexicans to his assurance that a "natural boundary" at the Rio Grande River would work to the mutual benefit of both nations. Such a boundary, Jackson insisted, would eliminate "collisions" that two peoples of "conflicting laws, habits and interests" were bound to have. Moreover, it would provide the Mexicans with needed cash to bolster their economy: the President was willing to go as high as five million dollars to purchase the territory. Failure of the sale was sure to encourage the many Americans who had moved to Texas over the previous ten years to establish an independent republic. And such a turn of events, the President feared, would sever the "bonds of amity and good understanding" between the United States and Mexico.

Since the early 1820s, Americans had been migrating to Texas, particularly from the South and West. Motivated to a large extent by the hard times generated by the Panic of 1819, they sought relief in Texas because the Mexicans encouraged them to settle there. Led by Moses Austin and his son Stephen F., they established an American colony in Texas and accepted Mexican authority. Slave owners from Alabama, Mississippi, and Tennessee were particularly attracted to this haven. By 1830 over twelve thousand Americans had emigrated to Texas, and Mexico, alarmed, eventually prohibited all immigration from the north.

Many Texans desired immediate annexation by the United States, especially after 1829, when slavery was forbidden throughout Mexican territory. The blatant and hostile intentions of these Texans naturally provoked the Mexicans, and Jackson's fumbling efforts to purchase the territory only exacerbated an already worsening situation. Despite his passion for Texas, the President wanted neither war with Mexico nor domestic strife over the wisdom of adding what might become another slave state. Still, he would not abandon his dream of territorial expansion. "The boundary between the U. States and Mexico," he jotted into his private memorandum book, ". . . must be altered."

Jackson's apprehensions deepened when he learned that his old friend and protégé, Sam Houston, late governor of Tennessee, had fled to Texas after a disastrous marriage and reportedly "would conquer Mexico or Texas, & be worth two millions in two years." These were the "efusions of a distempered brain," said Jackson; Houston would never place millions before the welfare of his country, but that did not guarantee a peaceful resolution to the problem.

Perhaps, given Mexico's stiff opposition to territorial dismemberment, no one in the United States possessed the diplomatic skill to bring about the peaceful acquisition of this valuable and strategically important landmass. But certainly Jackson botched what little chance he may have had by appointing Butler and then keeping him long after Jackson had reason to believe that his minister was a scoundrel. Gen. Antonio López de Santa Anna was convinced that the United States had acted dishonorably and had violated its neutrality laws by encouraging filibustering expeditions into Texas and by arming Americans to instigate revolution.

The failure of American diplomacy did indeed spur the Texans to take matters into their own hands. A war party was formed at the same time that the Mexican government was moving to centralize control over all parts of the Mexican republic, including Texas. The struggle for independence ignited in October 1835 and roared to its climax when General Santa Anna marched into Texas at the head of a five-thousand-man army. Texas proclaimed its independence on March 2, 1836, and on April 21 a Texan army commanded by Sam Houston defeated Santa Anna at the Battle of San Jacinto. Santa Anna himself was captured and forced to sign a treaty (later repudiated) recognizing Texan independence.

No American doubted that annexation by the United States would soon follow. Some Texans might have preferred to remain a republic, but probably many more desired eventual statehood.

The Mexican minister to the United States, Manuel Eduardo de Gorostiza, peppered President Jackson with angry protests. He raged against American treachery and ultimately demanded his passports. Relations between Mexico and the United States rapidly deteriorated, and within two months it appeared that war between the two countries would break out momentarily. The secretary of the Navy, Mahlon Dickerson, reported at a cabinet meeting that Com Alexander J. Dallas had notified him that the American consul and residents at Tampico had suffered innumerable "indignities" at the hands of Mexican authorities. Moreover, American armed vessels in the area had been refused water, and their officers had been denied permission to go ashore. Worse, these authorities had threatened to put to death all Americans in Tampico in retaliation for the capture of Santa Anna.

Dickerson concluded his report. [Attorney General] Benjamin Butler, in a letter to his wife, explained what happened next. Jackson "broke out in his most impassioned manner." He jumped to his feet, gesticulated wildly, and shook his fist at invisible enemies. It was one of the most frightening displays of the President's anger that the cabinet had ever witnessed. The members sat frozen, staring; nobody dared interrupt the wild outburst.

Then, wrote Butler, Old Hickory barked, "Write immediately to Commodore Dallas & order him to *blockade* the harbour of Tampico, & to suffer nothing to enter till they allow him to land and obtain his supplies of water & communicate with the Consul, & if they touch the hair of the head of one of our citizens, tell him *to batter down & destroy their town & exterminate the inhabitants from the face of the earth!"*

The cabinet sucked in its collective breath, but said nothing. Could he be serious?

Finally, Jackson addressed his secretary of state, John Forsyth. "Have you rec[eived] any information on this subject?"

Forsyth shook his head.

"Then let the Secy of the Navy furnish you the papers," Jackson ordered, "& do you write immediately to Mr. Gorostiza informing him of the orders we have given to Commodore Dallas, & that we shall not permit a jot or tittle of the treaty to be violated, or a citizen of the United States to be injured without taking immediate redress."

Fortunately, cooler heads on both sides prevented the extermination of the citizens of Tampico, but American-Mexican relations continued to deteriorate: Texans were doing everything possible to force U.S. recognition of their independence and eventual annexation. Commissioners dispatched to lobby in Washington were all warmly received by the President. During one such meeting Jackson turned to Special Commissioner Samuel Carson and said. "Is it true, Mr. Carson, that your Government has sent Santa Anna back to Mexico?" Carson responded that Santa Anna was indeed expected to depart shortly to assist in winning ratification of the treaty recognizing the independence of Texas.

"Then I tell you, Sir," said Jackson, "if ever he sets foot on Mexican ground, your Government may whistle; he, Sir, will give you trouble, if he escapes, which you dream not of."

Then there would be war, Carson said.

"Where is your means, Sir, to carry on an offensive war against Mexico?"

"In the enthusiasms of the American people," said Carson happily, "their devotion to the cause of Liberty are the ways and means, to defray the expenses of the War."

Jackson blanched. It was one thing for the President of the United States to threaten war, quite another for "outsiders" from Texas to presume they could manipulate this country into one. The United States had a treaty with Mexico, and the annexation of Mexican territory would most certainly be viewed around the world as a betrayal. Civilized countries would label it a brutal and aggressive act, a violation of the "law of nations." The "Texians," as Jackson frequently called them, must realize that annexation would take time and careful planning. Thus, when Stephen F. Austin sent him an impassioned letter requesting assistance, Jackson wrote the following endorsement: "[Austin] does not reflect that we have a treaty with Mexico, and our national faith is pledged to support it. The Texians before they took the step to declare themselves Independent, which has aroused and united all Mexico against them ought to have pondered well, it was a rash and premature act. Our nutrality must be faithfully maintained."

And there were other problems. Abolitionists, for one. These troublemakers would exploit any issue to attack slavery, said Jackson, even if it ruptured relations between the North and South. They intended to oppose the admission of Texas because it represented the continued expansion of slavery. Texas, therefore, posed a possible threat to the Union, which hobbled Jackson's efforts to negotiate a swift treaty of admission. His passion for Texas could never match his passion for the Union. "Prudence," he later wrote, seemed to dictate that "we should stand aloof" and see how things would develop. No doubt he was also fearful of jeopardizing the election of his hand-picked successor to the Presidency, Martin Van Buren.

At this juncture Sam Houston decided to send Santa Anna to Washington to meet Jackson in the hope that their talks together would help the cause of Texas annexation. Houston released the Mexican, presented him with a handsome horse, and headed him (under armed escort) to the capital. Santa Anna arrived on January 17, 1837.

At the moment, Old Hickory was recovering from a severe "hemorrhage of the lungs" that had almost ended his life. For months he remained in his room, not daring to expose himself to a relapse by needless movement around the White House. In fact, he left his room only four times during the final six months of his administration. Still, on state occasions, Jackson could muster great presence and exude the appearance of enormous strength. For his part, Santa Anna, despite his long trip, looked refreshed and relaxed. He was amused and rather pleased by the notoriety that his arrival in the capital had provoked. Many assumed he would look malevolent. They were surprised to find him a gracious and cultivated man of impeccable manners and dress.

On Thursday, January 19, 1837, the Mexican general was escorted into the presence of the American general at the White House. The two men greeted one another politely and with a degree of dignified reserve. Always the gentleman, Old Hickory assured his guest that he was most welcome in Washington and expressed pleasure in meeting him at long last. "General Andrew Jackson greeted me warmly," Santa Anna later wrote, "and honored me at a dinner attended by notables of all countries." Jackson treated him not as an enemy but as a head of state, even though Santa Anna had been succeeded in Mexico by Anastasio Bustamante.

The official greeting, reception, and dinner went extremely well, but the conversations involved nothing of substance. Not until the following day did the two men turn to the matter that had brought them together.

Santa Anna began by proposing the cession of Texas for a "fair consideration." The United States, responded Jackson, could do nothing about a cession until the "disposition of the Texians" was resolved. "Until Texas is acknowledged Independent," said the President, this nation could make no official move. At some point in the conversation, Jackson outlined a proposal for the Mexican to take back to his country. Beginning with the supposition that Mexico would officially acknowledge the independence of Texas at some point early on, Jackson suggested that the boundary of the United States be extended to include Texas and northern California—in effect, this would run the "line of the U. States to the Rio grand—up that stream to latitude 38 north & then to the pacific including north California." In return the United States would compensate Mexico with $3,500,000. "But before we promise anything," Jackson continued, "Genl Santana must say that he will use his influence to suspend hostilities." The President assured his visitor that the principal objective of the United States was not territorial acquisition or the further embarrassment of the Mexican Republic, but rather to "secure peace & tranquility on our respective borders & lay the foundation of a permanent tranquility between the U.S. and Mexico."

The interview ended on a polite but indefinite note. President Jackson provided Santa Anna with a warship to carry him to Veracruz, and the Mexican had nothing but gratitude for his treatment.

A little later Jackson mentioned his conversation with Santa Anna to William Wharton, recently arrived in Washington to represent Texas. Wharton protested: Texan independence was an accomplished fact achieved through her own military power, and Mexico had no right to make a treaty that in any way bound her. What the United States must do, insisted Wharton, was to recognize Texan independence; then the nation could move on to the question of possible annexation.

Jackson grimaced. Perhaps, suggested the President to Wharton, as a way of quieting the sectional rivalry that recognition was sure to provoke, Texas might claim California in order to "paralyze" Northern opposition to annexation. Acquisition of California along with Texas meant the continuation of representational balance in the Senate between free and slave states. The suggestion did not elicit much enthusiasm from Wharton. Texas could never legitimately claim California or undertake a war to assert its claim. California was simply not on the negotiating table.

Congress, however, responded to the wishes of the "Texians" without grappling with the sectional consequences and, during the final days of Jackson's administration, recognized the independence of the Texas Republic. The President quickly appointed Alcée Louis La Branche of Louisiana as chargé d'affaires to Texas, and the Senate confirmed the nomination only hours before the final adjournment of Congress. Around midnight, when word came that La Branche had been confirmed, Jackson met with Wharton and a few others to celebrate. They lifted their glasses in a single toast: Texas!

But Jackson returned home defeated in his one great effort to reach the Rio Grande. He rightly feared his failure might jeopardize the integrity and tranquility of the Union.

The more he thought about it, as he sat in his study at the Hermitage reading the reports that arrived daily from Washington, the more he convinced himself that the security of the United States demanded the acquisition of Texas. Never mind the machinations of abolitionists. They were nothing compared with the danger posed by foreign enemies: Great Britain, for example.

If Britain should decide to reenter the continent through Texas and attempt a linkup with Canada, then war would be inevitable. "The safety of the republic being the supreme law, and Texas having offered us the key to the safety of our country from all foreign intrigues and diplomacy," Jackson wrote, "I say accept the key . . . and bolt the door at once." If England concluded an alliance with the "Texians"—which seemed under way at that very moment—then she would most likely move "an army from canady, along our western frontier," march through Arkansas and Louisiana, seize New Orleans, "excite the negroes to insurrection," "arouse the Indians on our west to war," and "throw our whole west into flames that would cost oceans of blood & hundreds of millions of money to quench, & reclaim. . . ." As he wrote these words, Jackson worked himself into a passion. "Texas must be ours," he raged. "Our safety requires it." Later he repeated his demand with a little less passion but with the same determination. We must have Texas, "peaceably if we can, forcibly if we must."

Despite strong Northern pressure, the new President, John Tyler, obtained a treaty of annexation signed by representatives of Texas and the United States in April 1844 and submitted it to the Senate for ratification. It was accompanied by an extraordinary letter to the British minister to Washington, Richard Pakenham, written by the secretary of state, John C. Calhoun. In it Calhoun contended that the treaty had been signed for the express purpose of protecting American slavery from British attempts to bring about universal emancipation. The extension of the American slave interests into Texas, he said, would nullify that "reprehensible" goal.

Friends of annexation groaned when they read copies of Calhoun's provocative letter. The secretary had placed annexation "*exclusively* upon the ground of *protection of Slavery* in the *Southern States!*" and the senators from the nonslaveholding states who favored annexation were furious because "it would be death to them, politically, if they were to vote for the Treaty based on such principles."

Why had Calhoun done it? Why had he jeopardized the treaty by the gratuitous mention of slavery? Maj. William B. Lewis, one of Jackson's oldest friends, claimed to know. The secretary of state meant to kill the treaty, he wrote, in order to "drive off every Northern man from the reannexation" and thereby give him a "pretext to unite the whole South upon himself as the Champion of its cause." Put simply, he meant to divide the Union, create a Southern confederacy, and make himself the "great man of this fragment which he expects to tear from the embrace of our glorious Govt." Like abolitionists, Lewis added, Southern hotheads were determined to disrupt the Union to achieve their own selfish objectives. Unfortunately, Texas had become a pawn in the fatal game of personal ambition. As far as Jackson was concerned, between "that arch fiend, J. Q. Adams" and that "*Cateline,*" John C. Calhoun, they were tearing the Union apart.

So the treaty failed. And shortly thereafter the ostensible Whig and Democratic candidates for the Presidency in the next election, Henry Clay and Martin Van Buren, publicly announced their opposition to annexation. Clay (himself a slave owner) regarded annexation as dangerous to the country because it might provoke a war with Mexico, excite sectional passions over slavery, and prove financially disastrous, since the $10 million Texas debt would have to be assumed by the United States. Van Buren was especially concerned over the sectional rancor and possibility of war.

Jackson "shed tears of regret" when he read the letter of his old friend Martin Van Buren. "I would to god I had been at Mr. V. B. elbow when he closed his letter. I would have brought to his view *the proper conclusion.*" The only course of action left was to dump Van Buren as a presidential candidate and nominate someone else, someone who "is an annexation man," he wrote, "and from the Southwest." Other Democrats agreed, and at the national nominating convention in Baltimore, they "arranged" to replace Van Buren with James K. Polk.

Clay and Polk ran a close race. Among other things, Polk promised to "rean-nex" Texas, claiming like Jackson that it was part of the Louisiana Purchase and had been shamefully surrendered by that "crazy old man, John Quincy Adams." In the election, he won 170 electoral votes to Clay's 105. The popular vote was even closer: 1,337,243 to 1,299,062. Polk defeated Clay by a 1.4 percent margin. "A mere *Tom Tit*," growled John Quincy Adams, had triumphed over the "old Eagle. The partial associations of Native Americans, Irish Catholics, abolition societies, liberty party, the Pope of Rome, the Democracy of the sword, and the dotage of a ruffian [Andrew Jackson] are sealing the fate of this nation, which nothing less than the in-terposition of Omnipotence can save."

Between the time of his election and inauguration, Polk met several times with Jackson at the Hermitage. Old Hickory instructed his friend on the necessity of an-nexing Texas in order to "put to rest the vexing question of abolitionism, the dan-gerous rock to our Union, and put at defiance all combined Europe, if combined to invade us." But Polk needed no instruction. Upon his arrival in Washington, he was queried by many members of Congress about his plans and goals. "He is for Texas, Texas, Texas," reported Sen. Willie P. Mangum of North Carolina, "& talks of but little else."

The outgoing President, John Tyler, saw his opportunity to capitalize on Polk's victory, and he helped arrange a joint resolution of annexation for both houses of Congress. After considerable politicking the House and Senate gave their approval, and Tyler signed the resolution on March 1, 1845, just three days before he was to leave office. A messenger was immediately dispatched to Texas with the "glorious" news.

"Texas is ours," trumpeted the newspapers. "The Union is safe." A feeble old man who had only a few months to live added his voice to the general acclaim. An-drew Jackson thanked God that he had lived to see this happy day. "I . . . congratu-late my beloved country [that] Texas is reannexed," he wrote, "and the safety, pros-perity, and the greatest interest of the whole Union is secured by this . . . great and important national act."

But others expressed more disturbing views. They feared that the admission of Texas would lead inevitably to war with Mexico and possibly civil war. And their direst predictions proved correct. Texas ratified annexation on July 4 and was ad-mitted into the Union as a slave state on December 29, 1845. The following spring—on May 11, 1846—the United States declared war against Mexico. Later the North and South submitted their dispute over slavery to a frightful test of arms. Within twenty years the Union cracked apart, and to weld it back together did in-deed take "oceans of blood & hundreds of millions of money."

6 Antebellum Society

William Sidney Mount was a founder of the American school of democratic genre art. In Rustic Dance After a Sleigh Ride *(1830, detail), he portrayed antebellum society with lighthearted candor.*

Religion on the Frontier

Bernard A. Weisberger

The following essay illustrates how exotic and colorful historical material can be presented in all its vigor without the historian's surrendering the obligation to analyze and explain the significance of the subject he or she is describing. Indeed, in this case the discussion of the "meaning" of a backwoods revivalism adds greatly to the verisimilitude of the strange events themselves. Portraits of the emotionally charged religious camp meetings of the nineteenth-century frontier easily degenerate into caricature. Bernard A. Weisberger studiously avoids this trap both by showing that the meetings were complex affairs (to which many kinds of people, driven by differing urges, came) and by pointing out the rational bases for the meetings and the emotional excesses they generated. He takes a relatively narrow subject, frontier religion, and relates it to a wide range of larger questions: American democracy; east–west conflicts; the nature of nationalism; human nature itself.

Dr. Weisberger, formerly a professor of history at Chicago, Rochester, and other universities, is currently devoting himself full time to historical research and writing. Among his books are *They Gathered at the River*, a study of revivalism, *The American Newspaperman*, and *The New Industrial Society*.

The great revival in the West, or the Kentucky Revival of 1800, as it was sometimes called, was a landmark in American history. It was not some accidental outburst of religious hysteria that crackled through the clearings. Rather, it was one of many answers to a question on which America's destiny hung during Thomas Jefferson's Presidency. Which way would the West go? It was filling up fast in 1800, and yet it still remained isolated behind the mountain barriers, only thinly linked to the nation by a cranky, awkward, and dangerous transportation "system" of trails and rivers. Could it be held within the bounds of American institutions as they had developed over 175 colonial years? Would its raw energies pull it into some new orbit—say, an independent confederation? Or, if it stayed in the Union, would it send representatives swarming back eastward to crush old patterns under the weight of numbers?

No group asked this question more anxiously than eastern clergymen. For, in 1800, they saw that their particular pattern was being abandoned on the frontier. From Kentucky, Tennessee, the western Carolinas, and Virginia, reports came back of a world that was shaggy, vicious, and churchless. The hard-living men and women of the forest clearings were not raising temples to God. Their morals (to eastern eyes) were parlous. Corn liquor flowed freely; marriages were celebrated long after children had arrived; gun and rope settled far too many legal disputes. The West was crowded with Sabbath-breakers and profane swearers, thieves, murderers, and blasphemers, with neither courts of law nor public opinion to raise a rebuke. The whole region seemed "hair-hung and breeze-shaken" over Hell's vault. And this was a matter of life-or-death seriousness to the churches. It was clear even then that America's future lay beyond the mountains. And if the West grew up Godless, then the entire nation would one day turn from His ways, to its destruction. It was no wonder that pious folk of the seaboard dug into their pocketbooks to scrape up funds for "home missionary" societies aimed at paying the way of parsons traveling westward. Or that church assemblies warned of crises ahead and called for special days of fasting, humiliation, and prayer for the West.

Yet, for a fact, the easterners were wrong. They misjudged their pioneers. Western people wanted and needed the church just as badly as the church needed their support for survival. Religion had a part to play in the hard-driven lives of the frontier settlers. It was more than a mere foundation for morality. It offered the hope of a bright future, shining beyond the dirt-floored, hog-and-hominy present. It offered an emotional outlet for lives ringed with inhibition. It was a social thing, too, furnishing occasions on which to lay aside axe and gun and skillet and gather with neighbors, to sing, to weep, to pray, or simply to talk with others. The West had to have religion—but religion of its own special kind. The West was not "lost" in 1800, but on the verge of being saved. Only it was going to be saved the same way it did everything else: on its own individualistic terms.

The East found this hard to understand. The East had trouble taking stock of such a man as the father of the western revival, James McGready. McGready was an angular, black-eyed Scotch-Irishman, born on the Pennsylvania frontier. He came of a hard-working and pious stock that had filled the western stretches of the Colonies in the sixty years before the Revolution. McGready was true to the spirit of his Highland Calvinistic ancestors, who worked, prayed, and fought heartily. He grew to adolescence without becoming a swearer, drinker, or Sabbath-breaker, which made him something of a God-fearing rarity among frontier youth. So his family sent him to a private school conducted by a minister, where he wrestled with Scripture in the morning and did farm chores in the afternoon for his "tuition." In 1788, he was licensed to preach, and came down to western North Carolina's Guilford County, where his family had moved. Thus, McGready was a product of western Presbyterianism.

That was important. In the 1790s, the religious picture in the United States already showed considerable (and characteristic) variety. Episcopalianism was solidly rooted among the landed gentry of the South. The Dutch Reformed Church carried on the heritage established when the flag of Holland flapped over New York. Various shoots of Lutheranism pushed up out of the soil of German settlements. Baptism and Methodism were small but growing faiths. There were little wedges in the pie of church membership labeled "Quaker," "Catholic," and "Jewish." A few bold souls called themselves Deists. A few more were on the way to becoming Unitarians. American worship wore a coat of many colors. But in New England and the mid-Atlantic states, the Presbyterian and Congregational bodies were unquestionably in the forefront. Both were rooted in the preceding century's Puritanism. Both officially believed in "predestination" and "limited election"—God had chosen a few individuals to be saved from general damnation, and the list, made up from the beginning of eternity, was unchangeable. These chosen "saints" were born in sin, but in His own way God would convert them to holiness during their lifetimes. Meanwhile, the laws of God must be interpreted and explained to mankind. In order to do this, the Presbyterians and Congregationalists had raised up colleges to train their ministers, the most famous among them by 1800 being Harvard, Yale, and Princeton. Graduates of these schools thundered of Jehovah's wrath to their congregations in two-hour sermons rich with samples of their learning. During the week they warmed their study chairs ten hours a day, writing black-bound volumes of theology.

Religion of this sort lacked appeal for the Scotch-Irish migrants pushing into the frontier regions. They were Presbyterians in name. But their wild surroundings did something to them. They came to resent authority—whether exercised by excise collectors, land speculators, lawyers, or, finally, ministers. What was more, they wanted a little stronger assurance of salvation than a strict reading of limited election gave them. There was a need, in this fur-capped, bewhiskered Christian world, for more promise in life, and more passion too. Learned lectures might do for townspeople, but not for pioneers.

Among common folk, both East *and* West, a ferment of resentment against the "aristocratic" notion of election was at work. In the 1740s it had exploded in a revival called the Great Awakening. Baptist, Presbyterian, Congregationalist, Anglican, and Dutch-Reformed Christians were caught up in a common whirlwind of handclapping, shouting, and hosannaing. A good many new leaders, and a number of unpleasant schisms, had risen out of this storm. And in western Pennsylvania, revival-minded Presbyterians had founded a number of little academies to train their preachers. Derisively dubbed "log colleges" by the learned, they took the name proudly. Their graduates were short on Greek and exegesis but long on zeal. When the Great Awakening sputtered out before the Revolution, these colleges remained, helping to keep the sparks alive. Now, with the new nation established, the fire was ready to blaze again. McGready, himself a log-college graduate, was one of the first to blow on it.

McGready got to grips with the powers of darkness in North Carolina without wasting any time. He began to preach against the "formality and deadness" of the local churches. Besides that, he demanded some concrete testimony of good living from his flock, and the particular evidence he asked for was highly exacting. The new preacher insisted that strong drink was a slippery path to Hell. In Guilford County this did not sit well. Frontiersmen saw no harm in lightening a hard life with a dram or two, and they wanted no lectures on the subject from men of the cloth. In point of fact, there was no cloth. Pioneer ministers wore buckskin, and took their turn with the next man at hoeing corn or splitting kindling. McGready got nowhere—at least nowhere in North Carolina. After a futile battle, he left to seek a more promising future in Kentucky—some said by request of the congregation.

In Kentucky, circumstances were riper for him. Despite eastern concern, a new Christian community was taking shape in that rugged, bear-and-savage-haunted wilderness province, where crude living went along with high dreaming. It was a community ready to be stirred into life, and McGready was the man to seize the stick. In Logan County, in the southwestern part of the state—a region well-known for unregenerate doings—he had three small congregations: at Red River, Gasper River, and Muddy River. He began to preach to these congregations, and he did not deal with such recondite matters as the doctrines contained in Matthew, or their applications. Instead he would "so describe Heaven" that his listeners would "see its glories and long to be there." Then he went on to "array hell and its horrors" so that the wicked would "tremble and quake, imagining a lake of fire and brimstone yawning to overwhelm them." With that brimstone smoking away in the background, McGready struck for bedrock. The whole point of Christianity, for him, was in the conversion of sinners to saints assured of eternal bliss. His question of questions was dagger-sharp: "If I were converted, would I feel it and know it?" A McGready parishioner was not going to be allowed to rest in self-satisfaction merely because he attended worship and avoided the grosser forms of indecency.

Under such spurring, results began to show among the faithful. In 1799, during a service at Gasper River, many fell to the ground and lay "powerless, groaning, praying and crying for mercy." Women began to scream. Big, tough men sobbed like hysterical children. What could explain this? Simply the fact that belly-deep fear was taking over. For it is well to remember that in those days conversion was the *only* token of salvation. No matter how young one was, no matter how blameless a life he had led, until the moment of transformation one was a sinner, bound for torment. If death stepped in before conversion was completed, babes and grandsires alike sank screaming into a lake of burning pitch—a lake that was not metaphorical, not symbolical, but *real* and eternal. And death on the frontier was always around the corner—in the unexpected arrow, the milk sickness, the carelessly felled tree, the leap of the wounded grizzly. Frontiersmen bottled up their fear. It was the price of sanity and survival. But when a religious service provided an acceptable excuse for breaking down the barriers, it was no wonder that men shivered and wept.

After shaking up the dry bones of the Gasper River settlement, McGready moved on in June of 1800 to Red River. He meant to hold a sacramental service, at the end of which church members would take the Lord's Supper together. What he got was something more uncontrolled. In a meetinghouse of undressed logs McGready shared his pulpit with three other Presbyterian ministers. A Methodist preacher was also present. That was not unusual. Frontier preachers were a small band. They knew each other well. A service was a social occasion, and therefore a treat, and several ministers often took part in order to draw it out.

The Presbyterian shepherds did their preaching, and what they said has not come down to us, but they must have dragged a harrow through the congregation's feelings. When John McGee, the Methodist, arose, an awesome hush had fallen on the house. McGee faced a problem. The Methodists were relative newcomers to America, officially on the scene only since 1766. They were frowned on by more established groups, mainly because they gave emotion free rein in their worship. It was not unusual at a Methodist meeting for women to faint, men to shout in strange tongues, and the minister himself to windmill his arms and bawl himself red-faced. For the more formal Presbyterians, such conduct was out of bounds. McGee knew this, and wanted to mind his ecclesiastical manners. But he knew a ripe audience when he saw one, too, and after an apparent debate with himself, he made his move. Rising, he shouted that everyone in the house should submit to "the Lord Omnipotent." Then he began to bounce from backless bench to backless bench, pleading, crying, shouting, shaking, and exhorting, "with all possible energy and ecstasy."

That broke the dam. The sinners of Red River had spent a lonely winter with pent-up terrors gnawing at them. McGee's appeal was irresistible. In a moment the floor was "covered with the slain; their screams for mercy pierced the heavens." Cursers, duelers, whiskey-swillers, and cardplayers lay next to little children of ten and eleven, rolling and crying in "agonies of distress" for salvation. It was a remarkable performance for a region "destitute of religion." When it was through, a new harvest of souls had been gathered for the Lord.

Word of the Red River meeting whisked through the territory. When McGready got to Muddy River, his next congregation, new scenes of excitement were enacted. During the meeting, sinners prayed and cried for mercy once again, and some of them, overwhelmed by feeling, bolted from the house and rushed in agony into the woods. Their cries and sobs could be heard ringing through the surrounding trees. And when this meeting had yielded up its quota of saved, the Kentucky Revival was not only a fact, but a well-known one. McGready announced another sacramental meeting for Gasper River, and before long, dozens, perhaps hundreds, of Kentuckians who did not belong to his district were threading the trails on their way to the service. Some came as far as a hundred miles, a hard week's trip in the back country. In wagons, on horseback, and on foot came the leathershirted men, rifles balanced on their shoulders, and their pinched-looking, tired women, all looking for blessed assurance and a washing away of their sins.

At Gasper River, history was made. The cabins of the neighborhood could not hold the influx of visitors, so the newcomers came prepared to camp out. They brought tents—some of them—and cold pork, roasted hens, slabs of corn bread, and perhaps a little whiskey to hold them up through the rigors of a long vigil. The Gasper River meetinghouse was too small for the crowd, so the men got out their educated axes, and in a while the clop-clop of tree-felling formed an overture to the services. Split-log benches were dragged into place outdoors, and the worshipers adjourned to God's first temple. What was taking place was an outdoor religious exercise, meant to last two or three days, among people who camped on the spot. This was the camp meeting. Some claimed that Gasper River sheltered the very first of them. That claim has been challenged in the court of historical inquiry. But whether it stands up or not, the Gasper River meeting was something new in worship. It took its form from its western surroundings. Outsiders were a long time in understanding it, because they saw its crude outside and not its passionate heart.

The outside was raw enough. Once again McGready exhorted, and once again sinners fell prostrate to the ground. Night came on; inside the meetinghouse, candlelight threw grotesque, waving shadows on the walls. Outside, the darkness deepened the sense of mystery and of eternity's nearness. Preachers grew hoarse and exhausted, but insatiable worshipers gathered in knots to pray together, and to relieve their feelings by telling each other of "the sweet wonders which they saw in Christ." Hour followed hour, into dawn. For people who had to rise (and generally retire) with the sun each day of their lives, this alone was enough to make the meeting memorable for the rest of their lives. Lightheaded and hollow-eyed, the "mourn-ers," or unconverted, listened alternately to threats of sulphur and promises of bliss, from Saturday until Monday. On Tuesday, after three throbbing days, they broke it up. Forty-five had professed salvation. Satan had gotten a thorough gouging.

Now the tide of camp-meeting revivalism began to roll northward. One of the visitors at the Logan County meetings was a young Presbyterian clergyman whose life was something of a copy of McGready's. Barton Warren Stone too had learned on the frontier to revere God Almighty and to farm well. He too had studied reli-gion in a log college. But more than this, he was one of McGready's own converts, having fallen under the power of the older man's oratory in North Carolina. Stone liked what he observed in Logan County, and he took McGready's preaching meth-ods and the camp-meeting idea back to his own congregations in Bourbon County, well to the north and east. Soon he too had imitators, among them Richard McNe-mar, who had small Presbyterian charges across the river in Ohio.

But it was Stone himself who touched off the monster camp meeting of the re-gion's history. He set a sacramental service for August 6, 1801, at Cane Ridge, not far from the city of Lexington. Some undefinable current of excitement running from cabin to cabin brought out every Kentuckian who could drop his earthly con-cerns and move, by horseflesh or shoe leather, toward the campground. Later on, some people estimated that 25,000 were on hand, but that figure is almost too fan-tastic for belief. In 1800, Kentucky had only a quarter of a million residents, and Lexington, the largest town, numbered under two thousand. But even a crowd of three or four thousand would have overwhelmed anything in the previous experi-ence of the settlers.

Whatever the actual number, there was a sight to dazzle the eyes of the minis-ters who had come. Technically the meeting was Presbyterian, but Baptist and Methodist parsons had come along, and there was room for them, because no one man could hope to reach such a mob. Preaching stands built of logs were set up outdoors. One man remembered a typical scene—a crowd spilling out of the doors of the one meetinghouse, where two Presbyterian ministers were alternately hold-ing forth, and three other groups scattered within a radius of a hundred yards. One cluster of sinners was gathered at the feet of a Presbyterian preacher, another gave ear to a Methodist exhorter, and lastly, a knot of Negroes was attending on the words of some orator of their own race. All over the campground, individual speak-ers had gathered little audiences to hear of *their* experiences. One observer said that there were as many as three hundred of these laymen "testifying."

So Cane Ridge was not really a meeting, but a series of meetings that gathered and broke up without any recognizable order. One Methodist brother who could not find a free preaching-stand ventured up the slanting trunk of a partly fallen tree. He found a flat spot, fifteen feet off the ground, and he spoke from this van-tage point while a friend on the ground held up an umbrella on a long pole to shel-ter him from the weather. Within a few moments, this clergyman claimed, he had gathered an audience of thousands. Undoubtedly they stayed until lured away by some fresh address from a stump or the tail of a wagon. For the crowds were with-out form as they collected, listened, shouted "Amen!" and "Hallelujah!" and drifted off to find neighbors or refreshments or more preaching. The din can only be guessed at. The guilty were groaning and sometimes screaming at the top of their lungs, and those who felt that they were saved were clapping their hands, shouting hymns, and generally noising out their exultation. There were always hecklers at the meetings too, and some of them were no doubt shouting irreverent remarks at the faithful. Crying children added their bit, and tethered horses and oxen stamped, bawled, and whinnied to make the dissonance complete. Someone said that the meeting sounded from afar like the roar of Niagara. At night the campfires threw weird shadow-patterns of trees across the scene, and the whole moving, re-sounding gathering appeared to be tossing on the waves of some invisible storm. As if to etch the experience into men's memories, there were real rainstorms, and the drenched participants were thrown into fresh waves of screaming as thunder and lightning crashed around them.

All in all, a memorable enough episode. And yet still stranger things happened to put the brand of the Lord's sponsorship on Cane Ridge's mass excitement. Over-whelmed with their sensations, some men and women lay rigid and stiff on the ground for hours in a kind of catalepsy. One "blasphemer" who had come to scoff at the proceedings tumbled from his saddle unconscious and remained so for a day and a half. There was something incredibly compelling in what was going on. One remembered testimony came from a reasonably hard-headed young man named James Finley. Later in life Finley became a Methodist preacher, but in 1801 he was, except for a better-than-average education, a typical frontiersman. He had a small farm, a new wife, and a vigorous love of hunting. He had come to the Cane Ridge meeting out of curiosity, but as he looked on, he was taken with an uncontrollable trembling and feelings of suffocation. He left the campground, found a log tavern, and put away a glass of brandy to steady his nerves. But they were beyond steadying. All the way home he kept breaking out in irrational fits of laughter or tears. Many a spirit, returning from Cane Ridge, must have been moved in the same near-hysteri-cal way.

A holy frenzy seemed to have taken hold of the West. Throughout the frontier communities, the ecstasy of conversion overflowed into the nervous system. At Cane Ridge, and at a hundred subsequent meetings, the worshipers behaved in ways that would be unbelievable if there were not plenty of good testimony to their truth. Some got the "jerks," a spasmodic twitching of the entire body. They were a fearful thing to behold. Some victims hopped from place to place like bouncing balls. Sometimes heads snapped from side to side so rapidly that faces became a blur, and handkerchiefs whipped off women's heads. One preacher saw women taken with the jerks at table, so that teacups went flying from their hands to splash against log walls. Churchmen disagreed about the meaning of these symptoms. Were they signs of conversion? Or demonstrations of the Lord's power, meant to convince doubters? Peter Cartwright, a famous evangelist of a slightly later era, be-lieved the latter. He told of a skeptic at one of his meetings who was taken with the jerks and in a particularly vicious spasm snapped his neck. He died, a witness to the judgment of Omnipotence but gasping out to the last his "cursing and bitterness." Besides the jerks, there were strange seizures in which those at prayer broke into uncontrollable guffaws or intoned weird and wordless melodies or barked like dogs.

It was wild and shaggy, and very much a part of life in the clearings. Westerners wanted to feel religion in their bones. In their tough and violent lives intellectual exercises had no place, but howls and leaps were something that men who were "half-horse and half-alligator" understood. It was natural for the frontier to get religion with a mighty roar. Any other way would not have seemed homelike to people who, half in fun and half in sheer defensiveness, loved their brag, bluster, and bluff.

Yet there was something deeper than mere excitement underneath it all. Something fundamental was taking place, some kind of genuine religious revolution, bearing a made-in-America stamp. The East was unhappy with it. For one thing, camp-meeting wildness grated on the nerves of the educated clergy. All of this jigging and howling looked more like the work of Satan than of God. There were ugly rumors too, about unsanctified activities at the meetings. Some candidates for salvation showed up with cigars between their teeth. Despite official condemnation, liquor flowed free and white-hot on the outskirts of the gatherings. It might be that corn did more than its share in justifying God's ways to man. Then there were stories that would not down which told how, in the shadows around the clearing, excited men and women were carried away in the hysteria and, as the catch phrase had it, "begot more souls than were saved" at the meeting. All these tales might have had some partial truth, yet in themselves they did not prove much about frontier religion. As it happened, a part of every camp-meeting audience apparently consisted of loafers and rowdies who came for the show and who were quite capable of any sin that a Presbyterian college graduate was likely to imagine.

Yet it was not the unscrubbed vigor of the meetings that really bothered conservatives in the Presbyterian Church. Their fundamental problem was in adjusting themselves and their faith to a new kind of democratic urge. Enemies of the revivals did not like the success of emotional preaching. What would happen to learning, and all that learning stood for, if a leather-lunged countryman with a gift for lurid word pictures could be a champion salvationist? And what would happen— what *had* happened—to the doctrine of election when the revival preacher shouted "Repent!" at overwrought thousands, seeming to say that any Tom, Dick, or Harry who felt moved by the Spirit might be receiving the promise of eternal bliss? Would mob enthusiasm replace God's careful winnowing of the flock to choose His lambs? The whole orderly scheme of life on earth, symbolized by a powerful church, an educated ministry, and a straight and narrow gate of salvation, stood in peril.

Nor were the conservatives wrong. In truth, when the McGreadys and Stones struck at "deadness" and "mechanical worship" in the older churches, they were going beyond theology. They were hitting out at a view of things that gave a plain and unlettered man little chance for a say in spiritual affairs. A church run by skilled theologians was apt to set rules that puzzled simple minds. A church which held that many were called, but few chosen, *was* aristocratic in a sense. The congregations of the western evangelists did not care for rules, particularly rules that were not immediately plain to anyone. In their view, the Bible alone was straightforward enough. Neither would they stand for anything resembling aristocracy, whatever form it might take. They wanted cheap land and the vote, and they were getting these things. They wanted salvation as well—or at least free and easy access to it— and they were bound to have that too. If longer-established congregations and their leaders back east did not like that notion, the time for a parting of the ways was at hand. In politics, such a parting is known as a revolution; in religion, it is schism. Neither word frightened the western revivalists very much.

The trouble did not take long to develop. In McGready's territory, a new Cumberland Presbytery, or subgroup, was organized in 1801. Before long it was in a battle with the Kentucky Synod, the next highest administrative body in the hierarchy. The specific issue was the licensing of certain "uneducated" candidates for the ministry. The root question was revivalism. The battle finally went up to the General Assembly, for Presbyterians a sort of combined Congress and Supreme Court. In 1809 the offending revivalistic presbytery was dissolved. Promptly, most of its congregations banded themselves into the separate Cumberland Presbyterian Church. Meanwhile, Barton Stone, Richard McNemar, and other members of the northern Kentucky wing of camp-meeting Presbyterianism were also in trouble. They founded a splinter group known as the "New Lights," and the Kentucky Synod, as might have been foreseen, lost little time in putting the New Lights out, via heresy proceedings. Next, they formed an independent Springfield Presbytery. But like all radicals, they found it easier to keep going than to apply the brakes. In 1804 the Springfield Presbytery fell apart. Stone and some of his friends joined with others in a new body, shorn of titles and formality, which carried the magnificently simple name of the Christian Church. Later on, Stone went over to the followers of Thomas and Alexander Campbell, who called themselves Disciples of Christ. Richard McNemar, after various spiritual adventures, became a Shaker. Thus, ten years after Cane Ridge, the score was depressing for Presbyterians. Revivalism had brought on innumerable arguments, split off whole presbyteries, and sent ministers and congregations flying into the arms of at least four other church groups. That splintering was a stronger indictment than any conservative could have invented to bring against Cane Ridge, or against its western child, the camp meeting.

A dead end appeared to have been reached. But it was only a second-act curtain. In the first act, religion in the West, given up for lost, had been saved by revivalism. In the second, grown strong and rambunctious, it had quarreled with its eastern parents. Now the time was at hand for a third-act resolution of the drama. Both sides would have to back down and compromise. For the lesson of history was already plain. In religious matters, as in all matters, East and West, metropolis and frontier, were not really warring opposites. Each nourished the other, and each had an impact on the other. Whatever emerged as "American" would carry some of the imprint of both, or it would perish.

On the part of the West, the retreat consisted of taming the camp meeting. Oddly enough, it was not the Presbyterians who did that. By 1812 or so, they had drawn back from it, afraid of its explosive qualities. But the Methodists were in an excellent position to make use of revivalism and all its trappings. They had, at that time at least, no educated conservative wing. They welcomed zealous backwood preachers, even if they were grammatically deficient. In fact, they worked such men into their organization and sent them, under the name of "circuit-riders," traveling tirelessly on horseback to every lonely settlement that the wilderness spawned. The result was that the Methodists were soon far in the lead in evangelizing the frontier. They did not have to worry about the claims of limited election either. Their formal theology did not recognize it. With a plain-spoken and far-reaching ministry freely offering salvation to all true believers,

With the help of the Word—and sometimes the bottle—frontier camp meetings went on for days and reaped rich harvests of converts.

Methodism needed only some kind of official harvest season to count and bind together the converts. The camp meeting was the perfect answer. By 1811, the Methodists had held four or five hundred of them throughout the country; by 1820, they had held a thousand—by far the majority of all such gatherings in the nation.

But these meetings were not replicas of Cane Ridge. They were combed, washed, and made respectable. Permanent sites were picked, regular dates chosen, and preachers and flocks given ample time to prepare. When meeting time came, the arriving worshipers in their wagons were efficiently taken in charge, told where to park their vehicles and pasture their teams, and given a spot for their tents. Orderly rows of these tents surrounded a preaching area equipped with sturdy benches and preaching stands. The effect was something like that of a formal bivouac just before a general's inspection. Tight scheduling kept the worship moving according to plan—dawn prayers, eight o'clock sermons, eleven o'clock sermons, dinner breaks, afternoon prayers and sermons, meals again, and candlelight services. Years of experience tightened the schedules, and camp-meetings manuals embodied the fruits of practice. Regular hymns replaced the discordant bawling of the primitive era. Things took on a generally homelike look. There were Methodist ladies who did not hesitate to bring their best feather beds to spread in the tents, and meals tended to be planned and ample affairs. Hams, turkeys, gravies, biscuits, preserves, and melons produced contented worshipers and happy memories.

There were new rules to cope with disorderliness as well. Candles, lamps and torches fixed to trees kept the area well lit and discouraged young converts from amorous ways. Guards patrolled the circumference of the camp, and heroic if sometimes losing battles were fought to keep whiskey out. In such almost decorous surroundings jerks, barks, dances and trances became infrequent and finally nonexistent.

Not that there was a total lack of enthusiasm. Hymns were still yelled and stamped as much as sung. Nor was it out of bounds for the audience to pepper the sermon with ejaculations of "Amen!" and "Glory!" Outsiders were still shocked by some things they saw. But they did not realize how far improvement had gone.

Eastern churchmen had to back down somewhat, too. Gradually, tentatively, they picked up the revival and made it part of their religious life. In small eastern towns it became regularized into an annual season of "ingathering," like the harvest or the election. Yet it could not be contained within neat, white-painted meetinghouses. Under the "sivilized" clothing, the tattered form of Twain's Pap Finn persisted. Certain things were taken for granted after a time. The doctrine of election was bypassed and, in practice, allowed to wither away.

Moreover, a new kind of religious leader, the popular evangelist, took the stage. Men like Charles G. Finney in the 1830s, Dwight L. Moody in the 1870s, and Billy Sunday in the decade just preceding the First World War flashed into national prominence. Their meetings overflowed church buildings and spilled into convention halls, auditoriums, and specially built "tabernacles." As it happened, these men came from lay ranks into preaching. Finney was a lawyer, Moody a shoe salesman, and Sunday a baseball player. They spoke down-to-earth language to their massed listeners, reduced the Bible to basic axioms, and drew their parables from the courtroom, the market, and the barnyard. They made salvation the only goal of their service, and at the meeting's end they beckoned the penitents forward to acknowledge the receipt of grace. In short, they carried on the camp-meeting tradition. By the closing years of the nineteenth century, however, the old campgrounds for the most part were slowly abandoned. Growing cities swallowed them up, and rapid transportation destroyed the original reason for the prolonged camp-out. But the meetings were not dead. Mass revivalism had moved them indoors and made them a permanent part of American Protestantism.

All of this cost something in religious depth, religious learning, religious dignity. Yet there was not much choice. The American churches lacked the support of an all-powerful state or of age-old traditions. They had to move with the times. That is why their history is so checkered with schismatic movements—symptoms of the struggle to get in step with the parade. Hence, if the West in 1800 could not ignore religion, the rest of the country, in succeeding years, could not ignore the western notion of religion. One student of the camp meeting has said that it flourished "side by side with the militia muster, with the cabin raising and the political barbecue." That was true, and those institutions were already worked deeply into the American grain by 1840. They reflected a spirit of democracy, optimism, and impatience that would sweep us across a continent, sweep us into industrialism, sweep us into a civil war. That spirit demanded some religious expression, some promise of a millennium in which all could share.

The camp meeting was part of that religious expression, part of the whole revival system that channeled American impulses into church-going ways. In the home of the brave, piety was organized so that Satan got no breathing spells. Neither, for that matter, did anyone else.

The Education of Women

Elaine Kendall

The great contemporary interest in the position of women in American society has led to many historical investigations in an attempt to throw light on how the current situation came to be. Much of this work has centered on the long struggle of feminists to obtain equal treatment before the law: the vote, equal pay for equal work, even such basic rights as that of married women to own property in their own names and to make wills without their husbands' approval. But historical attention has also been focused on other aspects of women's place—on such interesting questions as family structure and function in different periods and, as in the following essay, on female education. The author, Elaine Kendall, traces the history of how girls were educated in America from colonial times to the middle of the nineteenth century. This is a story of progress, but of limited progress, one that helps explain both the strength of the feminists' demands for reform and the slowness with which these demands were achieved. Kendall is the author of a history of women's education, appropriately titled, as readers of her essay here will understand, *Peculiar Institutions*.

"Could I have died a martyr in the cause, and thus ensured its success, I could have blessed the faggot and hugged the stake." The cause was state support for female education, the would-be Saint Joan was Emma Willard, and the rhetorical standards of the 1820s were lofty and impassioned. The most militant feminists rarely scale such heights today. For one thing, dogged effort has finally reduced the supply of grand injustices; and today's preference for less florid metaphor has deprived the movement of such dramatic images. Comparatively speaking, the rest of the struggle is a downhill run, leading straight to twenty-four-hour daycare centers, revised and updated forms of marriage, free access to the executive suite, and rows of "Ms's" on Senate office doors. Glorying in our headway, we easily forget that leverage comes with literacy, and literacy for women is a relative novelty.

Long before the Revolution, American males already had Harvard, Yale, and Princeton, as well as a full range of other educational institutions—grammar schools, academies, seminaries, and numerous smaller colleges. American girls had only their mother's knee. By 1818, the year in which Emma Willard first introduced her *Plan for the Improvement of Female Education,* the gap was almost as wide as ever. Public schooling was a local option, quite whimsically interpreted. The towns could provide as much or as little as they wished, extending or restricting attendance as they saw fit. Ms. Willard presented her novel proposals to the New York State legislature, which dealt with the question by putting it repeatedly at the bottom of the agenda until the session was safely over. Lavish tributes to Mother's Knee filled the halls of Albany. In the opinion of the senators, M.'s K. not only outshone our men's colleges but also Oxford, Cambridge, and Heidelberg as an institution of female edification. Despite the support of De Witt Clinton, John Adams, and Thomas Jefferson, it was three more years—when a building and grounds were offered independently by the town of Troy—before the Willard Seminary actually got under way. The academy still flourishes and claims to "mark the beginning of higher education for women in the United States." Since that is not precisely the same as being the first such school and the rival contenders have either vanished or metamorphosed into other sorts of institutions entirely, there is no reason to dispute it. The pre-Revolutionary South did have a few early convents, including one at New Orleans that was established by the Ursuline order in 1727 and taught religion, needlework, and something of what was called basic skills. Other religious groups, particularly the Moravians and Quakers, supported female seminaries during the eighteenth century, but these places did not really attempt to offer advanced education—a commodity for which there was little market in an era when girls were unwelcome in elementary schools. A few New England clergymen opened small academies for girls during the first decade of the nineteenth century, but these noble and well-intentioned efforts were ephemeral, never outlasting their founders. Until Emma Willard succeeded in extracting that bit of real estate from Troy, public and private support for such ventures was virtually nonexistent.

Some few ambitious and determined girls did succeed in learning to read and write in colonial America, but hardly ever at public expense and certainly not in comfort. Their number was pitifully small, and those who gained more than the rudiments of literacy would hardly have crowded a saltbox parlor. . . .

As the grip of Puritanism gradually relaxed, the image of a learned female improved infinitesimally. She was no longer regarded as a disorderly person or a heretic but merely as a nuisance to her husband, family, and friends. A sensible woman soon found ways to conceal her little store of knowledge or, if hints of it should accidentally slip out, to disparage or apologize for it. Abigail Adams, whose wistful letters show a continuing interest in women's education, described her own with a demurely rhymed disclaimer:

The little learning I have gained
Is all from simple nature drained.

In fact, the wife of John Adams was entirely self-educated. She disciplined herself to plod doggedly through works of ancient history whenever her household duties permitted, being careful to do so in the privacy of her boudoir. In her letters she deplored the fact that it was still customary to "ridicule female learning" and even in the "best families" to deny girls more than the barest rudiments.

The prevailing colonial feeling toward female education was still so unanimously negative that it was not always thought necessary to mention it. Sometimes this turned out to be a boon. A few villages, in their haste to establish schools for boys, neglected to specify that only males would be admitted. From the beginning they wrote their charters rather carelessly, using the loose generic term "children." This loophole was nearly always blocked as soon as the risks became apparent, but in the interim period of grace girls were occasionally able to pick up a few crumbs of knowledge. They did so by sitting outside the schoolhouse or on its steps, eavesdropping on the boys' recitations. More rarely, girls were tolerated in the rear of the schoolhouse behind a curtain, in a kind of makeshift seraglio. This Levantine arrangement, however, was soon abandoned as inappropriate to the time and place, and the attendance requirements were made unambiguous. New England winters and Cape Cod architecture being what they are, the amount of learning that one could have acquired by these systems was necessarily scanty. Still it was judged excessive. The female scholars in the yard and on the stairs seemed to suffer disproportionately from pleurisy and other respiratory ailments. Further proof of the divine attitude toward the educating of women was not sought. Girls were excluded for their own good, as well as to ensure the future of the Colonies.

After the Revolution the atmosphere in the New England states did become considerably more lenient. Here and there a town council might vote to allow girls inside the school building from five to seven in the morning, from six to eight at night, or, in a few very liberal communities, during the few weeks in summer when the boys were at work in the fields or shipyards. This was a giant step forward and would have been epochal if teachers had always appeared at these awkward times. Unfortunately the girls often had to muddle through on their own without benefit of faculty. The enlightened trend, moreover, was far from general. In 1792 the town of Wellesley, Massachusetts, voted "not to be at any expense for schooling girls," and similarly worded bylaws were quite usual throughout the northern states until the 1820s. In the southern Colonies, where distances between the great estates delayed the beginnings of any public schooling even longer, wealthy planters often imported tutors to instruct their sons in academic subjects. If they could afford the additional luxury, they might also engage singing and dancing masters for the daughters, who were not expected to share their brothers' more arduous lessons. In a pleasant little memoir of the South, *Colonial Days and Dames,* Anne Wharton, a descendant of Thomas Jefferson, noted that "very little from books was thought necessary for a girl. She was trained to domestic matters . . . the accomplishments of the day . . . to play upon the harpischord or spinet, and to work impossible dragons and roses upon canvas."

Although the odds against a girl's gaining more than the sketchiest training during this era seem to have been overwhelming, there were some remarkable exceptions. The undiscouraged few included Emma Willard herself; Catherine and Harriet Beecher, the clergyman's daughters, who established an early academy at Hartford; and Mary Lyon, who founded the college that began in 1837 as Mount Holyoke Seminary. Usually, however, the tentative and halfhearted experiments permitted by the New England towns served only to give aid and comfort to the opposition. They seemed to show that the female mind was not inclined to scholarship and the female body was not strong enough to withstand exposure—*literal* exposure, in many cases—to it. By 1830 or so primary education had been grudgingly extended to girls almost everywhere, but it was nearly impossible to find anyone who dared champion any further risks. Boston had actually opened a girls' high school in 1826 only to abolish it two years later. . . .

Public schools obviously were not the only route to learning or most female American children up through colonial times would have been doomed to total ignorance. Fathers, especially clergymen fathers, would often drill their daughters in the Bible and sometimes teach them to read and do simple sums as well. Nothing that enhanced an understanding of the Scriptures could be entirely bad, and arithmetic was considered useful in case a woman were to find herself the sole support of her children. Brothers would sometimes lend or hand down their old school books, and fond uncles might help a favorite and clever niece with her sums. The boys' tutor was often amenable to a pretty sister's pleas for lessons. For those girls not fortunate enough to be the daughters of foresighted New England parsons or wealthy tobacco and cotton factors, most colonial towns provided dame schools. These catered to boys as well as to girls of various ages. They offered a supplement to the curriculum at Mother's Knee, but only just. Because these schools were kept by women who had acquired their own learning haphazardly, the education they offered was motley at best. The solitary teacher could impart no more than she herself knew, and that rarely exceeded the alphabet, the shorter catechism, sewing, knitting, some numbers, and perhaps a recipe for baked beans and brown bread. The actual academic function of these early American institutions seems to have been somewhat exaggerated and romanticized by historians. Dame schools were really no more than small businesses, managed by impoverished women who looked after neighborhood children and saw to it that idle little hands did not make work for the devil. The fees (tuition is too grand a word) were tiny, with threepence a week per child about par. That sum could hardly have paid for a single hornbook for the entire class. The dame school itself was an English idea, transplanted almost intact to the Colonies. Several seem to have been under way by the end of the seventeenth century. . . .

As the country became more affluent, schoolkeeping gradually began to attract more ambitious types. Older girls were still being excluded from the town seminaries and in many places from the grammar schools as well. A great many people quickly realized that there was money to be made by teaching the children of the new middle class and that they could sell their services for far more than pennies. No special accreditation or qualification was required, and there was no competition from the state. Toward the end of the eighteenth century and at the beginning of the nineteenth, platoons of self-styled professors invaded American towns and cities, promising to instruct both sexes and all ages in every known art, science, air, and grace. These projects were popularly known as adventure schools, a phrase that has a pleasant modern ring to it, suggesting open classrooms, free electives, and individual attention.

That, however, is deceptive. The people who ran such schools were usually adventurers in the not very admirable sense of the word: unscrupulous, self-serving, and of doubtful origins and attainments. Many simply equipped themselves with false diplomas and titles from foreign universities and set up shop. The schools continued to operate only as long as they turned a profit. When enrollment dropped, interest waned, or fraud became obvious, the establishment would simply fold and the proprietors move to another town for a fresh start. The newer territories were particularly alluring to the worst of these entrepreneurs, since their reputations could neither precede nor follow them there. A new name, a new prospectus, an ad in the gazette, and they were in business again until scandal or mismanagement obliged them to move on. Such "schools" were not devised for the particular benefit of girls; but because they were independent commercial enterprises, no solvent person was turned away. Thousands of young women did take advantage of the new opportunity and were, in many cases, taken advantage of in return. For boys the adventure schools were an alternative to the strict classicism and religiosity of the academies and seminaries, but for girls they were the only educational possibility between the dame school and marriage.

There was little effort to devise a planned or coherent course of study, though elaborately decorated certificates were awarded upon completion of a series of lessons. The scholar could buy whatever he or she fancied from a mind-bending list. One could take needlework at one place, languages at another, dancing or "ouranology" at a third. (It was a pompous era, and no one was fonder of polysyllables than the professors. Ouranology was sky-watching, but it sounded impressive.) There were no minimum or maximum course requirements, though the schoolmasters naturally made every effort to stock the same subjects offered by the competition, in order to reduce the incidence of school-hopping. . . .

Many of the adventure schools hedged their financial risks by functioning as a combination store and educational institution, selling fancywork, "very good Orange-Oyl," sweetmeats, sewing notions, painted china, and candles along with lessons in dancing, foreign languages, geography, penmanship, and spelling. Usually they were mama-and-papa affairs, with the wife instructing girls in "curious works" and the husband concentrating upon "higher studies." Curious works covered a great deal of ground—the making of artificial fruits and flowers, the "raising of paste," enamelling, japanning, quilting, fancy embroidery, and in at least one recorded case "flowering on catgut," an intriguing accomplishment that has passed into total oblivion, leaving no surviving examples.

The adventure schools advertised heavily in newspapers and journals of the period, often in terms indicating that teaching was not an especially prestigious profession. One Thomas Carroll took several columns in a May, 1765, issue of the New York *Mercury* to announce a curriculum that would have taxed the entire faculty of Harvard and then proceeded to explain that he "was not under the necessity of coming here to teach, he had views of living more happy, but some unforeseen, and unexpected events have happened since his arrival here. . . ," thus reducing this Renaissance paragon to schoolkeeping and his lady to teaching French knots and quilting.

While they lasted adventure schools attempted to offer something for everyone, including adults, and came in all forms, sizes, and price ranges. They met anywhere and everywhere: "at the Back of Mr. Benson's Brew-House," in rented halls, in borrowed parlors, at inns, and from time to time in barns or open fields. The adventurer was usually available for private lessons as well, making house calls "with the utmost discretion," especially in the case of questionable studies like dancing or French verbs. The entire physical plant usually fitted into a carpetbag. . . .

The pretentious and empty promises of the adventure schools eventually aroused considerable criticism. Americans may not yet have appreciated the value of female education, but they seem always to have known the value of a dollar. It was not long before the public realized that flowering on catgut was not so useful an accomplishment for their daughters as ciphering or reading. The more marginal operators began to melt away, and those schoolmasters who hung on were obliged to devote more attention to practical subjects and eliminate many of the patent absurdities. . . .

Certain religious groups, particularly the Moravians and the Quakers, had always eschewed frippery and pioneered in the more realistic education of women. Friends' schools were organized as soon as the size and prosperity of the settlements permitted them. This training emphasized housewifery but did include the fundamentals of literacy. Many of the earliest eighteenth-century Quaker primary schools were co-educational, though access to them was limited to the immediate community. Because these were concentrated in the Philadelphia area, girls born in Pennsylvania had a much better chance of acquiring some education than their contemporaries elsewhere. The Moravians (who also settled in the southeastern states) quickly recognized the general lack of facilities in the rest of the Colonies and offered boarding arrangements in a few of their schools. The student body soon included intrepid and homesick girls from New England and even the West Indies. These institutions were purposeful and rather solemn, the antithesis of superficiality. The Moravians insisted upon communal household chores as well as domestic skills, and in the eighteenth century these obligations could be onerous; dusting, sweeping, spinning, carding, and weaving came before embroidery and hemstitching. These homely lessons were enlivened by rhymes celebrating the pleasure of honest work. Examples survive in the seminary archives and supply a hint of the uplifting atmosphere:

> *I've spun seven cuts, dear companions allow*
> *That I am yet little, and know not right how;*
>
> *Mine twenty and four, which I finished with joy,*
> *And my hands and my feet did willing employ.*

Though the teaching sisters in these sectarian schools seem to have been kind and patient, the life was rigorous and strictly ordered, a distinct and not always popular alternative to pleasant afternoons with easygoing adventure masters. In an era when education for women was still widely regarded as a luxury for the upper classes, the appeal of the pioneering religious seminaries tended to be somewhat narrow. If a family happened to be sufficiently well-off to think of educating their girls, the tendency was to make fine ladies of them. As a result there were many young women who could carry a tune but not a number, who could model a passable wax apple but couldn't read a recipe, who had memorized the language of flowers but had only the vaguest grasp of English grammar. There seemed to be no middle ground between the austerities of the religious schools and the hollow frivolities offered by commercial ventures. Alternatives did not really exist until the

1820s, when the earliest tentative attempts were made to found independent academies and seminaries.

Catherine and Harriet Beecher, who were among the first to open a school designed to bridge the gulf, believed almost as strongly as the Moravians in the importance of domestic economy. They were, however, obliged by public demand to include a long list of dainty accomplishments in their Hartford curriculum. Many girls continued to regard the new secular seminaries as they had the adventure schools—as rival shops where they could browse or buy at will, dropping in and out at any time they chose. To the despair of the well-intentioned founders few students ever stayed to complete the course at any one place. Parents judged a school as if it were a buffet table, evaluating it by the number and variety of subjects displayed. In writing later of the difficult beginnings of the Hartford Seminary, Catherine Beecher said that "all was perpetual haste, imperfection, irregularity, and the merely mechanical commitment of words to memory, without any chance for imparting clear and connected ideas in a single branch of knowledge. The review of those days is like the memory of a troubled and distracting dream."

Public opinion about the education of girls continued to be sharply (if never clearly) divided until after the Civil War. Those who pioneered in the field were at the mercy of socially ambitious and ambivalent parents, confused and unevenly prepared students, and constantly shifting social attitudes. In sudden and disconcerting switches "the friends" of women's education often turned out to be less than wholehearted in their advocacy. Benjamin Rush, whose *Thoughts Upon Female Education,* written in 1787, influenced and inspired Emma Willard, Mary Lyon, and the Beecher sisters, later admitted that his thoughtful considerations had finally left him "not enthusiastical upon the subject." Even at his best, Rush sounds no more than tepid; American ladies, he wrote, "should be qualified to a certain degree by a peculiar and suitable education to concur in instructing their sons in the principles of liberty and government." During her long editorship of *Godey's Lady's Book* Sarah Josepha Hale welcomed every new female seminary and academy but faithfully reminded her readers that the sanctity of the home came first: ". . . on what does social well-being rest but in our homes. . . ?" "Oh, spare our homes!" was a constant refrain, this chorus coming from the September, 1856, issue. *Godey's Lady's Book* reflects the pervasive nineteenth-century fear that the educated woman might be a threat to the established and symbiotic pattern of American family life. The totally ignorant woman, on the other hand, was something of an embarrassment to the new nation. The country was inundated by visiting European journalists during this period, and they invariably commented upon the dullness of our social life and the disappointing vacuity of the sweet-faced girls and handsome matrons they met. Though Americans themselves seemed to feel safer with a bore than with a bluestocking, they were forced to give the matter some worried thought.

"If all our girls become philosophers," the critics asked, "who will darn our stockings and cook the meals?" It was widely, if somewhat irrationally, assumed that a maiden who had learned continental stichery upon fine lawn might heave to and sew up a shirt if necessary, but few men believed that a woman who had once tasted the heady delights of Shakespeare's plays would ever have dinner ready on time— or at all.

13

HORIZONTAL BAR.

14

THE TRIANGLE.

15

STOOPING FORWARD.

16

BENDING BACKWARD.

A series of genteel exercises for genteel young ladies from Godey's Lady's Book. *How the young ladies managed to perform much, if any, serious exercise swathed in those voluminous skirts remains something of a mystery.*

The founders of female seminaries were obliged to cater to this unease by modifying their plans and their pronouncements accordingly. The solid academic subjects were so generally thought irrelevant for "housewives and helpmates" that it was usually necessary to disguise them as something more palatable. The Beechers taught their girls chemistry at Hartford but were careful to assure parents and prospective husbands that its principles were applicable in the kitchen. The study of mathematics could be justified by its usefulness in running a household. Eventually the educators grew more daring, recommending geology as a means toward understanding the Deluge and other Biblical mysteries and suggesting geography and even history as suitable because these studies would "enlarge women's sphere of thought, rendering them more interesting as companions to men of science." There is, however, little evidence that many were converted to this extreme point of view. The average nineteenth-century American man was not at all keen on chat with an interesting companion, preferring a wife like the one in the popular jingle *"who never learnt the art of schooling/Untamed with the itch of ruling."* The cliché of the period was "woman's sphere." The phrase was so frequently repeated that it acquires almost physical qualities. Woman's Sphere—the nineteenth-century woman was fixed and sealed within it like a model ship inside a bottle. To tamper with the arrangement was to risk ruining a complex and fragile structure that had been painstakingly assembled over the course of two centuries. Just one ill-considered jolt might make matchwood of the entire apparatus.

In 1812 the anonymous author of *Sketches of the History, Genius, and Disposition of the Fair Sex* wrote that women are "born for a life of uniformity and dependence. . . . Were it in your power to give them genius, it would be almost always a useless and very often a dangerous present. It would, in general, make them regret the station which Providence has assigned them, or have recourse to unjustifiable ways to get from it." The writer identified himself only as a "friend of the sex" (not actually specifying which one).

This century's feminists may rage at and revel in such quotes, but the nineteenth-century educators were forced to live with this attitude and work within and around it. In order to gain any public or private support for women's secondary schools they had to prove that a woman would not desert her husband and children as soon as she could write a legible sentence or recite a theorem. That fear was genuine, and the old arguments resurfaced again and again. What about Saint Paul's injunction? What about the sanctity of the home? What about the health of the future mothers of the race? What about supper?

Advocates of secondary education for women, therefore, became consummate politicians, theologians, hygienists, and, when necessary, apologists. "It is desirable," wrote Mary Lyon in 1834 of her Mount Holyoke Female Seminary project, "that the plans relating to the subject should not seem to originate with us but with benevolent *gentlemen*. If the object should excite attention there is danger that many good men will fear the effect on society of so much female influence and what they will call female greatness." New and subtle counterarguments were presented with great delicacy. God had entrusted the tender minds of children to women; therefore women were morally obliged to teach. The home would be a holier place if the chatelaine understood religious principles and could explain them. The founders of Abbot Academy proclaimed that "to form the immortal mind to habits suited to an immortal being, and to instill principles of conduct and form the character for an immortal destiny, shall be subordinate to no other care." All that harping on immortality went down smoothly in the evangelistic atmosphere of the 1820s. A thick coating of religion was applied to every new educational venture. The parents of prospective students were assured that their daughters would not only study religion in class but would have twice-daily periods of silent meditation, frequent revival meetings, and a Sunday that included all of these. In reading the early seminary catalogues, one finds it hard to see where secular studies could have fit in at all. To the religious guarantees were appended promises of careful attention to health. The educators lost no time in adding the new science of calisthenics to their curricula. They had the medical records of their students compared to that of the public at large and published the gratifying results in newspapers and magazines. Domestic work was also to be required of girls who attended the new seminaries, partly for economy's sake but mainly so that they would not forget their ultimate destiny.

All of this was calming and persuasive, but nothing was so effective as simple economics. By the 1830s most states had begun a program of primary public education. As the West followed suit the need for teachers became acute and desperate. Men were not attracted to the profession because the pay was wretched, the living conditions were lonely, and the status of a schoolmaster was negligible if not downright laughable. Saint Paul was revised, updated, and finally reversed. He had not, after all, envisioned the one-room schoolhouses of the American prairies, the wages of three dollars a month, or the practice of "boarding around."

Within an astonishingly short time fears for female health subsided. The first women teachers proved amazingly durable, able to withstand every rigor of frontier life. In a letter to her former headmistress one alumna of the Hartford Seminary described accommodations out west:

> I board where there are eight children, and the parents, and only two rooms in the house. I must do as the family do about washing, as there is but one basin, and no place to go to wash but out the door. I have not enjoyed the luxury of either lamp or candle, their only light being a cup of grease with a rag for a wick. Evening is my only time to write, but this kind of light makes such a disagreeable smoke and smell, I cannot bear it, and do without light, except the fire. I occupy a room with three of the children and a niece who boards here. The other room serves as a kitchen, parlor, and bedroom for the rest of the family. . . .

Other graduates were just as stoical and often no more comfortable:

> I board with a physician, and the house has only two rooms. One serves as kitchen, eating, and sitting room; the other, where I lodge, serves also as the doctor's office, and there is no time, night or day, when I am not liable to interruption.
>
> My school embraces both sexes, and all ages from five to seventeen, and not one can read intelligibly. They have no idea of the proprieties of the schoolroom or of study. . . . My furniture consists now of . . . benches, a single board put up against

the side of the room for a writing desk, a few bricks for andirons, and a stick of wood for shovel and tongs.

These letters were collected by Catherine Beecher in her book *True Remedy for the Wrongs of Women,* which advanced the cause of women's education by showing the worthwhile uses to which it could be put. Delighted with the early results, several states quickly set up committees to consider training women teachers on a larger scale. Their findings were favorable, though couched in oddly ambiguous language. New York's group reported that women seemed to be "endued with peculiar faculties" for the occupation. "While man's nature is rough, stern, impatient, ambitious, hers is gentle, tender, enduring, unaspiring." That was most encouraging, but the gentlemen also generously acknowledged that "the habits of female teachers are better and their morals purer; they are much more apt to be content with, and continue in, the occupation of teaching." A Michigan report stated in 1842 that "an elementary school, where the rudiments of an English education only are taught, such as reading, spelling, writing, and the outlines barely of geography, arithmetic, and grammar, requires a female of practical common sense with amiable and winning manners, a patient spirit, and a tolerable knowledge of the springs of human action. A female thus qualified, carrying with her into the schoolroom the gentle influences of her sex, will do more to inculcate right morals and prepare the youthful intellect for the severer discipline of its after years, than the most accomplished and learned male teacher." Far from objecting to these rather condescending statements, the founders of the struggling seminaries were more than happy to hear them. Even the miserable wages offered to teachers could be regarded as an advantage, since they provided the single most effective argument for more female academies. "But where are we to raise such an army of teachers as are required for this great work?" asked Catherine Beecher in the same book that contained the letters from her ex-students. "Not from the sex which finds it so much more honorable, easy, and lucrative, to enter the many roads to wealth and honor open in this land. . . . It is WOMAN who is to come [forth] at this emergency, and meet the demand—woman, whom experience and testimony have shown to be the best, as well as the cheapest guardian and teacher of childhood, in the school as well as the nursery."

Teaching became a woman's profession by default and by rationalization. Clergymen and theologians suddenly had nothing but praise for women teachers. God must have meant them to teach because he made them so good at it. They would work for a half or a third of the salary demanded by a man. What, after all, was a schoolroom but an extension of the home, woman's natural sphere? And if females had to have schools of their own to prepare them for this holy mission, then so be it. Future American generations must not be allowed to suffer for want of instruction when a Troy, Hartford, or Mount Holyoke girl asked no more than three dollars a month, safe escort to the boondocks, and a candle of her own.

Everyday Life Before the Civil War

Jack Larkin

Some of the most difficult things to learn about the past are not the things that were obscure and unusual but those that were so obvious that the people of the time did not think them worth mentioning. Matters that historians have had the greatest difficulty discovering are often ones that at the time almost no one thought worth describing because they were common knowledge. Much that we know about life in early America we know because foreign travelers were struck by manners and customs of the people that to them seemed different from those of their native lands. But the very reason the behavior seemed notable to an outsider—that it was characteristic of the society—often meant that to Americans it was ordinary or "normal," something "everyone" already knew. Similarly, while people naturally take care of and preserve fine jewelry and expensive furniture, "everyday" objects central to their existence tend to get used up and discarded and thus are rare and hard to find in later years.

Of course everyday objects and attitudes can be discovered and recovered, and from them historians can learn an enormous amount about why people did the "unimportant" things that interest us today and why they held the beliefs that led to those actions. In this essay Jack Larkin, Chief Historian at Old Sturbridge Village restoration in Massachusetts, presents a miscellany of information about early nineteenth-century life, information that Americans of those years would have taken for granted but that to modern readers is fascinating.

Contemporary observers of early-nineteenth-century America left a fragmentary but nonetheless fascinating and revealing picture of the manner in which rich and poor, Southerner and Northerner, farmer and city dweller, freeman and slave presented themselves to the world. To begin with, a wide variety of characteristic facial expressions, gestures, and ways of carrying the body reflected the extraordinary regional and social diversity of the young republic.

When two farmers met in early-nineteenth-century New England, wrote Francis Underwood, of Enfield, Massachusetts, the author of a pioneering 1893 study of small-town life, "their greeting might seem to a stranger gruff or surly, since the facial muscles were so inexpressive, while, in fact, they were on excellent terms." In courtship and marriage, countrymen and women were equally constrained, with couples "wearing all unconsciously the masks which custom had prescribed; and the onlookers who did not know the secret . . . would think them cold and indifferent."

The Yankees, however, were not the stiffest Americans. Even by their own impassive standards, New Englanders found New York Dutchmen and Pennsylvania German farmers "clumsy and chill" or "dull and stolid." But the "wild Irish" stood out in America for precisely the opposite reason. They were not "chill" or "stolid" enough, but loud and expansive. Their expressiveness made Anglo-Americans uncomfortable.

The seemingly uncontrolled physical energy of American blacks left many whites ill at ease. Of the slaves celebrating at a plantation ball, it was "impossible to describe the things these people did with their bodies," Frances Kemble Butler, an English-born actress who married a Georgia slave owner, observed, "and above all with their faces. . . ." Blacks' expressions and gestures, their preference for rhythmic rather than rigid bodily motion, their alternations of energy and rest made no cultural sense to observers who saw only "antics and frolics," "laziness," or "savagery." Sometimes perceived as obsequious, childlike, and dependent, or sullen and inexpressive, slaves also wore masks—not "all unconsciously" as Northern farm folk did, but as part of their self-protective strategies for controlling what masters, mistresses, and other whites could know about their feelings and motivations.

American city dwellers, whose daily routines were driven by the quicker pace of commerce, were easy to distinguish from "heavy and slouching" farmers attuned to slow seasonal rhythms. New Yorkers, in particular, had already acquired their own characteristic body language. The clerks and commercial men who crowded Broadway, intent on their business, had a universal "contraction of the brow, knitting of the eyebrows, and compression of the lips . . . and a hurried walk." It was a popular American saying in the 1830s, reported Frederick Marryat, an Englishman who traveled extensively in the period, that "a New York merchant always walks as if he had a good dinner before him, and a bailiff behind him."

Early-nineteenth-century Americans lived in a world of dirt, insects, and pungent smells. Farmyards were strewn with animal wastes, and farmers wore manure-spattered boots and trousers everywhere. Men's and women's working clothes alike were often stiff with dirt and dried sweat, and men's shirts were often stained with "yellow rivulets" of tobacco juice. The locations of privies were all too obvious on warm or windy days. Unemptied chamber pots advertised their presence. Wet baby "napkins," today's diapers, were not immediately washed but simply put by the fire to dry. . . .

Densely populated, but poorly cleaned and drained, America's cities were often far more noisome than its farmyards. Horse manure thickly covered city streets, and few neighborhoods were free from the spreading stench of tanneries and slaughterhouses. New York City accumulated so much refuse that it was generally believed the actual surfaces of the streets had not been seen for decades. During her stay in Cincinnati, the English writer Frances Trollope followed the practice of the vast majority of American city housewives when she threw her household "slops"—refuse food and dirty dishwater—out into the street. An irate neighbor soon informed her that municipal ordinances forbade "throwing such things at the sides of the streets" as she had done; "they must just all be cast right into the middle and the pigs soon takes them off." In most cities hundreds, sometimes thousands, of free-roaming pigs scavenged the garbage; one exception was Charleston, South Carolina, where buzzards patrolled the streets. By converting garbage into pork, pigs kept city streets cleaner than they would otherwise have been, but the pigs themselves befouled the streets and those who ate their meat—primarily poor families—ran greater than usual risks of infection.

A runaway pig creates mayhem on a city street.

The most visible symbols of early American sanitation were privies or "necessary houses." But Americans did not always use them; many rural householders simply took to the closest available patch of woods or brush. However, in more densely settled communities and in regions with cold winters, privies were in widespread use. They were not usually put in out-of-the-way locations. The fashion of some Northern farm families, according to Robert B. Thomas's *Farmer's Almanack* in 1826, had long been to have their "necessary planted in a garden or other conspicuous place." Other countryfolk went even further in turning human wastes to agricultural account and built their outhouses "within the territory of a hog yard, that the swine may root and ruminate and devour the nastiness thereof." Thomas was a long-standing critic of primitive manners in the countryside and roundly condemned these traditional sanitary arrangements as demonstrating a "want of taste, decency, and propriety." . . .

Sleeping accommodations in American country taverns were often dirty and insect-ridden. The eighteenth-century observer of American life Isaac Weld saw "filthy beds swarming with bugs" in 1794; in 1840 Charles Dickens noted "a sort of game not on the bill of fare." Complaints increased in intensity as travelers went south or west. Tavern beds were uniquely vulnerable to infestation by whatever insect guests travelers brought with them. The bedding of most American households was surely less foul. Yet it was dirty enough. New England farmers were still too often "tormented all night by bed bugs," complained *The Farmer's Almanack* in 1837, and books of domestic advice contained extensive instructions on removing them from feather beds and straw ticks.

Journeying between Washington and New Orleans in 1828, Margaret Hall, a well-to-do and cultivated Scottish woman, became far more familiar with intimate insect life than she had ever been in the genteel houses of London or Edinburgh. Her letters home, never intended for publication, gave a graphic and unsparing account of American sanitary conditions. After sleeping in a succession of beds with the "usual complement of fleas and bugs," she and her party had themselves become infested: "We bring them along with us in our clothes and when I undress I find them crawling on my skin, nasty wretches." New and distasteful to her, such discoveries were commonplace among the ordinary folk with whom she lodged. The American children she saw on her Southern journey were "kept in such a state of filth," with clothes "dirty and slovenly to a degree," but this was "nothing in comparison with their heads . . . [which] are absolutely crawling!" In New Orleans she observed women picking through children's heads for lice, "catching them according to the method depicted in an engraving of a similar proceeding in the streets of Naples."

Americans were not "clean and decent" by today's standards, and it was virtually impossible that they should be. The furnishings and use of rooms in most American houses made more than the most elementary washing difficult. In a New England farmer's household, wrote Underwood, each household member would "go down to the 'sink' in the lean-to, next to the kitchen, fortunate if he had not to break ice in order to wash his face and hands, or more fortunate if a little warm water was poured into his basin from the kettle swung over the kitchen fire." Even in the comfortable household of the prominent minister Lyman Beecher in Litchfield, Connecticut, around 1815, all family members washed in the kitchen, using a stone sink and "a couple of basins."

Southerners washed in their detached kitchens or, like Westerners in warm weather, washed outside, "at the doors . . . or at the wells" of their houses. Using basins and sinks outdoors or in full view of others, most Americans found anything more than "washing the face and hands once a-day," usually in cold water, difficult, even unthinkable. Most men and women also washed without soap, reserving it for laundering clothes; instead they used a brisk rubbing with a coarse towel to scrub the dirt off their skins.

Gradually the practice of complete bathing spread beyond the topmost levels of American society and into smaller towns and villages. This became possible as families moved washing equipment out of kitchens and into bedchambers, from shared space to space that could be made private. As more prosperous households furnished one or two of their chambers with washing equipment—a washstand, a basin, and a ewer, or large-mouthed pitcher—family members could shut the chamber door, undress, and wash themselves completely. The daughters of the Larcom family, living in Lowell, Massachusetts, in the late 1830s, began to bathe in a bedchamber in this way; Lucy Larcom described how her oldest sister started to take "a full cold bath every morning before she went to her work . . . in a room without a fire," and the other young Larcoms "did the same whenever we could be resolute enough." By the 1830s better city hotels and even some country taverns were providing individual basins and pitchers in their rooms.

At a far remove from "primitive manners" and "bad practices" was the genteel ideal of domestic sanitation embodied in the "chamber sets"—matching basin and ewer for private bathing, a cup for brushing the teeth, and a chamber pot with cover to minimize odor and spillage—that American stores were beginning to stock. By 1840 a significant minority of American households owned chamber sets and washstands to hold them in their bedchambers. For a handful there was the very faint dawning of an entirely new age of sanitary arrangements. In 1829 the new Tremont House hotel in Boston offered its patrons indoor plumbing: eight chambers with bathtubs and eight "water closets." In New York City and Philadelphia, which had developed rudimentary public water systems, a few wealthy households had water taps and, more rarely, water closets by the 1830s. For all others flush toilets and bathtubs remained far in the future. . . .

In the early part of the century America was a bawdy, hard-edged, and violent land. We drank more than we ever had before or ever would again. We smoked and chewed tobacco like addicts and fought and quarreled on the flimsiest pretexts. The tavern was the most important gateway to the primarily male world of drink and disorder: in sight of the village church in most American communities, observed Daniel Drake, a Cincinnati physician who wrote a reminiscence of his Kentucky boyhood, stood the village tavern, and the two structures "did in fact represent two great opposing principles."

The great majority of American men in every region were taverngoers. The printed street directories of American cities listed tavernkeepers in staggering numbers, and even the best-churched parts of New England could show more "licensed houses" than meetinghouses. In 1827 the fast-growing city of Rochester, New York, with a population of approximately eight thousand, had nearly one hundred establishments licensed to sell liquor, or one for every eighty inhabitants.

America's most important centers of male sociability, taverns were often the scene of excited gaming and vicious fights and always of hard drinking, heavy smoking, and an enormous amount of alcohol-stimulated talk. City men came to their neighborhood taverns daily, and "tavern haunting, tippling, and gaming," as Samuel Goodrich, a New England historian and publisher, remembered, "were the chief resources of men in the dead and dreary winter months" in the countryside.

City taverns catered to clienteles of different classes: sordid sailors' grogshops near the waterfront were rife with brawling and prostitution; neighborhood taverns and liquor-selling groceries were visited by craftsmen and clerks: well-appointed and relatively decorous places were favored by substantial merchants. Taverns on busy highways often specialized in teamsters or stage passengers, while country inns took their patrons as they came.

Taverns accommodated women as travelers, but their barroom clienteles were almost exclusively male. Apart from the dockside dives frequented by prostitutes, or the liquor-selling groceries of poor city neighborhoods, women rarely drank in public. . . .

By almost any standard, Americans drank not only nearly universally but in large quantities. Their yearly consumption at the time of the Revolution has been estimated at the equivalent of three and one-half gallons of pure two-hundred-proof alcohol for each person. After 1790 American men began to drink even more. By the late 1820s their imbibing had risen to an all-time high of almost four gallons per capita.

Along with drinking went fighting. Americans fought often and with great relish. York, Pennsylvania, for example, was a peaceable place as American communities went, but the Miller and Weaver families had a long-running quarrel. It had begun in 1800 when the Millers found young George Weaver stealing apples in their yard and punished him by "throwing him over the fence," injuring him painfully. Over the years hostilities broke out periodically. Lewis Miller remembered walking down the street as a teenaged boy and meeting Mrs. Weaver, who drenched him with the bucket of water she was carrying. He retaliated by "turning about and giving her a kick, laughing at her, this is for your politeness." Other York households had their quarrels too; in "a general fight on Beaver Street," Mistress Hess and Mistress Forsch tore each other's caps from their heads. Their husbands and then the neighbors interfered and "all of them had a knock down.". . .

. . . White Southerners lived with a pervasive fear of the violent potential of their slaves, and the Nat Turner uprising in Virginia in 1831, when a party of slaves rebelled and killed whites before being overcome, gave rise to tighter and harsher controls. But in daily reality slaves had far more to fear from their masters.

Margaret Hall was no proponent of abolition and had little sympathy for black Americans. Yet in her travels south she confronted incidents of what she ironically called the "good treatment of slaves" that were impossible to ignore. At a country tavern in Georgia, she summoned the slave chambermaid, but "she could not come" because "the mistress had been whipping her and she was not fit to be seen. Next morning she made her appearance with her face marked in several places by the cuts of the cowskin and her neck handkerchief covered with spots of blood."

Southern stores were very much like Northern ones, Francis Kemble Butler observed, except that they stocked "negro-whips" and "mantraps" on their shelves. A few slaves were never beaten at all, and for most, whippings were not a daily or weekly occurrence. But they were, of all Americans, by far the most vulnerable to violence. All slaves had, as William Wells Brown, an ex-slave himself, said, often "heard the crack of the whip, and the screams of the slave" and knew that they were never more than a white man's or woman's whim away from a beating. . . .

Although it remained a powerful force in many parts of the United States, the American way of drunkenness began to lose ground as early as the mid-1820s. The powerful upsurge in liquor consumption had provoked a powerful reaction, an unprecedented attack on all forms of drink that gathered momentum in the Northeast. Some New England clergymen had been campaigning in their own communities as early as 1810, but their concerns took on organized impetus with the founding of the American Temperance Society in 1826. Energized in part by a concern for social order, in part by evangelical piety, temperance reformers popularized a radically new way of looking at alcohol. The "good creature" became "demon rum"; prominent physicians and writers on physiology, like Benjamin Rush, told Americans that alcohol, traditionally considered healthy and fortifying, was actually a physical and moral poison. National and state societies distributed anti-liquor tracts, at first calling for moderation in drink but increasingly demanding total abstinence from alcohol.

To a surprising degree these aggressive temperance campaigns worked. By 1840 the consumption of alcohol had declined by more than two-thirds, from close to four gallons per person each year to less than one and one-half. Country storekeepers gave up the sale of spirits, local authorities limited the number of tavern licenses, and farmers even abandoned hard cider and cut down their apple orchards. The shift to temperance was a striking transformation in the everyday habits of an enormous number of Americans. "A great, though silent change," in Horace Greeley's words, had been "wrought in public sentiment."

But although the "great change" affected some Americans everywhere, it had a very uneven impact. Organized temperance reform was sharply delimited by geography. Temperance societies were enormously powerful in New England and western New York, and numerous in eastern New York, New Jersey, and Pennsylvania. More than three-fourths of all recorded temperance pledges came from these states. In the South and West, and in the laborers' and artisans' neighborhoods of the cities, the campaign against drink was much weaker. In many places drinking ways survived and even flourished, but as individuals and families came under the influence of militant evangelical piety, their "men of business and sobriety" increased gradually in number. . . .

Whipping and the pillory, with their attentive audiences, began to disappear from the statute book, to be replaced by terms of imprisonment in another new American institution, the state penitentiary. Beginning with Pennsylvania's abolition of flogging in 1790 and Massachusetts's elimination of mutilating punishments in 1805, several American states gradually accepted John Hancock's view of 1796 that "mutilating or lacerating the body" was less an effective punishment than "an indignity to human nature." Connecticut's town constables whipped petty criminals for the last time in 1828.

Slaveholding states were far slower to change their provisions for public punishment. The whipping and mutilation of blacks may have become a little less ferocious over the decades, but the whip remained the essential instrument of punishment and discipline. "The secret of our success," thought a slave owner, looking back after emancipation, had been "the great motive power contained in that little instrument." Delaware achieved notoriety by keeping flogging on the books for whites and blacks alike through most of the twentieth century.

Although there were important stirrings of sentiment against capital punishment, all American states continued to execute convicted murderers before the mid-1840s. Public hangings never lost their drawing power. But a number of American public officials began to abandon the long-standing view of executions as instructive communal rituals. They saw the crowd's holiday mood and eager participation as sharing too much in the condemned killer's own brutality. Starting with Pennsylvania, New York, and Massachusetts in the mid-1830s, several state legislatures voted to take executions away from the crowd, out of the public realm. Sheriffs began to carry out death sentences behind the walls of the jailyard, before a small assembly of representative onlookers. Other states clung much longer to tradition and continued public executions into the twentieth century.

Early-nineteenth-century Americans were more licentious than we ordinarily imagine them to be.

"On the 20th day of July" in 1830, Harriet Winter, a young woman working as a domestic in Joseph Dunham's household in Brimfield, Massachusetts, "was gathering raspberries" in a field west of the house. "Near the close of day," Charles Phelps, a farm laborer then living in the town, "came to the field where she was," and in the gathering dusk they made love—and, Justice of the Peace Asa Lincoln added in his account, "it was the Sabbath." American communities did not usually document their inhabitants' amorous rendezvous, and Harriet's tryst with Charles was a commonplace event in early-nineteenth-century America. It escaped historical oblivion because she was unlucky, less in becoming pregnant than in Charles's refusal to marry her. Asa Lincoln did not approve of Sabbath evening indiscretions, but he was not pursuing Harriet for immorality. He was concerned instead with economic responsibility for the child. Thus he interrogated Harriet about the baby's father—while she was in labor, as was the long-customary practice—in order to force Charles to contribute to the maintenance of the child, who was going to be "born a bastard and chargeable to the town."

Some foreign travelers found that the Americans they met were reluctant to admit that such things happened in the United States. They were remarkably straitlaced about sexual matters in public and eager to insist upon the "purity" of their manners. But to take such protestations at face value, the unusually candid Englishman Frederick Marryat thought, would be "to suppose that human nature is not the same everywhere."

The well-organized birth and marriage records of a number of American communities reveal that in late-eighteenth-century America pregnancy was frequently the prelude to marriage. The proportion of brides who were pregnant at the time of their weddings had been rising since the late seventeenth century and peaked in the turbulent decades during and after the Revolution. In the 1780s and 1790s nearly one-third of rural New England's brides were already with child. The frequency of sexual intercourse before marriage was surely higher, since some couples would have escaped early pregnancy. For many couples sexual relations were part of serious courtship. Premarital pregnancies in late-eighteenth-century Dedham, Massachusetts, observed the local historian Erastus Worthington in 1828, were occasioned by "the custom then prevalent of females admitting young men to their beds, who sought their company in marriage."

Pregnancies usually simply accelerated a marriage that would have taken place in any case, but community and parental pressure worked strongly to assure it. Most rural communities simply accepted the "early" pregnancies that marked so many marriages, although in Hingham, Massachusetts, tax records suggest that the families of well-to-do brides were considerably less generous to couples who had had "early babies" than to those who had avoided pregnancy. . . .

Most Americans—and the American common law—still did not regard abortion as a crime until the fetus had "quickened" or began to move perceptibly in the womb. Books of medical advice actually contained prescriptions for bringing on delayed menstrual periods, which would also produce an abortion if the woman happened to be pregnant. They suggested heavy doses of purgatives that created violent cramps, powerful douches, or extreme kinds of physical activity, like the "violent exercise, raising great weights . . . strokes on the belly . . . [and] falls" noted in William Buchan's *Domestic Medicine*, a manual read widely through the 1820s. Women's folklore echoed most of these prescriptions and added others, particularly the use of two American herbal preparations—savin, or the extract of juniper berries, and Seneca snakeroot—as abortion-producing drugs. They were dangerous procedures but sometimes effective.

Starting at the turn of the nineteenth century, the sexual lives of many Americans began to change, shaped by a growing insistence on control: reining in the passions in courtship, limiting family size, and even redefining male and female sexual desire.

Bundling was already on the wane in rural America before 1800; by the 1820s it was written about as a rare and antique custom. It had ceased, thought an elderly man from East Haddam, Connecticut, "as a consequence of education and refinement." Decade by decade the proportion of young women who had conceived a child before marriage declined. In most of the towns of New England the rate had dropped from nearly one pregnant bride in three to one in five or six by 1840; in some places prenuptial pregnancy dropped to 5 percent. For many young Americans this marked the acceptance of new limits on sexual behavior, imposed not by their parents or other authorities in their communities but by themselves.

These young men and women were not more closely supervised by their parents than earlier generations had been; in fact, they had more mobility and greater freedom. The couples that courted in the new style put a far greater emphasis on control of the passions. For some of them—young Northern merchants and professional men and their intended brides—revealing love letters have survived for the years after 1820. Their intimate correspondence reveals that they did not give up sexual expression but gave it new boundaries, reserving sexual intercourse for marriage. Many of them were marrying later than their parents, often living through long engagements while the husband-to-be strove to establish his place in the world. They chose not to risk a pregnancy that would precipitate them into an early marriage.

Many American husbands and wives were also breaking with tradition as they began to limit the size of their families. Clearly, married couples were renegotiating the terms of their sexual lives together, but they remained resolutely silent about how they did it. In the first two decades of the nineteenth century, they almost certainly set about avoiding childbirth through abstinence; coitus interruptus, or male withdrawal; and perhaps sometimes abortion. These contraceptive techniques had long been traditional in preindustrial Europe, although previously little used in America.

As they entered the 1830s, Americans had their first opportunity to learn, at least in print, about more effective or less self-denying forms of birth control. They could read reasonably inexpensive editions of the first works on contraception published in the United States: Robert Dale Owen's *Moral Physiology* of 1831 and Dr.

Charles Knowlton's *The Fruits of Philosophy* of 1832. Both authors frankly described the full range of contraceptive techniques, although they solemnly rejected physical intervention in the sexual act and recommended only douching after intercourse and coitus interruptus. Official opinion, legal and religious, was deeply hostile. Knowlton, who had trained as a physician in rural Massachusetts, was prosecuted in three different counties for obscenity, convicted once, and imprisoned for three months.

But both works found substantial numbers of Americans eager to read them. By 1839 each book had gone through nine editions, putting a combined total of twenty to thirty thousand copies in circulation. . . .

"Everyone smokes and some chew in America," wrote Isaac Weld in 1795. Americans turned tobacco, a new and controversial stimulant at the time of colonial settlement, into a crucially important staple crop and made its heavy use a commonplace—and a never-ending source of surprise and indignation to visitors. Tobacco use spread in the United States because it was comparatively cheap, a homegrown product free from the heavy import duties levied on it by European governments. A number of slave rations described in plantation documents included "one hand of tobacco per month." Through the eighteenth century most American smokers used clay pipes, which are abundant in colonial archeological sites, although some men and women dipped snuff or inhaled powdered tobacco.

Where the smokers of early colonial America "drank" or gulped smoke through the short, thick stems of their seventeenth-century pipes, those of 1800 inhaled it more slowly and gradually; from the early seventeenth to the late eighteenth century, pipe stems became steadily longer and narrower, increasingly distancing smokers from their burning tobacco.

In the 1790s cigars, or "segars," were introduced from the Caribbean. Prosperous men widely took them up; they were the most expensive way to consume tobacco, and it was a sign of financial security to puff away on "longnines" or "principe cigars at three cents each" while the poor used clay pipes and much cheaper "cut plug" tobacco. After 1800 in American streets, barrooms, stores, public conveyances, and even private homes it became nearly impossible to avoid tobacco chewers. Chewing extended tobacco use, particularly into workplaces; men who smoked pipes at home or in the tavern barroom could chew while working in barns or workshops where smoking carried the danger of fire.

"In all the public places of America." wrote Charles Dickens, multitudes of men engaged in "the odious practice of chewing and expectoration," a recreation practiced by all ranks of American society. Chewing stimulated salivation and gave rise to a public environment of frequent and copious spitting, where men every few minutes were "squirting a mouthful of saliva through the room."

Spittoons were provided in the more meticulous establishments, but men often ignored them. The floors of American public buildings were not pleasant to contemplate. A courtroom in New York City in 1833 was decorated by a "mass of abomination" contributed to by "judges, counsel, jury, witnesses, officers, and audience."

The Americans of 1820 would have been more recognizable to us in the informal and egalitarian way they treated one another. The traditional signs of deference before social superiors—the deep bow, the "courtesy," the doffed cap, lowered

head, and averted eyes—had been a part of social relationships in colonial America. In the 1780s, wrote the American poetess Lydia Huntley Sigourney in 1824,
there were still "individuals . . . in every grade of society" who had grown up "when
a bow was not an offense to fashion nor . . . a relic of monarchy." But in the early
nineteenth century such signals of subordination rapidly fell away. It was a natural
consequence of the Revolution, she maintained, which, "in giving us liberty, obliterated almost every vestige of politeness of the 'old school.'" Shaking hands became the accustomed American greeting between men, a gesture whose symmetry
and mutuality signified equality. Frederick Marryat found in 1835 that it was "invariably the custom to shake hands" when he was introduced to Americans and that
he could not carefully grade the acknowledgement he would give to new acquaintances according to their signs of wealth and breeding. He found instead that he
had to "go on shaking hands here, there and everywhere, and with everybody."
Americans were not blind to inequalities of economic and social power, but they
less and less gave them overt physical expression. Bred in a society where such distinctions were far more clearly spelled out, Marryat was somewhat disoriented in
the United States; "it is impossible to know who is who," he claimed, "in this land of
equality."

Well-born British travelers encountered not just confusion but conflict when
they failed to receive the signs of respect they expected. Margaret Hall's letters
home during her Southern travels outlined a true comedy of manners. At every
stage stop in the Carolinas, Georgia, and Alabama, she demanded that country tavernkeepers and their households give her deferential service and well-prepared
meals; she received instead rancid bacon and "such an absence of all kindness of
feeling, such unbending frigid heartlessness." But she and her family had a far
greater share than they realized in creating this chilly reception. Squeezed between the pride and poise of the great planters and the social debasement of the
slaves, small Southern farmers often displayed a prickly insolence, a considered
lack of response, to those who too obviously considered themselves their betters.
Greatly to their discomfort and incomprehension, the Halls were experiencing
what a British traveler more sympathetic to American ways, Patrick Shirreff, called
"the democratic rudeness which assumed or presumptuous superiority seldom fails
to experience."

In the seventeenth century white American colonials were no taller than their
European counterparts, but by the time of the Revolution they were close to their
late-twentieth-century average height for men of slightly over five feet eight inches.
The citizens of the early republic towered over most Europeans. Americans' early
achievement of modern stature—by a full century and more—was a striking consequence of American abundance. Americans were taller because they were better
nourished than the great majority of the world's peoples.

Yet not all Americans participated equally in the nation's abundance. Differences in stature between whites and blacks, and between city and country dwellers,
echoed those between Europeans and Americans. Enslaved blacks were a full inch
shorter than whites. But they remained a full inch taller than European peasants
and laborers and were taller still than their fellow slaves eating the scanty diets afforded by the more savagely oppressive plantation system of the West Indies. And

by 1820 those who lived in the expanding cities of the United States—even excluding immigrants whose heights would have reflected European, not American, conditions—were noticeably shorter than the people of the countryside, suggesting an increasing concentration of poverty and poorer diets in urban places.

Across the United States almost all country households ate the two great American staples: corn and "the eternal pork," as one surfeited traveler called it, "which makes its appearance on every American table, high and low, rich and poor." Families in the cattle-raising, dairying country of New England, New York, and northern Ohio ate butter, cheese, and salted beef as well as pork and made their bread from wheat flour or rye and Indian corn. In Pennsylvania, as well as Maryland, Delaware, and Virginia, Americans ate the same breadstuffs as their Northern neighbors, but their consumption of cheese and beef declined every mile southward in favor of pork.

Farther to the south, and in the West, corn and corn-fed pork were truly "eternal"; where reliance on them reached its peak in the Southern uplands, they were still the only crops many small farmers raised. Most Southern and Western families built their diets around smoked and salted bacon, rather than the Northerners' salt pork, and, instead of wheat or rye bread, made cornpone or hoecake, a coarse, strong bread, and hominy, pounded Indian corn boiled together with milk.

Before 1800, game—venison, possum, raccoon, and wild fowl—was for many American households "a substantial portion of the supply of food at certain seasons of the year," although only on the frontier was it a regular part of the diet. In the West and South this continued to be true, but in the Northeast game became increasingly rare as forests gave way to open farmland, where wild animals could not live. . . . The old ways, so startlingly unfamiliar to the modern reader, gradually fell away. Americans changed their assumptions about what was proper, decent, and normal in everyday life in directions that would have greatly surprised most of the men and women of the early republic. Some aspects of their "primitive manners" succumbed to campaigns for temperance and gentility, while others evaporated with the later growth of mass merchandising and mass communications.

Important patterns of regional, class, and ethnic distinctiveness remain in American everyday life. But they are far less powerful, and less central to understanding American experience, than they once were. Through the rest of the nineteenth century and into the twentieth, the United States became ever more diverse, with new waves of Eastern and Southern European immigrants joining the older Americans of Northern European stock. Yet the new arrivals—and even more, their descendants—have experienced the attractiveness and reshaping power of a national culture formed by department stores, newspapers, radios, movies, and universal public education. America, the developing nation, developed into us. And perhaps our manners and morals, to some future observer, will seem as idiosyncratic and astonishing as this portrait of our earlier self.

Prison "Reform" in America

Roger T. Pray

One of the puzzles about American society is the fact that while throughout its history the country has been one of the richest and most free in the world, a land of opportunity and a happy place where (in Jefferson's words) there was enough land to support "a thousand generations" of future citizens, it has also had a reputation for lawlessness, home to an extremely large number of criminals. It has also, as Roger T. Pray points out in this essay, been a country where much attention has been devoted to the search for ways to prevent crime, showing criminals the error of their ways by locking them up and attempting to reform them. As early as the 1830s American methods of treating criminals were famous. One of the greatest European students of American society, the Frenchman Alexis de Tocqueville, developed his understanding of America while on an official mission to examine American prison systems.

Roger T. Pray is a prison psychologist, currently a researcher with the Utah Department of Correction.

Prisons are a fact of life in America. However unsatisfactory and however well-concealed they may be, we cannot imagine doing without them. They remain such a fundamental bulwark against crime and criminals that we now keep a larger portion of our population in prisons than any other nation except the Soviet Union and South Africa, and for terms that are longer than in many countries. Furthermore, we Americans invented the prison.

It was created by humanitarians in Philadelphia in 1790 and spread from there to other cities in the United States and Europe. The stubborn questions that perplex us today about how prisons can and should work—what they can achieve and how they might fail—began to be asked almost as soon as the first one opened. The history of prisons in America is the history of a troubled search for solutions.

Before there were prisons, serious crimes were almost always redressed by corporal or capital punishment. Institutions like the Bastille and the Tower of London mainly held political prisoners, not ordinary criminals. Jails existed, but primarily for pretrial detention. The closest thing to the modern prison was the workhouse, a place of hard labor almost exclusively for minor offenders, derelicts, and vagrants. Once a felon was convicted, he was punished bodily or fined but not incarcerated. Today's system, where imprisonment is a common penalty for a felony, is a historical newcomer.

The colonists did not have prisons. Until the Revolution they were required to follow the British criminal code, which depended heavily on corporal and capital punishment. The code applied to religious offenses as well as secular ones, and it was sometimes hard to tell the difference. A condemned man about to be executed commonly had to face his coffin while a clergyman exhorted the congregation to avoid this soul's plight. Crimes that didn't warrant the death penalty were dealt with by fines (especially for the rich) or "sanguinary" punishments, such as flogging and mutilation (more often for the less well-off).

Many colonial punishments were designed to terrorize offenders and hold them up to ridicule. The ducking stool, the stocks and the pillory, branding of the hand or forehead, and public flogging were all commonplace.

Many crimes were punishable by death. In Pennsylvania between 1718 and 1776, under the British penal code, execution could be prescribed for high treason, petty treason, murder, burglary, rape, sodomy, buggery, malicious maiming, manslaughter by stabbing, witchcraft by conjuration, and arson. All other felonies were capital on a second conviction. The death penalty was usually carried out by hanging, although stoning, breaking on the rack, and burning at the stake were not unknown.

Toward the end of the 1700s people began to realize that cruel physical retribution did little to curb crime; more important, society was experiencing changes that would profoundly affect penology. The nation's population began to increase dramatically. As people began to move around more frequently and easily, the effectiveness of ridicule naturally declined. People began to perceive the old penal code and its punishments as not only obsolete and barbaric but also foreign, left over from the hated British. A more just American solution should and could be developed.

Ironically the search for new punishments was to rely heavily on new ideas imported from Europe in the writings of such social thinkers of the Enlightenment as the baron de Montesquieu, Voltaire, Thomas Paine, and Cesare Beccaria. Whereas the Calvinists of colonial times had regarded man as basically depraved, these thinkers saw him as essentially good. It followed that a criminal could be rehabilitated. And since all men now were held to be born free and equal, even the worst were entitled to certain elementary rights to life, ultimate liberty, and at least some chance to pursue happiness.

The European theorizer who had the most direct influence upon penology was Beccaria, the Italian author of an influential 1764 essay, *On Crimes and Punishments*. Beccaria, a nobleman, had become deeply concerned about the deplorable treatment of criminals in his country. His work had a profound effect on criminal punishment the world over.

Beccaria wrote that "the purpose of punishment is not to torment a sensible being, or to undo a crime [but] is none other than to prevent the criminal from doing further injury to society and to prevent others from committing the like offense." He urged that accused criminals be treated humanely prior to trial and be afforded every opportunity to present evidence in their own behalf. Trials should be speedy, and secret accusations and torture to extract confessions abolished. He also wrote that overly harsh and inequitably applied laws caused more problems than they alleviated. "The severity of the punishment," he wrote, "of itself emboldens men to commit the very wrongs it is supposed to prevent. They are driven to commit additional crimes to avoid the punishment for a single one. . . . The certainty of a punishment, even if it be moderate, will always make a stronger impression than the fear of another which is more terrible but combined with the hope of impunity."

Beccaria believed the answer was to make punishments fit specific crimes. His writings had such enormous impact in this country that by the early 1800s most states had amended their criminal codes and strictly limited the death penalty to a few of the most serious crimes.

The largest ground swell for reform in America came from Quakers, and they played a crucial role in inventing the prison. Most of them lived in Pennsylvania and western New Jersey—in and around the nation's most important city, Philadelphia—and they were the only significant religious group to find brutal criminal punishments irreconcilable with their Christian beliefs. Toward the end of the eighteenth century, as new ideas about punishment spread, the Quakers set about to transform penal practices.

First, in 1786 they persuaded the Pennsylvania legislature to limit the death penalty to murder, treason, rape, and arson. People convicted of robbery, burglary, sodomy, or buggery would now have to give up their possessions and be imprisoned for up to ten years; if convicted of larceny, they could have to make double restitution (half to the state) and spend up to three years in prison. Next, the Quakers took on the terrible conditions in jails. Philadelphia jails locked up men and women in the same rooms at night. Inmates were thrown together with no regard for age, seriousness of offense, or ability to defend themselves. Liquor was sold on the premises. And detainees had to pay a fee to underwrite their own incarcerations, even if they were found innocent of any crime.

In 1787 the Quakers and their sympathizers formed the Philadelphia Society for Alleviating the Miseries of Public Prisons. Many prominent citizens took up the banner. In March, Dr. Benjamin Rush gave a lecture at the home of Benjamin Franklin in which he recommended dividing a large house into apartments for convicts, with special cells for the solitary confinement of troublesome inmates.

The Philadelphia Society soon persuaded the Pennsylvania legislature to convert a jail on Walnut Street into a prison for the confinement of convicted criminals from across the state. It was designed for two classes of inmates: serious offenders would be housed in sixteen solitary cells; less hardened ones would sleep in large rooms and would work together in shops. This became the first prison as we know it.

The creation of the Walnut Street prison in 1790 elicited tremendous enthusiasm in Philadelphia. It promised a vast improvement in the treatment of jailed offenders. And the initial results were very promising. Yearly commitments dropped from 131 in 1789 to just 45 in 1793. Burglars and pickpockets seemed to disappear from Philadelphia, and few discharged prisoners were caught committing new crimes. The Pennsylvania legislature was so impressed that it again amended the law in 1794 to reduce the number of crimes calling for capital punishment to just one: first-degree murder.

When society began putting into practice the new theories of penology, Americans became confident that a rational system of certain but humane punishment would vastly reduce crime. If colonial laws had contributed to crime, new laws would deter it. The prison was necessary, but the focus was on the laws, not on the

The prison at Walnut Street, established in Philadelphia in 1790, was the first in the world. By 1817 conditions had so deteriorated that it was considered a failure and described as a "seminar for vice."

nature of the prison. No one was yet arguing that life inside a prison would improve anybody.

The Walnut Street prison, the first in the world, served as the prototype for all other prisons built in this country over the next thirty years. But just as the Walnut Street Prison represented a dramatic departure from colonial practices, so developments in New York and Pennsylvania in the 1820s represented another departure of even greater magnitude—one that was to make even Europe vitally interested in the course of American penology. Before that happened, things went to pieces in Walnut Street.

Despite the initial enthusiasm over the prison, conditions soon became dreadful. As yet no one had very clear ideas about what prisons should look like or how they should be run. Between 1790 and 1820 they tended to be like houses where all prisoners not in solitary confinement lived in common rooms and ate in large dining halls. It was difficult to avoid putting more and more offenders in the large rooms, and this caused overcrowding and management problems. Moreover, it was hard to make inmates work. Difficulties with uncooperative prisoners led to a gradual resurrection of the very corporal punishments the prison had been created to eliminate, although some prisons did try using isolation and the withholding of rations to control inmates.

By the early 1800s Walnut Street and other prisons were gruesome places. The early prison historian Richard Phelps described the prison established in 1790 in an abandoned copper mine at Simsbury, Connecticut—one of the first after Walnut Street: "The passage down the shaft into the cavern was upon a ladder fastened upon one side and resting on the bottom. At the foot of this passage commences a gradual descent for a considerable distance, all around being solid rock or ore. . . . On the sides, in the niches of the cavern, platforms were built of boards for the prisoners, on which straw was placed for their beds. The horrid gloom of this dungeon can scarcely be realized. The impenetrable vastness supporting the awful mass above impending as if ready to crush one to atoms; the dripping water trickling like tears from its sides; the unearthly echoes, all conspired to strike aghast with amazement and horror. A bell summoning the prisoners to work brought them up from the cavern beneath through a trapdoor, in regular numbers, two or three together. . . . The prisoners were heavily ironed and secured by fetters and being therefore unable to walk made their way by jumps and hops. On entering the smithy some went to the side of the forges where collars dependent by iron chains from the roof were fastened around their necks and others were chained in pairs to wheelbarrows. The attendants delivered pickled pork to the prisoners for dinner at their forges, a piece for each thrown on the floor and left to be washed and boiled in the water used for cooling the iron wrought at the forges. Meat was distributed in a similar manner for breakfast."

By 1817 the Philadelphia Society acknowledged that Walnut Street had so degenerated that as many as forty prisoners were being housed in an eighteen-by-eighteen-foot room, that it was now no different from a European jail, and that it had become a virtual "seminary for vice." As a remedy the society persuaded the Pennsylvania legislature to build two new prisons—one in eastern and one in western Pennsylvania. These were to be built with only single cells, so that every inmate could be kept alone, eliminating all the problems of congregate living.

The criminal justice situation in New York before the 1790s had been similar to that in Pennsylvania: many crimes called for capital punishment, and corporal punishment was extensive. In 1794 reformers from New York visited Philadelphia and decided to emulate Walnut Street. New York reduced its list of capital crimes to just murder and treason, and two prisons were built—one at Albany and one in Greenwich Village. As in Pennsylvania, they soon became overcrowded. Conditions so degenerated that in 1816 a third and very different prison was authorized, at Auburn.

The Auburn prison followed a new scheme: the worst offenders went into solitary confinement; but a second class was put in separate cells three days a week, and minor offenders were allowed to work together six days a week. By 1823 most of the Auburn inmates serving long terms in solitary had suffered mental breakdowns. Isolation was discontinued, and the governor pardoned most of the remaining isolated inmates. The Auburn system was now revamped to allow congregate work by day for all (with a rule of total silence) and solitary confinement by night. This was essentially a compromise between total group living, which had led to such horrendous conditions earlier, and total isolation, which bred insanity.

These developments in Pennsylvania and New York became the basis for a tremendous thirty-five-year rivalry between what were seen as the two basic forms of the prison: the individual system, represented by Pennsylvania, and the congregate system, represented by Auburn. The supporters of the Pennsylvania system (the Philadelphia Society) called Auburn a cheap imitation. Auburn's defenders (the Boston Prison Discipline Society) called the individual system extravagant and claimed it led to death and insanity while failing to eliminate interaction between inmates, since heat ducts and water pipes still allowed clandestine communication.

As various states contemplated prison construction, they moved firmly into one camp or the other. The Reverend Louis Dwight, self-styled spokesman for the Boston Prison Discipline Society, made sure that state legislatures contemplating building prisons received copies of his annual reports. He promoted the Auburn system with religious zeal and regarded any opposition as heretical. His reports were quite misleading—as were those promulgated by advocates of the individual system—but he was very effective in encouraging other states to emulate Auburn.

Prison reformers in both camps agreed that the great mistake of the 1790s had been the failure to keep inmates from associating with one another. The only issue was whether they should labor and eat silently in groups or remain alone in their cells. For this reason prison architecture—the layout of cells, eating and sleeping arrangements, and work facilities—became a vital concern.

Attitudes had already changed drastically since the prison's first years. Whereas the focus had been on more humane laws, which were supposed to eliminate crime from society, now it was believed that laws had failed but the internal routine of the prison could reform offenders before returning them to society. In 1829 and 1830 inspectors at the Auburn prison interviewed inmates about to be released in hope of uncovering clues to the origins of their criminality. It emerged that most of them had come from broken or otherwise unwholesome homes. The inspectors concluded that a lack of rigorous childhood training in discipline and obedience was, along with exposure to vice, a major cause of crime. If so, order and discipline in the penitentiary should inculcate criminals with proper values and work habits, and isolation from evil influences should allow the basic goodness in man to emerge.

So much effort was expended to isolate inmates from the evils of society that even newspapers were banned from one prison. Correspondence with one's family was typically either forbidden or limited to one letter during the whole confinement. The occasional visitor had to be of unquestioned moral character. The warden of Sing Sing (established in 1824) told inmates in 1826: "It is true that while confined here you can have no intelligence concerning relatives or friends. . . . You are to be literally buried from the world."

The Pennsylvania system isolated the inmate for his entire stay. He was to leave the institution as ignorant of his fellow convicts as when he arrived. A convict arriving at Pennsylvania's Eastern Penitentiary was examined by a physician and then given a hot bath and some clothes. Later he was blindfolded and led to a central rotunda, where the superintendent explained the rules and operation of the prison. Then, still blindfolded, he was taken to his cell, whose number became his name. He was allowed to exercise in the little yard next to his cell only when the inmates in the adjoining yards were not present. He was left alone except when brought meals. After a few days he was asked if he would like some work—an offer usually accepted because of boredom. If he behaved, he would be allowed a Bible. So isolated were the prisoners that they did not hear for months about a cholera epidemic that decimated Philadelphia, and not one inmate caught the disease.

At Auburn prisoners slept alone in their cells at night but worked and ate in groups. They were forbidden to converse or even to exchange glances with other inmates. Strict routines were established to maintain this silence. Since Auburn officials couldn't have inmates casually walking from place to place, they invented the lockstep. Standing immediately behind one another, each looking over the shoulder of the man ahead, with faces turned down and to the right to prevent conversation, prisoners shuffled along in unison. The lockstep survived until the 1930s.

The routine at Auburn was described graphically, if uncritically, in an 1826 report of the Boston Prison Discipline Society: "The unremitted industry, the entire subordination, and subdued feeling among the convicts, has probably no parallel among any equal number of convicts. In their solitary cells, they spend the night with no other book than the Bible, and at sunrise they proceed in military order, under the eye of the turnkey, in solid columns, with the lock march to the workshops, thence in the same order at the hour of breakfast, to the common hall, where they partake of their wholesome and frugal meal in silence. Not even a whisper might be heard through the whole apartment.

"Convicts are seated in single file, at narrow tables with their backs toward the center, so that there can be no interchange of signs. If one has more food than he wants, he raises his left hand, and if another has less, he raises his right hand, and the waiter changes it. . . . There is the most perfect attention to business from morning till night, interrupted only by the time necessary to dine—and never by the fact that the whole body of prisoners have done their tasks and the time is now their own, and they can do as they please.

"At the close of the day, a little before sunset, the work is all laid aside, at once, and the convicts return in military order, to the silent cells where they partake of their frugal meal, which they are permitted to take from the kitchen, where it is furnished for them, as they returned from the shop. After supper, they can, if they choose, read the scriptures, undisturbed, and can reflect in silence on the error of their lives. They must not disturb their fellow prisoners by even a whisper."

Many important Europeans came to visit these institutions with the hope of applying the new systems at home. In fact, the typical distinguished foreigner would no more have passed up a chance to visit a prison than he would have missed seeing a Southern plantation or a Lowell, Massachusetts, textile mill. Alexis de Tocqueville's second main objective during his visit, after studying our form of government, was the examination of our prisons. He found strengths and weaknesses in both systems. In his view, inmates at Auburn were treated more harshly, but at Pennsylvania they were more unhappy. He concluded that seclusion was physically unhealthy but morally effective; and that although the Pennsylvania system was more expensive to construct and operate, it was easier to administer. . . .

Theories were one thing; in actual practice and with the passage of time, the new prison systems deteriorated. By the mid-1800s prisons everywhere scarcely reflected the designs that had been so fiercely debated. The rigorous routine at Auburn and the solitary confinement of Pennsylvania both had been virtually abandoned.

The major reason was overcrowding. Sentences were extremely long and of fixed duration. With no provisions for early release or parole, prisons filled up fast. Overcrowding led to a relaxation of rules, and this in turn enabled inmates to mix freely. Prisons again began to experience the old problems of congregate living.

Part of the trouble was that prisoners were not segregated by age or criminal record, and rules and regulations were geared to the worst offenders.

It had originally been anticipated that inmates would read the Bible, talk with and emulate those exemplary outsiders approved to enter their institution, and contemplate their sins in silence. But most inmates couldn't read and had no use for do-gooders. Whereas the fathers of the penitentiary had expected inmates to be amenable to change, most were hardened criminals serving long sentences and had little to lose by making trouble or trying to escape. So wardens concentrated on maintaining order, and almost every form of brutality found its way back into the penitentiary. Floggings were so common that the public became appalled when it found out about them. At Sing Sing in 1843 as many as three thousand lashes per month were administered.

Many of the punishments had a medieval cast. Prisoners were tied up by their hands with their toes barely touching the floor. They were strapped on their backs to boards or bars for twenty days at a time. They were placed in sweatboxes—unventilated cells on either side of a fireplace. Alcohol was poured on epileptics having seizures and then ignited to detect shamming. New Jersey investigators in 1829 discovered a fourteen-year-old boy who had been imprisoned with hardened criminals and also physically restrained because he could fit through the gratings in prison doors. Prison officials had placed an iron yoke around his head and fastened his hands to it twenty inches apart at shoulder level.

The distressing aspects of the penitentiary did not stop at the prison walls. In the 1830s inmate labor was often leased to private contractors. Its low price meant a valuable competitive advantage, and the awarding of contracts for it unavoidably invited graft and corruption. Some states began to restrict the use of inmate labor by the mid-1840s.

By the last half of the nineteenth century, citizens had lost faith in the idea that a properly structured environment could cure society's crime problem.

Black Slaveowners

Philip Burnham

In 1830, Philip Burnham points out in this essay, more than 12,000 American slaves were owned by Americans who were themselves black. How this came to be is, as Burnham also notes, a fascinating and complex story.

It is, of course, common knowledge that throughout pre–Civil War American history many persons of color had one way or another obtained their freedom. That a small but important minority of them owned slaves is less well known. Why they invested in slaves and how their ownership affected the slave–master relationship (and also the larger question of how free blacks in general related to the mass of those held in bondage) is the subject of Burnham's study. Southern whites commonly referred to slavery as their "peculiar institution." By peculiar they meant "particular" or "unique," but how the situation worked out when blacks were owned by other blacks was often peculiar also, in the sense of odd.

Philip Burnham is a Washington-based journalist who specializes in issues of concern to minorities.

In the 1640s John Casor was brought from Africa to America, where he toiled as a servant for a Virginia landowner. In 1654 Casor filed a complaint in Northampton County Court, claiming that his master Anthony Johnson, had unjustly extended the terms of his indenture with the intention of keeping Casor his slave for life. Johnson, insisting he knew nothing of any indenture, fought hard to retain what he regarded as his personal property. After much wrangling, on March 8, 1655, the court ruled that "the said Jno Casor Negro shall forthwith bee returned unto the service of his master Anthony Johnson," consigning him to a lifetime of bondage. Given the vulnerable legal status of servants—black and white—in colonial America, the decision was not surprising. But the documents reveal one additional fact of interest: Anthony Johnson, like his chattel, Casor, was black.

Johnson's life in America has something in it of a rags-to-riches tale. He appears to have arrived in Virginia in 1621 and is noted in the early records simply as "Antonio, a Negro." Though the general-muster rolls of 1625 list his occupation as "servant," twenty-five years later he had somehow accumulated a respectable surname and two hundred and fifty acres of land on Virginia's Eastern Shore. Surviving both a fire that damaged their plantation and the protracted legal tiff with Casor, Anthony and his wife, Mary, moved to the Eastern Shore of Maryland in the early 1660s, their contentious slave in tow. In 1666 Johnson leased a lot of three hundred acres, on which the prosperous landowner remained until his death. As for Casor, he stayed on as a "servant," witnessing Mary Johnson's will of 1672 and registering his own livestock brand in the same year, apparently something of a colonial success story himself.

By the early eighteenth century the Johnson family had disappeared from the historical record. But in the hundred and fifty years that followed, many other black slaveowners imitated Johnson's example, and for a variety of reasons. According to 1830 U.S. census records, 3,775 free blacks—living mostly in the South—owned a total of 12,760 slaves. Though the vast majority of these owned no more than a few slaves, some in Louisiana and South Carolina held as many as seventy or eighty. Nor was the South the only region to know black slaveowners. Their presence was recorded in Boston by 1724 and in Connecticut by 1783. As late as 1830 some blacks still owned slaves in Rhode Island, Connecticut, Illinois, New Jersey, and New York, as well as in the border states and the District of Columbia.

The motives that guided black slaveowners were many and complex. Most of them appear to have "owned" slaves for the benevolent purpose of protecting family members from a society that habitually regarded free black people with deep suspicion. But a significant minority did so for the same reasons that motivated white slaveowners: commercial profit and prestige. Slave-owning on the part of this latter group was a strategy for assimilation in a mistrustful and potentially explosive social atmosphere. Not only were black slaveowners sometimes reviled by other blacks, but they were equally feared by the white middle class as potential usurpers. Whatever our stereotype of the American master in the antebellum era, neither the commercial nor the humanitarian black slaveowner easily fits it.

A crucial prerequisite for slave-owning was, of course, freedom. At the time of the 1830 census, nearly one out of eight blacks in the United States was a "free person of color," whether by birthright, manumission, or the purchase of his or her freedom. Whatever their improved legal status, free people of color still experienced many of the same difficulties that slaves did. The laws differed according to period and region, but free blacks of the antebellum era were generally forbidden the right to vote, to bear arms, and to testify against whites in a court of law. They were often denied credit, consigned to segregated churches, prevented from establishing permanent residences, and even denied licenses to sell liquor. They often lived side by side with slaves—on occasion marrying them—and their white neighbors tended to see them as a potentially disruptive force. Most free people of color were poor. They lived, as the historian John Hope Franklin has put it, in a state of "quasi-freedom."

There was often deep mistrust between free and enslaved black people. Free blacks only rarely expressed open sympathy for slaves. Most tended to guard jealously the few privileges they had secured: generally, the higher they rose, the more advantages they hoped to protect. And though free people of color might embrace racial equality as a worthy ideal, many used their intermediate status to exploit those at the bottom. What's more, such tensions, as the historian Ira Berlin has noted, in *Slaves Without Masters,* "often divided free Negroes from one another as much as it divided them from whites."

In absolute terms the number of slaveowning blacks was always small. In antebellum North Carolina, for example, only about 10 percent of free blacks owned any kind of property at all, let alone slaves. In the America of 1830 more than three hundred thousand people of color were free; of these, about 2 percent were slaveholders. One scholar has estimated that from 1790 to 1860 just one in eighty free blacks was a slaveowner. Blacks who owned slaves were thus a tiny minority within a minority. Of course, white slaveowners were a minority too—though a much larger one—composing about a third of white families in the first half of the nineteenth century. Booker T. Washington, born to slavery in Virginia, revealed in 1905 that he did not even know black slaveowners had existed. Perhaps he did not want to, for black masters, though few, were widespread, their presence, as John Russell wrote in his 1916 history of early Virginia, "so common in the period of the Commonwealth as to pass unnoticed and without criticism by those who consciously recorded events of the times."

It is not unusual to find that people of color who owned slaves did so for humanitarian motives. In the 1830s John Barry Meachum, a St. Louis minister, bought bondsmen and then invited them to purchase their freedom on easy terms. A woman from Charleston, South Carolina, sold a slave in 1828 on the condition that "he is kindly treated and is never sold, he being an unfortunate individual and requiring much attention." In one extraordinary case a Baptist Negro church in Lexington, Kentucky, is said to have gained a slave preacher by paying for him on the installment plan, passing the Sunday collection plate to pay the deacons of a local white congregation who had purchased him.

Most often black slaveowners were men who had bought their own family members. For instance, Mosby Shepherd, manumitted by the Virginia legislature for giving information concerning the Gabriel insurrection of 1800, bought his own son with the express purpose of later freeing him. Owning blood relatives could be a convenient legal fiction to protect them from the hostility that free blacks attracted. Often it was a way to evade stringent laws requiring newly freed slaves to leave the state within a certain period. Sometimes free blacks married slaves and raised families. If the slave in such a union was owned by a third party and "threatened" with freedom, the spouse could purchase him or her. Some laws even made it easier for blacks to own family members than to manumit them.

Frequently terrible decisions would have to be made, as when children had to be sold off to purchase a spouse. Rose Petepher of New Bern, North Carolina, bought her husband, Richard Gasken, a runaway who had spent several years roaming the woods: They raised several children later hired out as slaves, presumably to keep family finances afloat. Daniel Brown of Norfolk, Virginia, purchased his freedom through hard work and was sold to his wife, Ann, to avoid the law requiring newly manumitted slaves to leave Virginia. When Brown decided he wanted to emigrate to Liberia, his wife balked, not only refusing him permission to go but threatening to sell him. After great effort he persuaded her to manumit him, and he shipped out for Liberia. In 1854 Brown wrote from Monrovia pleading that "Liberia is the place for us and our children, and no where else but here." Later that year Ann finally decided to join him.

Ownership could, of course, add a strange dimension to ordinary family squabbles. Dilsey Pope of Columbus, Georgia, a free woman of color, owned her husband. After they quarreled, she sold him to a white slaveowner; he refused to sell him back once the couple had reconciled. Carter Woodson, the historian who in the 1920s published the research on black slaveholders in the 1830 census, recalled an acquaintance whose mother had been purchased out of slavery by her husband, himself a former slave. When later she grew enamored of another man—a slave, it turned out—and secretly bestowed upon him her husband's manumission papers, the police, thinking the husband had conspired to give up his papers, arrested him and brought him to trial. To cover his legal expenses, the angry husband sold his wife for five hundred dollars.

Black slaveowners, like white ones, sometimes bid for their charges on the open market. Many, however, did not actively seek to obtain slaves but inherited them from family members or white neighbors. In the latter case the person inherited often appears to have been the product of a secret sexual liaison. Henry Lipscomb, a white slaveowner from Cumberland County, Virginia, willed several slaves—probably his own children—to a black family by the same name, headed by Nancy Lipscomb, a "free woman of color." Another black woman, Priscilla Ivey of Mecklenburg County, Virginia, inherited several slaves from a white man in 1821 and held them for thirty-five years, eventually willing them to her children.

Humanitarian motives didn't always play a part in the black slaveowner's trade. Nat Butler, of Aberdeen, Maryland, obtained slaves by a gambit worthy of Simon Legree. Something of a rarity, Butler specialized in turning high hopes to abject misery. He was known to help runaways, providing them with a hiding place while they waited to escape North. At the same time, posing as a slave catcher, he would offer to resell the runaways to their original owners. If the price offered was too low, Butler would sell the slaves to a third party for a neat profit.

Like their white counterparts, black slaveowners advertised for runaways. Sarah Johnson, a seamstress from Charleston, South Carolina, placed an ad in a local paper in August 1836 to locate a servant of "small stature a little pitted with small pox her front teeth much decayed had on when she went away a striped blue frock. It is suspected that she will try and go into the country. . . . I will pay any reasonable reward." In 1859 Eliza McNellage offered a reward of twenty dollars in the Charleston *Mercury* for a sixteen-year-old named Mary who was "well known in the vicinity of Market and Archdale Streets."

Some owners mingled their more generous instincts with economic self-interest. Samuel Smith of Chesterfield, Virginia, willed his slave family to his daughter-in-law "to hold the above-mentioned slaves during her natural life, and at the death of the above named Betsy Smith, I desire that they shall be free." Smith had earlier used a child as collateral for a loan, stipulating that should he not repay the outstanding debt, his creditor should "expose the said Negro boy for sale." The evidence suggests that the child was Smith's own son.

In 1845 Ricksum Webb, of Caroline County, Maryland, willed to his son a slave named Jerry, to be kept for ten years and then freed. The will provided good incentive for the bondsman to accept his lot. "Should Jerry abscond from service and be taken," the document read, he was "to be sold for life to the highest bidder." Richard Parsons, a farmer and boatman of Campbell County, Virginia, set free his slave children in a will of 1842 but made no such provisions for nine other slaves he considered simply to be property. In a particularly complex case Judith Angus of Petersburg, Virginia, willed her estate to her sons, George, Moses, and Frank. Moses was free at the time; the other two were slaves. The 1832 will stipulated that George was to be freed—unless Moses returned to Petersburg, in which case the former was

The African House, Melrose Plantation, was built by the Metoyer family. Thomas Metoyer, a Frenchman, married Marie Therese, a former slave; they in turn were slaveholders.

to be "at his disposal." If George did remain a slave, he was to be hired out, the funds from his labor to be used to buy free the third son, Frank, owned by another party. Among black slaveowners, family hierarchy could have its harsh prerogatives.

The legal complications encountered by families part slave and part free were nothing short of Byzantine, and in many cases Solomon himself would have been hard pressed to mete out justice. A slave named Miles took a slave wife in North Carolina. He was freed by his master and then purchased his wife, whom he in turn freed. One of their children was born when the mother was a slave, the others when she was free. When the mother died, Miles remarried a free woman of color by whom he had several more children. In 1857 Miles died intestate; the children of both mothers disputed the division of property. The North Carolina Supreme Court reasoned that the children of the first marriage had no claim to the estate since slaves could not make contracts that were legally binding. Thus Miles's original marriage was a "fiction," the children not recognized as legal heirs. He had, in short, failed to legitimize the marriage once he and his wife had become free.

Many black slaveowners lived in cities, where they freely mixed with local slaves and occasionally bought and sold them. Urban slaveowners engaged in a variety of occupations: they were barbers, livery stable men, blacksmiths, mechanics, grocers, even prostitutes. In South Carolina and Louisiana a powerful mulatto caste developed in the large cities, comprising lighter-skinned people of color who separated themselves at all costs from the lowly slaves who worked the plantations. The slaveowners among them amassed considerable commercial power, often parlaying it into greater social acceptance and educational advancement.

Like slaves, most free blacks were illiterate. But along the lower Mississippi some obtained more than a rudimentary education and left letters and diaries that offer fascinating glimpses into the lives of antebellum black slaveowners. Among these was William Johnson, a slave turned free man of color in Natchez, Mississippi.

Granted his freedom in 1830, Johnson set up business in Natchez as a barber and moneylender until he purchased a nearby farm. At the time of his death in 1851 he owned fifteen slaves, with an eye to turning a profit. And yet, his diary indicates, some of them evoked in him a turbulent mixture of emotions. "To day has been to me a very Sad Day," he wrote on December 31, 1843. "Many tears were in my Eyes to day On acct. of my Selling poor Steven. I went under the hill this Evening to See him of[f] but the Boat did not Cross over again and Steven got drunk in a few minutes and I took him Home & made him Sleep in the garret and Kept him Safe." Johnson, who had bought Steven in 1832 for $455, had just sold him for $600. The next day the former slave still grappled with his conscience: "I felt hurt but Liquor is the Cause of his troubles; I would not have parted with Him if he had Only have Let Liquor alone but he Cannot do it I believe."

As a black slaveholder Johnson was caught in a tangle of ironies. His diaries reveal the rancor he felt toward the arrogant white slaveowners of his area, though he was cautious to keep his resentment under wraps. While he expressed considerable compassion for his slaves, the only one who ever escaped from him was helped to freedom by a man he called "a white scoundrel." Johnson was murdered in 1851, apparently by a mulatto whose race the courts had difficulty ascertaining. Baylor Winn—who claimed Indian and white ancestry—was never found guilty of murdering Johnson because it could not be proved that Winn was a "Negro." Mississippi law forbade the testimony of black witnesses against white people, and as the only witnesses for the prosecution were people of color, Winn was never convicted.

Andrew Durnford, a free man of color in nearby Louisiana, was a sugar planter who owned seventy-seven slaves at his death in 1859. In his correspondence Durnford describes his 1835 visit to a slave auction in Richmond, Virginia. "I went to see a family of four children, father & mother for 1800$ of yellow complexion," he wrote to a Louisiana friend. "I acted and played the indifferent saying they were too high. An other family of a father & mother with two children for 1200$. I was requested to make an offer, butt would nott do it as I find that some of the farmers . . . don't like to sell to Negro traders butt will, to anybody that buys for their own use."

In fact, Durnford *was* buying for his own use on the sugar plantation he called St. Rosalie, thirty miles south of New Orleans. A man of business, he lamented the high cost of slaves, complaining that Alabamians had bid too high and driven up the market price. "I could have bought some cheaper but, they are what I call rotten people." After buying twenty-five slaves, he encountered some difficulty getting them home. "I wrote in Baltimore to get a passage on board of the brig Harriet cleared for New Orleans, but the captain would not agree to take Blacks."

Durnford's correspondence is richly revealing of the complicated lives led by antebellum mulatto planters. His letters from Richmond are addressed to John McDonogh of New Orleans, a white friend and creditor who later served as a vice president to the American Colonization Society, which resettled freed slaves in Liberia. McDonogh, an unusual master by any standards, sent eighty-five of his slaves to this African republic and later provided in his will for the manumission of many others. Durnford was not so sanguine about the prospects of manumission, though he did free four slaves during his life. "Self interest is too strongly rooted in the bosom of all that breathes the American atmosphere," he wrote in 1843. "Self interest is al la mode." Paternalism and cruelty went hand in hand at Durnford's plantation. "Jackson has just left here," he wrote of a runaway in 1836. "I ordered five rounds to be given him yesterday for cutting my cane and corn. He is a wicked fellow. Was he not a relic I would gett clear of him."

As the Civil War approached, more restrictions were imposed on black slaveowners, and the abolitionist press made white Southerners warier still of this unusual group in their midst. As Northern cries for manumission grew stronger, certain states denied free blacks property rights. In 1860 the North Carolina legislature formally forbade blacks to "buy, purchase, or hire for any length of time any slave or slaves, or to have any slave or slaves bound as apprentice or apprentices."

As public opinion turned against free blacks, William Ellison, Jr., a free mulatto whose father owned dozens of slaves, attempted to leave South Carolina in 1860. The agents for a Philadelphia steamer refused Ellison and his children passage, claiming that if they turned out to be escaped slaves, anyone found guilty of helping them leave the South could be executed. They suggested instead that Ellison declare his children slaves—though they were not—and put them in the charge of a white passenger. Sensing danger, he obtained passage for them on another ship by using his influence and financial resources. Clearly even the wealthy mulatto caste had come to feel threatened by the eve of the Civil War.

Elsewhere in the Deep South the landowning mulatto caste was anxious to prove its loyalty to the cause. Several black slaveowners in the Delta region wrote jointly to the New Orleans *Daily Delta* in December 1860 that "the free colored population (native) of Louisiana . . . own slaves, and they are dearly attached to their native land . . . and they are ready to shed their blood for her defence. They have no sympathy for abolitionism; no love for the North, but they have plenty for Louisiana." Thus the Emancipation Proclamation of 1863 struck as much of a blow to commercial black slaveowners—like the descendants of William Johnson and Andrew Durnford—as it did to their white counterparts. And where owners were compensated for their losses, even those with benevolent motives profited, providing a windfall for people who had been protecting family members. In the District of Columbia, for example, where slavery was abolished in 1862 in advance of the Proclamation, Robert Gunnell received three hundred dollars each for his wife, children, and grandchildren, eighteen people in all.

That black people could have owned slaves at all is a strange irony of American history, one that has led to all manner of theorizing, much of it untenable. It would be a mistake, for example, to think that black slaveholders turned the entire institution of slavery on its head, for even the most powerful black planters could own only people of color, not whites. Though whites were commonly employed as indentured servants in the colonial era, they were never held as slaves as the term is normally used. It is true that free people of color sometimes hired white laborers for temporary work. "I send Noel up to let you know that I will do without dutch people this year," wrote Andrew Durnford to John McDonogh. But as a Virginia statute from 1670 proclaims: "No negro or Indian though baptized and enjoyed their own freedome shall be capable of any purchase of Christians but yet not debarred from buying any of their owne nation." The existence of the statute seems to suggest that holding white "slaves"—or servants—was conceivable for a black only in the early years of colonial Virginia. Such a practice, had it endured, would have undermined the entire social foundation of slavery, resting as it did on the oppression of people of color.

Over the years a number of unconvincing apologies have been offered on behalf of the black slaveholder. The historian Luther Porter Jackson has argued that the 1830 census figures for black slaveowners were inflated, since some of those who appear on the rolls were people of color who had *hired* slaves, not purchased them. Even so, it's difficult to claim that people who "hired" others from their owners were not profiting participants in the peculiar institution. It has rightly been noted that many black slaveholders were, at least in their intentions, benevolent, but it's also clear that not all slaves owned by family members—ostensibly sympathetic masters—were treated with much compassion. Benevolent slaveowning in the Northern states is even more difficult to rationalize, since the act of manumission there was less fraught with legal difficulties. Examined in all its variety, the story of black slaveowners gives powerful evidence that slavery was just as complex an institution for them—as they grappled with economic forces and social realities—as it was for whites.

Anthony Johnson and his spiritual descendants remind us that however much we may generalize, the experience of individuals ranges from the heights of human compassion to the depths of profound greed—and all variations therein. As Andrew Durnford wrote in his will, "I also hereby emancipate and order to be emancipated, the boy of my servant Wainy born the 2d of January 1857 and when the Said boy shall be ten years old I hereby give him two thousand dollars to contribute to give Said boy a good education." The boy, it turns out, wasn't just anyone: He was Durnford's son by a slave mistress. Even after death Durnford was looking out for his own. As the planter himself had once put it in a letter to McDonogh, "self interest is al la mode."

7

Civil War and Reconstruction

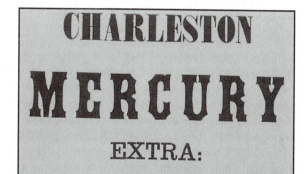

CHARLESTON

MERCURY

EXTRA:

Passed unanimously at 1.15 o'clock, P. M., December 20th, 1860.

AN ORDINANCE

To dissolve the Union between the State of South Carolina and other States united with her under the compact entitled "The Constitution of the United States of America."

We, the People of the State of South Carolina, in Convention assembled, do declare and ordain, and it is hereby declared and ordained,

That the Ordinance adopted by us in Convention, on the twenty-third day of May, in the year of our Lord one thousand seven hundred and eighty-eight, whereby the Constitution of the United States of America was ratified, and also, all Acts and parts of Acts of the General Assembly of this State, ratifying amendments of the said Constitution, are hereby repealed; and that the union now subsisting between South Carolina and other States, under the name of "The United States of America," is hereby dissolved.

THE

UNION

IS

DISSOLVED!

A South Carolina newspaper announces the dissolution of the Union. South Carolina's secession was celebrated in the South with bonfires, parades, and fireworks.

A War That Never Goes Away

James M. McPherson

As is true of all complex and pivotal events, explanations of the causes of the Civil War are almost without number. Slavery, states' rights, economic conflicts, human blundering, and sordid political demagoguery have all been said to have brought about the war. While all of these phenomena affected the course of events in the decades before 1861, what weight should be assigned to each is the cause of endless debate.

In this article, Professor James M. McPherson of Princeton University discusses most of these explanations, but he is primarily concerned with different questions: Why were so many patriotic Americans on both sides willing to risk their lives, even to fight brother against brother, either to preserve or break up the Union? And why have later generations of historians and countless ordinary citizens been so obsessed with understanding the conflict and rehashing the events that made it up? Why, in other words, does the Civil War remain of such intense contemporary interest since the issues that caused the war were resolved so long ago?

Professor McPherson is the author of *Battle Cry of Freedom* and other books about the Civil War.

"Americans just can't get enough of the Civil War." So says a man who should know, Terry Winschel, historian of the Vicksburg National Military Park. . . .

. . . As a beneficiary of this popular interest in the Civil War, I am often asked to explain what accounts for it—in particular, to explain why my own recent contribution to the literature on the war and its causes, *Battle Cry of Freedom*, was on national best-seller lists. . . . I have a few answers.

First, for Americans, the human cost of the Civil War was by far the most devastating in our history. The 620,000 Union and Confederate soldiers who lost their lives almost equaled the 680,000 American soldiers who died in all the other wars this country has fought combined. When we add the unknown but probably substantial number of civilian deaths—from disease, malnutrition, exposure, or injury—among the hundreds of thousands of refugees in the Confederacy, the toll of Civil War dead may exceed war deaths in all the rest of American history. Consider two sobering facts about the Battle of Antietam, America's single bloodiest day. The 25,000 casualties there were nearly four times the number of American casualties on D-day, June 6, 1944. The 6,500 men killed and mortally wounded in one day near Sharpsburg were nearly double the number of Americans killed and mortally wounded in combat in all the rest of the country's nineteenth-century wars combined—the War of 1812, the Mexican War, and the Spanish-American War.

This ghastly toll gives the Civil War a kind of horrifying but hypnotic fascination. As Thomas Hardy once put it, "War makes rattling good history; but Peace is poor reading." The sound of drum and trumpet, the call to arms, the clashing of armies have stirred the blood of nations throughout history. As the horrors and the seamy side of a war recede into the misty past, the romance and honor and glory forge into the foreground. Of no war has this been more true than of the Civil War, with its dashing cavaliers, its generals leading infantry charges, its diamond-stacked locomotives and paddle-wheeled steamboats, its larger-than-life figures like Lincoln, Lee, Jackson, Grant, and Sherman, its heroic and romantic women like Clara Barton and "Mother" Bickerdyke and Rose O'Neal Greenhow, its countless real-life heroines and knaves and heroes capable of transmutation into a Scarlett O'Hara, Rhett Butler, or Ashley Wilkes. If romance is the other face of horror in our perception of the Civil War, the poignancy of a brothers' war is the other face of the tragedy of a civil war. In hundreds of individual cases the war did pit brother against brother, cousin against cousin, even father against son. This was especially true in border states like Kentucky, where the war divided such famous families as the Clays, Crittendens, and Breckinridges and where seven brothers and brothers-in-law of the wife of the United States President fought for the Confederate States. But it was also true of states like Virginia, where Jeb Stuart's father-in-law commanded Union cavalry, and even of South Carolina, where Thomas F. Drayton became a brigadier general in the Confederate army and fought against his brother Percival, a captain in the Union navy, at the Battle of Port Royal. Who can resist the painful human interest of stories like these—particularly when they are recounted in the letters and diaries of Civil War protagonists, preserved through generations and published for all to read as a part of the unending stream of Civil War books?

Indeed, the uncensored contemporary descriptions of that war by participants help explain its appeal to modern readers. There is nothing else in history to equal it. Civil War armies were the most literate that ever fought a war up to that time, and twentieth-century armies censored soldiers' mail and discouraged diary keeping. Thus we have an unparalleled view of the Civil War by the people who experienced it. This has kept the image of the war alive in the families of millions of Americans whose ancestors fought in it. When speaking to audiences as diverse as Civil War buffs, Princeton students and alumni, and local literary clubs, I have sometimes asked how many of them are aware of forebears who fought in the Civil War. I have been surprised by the large response, which demonstrates not only a great number of such people but also their consciousness of events that happened so long ago yet seem part of their family lore today.

This consciousness of the war, of the past as part of the present, continues to be more intense in the South than elsewhere. William Faulkner said of his native section that the past isn't dead; it isn't even past. As any reader of Faulkner's novels knows, the Civil War is central to that past that is present; it is the great watershed of Southern history; it is, as Mark Twain put it a century ago after a tour through the South, "what A.D. is elsewhere; they date from it." The symbols of that past-in-present surround Southerners as they grow up, from the Robert E. Lee Elementary School or Jefferson Davis High School they attend and the Confederate battle flag that flies over their statehouse to the Confederate soldier enshrined in bronze or granite on the town square and the family folklore about victimization by Sherman's bummers. Some of those symbols remain highly controversial and provoke as much passion today as in 1863: the song "Dixie," for example, and the Confederate flag, which for many Southern whites continue to represent courage, honor, or defiance while to blacks they represent racism and oppression.

This suggests the most important reason for the enduring fascination with the Civil War among professional historians as well as the general public: Great issues were at stake, issues about which Americans were willing to fight and die, issues whose resolution profoundly transformed and redefined the United States. The Civil War was a total war in three senses: It mobilized the total human and material resources of both sides; it ended not in a negotiated peace but in total victory by one side and unconditional surrender by the other; it destroyed the economy and social system of the loser and established those of the winner as the norm for the future.

The Civil War was fought mainly by volunteer soldiers who joined the colors before conscription went into effect. In fact, the Union and Confederate armies mobilized as volunteers a larger percentage of their societies' manpower than any other war in American history—probably in world history, with the possible exception of the French Revolution. And Civil War armies, like those of the French Revolution, were highly ideological in motivation. Most of the volunteers knew what they were fighting for, and why. What were they fighting for? If asked to define it in a single word, many soldiers on both sides would have answered: liberty. They fought for the heritage of freedom bequeathed to them by the Founding Fathers. North and South alike wrapped themselves in the mantle of 1776. But the two sides interpreted that heritage in opposite ways, and at first neither side included the slaves in the vision of liberty for which it fought. The slaves did, however, and by the time of Lincoln's Gettysburg Address in 1863, the North also fought for "a new birth of freedom. . . ." These multiple meanings of freedom, and how they dissolved and reformed in kaleidoscopic patterns during the war, provide the central meaning of the war for the American experience.

When the "Black Republican" Abraham Lincoln won the Presidency in 1860 on a platform of excluding slavery from the territories, Southerners compared him to George III and declared their independence from "oppressive Yankee rule." "The same spirit of freedom and independence that impelled our Fathers to the separation from the British Government," proclaimed secessionists, would impel the "liberty loving people of the South" to separation from the United States government. A Georgia secessionist declared that Southerners would be "either *slaves in the Union or freemen out of it*." Young men from Texas to Virginia rushed to enlist in this "Holy Cause of Liberty and Independence" and to raise "the standard of Liberty and Equality for white men" against "our Abolition enemies who are pledged to prostate the white freemen of the South down to equality with negroes." From "the high and solemn motive of defending and protecting the rights which our fathers bequeathed to us," declared Jefferson Davis at the outset of war, let us "renew such sacrifices as our fathers made to the holy cause of constitutional liberty."

But most Northerners ridiculed these Southern professions to be fighting for the ideals of 1776. That was "a libel upon the whole character and conduct of the

This painting of the departure of the Seventh Regiment from New York conveys the sense of enthusiasm everyone had nearly in the war.

men of '76," said the antislavery poet and journalist William Cullen Bryant. The Founding Fathers had fought "to establish the rights of man . . . and principles of universal liberty." The South, insisted Bryant, had seceded "not in the interest of general humanity, but of a domestic despotism. . . . Their motto is not liberty, but slavery." Northerners did not deny the right of revolution in principle; after all, the United States was founded on that right. But "the right of revolution," wrote Lincoln in 1861, "is never a legal right. . . . At most, it is but a moral right, when exercised for a morally justifiable cause. When exercised without such a cause revolution is no right, but simply a wicked exercise of physical power." In Lincoln's judgment secession was just such a wicked exercise. The event that precipitated it was Lincoln's election by a constitutional majority. As Northerners saw it, the Southern states, having controlled the national government for most of the previous two generations through their domination of the Democratic party, now decided to leave the Union just because they had lost an election.

For Lincoln and the Northern people, it was the Union that represented the ideals of 1776. The republic established by the Founding Fathers as a bulwark of liberty was a fragile experiment in a nineteenth-century world bestridden by kings, emperors, czars, and dictators. Most republics through history had eventually been overthrown. Some Americans still alive in 1861 had seen French republics succumb twice to emperors and once to the restoration of the Bourbon monarchy. Republics in Latin America came and went with bewildering rapidity. The United States in 1861 represented, in Lincoln's words, "the last, best hope" for the survival of republican liberties in the world. Would that hope also collapse? "Our popular government has often been called an experiment," Lincoln told Congress on July 4, 1861. But if the Confederacy succeeded in splitting the country in two, it would set a fatal precedent that would destroy the experiment. By invoking this precedent, a minority in the future might secede from the Union whenever it did not like what the majority stood for, until the United States fragmented into a multitude of petty, squabbling autocracies. "The central idea pervading this struggle," said Lincoln, "is the necessity . . . of proving that popular government is not an absurdity. We must settle this question now whether, in a free government, the minority have the right to break up the government whenever they choose."

Many soldiers who enlisted in the Union army felt the same way. A Missourian joined up as "a duty I owe my country and to my children to do what I can to preserve this government as I shudder to think what is ahead of them if this government should be overthrown." A New England soldier wrote to his wife on the eve of the First Battle of Bull Run: "I know . . . how great a debt we owe to those who went before us through the blood and sufferings of the Revolution. And I am willing—perfectly willing—to lay down all my joys in this life, to help maintain this government, and to pay that debt."

Freedom for the slaves was not part of the liberty for which the North fought in 1861. That was not because the Lincoln administration supported slavery; quite the contrary. Slavery was "an unqualified evil to the negro, to the white man . . . and to the State," said Lincoln on many occasions in words that expressed the sentiments of a Northern majority. "The monstrous injustice of slavery . . . deprives our republican example of its just influence in the world—enables the enemies of free institutions, with plausibility, to taunt us as hypocrites. . . ." Yet in his first inaugural address, Lincoln declared that he had "no purpose, directly or indirectly, to interfere with . . . slavery in the States where it exists." He reiterated this pledge in his first message to Congress, on July 4, 1861, when the Civil War was nearly three months old.

What explains this apparent inconsistency? The answer lies in the Constitution and in the Northern polity of 1861. Lincoln was bound by a constitution that protected slavery in any state where citizens wanted it. The republic of liberty for whose preservation the North was fighting had been a republic in which slavery was legal everywhere in 1776. That was the great American paradox—a land of freedom based on slavery. Even in 1861 four states that remained loyal to the Union were slave states, and the Democratic minority in free states opposed any move to make the war for the Union a war against slavery.

But as the war went on, the slaves themselves took the first step toward making it a war against slavery. Coming into Union lines by the thousands, they voted with their feet for freedom. As enemy property they could be confiscated by Union forces as "contraband of war." This was the thin edge of the wedge that finally broke apart the American paradox. By 1863 a series of congressional acts plus Lincoln's Emancipation Proclamation had radically enlarged Union war aims. The North henceforth fought not just to restore the old Union, not just to ensure that the nation born in 1776 "shall not perish from the earth," but to give that nation "a new birth of freedom."

Northern victory in the Civil War resolved two fundamental, festering issues left unresolved by the Revolution of 1776: whether this fragile republican experiment called the United States would survive and whether the house divided would continue to endure half slave and half free. Both these issues remained open questions until 1865. Many Americans doubted the Republic's survival: many European conservatives predicted its demise: some Americans advocated the right of secession and periodically threatened to invoke it; eleven states did invoke it in 1860 and 1861. But since 1865 no state or region has seriously threatened secession, not even during the "massive resistance" to desegregation from 1954 to 1964. Before 1865 the United States, land of liberty, was the largest slaveholding country in the world. Since 1865 that particular "monstrous injustice" and "hypocrisy" has existed no more.

In the process of preserving the Union of 1776 while purging it of slavery, the Civil War also transformed it. Before 1861 the words *United States* were a plural noun: "The United States *are* a large country." Since 1865 *United States* has been a singular noun. The North went to war to preserve the *Union;* it ended by creating a *nation.* This transformation can be traced in Lincoln's most important wartime addresses. The first inaugural address contained the word *Union* twenty times and the word *nation* not once. In Lincoln's first message to Congress, on July 4, 1861, he used *Union* forty-nine times and *nation* only three times. In his famous public letter to Horace Greeley of August 22, 1862, concerning slavery and the war, Lincoln spoke of the Union nine times and the nation not at all. But in the Gettysburg Address fifteen months later, he did not refer to the Union at all but used the word *nation* five times. And in the second inaugural address, looking back over the past four years, Lincoln spoke of one side's seeking to dissolve the Union in 1861 and the other side's accepting the challenge of war to preserve the nation. The old decentralized Republic, in which the post-office was the only agency of national government that touched the average citizen, was transformed by the crucible of war into a centralized polity that taxed people directly and created an internal revenue bureau to collect the taxes, expanded the jurisdiction of federal courts, created a national currency and a federally chartered banking system, drafted men into the Army, and created the Freedman's Bureau as the first national agency for social welfare. Eleven of the first twelve amendments to the Constitution had limited the powers of the national government; six of the next seven, starting with the Thirteenth Amendment in 1865, radically expanded those powers at the expense of the states. The first three of these amendments converted four million slaves into citizens and voters within five years, the most rapid and fundamental social transformation in American history—even if the nation did backslide on part of this commitment for three generations after 1877.

From 1789 to 1861 a Southern slaveholder was President of the United States two-thirds of the time, and two-thirds of the Speakers of the House and presidents pro tem of the Senate had also been Southerners. Twenty of the thirty-five Supreme

Court justices during that period were from the South, which always had a majority on the Court before 1861. After the Civil War a century passed before another resident of a Southern state was elected President. For half a century after the war hardly any Southerners served as Speaker of the House or president pro tem of the Senate, and only nine of the thirty Supreme Court justices appointed during that half-century were Southerners. The institutions and ideology of a plantation society and a caste system that had dominated half of the country before 1861 and sought to dominate more went down with a great crash in 1865 and were replaced by the institutions and ideology of free-labor entrepreneurial capitalism. For better or for worse, the flames of Civil War forged the framework of modern America.

So even if the veneer of romance and myth that has attracted so many of the current Civil War camp followers were stripped away, leaving only the trauma of violence and suffering, the Civil War would remain the most dramatic and crucial experience in American history. That fact will ensure the persistence of its popularity and its importance as a historical subject so long as there is a United States.

John Brown: Father of American Terrorism

Ken Chowder

A few media commentators, rendered nearly speechless by the destruction of the World Trade Center on September 11, 2001, sought perspective on the event by comparing it to earlier instances of terrorism in American history. Some mentioned John Brown, whom Ken Chowder here identifies as the "father" of American terrorism. Historical analogies are always unsatisfactory, and John Brown, who led the Pottawatomie massacre in Kansas in 1855 and the botched raid on Harpers Ferry in 1859, little resembled Mohamed Atta, ringleader of the Arab terrorists who crashed airliners into the World Trade Center. Chowder describes Brown as a business failure and inadequate father, a religious fanatic who murdered defenseless people, a megalomaniac who believed himself to be doing God's work. Though some claim that Brown's higher purpose—the abolition of slavery—justified his violent actions, Chowder concludes that Brown himself represented the "many excesses" of antebellum American society. In addition to writing historical documentaries, Chowder is author of several books and a novel, *Blackbird Days* (1980).

On December 2, 1859, a tall old man in a black coat, black pants, black vest, and black slouch hat climbed into a wagon and sat down on a black walnut box. The pants and coat were stained with blood; the box was his coffin; the old man was going to his execution. He had just handed a last note to his jailer; "I John Brown am now quite *certain* that the crimes of this *guilty, land will* never be purged *away*; but with Blood. I had . . . *vainly* flattered myself that without *very much* bloodshed; it might be done."

As he rode on his coffin, John Brown gazed out over the cornfields of Virginia. "This *is* a beautiful country," he said. "I never had the pleasure of seeing it before."

The United States in 1859 was a nation that harbored a ticking time bomb: the issue of slavery. And it was a place where an astonishing number of men were willing to die for their beliefs, certain they were following a higher law. John Brown was one of those God-fearing yet violent men. And he was already more than a man; he was a legend. In fact, there were two competing legends. To slaveholders he was utter evil—fanatic, murderer, liar, and lunatic, and horse thief to boot—while to abolitionists he had become the embodiment of all that was noble and courageous.

After a lifetime of failure John Brown had at last found a kind of success. He was now a symbol that divided the nation and his story was no longer about one man; it was a prophecy. The United States, like John Brown, was heading toward a gallows—the gallows of war.

A scaffold had been built in a field outside Charlestown, Virginia. There were rumors of a rescue attempt, and fifteen hundred soldiers, commanded by Col. Robert E. Lee, massed in the open field. No civilians were allowed within hearing range, but an actor from Virginia borrowed a uniform so he could watch John Brown die. "I looked at the traitor and terrorizer," said John Wilkes Booth, "with unlimited, undeniable contempt." Prof. Thomas Jackson, who would in three years be known as Stonewall, was also watching: "The sheriff placed the rope around [Brown's] neck, then threw a white cap over his head. . . . When the rope was cut by a single blow, Brown fell through. . . . There was very little motion of his person for several moments, and soon the wind blew his lifeless body to and fro."

A Virginia colonel named J. T. L. Preston chanted: "So perish all such enemies of Virginia! All such enemies of the Union! All such foes of the human race!"

But hanging was not the end of John Brown; it was the beginning. Northern churches' bells tolled for him, and cannon boomed in salute. In Massachusetts, Henry David Thoreau spoke: "Some eighteen hundred years ago, Christ was cruci-fied; This morning, perchance, Captain Brown was hung. . . . He is not Old Brown any longer; he is an angel of light."

John Brown's soul was already marching on. But the flesh-and-blood John Brown—a tanner, shepherd, and farmer, a simple and innocent man who could kill in cold blood, a mixture of opposite parts who mirrored the paradoxical America of his time—this John Brown had already vanished, and he would rarely appear again. His life instead became the subject for 140 years of spin. John Brown has been used rather than considered by history; even today we are still spinning his story.

As far as history is concerned, John Brown was genuinely nobody until he was fifty-six years old—that is, until he began to kill people. Not that his life was without incident. He grew up in the wilderness of Ohio (he was born in 1800, when places like Detroit, Chicago, and Cleveland were still frontier stockades). He married at twenty, lost his wife eleven years later, soon married again, and fathered a total of twenty children. Nine of them died before they reached adulthood.

At seventeen Brown left his father's tannery to start a competing one. "I ac-knowledge no master in human form," he would say, many years later, when he was wounded and in chains at Harpers Ferry. The young man soon mastered the rural arts of farming, tanning, surveying, home building, and animal husbandry, but his most conspicuous talent seemed to be one for profuse and painful failure.

In the 1830s, with a growing network of canals making barren land worth thou-sands, Brown borrowed deeply to speculate in real estate—just in time for the disas-trous Panic of 1837. The historian James Brewer Stewart, author of *Holy Warriors*, says that "Brown was a typical story of someone who invested, as thousands did, and lost thousands, as thousands did as well. Brown was swept along in a current of de-fault and collapse."

He tried breeding sheep, started another tannery, bought and sold cattle—each time a failure. When one venture lost money, Brown quietly appropriated funds from a partner in a new business and used it to pay the earlier loss. But in the end his farm tools, furniture, and sheep went on the auction block.

When his farm was sold, he seemed to snap. He refused to leave. With two sons and some old muskets, he barricaded himself in a cabin on the property. "I was making preparation for the commencement and vigorous prosecution of a te-dious, distressing, wasteing, and long protracted war," Brown wrote. The sheriff got up a posse and briefly put him in the Akron jail. No shots were fired, but it was an incident people would remember, years later, when the old man barricaded himself at Harpers Ferry.

Brown's misadventures in business have drawn widely varying interpretations. His defenders say he had a large family to support; small wonder he wanted badly to make money. But others have seen his financial dreams as an obsession, a kind of fever that gave him delusions of wealth and made him act dishonestly.

Perhaps it was this long string of failures that created the revolutionary who burst upon the American scene in 1856. By that time Brown had long nurtured a vague and protean plan: He imagined a great event in which he—the small-time farmer who had failed in everything he touched—would be God's messenger, a latter-day Moses who would lead his people from the accursed house of slavery. He had already, for years, been active in the Underground Railroad, hiding runaways and guiding them north toward Canada. In 1837 he stood up in the back of a church in Ohio and made his first public statement on human bondage, a single pungent sentence: "Here before God, in the presence of these witnesses, I consecrate my life to the destruction of slavery." For years, however, this vow seemed to mean relatively little; in the early 1850s, as anger over slavery began to boil up all over the North, the frustrated and humiliated Brown was going from courtroom to courtroom embroiled in his own private miseries.

Finally it happened. The John Brown we know was born in the place called Bloody Kansas. Slavery had long been barred from the territories of Kansas and Nebraska, but in 1854 the Kansas-Nebraska Act decreed that the settlers of these territories would decide by vote whether to be free or slave. The act set up a competition between the two systems that would become indistinguishable from war.

Settlers from both sides flooded into Kansas. Five of John Brown's sons made the long journey there from Ohio. But Brown himself did not go. He was in his mid-fifties, old by the actuarial tables of his day; he seemed broken.

Then, in March of 1855, five thousand proslavery Missourians—the hard-drinking, heavily armed "Border Ruffians"—rode into Kansas. "We came to vote, and we are going to vote or kill every God-damned abolitionist in the Territory," their leader declared. The Ruffians seized the polling places, voted in their own legislature, and passed their own laws. Prison now awaited anyone who spoke against slavery.

In May, John Junior wrote to his father begging for his help. The free-soilers needed arms, "more than we need bread," he said. "Now we want you to get for us these arms." The very next day, Brown began raising money and gathering weapons and in August the old man left for Kansas, continuing to collect arms as he went.

In May 1856 a proslavery army sacked the free-soil town of Lawrence; not a single abolitionist dared fire a gun. This infuriated Brown. He called for volunteers to go on "a secret mission." The old man, in his soiled straw hat, stuck a revolver in his belt and led a company of eight men down toward Pottawatomie Creek. Proslavery people lived in the cabins there.

Late on the night of May 23, 1856, one of the group, probably Brown, banged on the door of James Doyle's cabin. He ordered the men of the family outside at gunpoint, and Brown's followers set upon three Doyles with broadswords. They split open heads and cut off arms. John Brown watched his men work. When it was over, he put a single bullet into the head of James Doyle.

His party went to two more cabins, dragged out and killed two more men. At the end bodies lay in the bushes and floated in the creek; the murderers had made off with horses, saddles, and a bowie knife.

What came to be called the Pottawatomie Massacre ignited all-out war in Kansas. John Brown, the aged outsider, became an abolitionist leader. In August some 250 Border Ruffians attacked the free-soil town of Osawatomie. Brown led thirty men in defending the town. He fought hard, but Osawatomie burned to the ground.

A few days later, when Brown rode into Lawrence on a gray horse, a crowd gathered to cheer "as if the President had come to town," one man said. The spinning of John Brown had already begun. A Scottish reporter named James Redpath had found Brown's men in their secret campsite, and "I left this sacred spot with a far higher respect for the Great Struggle than ever I had felt before." And what of Pottawatomie? Brown had nothing to do with it, Redpath wrote. John Brown himself even prepared an admiring account of the Battle of Osawatomie for Eastern newspapers. Less than two weeks after the fight, a drama called *Ossawattomie Brown* was celebrating him on Broadway.

That autumn, peace finally came to Kansas, but not to John Brown. For the next three years he traveled the East, occasionally returning to Kansas, beseeching abolitionists for guns and money, money and guns. His plan evolved into this: One night he and a small company of men would capture the federal armory and arsenal at Harpers Ferry, Virginia. The invaders would take the guns there and leave. Local slaves would rise up to join them, making an army; together they all would drive south, and the revolution would snowball through the kingdom of slavery.

On the rainy night of October 16, 1859, Brown led a determined little procession down the road to Harpers Ferry. Some twenty men were making a direct attack on the U.S. government; they would liberate four million souls from bondage. At first the raid went like clockwork. The armory was protected by just one man, and he quickly surrendered. The invaders cut telegraph lines and rounded up hostages on the street.

Then Brown's difficulties began. A local doctor rode out screaming, "Insurrection!," and by midmorning men in the heights behind town were taking potshots down at Brown's followers: Meanwhile, John Brown quietly ordered breakfast from a hotel for his hostages. As Dennis Frye, the former chief historian at Harpers Ferry National Historical Park, asks, "The question is, why didn't John Brown attempt to leave? Why did he stay in Harpers Ferry?" Russell Banks, the author of the recent John Brown novel *Cloudsplitter*, has an answer: "He stayed and he stayed, and it seems to me a deliberate, resigned act of martyrdom."

At noon a company of Virginia militia entered town, took the bridge, and closed the only true escape route. By the end of the day, John Brown's revolution was failing. Eight invaders were dead or dying. Five others were cut off from the main group. Two had escaped across the river; two had been captured. Only five raiders were still fit to fight. Brown gathered his men in a small brick building, the enginehouse, for the long, cold night.

The first light of October 18 showed Brown and his tiny band an armory yard lined with U.S. Marines, under the command of Col. Robert E. Lee. A young lieutenant, J. E. B. Stuart, approached beneath a white flag and handed over a note asking the raiders to surrender. Brown refused. At that Stuart jumped aside, waved his cap, and the Marines stormed forward with a heavy ladder. The door gave way. Lt. Israel Green tried to run Brown through, but his blade struck the old man's belt buckle; God, for the moment, had saved John Brown.

A few hours later, as he lay in a small room at the armory, bound and bleeding, Brown's real revolution began. Gov. Henry A. Wise of Virginia arrived with a retinue of reporters. Did Brown want the reporters removed? asked Robert E. Lee. Definitely not. "Brown said he was by no means annoyed," one reporter wrote. For the old man was now beginning a campaign that would win half of America. He told the reporters: "I wish to say . . . that you had better—all you people of the South—prepare yourselves for a settlement of this question. . . . You may dispose of me very easily—I am nearly disposed of now; but this question is still to be settled—this negro question I mean; the end of that is not yet."

His crusade for acceptance would not be easy. At first he was no hero. Leaders of the Republican party organized anti-Brown protests; "John Brown was no Republican," Abraham Lincoln said. Even the *Liberator,* published by the staunch abolitionist William Lloyd Garrison, called the raid "misguided, wild, and apparently insane."

In the South the initial reaction was derision—the Richmond *Dispatch* called the foray "miserably weak and contemptible"—but that soon changed to fear. Stuart's soldiers found a carpetbag crammed with letters from Brown's supporters; a number of prominent Northerners had financed the raid. It had been a conspiracy, a wide-ranging one. But how wide?

A reign of terror began in the South. A minister who spoke out against the treatment of slaves was publicly whipped; a man who spoke sympathetically about the raid found himself thrown in jail. Four state legislatures appropriated military funds. Georgia set aside seventy-five thousand dollars; Alabama, almost three times as much.

Brown's trial took just one week. As Virginia hurried toward a verdict, the Reverend Henry Ward Beecher preached, "Let no man pray that Brown be spared! Let Virginia make him a martyr!" John Brown read Beecher's words in his cell. He wrote "Good" beside them.

On November 2 the jury, after deliberating for forty-five minutes, reached its verdict. Guilty. Before he was sentenced, Brown rose to address the court: "I see a book kissed here, . . . the Bible. . . . [That] teaches me to 'remember them that are in bonds, as bound with them.' I endeavored to act up to that instruction. . . . I believe that to have interfered . . . in behalf of His despised poor was not wrong, but right. Now, if it is deemed necessary that I should forfeit my life . . ., and mingle my blood further with the blood of my children and with the blood of millions in this slave country whose rights are disregarded . . . I say let it be done!"

For the next month the Charlestown jail cell was John Brown's pulpit. All over the North, Brown knew, people were reading his words. He wrote, "You know that Christ once armed Peter. So also in my case I think he put a sword into my hand, and there continued it so long as he saw best, and then kindly took it from me."

The author of the Pottawatomie Massacre was now comparing himself to Jesus Christ. And he was not alone. Even the temperate Ralph Waldo Emerson called him "the new Saint whose fate yet hangs in suspense but whose martyrdom if it shall be perfected, will make the gallows as glorious as the cross." There were rescue plans, but John Brown did not want to escape. "I am worth inconceivably more to hang than for any other purpose," he wrote.

He got that wish on December 2, and the mythologizing of the man began in earnest. Thoreau, Emerson, Victor Hugo, Herman Melville, and Walt Whitman all wrote essays or poems immortalizing him. James Redpath eagerly waited for the moment when "Old B was in heaven"; just a month after the execution, he published the first biography. Forty thousand copies of the book sold in a single month.

Less than a year and a half later, the guns began firing on Fort Sumter. If the country had been a tinder box, it seemed to many that John Brown had been the spark. "Did John Brown fail?" Frederick Douglass wrote. ". . . John Brown began the war that ended American slavery and made this a free Republic."

His reputation seemed secure, impermeable. The first biographies of the man James Redpath called the "warrior saint" all glorified him. But then, in 1910, Oswald Garrison Villard, grandson of the abolitionist William Lloyd Garrison, wrote a massive and carefully researched book that pictured Brown as a muddled, pugnacious, bumbling, and homicidal madman. Nineteen years later Robert Penn Warren issued a similar (and derivative) study. Perhaps the most influential image of John Brown came, not surprisingly, from Hollywood: In *Santa Fe Trail* Raymond Massey portrayed him as a lunatic, pure and simple.

It wasn't until the 1970s that John Brown the hero re-emerged. Two excellent studies by Stephen B. Oates and Richard Owen Boyer captured the core of the conundrum: Brown was stubborn, monomaniacal, egotistical, self-righteous, and sometimes deceitful; yet he was, at certain times, a great man. Boyer, in particular, clearly admired him: At bottom Brown "was an American who gave his life that millions of other Americans might be free."

Among African-Americans, Brown's heroism has never been in doubt. Frederick Douglass praised him in print; W. E. B. Du Bois published a four-hundred-page celebration of him in 1909; Malcolm X said he wouldn't mind being with white people if they were like John Brown; and Alice Walker, in a poem, even wondered if in an earlier incarnation she herself hadn't once been John Brown.

But, as Russell Banks points out, Brown's "acts mean completely different things to Americans depending upon their skin color." And the image that most white people today have of John Brown is still of the wild-eyed, blood thirsty madman. After all, he believed that God spoke to him; he killed people at Pottawatomie in cold blood; he launched an attack on the U.S. government at Harpers Ferry with not even two dozen men. How sane could he have been?

Let's look at those charges one by one. First: *He conversed with God.* Brown's religious principles, everyone agrees, were absolutely central to the man. As a child he learned virtually the entire Bible by heart. At sixteen he traveled to New England to study for the ministry. He gave up after a few months but remained deeply serious about his Calvinist beliefs. Brown had a great yearning for justice for all men, yet a rage for bloody revenge. These qualities may seem paradoxical to us, but they were ones that John Brown had in common with his deity. The angry God of the Old Testament punished evil: An eye cost exactly an eye.

If God spoke directly to John Brown, He also spoke to William Lloyd Garrison and to the slave revolutionary Nat Turner. To converse with God, in Brown's day, did not mean that you were eccentric. In fact, God was on everyone's side. John Brown saw the story of Moses setting the Israelites free as a mandate for emancipation, but at the same time, others used the Bible to justify slavery (Noah did, after all, set an everlasting curse on all the dark descendants of Ham). It was all in the Bible, and Americans on both sides went to war certain that they were doing God's bidding. So it is that John Brown believed that God had appointed him "a special agent of death," "an instrument raised up by Providence to break the jaws of the wicked."

Second: *He killed in cold blood.* Brown was a violent man, but he lived in increasingly violent times. Slavery itself was of course a violent practice. In 1831 Nat Turner led seventy slaves to revolt; they killed fifty-seven white men, women, and children. A few years later a clergyman named Elijah Lovejoy was gunned down for speaking out against slavery. By the 1850s another distinguished clergyman, Thomas Wentworth Higginson, could lead a mob to the federal courthouse in Boston and attack the place with axes and guns. "I can only make my life worth living," Higginson vowed, "by becoming a revolutionist." During the struggle in Kansas Henry Ward Beecher's Plymouth Church in Brooklyn was blithely shipping Sharps rifles west; "there are times," the famous preacher said, "when self-defense is a religious duty." By the late fifties, writes the historian James Stewart, even Congress was "a place where fist fights became common . . . a place where people came armed . . . a place where people flashed Bowie knives." On February 5, 1858, a brawl broke out between North and South in the House of Representatives; congressmen rolled on the floor, scratching and gouging each other.

Brown's Pottawatomie Massacre was directly connected to this national chaos. On the very day Brown heard about the sacking of Lawrence, another disturbing report reached him from Washington: A Southern congressman had attacked Sen. Charles Sumner, a fierce abolitionist, on the floor of Congress, caning him almost to death for insulting the South. When the news got to Brown's campsite, according to his son Salmon, "the men went crazy—*crazy*. It seemed to be the finishing, decisive touch." Brown ordered his men to sharpen their broadswords and set off toward Pottawatomie, the creek whose name still stains his reputation.

So it is that "Brown is simply part of a very violent world," according to the historian Paul Finkelman. At Pottawatomie, Finkelman says, "Brown was going after particular men who were dangerous to the very survival of the free-state settlers in the area." But Dennis Frye has a less analytical (and less sympathetic) reaction: "Pottawatomie was cold-blooded murder. [It was] killing people up close based on anger and vengeance."

To Bruce Olds, the author of *Raising Holy Hell,* a 1995 novel about Brown, Pottawatomie was an example of conscious political terrorism: "Those killings took place in the middle of the night, in the dark—that was on purpose. In his writings, [Brown] uses the word 'terror' and the word 'shock.' He intended to produce both of those, and he did."

Maybe Pottawatomie was insane, and maybe it was not. But what about that Harpers Ferry plan—a tiny band attacking the U.S. government, hoping to concoct a revolution that would carry across the South? Clearly *that* was crazy.

Horace Pippin's John Brown Going to His Hanging, *1942. In this painting, Pippin catches the somber mood as Brown is moved through the streets on the way to his hanging. As crowds line the street to view the spectacle, a lone figure of a black female appears to turn away in sorrow.*

Yes and no. If it was crazy, it was not unique. Dozens of people, often bearing arms, had gone South to rescue slaves. Secret military societies flourished on both sides, plotting to expand or destroy the system of slavery by force. Far from being the product of a singular cracked mind, the plan was similar to a number of others, including one by a Boston attorney named Lysander Spooner. James Horton, a leading African-American history scholar, offers an interesting scenario. "Was Brown crazy to assume he could encourage slave rebellion? . . . Think about the possibility of Nat Turner well-armed, well-equipped. . . . Nat Turner might have done some pretty amazing things," Horton says. "It was perfectly rational and reasonable for John Brown to believe he could encourage slaves to rebel."

But the question of Brown's sanity still provokes dissension among experts. Was he crazy? "He was obsessed," Bruce Olds says, "he was fanatical, he was monomaniacal, he was a zealot, and . . . psychologically unbalanced." Paul Finkelman disagrees: Brown "is a bad tactician, he's a bad strategist, he's a bad planner, he's not a very good general—but he's not crazy."

Some believe that there is a very particular reason why Brown's reputation as a madman has clung to him. Russell Banks and James Horton make the same argument. "The reason white people think he was mad," Banks says, "is because he was a white man and he was willing to sacrifice his life in order to liberate black Americans." "We should be very careful," Horton says, "about assuming that a white man who is willing to put his life on the line for black people is, of necessity, crazy."

Perhaps it is reasonable to say this: A society where slavery exists is by nature one where human values are skewed. America before the Civil War was a violent society, twisted by slavery. Even sober and eminent people became firebrands. John Brown had many peculiarities of his own, but he was not outside his society; to a great degree, he represented it, in its many excesses.

The past, as always, continues to change, and the spinning of John Brown's story goes on today. The same events—the raid on Harpers Ferry or the Pottawatomie Massacre—are still seen in totally different ways. What is perhaps most remarkable is that elements at both the left and right ends of American society are at this moment vitally interested in the story of John Brown.

On the left is a group of historical writers and teachers called Allies for Freedom. This group believes that the truth about the Harpers Ferry raid has been buried by the conventions of history. Its informal leader, Jean Libby, author of *John Brown Mysteries,* says, "What we think is that John Brown was a black nationalist. His ultimate goal was the creation of an independent black nation." The Allies for Freedom believes, too, that far from being the folly of a lunatic, Brown's plan was not totally unworkable, that it came much closer to succeeding than historians have pictured. Libby thinks that many slaves and free blacks *did* join the uprising—perhaps as many as fifty. Why would history conceal the fact of active black participation in Harpers Ferry? "The South was anxious to cover up any indication that the raid might have been successful," Libby says, "so slaves would never again be tempted to revolt."

Go a good deal farther to the left, and there has long been admiration for John Brown. In 1975 the Weather Underground put out a journal called *Osawatomie.* In the late 1970s a group calling itself the John Brown Brigade engaged in pitched battles with the Ku Klux Klan; in one confrontation in Greensboro, North Carolina, in 1979, five members of the John Brown Brigade were shot and killed. Writers also continue to draw parallels between John Brown and virtually any leftist who uses political violence, including the Symbionese Liberation Army (the kidnappers of Patty Hearst in the 1970s), Ted Kaczynski, the Unabomber, and the Islamic terrorists who destroyed the World Trade Center.

At the same time, John Brown is frequently compared to those at the far opposite end of the political spectrum. Right-to-life extremists have bombed abortion clinics and murdered doctors; they have, in short, killed for a cause they believed in, just as John Brown did. Paul Hill was convicted of murdering a doctor who performed abortions; it was, Hill said, the Lord's bidding: "There's no question in my mind that it was what the Lord wanted me to do, to shoot John Britton to prevent him from killing unborn children." If that sounds quite like John Brown, it was no accident. From death row Hill wrote to the historian Dan Stowell that Brown's "example has and continues to serve as a source of encouragement to me. . . . Both of us looked to the scriptures for direction, [and] the providential similarities between the oppressive circumstances we faced and our general understandings of the appropriate means to deliver the oppressed have resulted in my being encouraged to pursue a path which is in many ways similar to his." Shortly before his execution Hill wrote that "the political impact of Brown's actions continues to serve as a powerful paradigm in my understanding of the potential effects the use of defensive force may have for the unborn."

Nor was the murder Hill committed the only right-wing violence that has been compared to Brown's. The Oklahoma City bombing in 1995 was a frontal attack on a U.S. government building, just like the Harpers Ferry raid. Anti-abortion murders, government bombings, anarchist bombs in the mail—nearly every time political violence surfaces, it gets described in the press as a part of a long American tradition of terrorism, with John Brown as a precursor and hero, a founding father of principled violence.

He gets compared to anarchists, leftist revolutionaries, and right-wing extremists. The spinning of John Brown, in short, is still going strong. But what does that make *him*? This much, at least, is certain: John Brown is a vital presence for all sorts of people today. In February PBS's *The American Experience* is broadcasting a ninety-minute documentary about him. Russell Banks's novel *Cloudsplitter* was a critical success and a bestseller as well. On the verge of his two hundredth birthday (this May 9 [1800]), John Brown is oddly present. Perhaps there is one compelling reason for his revival in this new millennium: Perhaps the violent, excessive, morally torn society John Brown represents so aptly was not just his own antebellum America but this land, now.

Stonewall Jackson

Robert K. Krick

Aside from Ulysses S. Grant and Robert E. Lee, the most famous Civil War general, and according to many historians actually the most brilliant commander, was Thomas J. "Stonewall" Jackson. He earned the nickname Stonewall for the stubborn defense made by his troops at the first Battle of Bull Run, but it was as a swift and decisive master of maneuver and attack that his modern reputation stands. Some authorities believe that his death (from what today would be called "friendly fire" at the Battle of Chancellorsville in 1863) was a more important turning point in the war than Lee's defeat at Gettysburg in July of that year.

Besides describing Jackson's military accomplishments in this essay, Robert K. Krick, author of *Conquering the Valley: Stonewall Jackson at Port Republic* (1996) presents an insightful portrait of Jackson's complex personality.

"There was a witchery in his name," a Mississippian wrote, "which carried confidence to friend and terror to foe." Northerners victimized by Stonewall Jackson's daring thrusts were hardly less laudatory. Gen. Gouverneur K. Warren, on the verge of becoming a Federal hero at Gettysberg, wrote on hearing of Jackson's death that he rejoiced for the Union cause, "and yet in my soldier's heart I cannot but see him the best soldier of all this war, and grieve at his untimely end." A New York newspaper praised Jackson as a "military genius" and declared, "Nowhere else will the name of Jackson be more honored."

Americans North and South marveled—and still do—at Jackson's exploits and at the rigid, pious, eminently determined person who produced them. He was in some ways so unlike his fellows but in many others so ordinary.

A Confederate attending an 1897 reunion in Los Angeles read a short poem to his assembled comrades. Its reminiscent look at the mythic images of Jackson and Robert E. Lee closes with a couplet that deftly evokes the two:

> *. . . now and then*
> *Through dimming mist we see*
> *The deadly calm of Stonewall's face*
> *The lion-front of Lee.*

That deadly calm continues to bemuse observers. It prompted a modern popular film producer in a fit of silliness to call Jackson a blue-eyed assassin. Serious students of the war respond to the imagery in ways that often reveal more about themselves than about the militant Presbyterian deacon who came, with Lee, to symbolize the Confederacy.

Thomas Jonathan Jackson (1824–63) reached the eve of the great American war without revealing any hint that he had the makings of a legend. For a land enamored of rags-to-riches tales, he personified the noble concept of rising from humble origins. Orphaned at an early age, sheltered in the homes of a series of relatives, ill educated, Tom Jackson reached his late teens without any real prospects for modern success, to say nothing of greatness. A chance to enter the United States Military Academy at West Point opened new vistas. It also threw in young Jackson's path the intimidating prospect of competing in a rigorous academic environment with boys vastly better prepared for the challenge.

Nothing soluble by sheer hard work ever daunted Jackson. The youngster from western Virginia stayed in the West Point Hotel's attic on June 19, 1842, and the next day began the academy's entrance examinations. When the testing ended, his name appeared dead last on the list approved for admission. He applied himself to West Point's curriculum with the same implacable determination that later made him a terror to his foes. A classmate recalled that his "efforts at the blackboard were sometimes painful to witness." Whatever the problem at hand, Jackson "would hang to it like a bull-dog, and in his mental efforts . . . great drops of perspiration would roll from his face, even in the coldest weather." Cadets joked that "he was certain to flood the section room."

The sweat—and long nights of cramming by candlelight—paid off. Jackson managed to finish fifty-first out of eighty-three class members at the end of his first year. He improved steadily to stand thirtieth and twentieth in succeeding classes, then graduated seventeenth in 1846. His grades the last year received a boost from the class on ethics (or logic), in which he reached the head of his class. At the end of his third year at West Point, the rigidly disciplined young man stood first in conduct among all 204 cadets. . . . The year Jackson graduated, his country went to war with Mexico. His experiences as an artillery subaltern in that conflict marked the young lieutenant as an officer of skill and promise, and promotions for bravery won during the bitter fighting in front of Mexico City earned him the title of major. He wore that designation with pride for fifteen years until in 1861 he became Stonewall, perhaps the most famous *nom de guerre* in American history.

Jackson's Mexican interlude also prompted the dawning of a religious awareness that would blossom into one of his defining characteristics. During his youth Jackson's irregular upbringing had included more horse racing than piety. A story about his siring an illegitimate child is unsubstantiated and probably inaccurate, but its acceptance by some of Jackson's Confederate staff suggests their awareness of a past completely alien to the rigidly decorous adult. In 1847 the Catholic culture of occupied Mexico stimulated Major Jackson to examine the Roman Church's tenets and practices with real interest. A few years later his religious nature settled on Calvinism, and he embraced Presbyterianism with all the zeal of a spectacularly ardent soul, becoming what his pastor called "the best deacon I ever had."

Jackson spent less than three years in the Army after leaving Mexico, being first posted to Fort Hamilton, near New York, and then to Fort Meade, in Florida. Proximity to New York's bookstores and libraries gave him an opportunity to exercise a relentless bent toward self-improvement. He wrote earnestly in 1849 to the congressman who years earlier had appointed him to West Point: "I propose with the blessings of providence to be a hard student and to make myself not only acquainted with military art and science, but with politics and . . . well versed in history." He pledged himself to read forty to fifty pages every day—more than fifteen thousand pages annually. Jackson's library survives in enough bulk to confirm his lifelong commitment to serious private study. It includes well-read books (most bearing his signature) in five languages, many with marginal notes in his hand; an extensive set of Shakespeare; scientific treatises; and more history and biography than any other genre. The uncomplicated T. J. Jackson of popular lore actually read almost encyclopedically across a very broad spectrum.

The Florida assignment offered little chance for self-improvement or anything else attractive. Fort Meade, not far southeast of Tampa, faced no Seminole threat; instead its warfare raged within the post, between Jackson and his commander, Maj. William H. French. One of Jackson's peers at West Point had noticed how a petty misdeed by another cadet, "prompted only by laziness," had seemed to Jackson "to show a moral depravity disgracing to humanity." That meddlesome inflexibility now led Major Jackson to attack French (whose pregnant wife was at the post) with an endless array of charges over what Jackson thought was moral turpitude involving a female nursemaid. Reviewing the flood of paper generated by the squabble leaves a modern reader uncertain about French's guilt—and not much interested in the question (which is about how the two officers' superiors felt at the time). A crusade that unquestionably struck Jackson as a solemn duty now looks like pettifoggery.

In the short term Jackson's righteous campaign at Fort Meade turned out badly for everyone involved, as could easily have been predicted. Weary and demoralized, he resigned to take a position at the emerging military college in Lexington, Virginia. The result was entirely salutary. He found contentment in Lexington, fell in love twice there, and developed into the mature man who would exploit the opportunities fate offered him a few years later. . . .

He also found satisfaction in his role in the community and with his neighbors, declaring himself "delighted with my duties, the place and the people." However, although the terse and somewhat eccentric professor clearly had the respect of his neighbors, he "certainly did not have their admiration," a contemporary wrote. Then and later he was as far from convivial as a man could readily be.

His rigidity, undiluted by pragmatism, made the Virginia Military Institute dislike him. They called him Square Box, a derisive tribute to his imposing boot size, and at times would sneak into his classroom to draw an immense foot on the chalkboard. Cadets delighted in falling into lockstep behind Jackson as he strode about campus; he never turned his head, so the jape went undetected. Students pulling a practice artillery piece by hand looked for opportunities to whirl it suddenly towards the professor, to make him dodge awkwardly. A cadet writing in 1855 bewailed his lot as a student of physics under "such a *hell of a fool*, whose name is Jackson," and launched some doggerel that concluded, "Great Lord Almighty, what a wonder,/ *Major Jackson, Hell & Thunder*." The disenchanted cadet-poet died fighting under Stonewall seven years later.

Jackson never did unravel the intricacies of effective public discourse, nor did he learn to endear himself to his charges. He weathered a formal investigation of his classroom performance by the Board of Visitors, made at the insistence of the institute's alumni association. . . .

For his part, Jackson liked much about academic life. He contemplated writing a textbook on optics and collaborated with a brother-in-law on the design of a military school in North Carolina. Had he taken to that new opportunity, he probably would have commanded North Carolina troops in 1861—with an impact on his career and on the course of the Civil War that is unknowable but fascinating to contemplate. The famed Stonewall Brigade, five sturdy Virginia regiments, never would have existed, nor could Jackson have become Stonewall at Manassas. Would Thomas Jackson sans nickname have succeeded as dramatically without the magical circumstances that attended his career in Virginia?

His professional experiences during the decade in Lexington did much to mold him, but his domestic life probably made an even deeper impression. Jackson's relationships with three women during the 1850s—two wives and a sister-in-law—reveal aspects of the man that do not fit the randomly constructed legend that obscures him. In the summer of 1853 Jackson married Elinor Junkin, the daughter of a Presbyterian minister who was president of Washington College. The major's tender, loving attentions to Ellie would have amazed those who saw only his public austerity. Fourteen months after their marriage Ellie Jackson died in childbirth (the baby, a boy, died too). . . .

In 1857 he was married again, to Mary Anna Morrison, the sweet-tempered daughter of another college president and Presbyterian preacher. Love letters, many of which survive, show again that Jackson's marriage was marked by a tenderness at odds with his public image. In November 1862 Anna bore his only surviving child. Stern notions of duty kept the proud father, by then a world-renowned lieutenant general, from going to see the baby—or even allowing his family to visit him—until late the next April. By then Jackson only had a few days to live. . . .

By 1861 Major Jackson had become a familiar figure to a few hundred residents of Lexington and its environs and a few hundred more Virginia Military Institute men. Had the Civil War not offered him a stringent new environment in which his remarkable abilities would be revealed, he would have remained all but unknown. It is hard to imagine that the histories of this his city and county, or even of the institute where he taught, would have mentioned him in more than a footnote next to other names now long forgotten. The war supplied a dramatically different stage upon which to strut, one for which he was uniquely suited.

One moment crucial to his career, and even more essential to the legend, came at the crisis of the Battle of First Manassas (or the First Battle of Bull Run, as the Yankees called it) on July 21, 1861. While the Confederate tactical situation deteriorated all around him, Jackson held his brigade of five Virginia regiments to their duty with characteristic resolution. A South Carolinian hoping to inspire his own troops pointed to Jackson standing "like a stone wall."

The general deserved every bit of the credit bestowed upon him for the stand at Manassas, but the nickname was of course pure happenstance. What he soon achieved at the head of his troops in Virginia catapulted him to worldwide renown. Had he accomplished precisely what he did, however, under a less riveting label than "Stonewall," the Jackson legend might not have maintained quite the grip it has on the popular imagination. Consider the Confederate generals Nathan G. ("Shanks") Evans, Sterling ("Old Pap") Price, Jerome B. ("Polly") Robertson, and H. H. ("Mud") Walker.

Jackson spent the twenty-two months of life left to him after First Manassas validating his *nom de guerre*. After a months-long *sitzkrieg* in Virginia and the collapse of Southern frontiers in the Western theater, he electrified the Confederacy with his dazzling Shenandoah Valley campaign during the Spring of 1862. Southerners used to bad news idolized the only one of their leaders demonstrating aggressive instincts and delivering good news. The fabulous Valley campaign demonstrates what made Jackson great. He began it with a mere thirty-five hundred troops. In addition to being overwhelmingly outnumbered, he faced a strategic imperative that limited his options: His paramount obligation was to keep as many Federals as possible anchored in the Valley and thus out of the force building against Richmond. To achieve that end, Jackson struck with characteristic boldness and energy at the Battle of Kernstown on March 23, 1862. He lost the tactical honors but forced his enemies to remain in the Valley when they had started to leave.

For the next six weeks Jackson either retreated or lurked in the arms of the mountains, patiently pulling Federals southward and isolating them from other duty. At the end of April the Confederates dashed east out of the Valley, only to return at once by train and then march rapidly west to win a victory in the Alleghenies at McDowell on May 8. Reinforcements available to Jackson because of that victory, and others he managed to wangle from east of the Valley, gave him the wherewithal to take the offensive for the first time. In a series of long, rapid marches and daring thrusts, he won battles at Front Royal and Winchester on May 23 and 25.

To magnify his successes, he boldly lunged all the way to the Potomac, with deadly effect on the thinking Federals in Washington. At the last possible moment he scurried back through a bottleneck between two Federal columns closing in on his line of retreat and marched south through torrential rains. The climax of the campaign came on June 8 and 9, with two incredible victories in succession, at Cross Keys and Port Republic. Jackson' carefully calculated daring had won its way past razor-thin enemy troops yet again.

The campaign revealed Stonewall Jackson's salient strengths with pellucid clarity: careful planning, consummate patience, methodical hard work, dazzling marches, unmatched daring, and (especially) immutable determination—but no intuitive pirouettes. Other generals who came to prominence during the war matched some of those skills; none employed them all in combination the way Jackson did.

With the Valley won, Jackson pushed east toward Richmond to help Robert E. Lee, newly in command of the Army of Northern Virginia, lift the encirclement of the capitol city. During the Seven Days' Battles the siege was ended, but more despite Stonewall's participation than because of it. For the only time during the war, Jackson failed, totally and unequivocally. The failure clearly originated in a collapse of his facilities because of what today would be recognized as stress fatigue. In 1862 observers wondered whether the general was selfish and could not cooperate. Had his meteoric performance in the Valley been a fluke? Some even thought that his failure one day before Richmond happened because his well-known religious zeal forbade Sunday marching and fighting.

But no one had any occasion to wonder about Jackson over the next ten months; he and Lee cemented a skilled collaboration ("I would follow him blindfolded," Jackson said) that discomfited the Federals at every turn. After he had won the Battle of Cedar Mountain as an independent commander on August 9, 1862, Stonewall joined Lee in a daring initiative that outmaneuvered the Unionists at Second Manassas. That victory opened the way for a raid across the Potomac during which Jackson captured thirteen thousand enemy troops at Harpers Ferry, then commanded half of Lee's line above Antietam Creek during the Battle of Antietam. In December Jackson's corps took part in the easy, bloody repulse of an immense Federal Army at Fredericksburg.

The deft complementary relationship between Lee and Jackson reached its pinnacle at Chancellorsville in May 1863. Although outnumbered by more than two to one (about 130,000 to 60,000), the two Virginians contrived to befuddle Gen. Joseph Hooker, commanding the opposing Army of the Potomac. In a maneuver that, typically, Lee proposed and Jackson executed flawlessly, the Confederates marched thirty thousand men around their enemy's flank. When Jackson's legions came screaming out of the woods behind Hooker's line, they routed one-third of the Federal Army. They also marked at that moment the apogee of the Confederate nation's fortunes.

A few hours later, Jackson fell mortally wounded, the victim of a mistaken volley of smoothbore musketry by some confused North Carolinians. Eight days later, Sunday, May 10, 1863, the stricken general declared piously that he had always hoped to die on the Sabbath. "Let us cross over the river and rest under the shade of the trees," he said; then, as on so many marches and battlefields, he led the way. The war in Virginia—in fact the entire course of American history—veered onto an altered course. . . .

What combination of characteristics had enabled the sometime artillery major and academic mediocrity to carve so glittering a swath as a Confederate leader? There certainly was little in his appearance to contribute to the mystique. Storied military men, including Lee, for instance, often looked like powerful figures; Thomas Jackson was modestly handsome, a fraction under six feet tall, with "light bluish gray eyes" that often occasioned comment ("as brilliant as a diamond," wrote one who knew him). The eyes burned in battle with a radiance that prompted the soldiers to call their general Old Blue Light or the Blue-Light Elder.

A mien either graceful or militant, combined with his ordinarily agreeable appearance, might have made Jackson look something like his legend. In fact, though, he was taciturn and marginally disheveled. A Fredericksburg woman who attended church in 1863 with Jackson summarized the contrast: The general was "decidedly interesting if not handsome in his appearance . . . and very young for his age. . . He has an embarrassed, diffident manner. Is a little deaf." A member of the 4th Alabama wrote that Jackson looked like an "old Virginia farmer." . . .

A vast array of images of Jackson provides modern students ample chance to see what he looked like, but none conveys the full dimensions of his contemporary impact. A Virginia colonel who had attended V.M.I. under Jackson wrote in 1867 to an artist at work on a Chancellorsville painting that every photograph, engraving, or painting of Stonewall that he had seen "unmistakably represent[ed] him" yet none really captured "a good likeness." Even though "every individual feature is

The mounted figures of Confederate President Jefferson Davis and Generals Robert E. Lee and Stonewall Jackson are depicted on Stone Mountain, the world's largest sculpture. This memorial carving, completed in 1970 after more than a half-century of work, sets the historical mood for Stone Mountain Park, located near Atlanta, Georgia.

good, and one artist has his profile perfect," no artist "succeeded in catching Jackson's *tout ensemble*, none of them have *painted his awkwardness.*"

Whatever his popular image, his subordinates, almost without exception, did not like him. Senior generals under his command used unrestrained language about their treatment. A.P. Hill called him "that crazy old Presbyterian fool"; Richard S. Ewell referred to him as "that enthusiastic fanatic"; and Charles S. Winder, in diary entries across three days full of maneuver and battle, declared: "Jackson is insane . . . growing disgusted with Jackson . . . requesting to leave his command."

Discomfort so pronounced suggests frustrated dealings with a superior either dishonest, lazy, selfishly ambitious, or simply stupid. Jackson was none of those things. What he was, instead, was painfully terse. In his sometimes awkward civilian dealings he once admitted, "I have no genius for *seeing.*" Officers—some of them major generals famous in their own right—came away from meetings horrified when he abruptly cut off even the most cursory forms of courteous discourse. The deadly determined Stonewall, his diligence reinforced by calm acceptance of doing God's work under fairly direct guidance, simply did not interact with others as most people do. Partial deafness exacerbated his taciturnity. Those who came to know him well, however, recognized the difference between his brusquely businesslike demeanor and actual rudeness. One of his staff wrote: "He is very reserved, not particularly companionable, but always . . . affable and polite."

The unusual personality that offended generals and colonels actually polished the patina of Stonewall's growing legend. A pre-war civilian observer noted—as did many others—that Thomas Jackson "never smiled and talked only when he had something to say," and added a remark about seeing "a most peculiar glint in his eye." Observers of that indefinable something in Jackson's gaze doubtless interpreted it more eagerly after he had become famous (famous for both his military prowess and his alleged eccentricity). It prompted one witness to suggest "that if [Jackson] were not a very good man he would be a very bad one." Tales of unconventional habits, such as sucking on lemons or rampant hypochondria, inevitably grew in the telling.

Americans expect at least a discernible tincture of colorful peculiarity in their legends. Muttering about crazy Stonewall turned into gleeful recounting of his valuable eccentricities once the string of gaudy victories had begun. The man of course had changed not one whit in the meanwhile. A Macon, Georgia, newspaper typified the glib switch in a June 1862 column: "Sometime ago, we accused Jackson of being of unsound mind. Since that time, he has exhibited not the least symptom of improvement. In fact he gets worse every day. Within the last two weeks he seems to have gone completely daft . . . He has been raving, ramping, roaring, rearing, snorting and cavorting up and down the Valley, chawing up Yankees by the thousands . . . Crazy or not, we but echo the voice of the whole Confederacy when we say 'God bless Old Stonewall.'"

For the men in the ranks who gasped and sweated through the general's epic marches, his oddities likewise became lovable quirks and his insanity genius. The men discovered that a victory lay at the end of each march, usually without excessive cost in blood. Trading sweat for blood, and exertion for victory, made great sense to them.

One aspect of Jackson's business-like style was his meticulousness. An intimate friend of the general at West Point (later a Confederate general himself) said aptly, "Jackson's mind seemed to do its work rather by perseverance than by quick penetration." Stonewall had little of the acute intuition popularly presumed to be essential in great generalship—an attribute much mooted in nineteenth-century military texts as the French *coup d'oeil* or the German *Fingerspitzengefuhl*. Lacking the ability to master terrain at a glance, he employed several able topographic engineers to prepare sketches and maps that included distance charts and other reminders.

Another manifestation of his meticulousness was his rigorous insistence on gathering enemy property of all kinds, cataloguing it in full detail, and defending it at all costs. The official list of all captured goods from the 1862 Shenandoah Valley campaign enumerates saddles and shoes and blankets—and six handkerchiefs, two and three-quarter dozen neckties, and one bottle of red ink. . . .

Anyone hoping to know Stonewall Jackson must come to terms with the depth and fervor of his religious experience. One Sunday morning a South Carolina officer received a telegram announcing that his wife was desperately ill. The worried husband's brigade and division commanders promptly granted the distraught man a compassionate leave. When the Carolinian sought final clearance from his corps commander, Jackson somewhat atypically granted it—but only after lecturing the man in the impropriety of conducting private business on the Sabbath.

Wearing his new battle name of Stonewall, the general wrote soon after Manassas to his pastor in Lexington. Townspeople awaiting the mail eagerly sought to learn the contents of the envelope from their newly famous neighbor, but he mentioned the battle not at all. Instead, he sent a check for the support of the Sunday school he had started (in contravention of law and social standard) for black youngsters. A few weeks later Jackson played host to a visiting minister from Lexington by putting the man of God up on his own cot; the general slept on the floor of the tent, "without bed or matrass," the amazed visitor wrote.

Jackson's letters to a confidant in the Confederate Congress included much about military affairs—requests for help with armaments and recruiting, suggestions for actions affecting the armies—but they also featured a steady flow of religious promptings. Should not the Congress forbid carrying the mail, to say nothing of actually delivering it, on the Sabbath? Why not ban distilleries, turning their copper tubing into cannon? (Jackson eschewed strong drink because, he said irrefragably, he liked the way it tasted.)

Deacon Jackson's unflinching piety sometimes led him astray in military matters, as when he chose as his chief of staff a favorite Presbyterian cleric with precisely nothing to commend him for a staff role. In most instances, however, the divine guidance that Jackson perceived worked in his favor. . . . Stonewall's salient characteristics, both personal and military, profited from a calm certainty that he was doing God's will. Flourish the sword of the Lord and of Gideon, and let the Philistines beware!

More than any other quality, Thomas Jackson displayed determination. That defining characteristic dominated his performance. On many a battlefield the unswerving resolve of one man had more effect than dozens of cannon or thousands of muskets. Earnest devotion to a single goal, no matter what the obstacles, made Jackson "the most one-idead man I ever saw," according to an observer. A member of the general's staff, in a manuscript note scribbled during the war, declared: "His will unsurpassed—fearless, unwearied, unchanging persistent & it worked marvelously." That most basic essence of Stonewall Jackson conveyed itself also to a South Carolinian who visited headquarters. Jackson's face, he wrote, reflected "self-command, perseverance, indomitable will."

Examination of his storied campaigns reveals that Jackson's military abilities at tactical level, especially early in the war, were no more than ordinary. On the intermediate military plane that is called "operational," midway between tactics and strategy, Jackson sometimes displayed marked skill. Strategically he excelled, crafting campaigns still studied as classics by military training programs. Even so, it is impossible to see in him the essential genius of a Frederick the Great or a Napoleon. What made him awesome in war was the clenched-jaw will that guided every decision at every level.

William Tecumseh Sherman

Victor Davis Hanson

In 1864 Union General William Tecumseh Sherman and his army of 70,000 seized Atlanta and then "marched to the sea" to Savannah, cutting a wide swath of destruction along the way. He sought not only to defeat opposing soldiers but also to shatter the Confederates' will to keep its armies in the field. Some historians have regarded Sherman's style of warfare as a harbinger of the "total wars" of the twentieth century, culminating in ethnic cleansing, concentration camps, genocide, and the indiscriminate bombing of civilians. But in this article Victor Hanson urges a more thoughtful consideration of whether Sherman's harsh manner of war justified its purposes, the destruction of the slave system. That slavery was immoral Hanson takes as a given; thus he focuses on Sherman's style of warfare: a slashing strike through the enemy's homeland. Insofar as war is always barbaric, Sherman's strategy was humane insofar as it constituted the best means of ending a just war in the shortest time and with the fewest casualties. Unlike Grant's bloody battles of attrition, the wasting struggles of trench warfare during the First World War, the protracted aerial bombardments of the Second World War, or the body counts of Vietnam, Sherman fought as did Patton, whose armored columns raced across the plains of northern Europe in 1945. War is terrible, concludes Hanson, but Sherman understood that its terrors "must be proportional, ideological, and rational." Hanson's most recent books include *Bonfire of the Humanities: Rescuing Classics in an Impoverished Age* (2001) and *Carnage and Culture: Landmark Battles in the Rise of Western Power* (2001).

By the fall of 1864 no army in either Europe or America was as mobile, self-supporting, and lethal as William Tecumseh Sherman's, which was composed of soldiers in prime physical condition expert in the handling of modern firearms. Their general was in some sense not merely the most powerful man in America but also the most dangerous person in the world. The Macon *Telegraph* warned its readers: "It would seem as if in him all the attributes of man were merged in the enormities of the demon, as if Heaven intended in him to manifest depths of depravity yet untouched by a fallen race. . . . Unsated still in his demoniac vengeance he sweeps over the country like a simoom of destruction."

The advent of Sherman's army must have been a terrifying experience for an agrarian society. . . .

For the next century critics would argue over the rectitude, effectiveness, and difficulty of the March to the Sea, asserting that what Sherman did in Georgia was either amoral or irrelevant to the Union cause. Others added that Sherman had not been assiduous in collecting freed slaves—purportedly more than fifty thousand directly in his path were ready to flee—and that he had wrecked the entire tradition of the practice of just war that once had expressly spared civilians. Before addressing these criticisms systematically, I must note the irony in each.

How in a moral sense could the March to the Sea be too barbaric in destroying Southern property yet at the same time not effective enough in killing Confederate soldiers? How could Sherman's men be too lax in freeing slaves? How could his march be considered too easy when Grant and Lincoln—men known for neither timidity nor hysteria—feared for the very destruction of Sherman's army when he requested permission to attempt it? And how else could Sherman move his colossal army to the east and be in position to march northward other than by living off the land and destroying property? Was he to pay for the food of slaveowners in prized Federal dollars with promises that such capital would not be forwarded to purchase more bullets for Lee and Johnston? Were his men to eat hardtack while secessionists fared better? Keep clear of railroads, as locomotives sped by with food, ammunition, and guns to kill Northerners in Virginia? Bypass slaveowning plantationists in a war to end slavery?

As for the charge that Sherman's brand of war was amoral, if we forget for a moment what constitutes "morality" in war and examine acts of violence per se against Southern civilians, we learn that there were few, if any, gratuitous murders on the march. There seem also to have been less than half a dozen rapes, a fact acknowledged by both sides. Any killing outside of battle was strictly military execution in response to the shooting of Northern prisoners. The real anomaly seems to be that Sherman brought more than sixty thousand young men through one of the richest areas of the enemy South without unchecked killing or mayhem. After the war a Confederate officer remarked of the march through Georgia: "The Federal army generally behaved very well in this State. I don't think there was ever an army in the world that would have behaved better, on a similar expedition, in an enemy country. Our army certainly wouldn't."

If civilians were not killed, tortured, or raped, was the march of the army nonetheless amoral? The historian John Bennett Walters has argued that it was, because soldiers traumatized and robbed noncombatants and wrecked their homes: "An invading army, without any claim on military necessity, had thrown away every inclination toward mercy for weakness and helplessness. The Federal troops had resorted to the sheer brutality of overpowering strength to despoil a people of their material resources and to injure irreparably their finer sensibilities."

The true moral question, though, is not whether civilians are fair game in war but whether the property and tranquillity of civilians who support chattel slavery and rebellion are fair game in a war precipitated over refusal to end that institution—whether, in other words, the supporters of apartheid have abandoned prior claim on the "finer sensibilities." If one believes that slavery is a great evil and that secession constitutes treason, then Sherman was surely right that the best mechanism to end both, short of killing civilians, was to destroy the property of both the state and the wealthy, thereby robbing those fighting on behalf of slaveholding and rebellion of both the material and psychological support of their own citizenry. That seems to me very much a "military necessity."

We must here make a vital distinction between "total" war and a war of "terror." Sherman surely waged the latter, seeking to shock the enemy through the destruction of its landscape and the wreckage of its hopes to such a degree that it would desist from supporting the killing of Union troops. But that terror was not total, and he never resorted to any of the barbarities of the modern age—ethnic cleansing, concentration camps, mass killing, indiscriminate bombing, and torture—to achieve his ends. His march has nothing in common with the dirty wars of the twentieth century, wherein revolutions, coups, and ethnic hatreds have usually had no moral agenda and have never been part of an effort to stop enslavement. When Sherman reached Savannah, Southern generals asked him for the protection of their own families, surely proof that they at least did not think they were entrusting their women and children to a terrorist.

The late twentieth century has increasingly come to declare *all* war evil. Since peace is considered the natural state of relations, we live in an era of "conflict resolution" and "peace studies," in which some degree of moral guilt is freely assessed equally both to those who kill to advance evil and those who kill to end it, to those who are aggressive and to those who resist aggrandizement. Regardless of cause or circumstances, we all in the end must become "victims" of those who have the greater power, which transcends national boundaries: politicians, corporations, the military. Indeed, "evil" itself is to be seen as a relative idea.

Yet there is always a timeless, absolute difference between slavery and freedom, and those who battle for abolition and those who kill to defend slavery are qualitatively different and can be recognized as such. There would have been a real difference between a Confederate America and a Union America. Sherman's war against property belongs to a particular context, inseparable from the question of slavery. So I am confused when present-day historians write that they are disturbed, for example, to learn that Sherman's men killed bloodhounds in Georgia, as if the gratuitous killing of pets, some of which were accomplished trackers of slaves and Union prisoners, mattered very much when half a million blacks in Georgia had been slaves until Bill Sherman's dog-killers set thousands of them free.

Once the free Southern leadership and its citizenry chose to fight and kill on behalf of human bondage, the destruction of their private property, unlike attacks against Northern farms, took on the logic of retribution and atonement. Was this a fair rationale for Union soldiers when their own Founding Fathers had owned slaves and had seen no reason to bar the practice in either the Constitution or the Bill of Rights? Lincoln grasped perfectly this American dilemma and thus sought to eradicate the evil of slavery, at least in the beginning of his efforts, peaceably, with compensation, and over time, as all American society might slowly evolve to a consensus about the immorality of bondage.

Southerners, in contrast, wanted no part of that national dialogue, because they knew precisely where it would end up: abolition and a federal government now strong enough to enforce its moral culture on particular states. Southern leaders precipitated the war because they correctly saw Federal policy as leading immutably to the end of their way of life—a way of life whose material riches for a few were to be perpetually supported by the bondage of African blacks.

Was Sherman's march effective? There seem to be two approaches involved in this answer, and both result in the affirmative. If for a moment we forget the actual material damage done the Confederacy and consider where Sherman's army started and where it finished, the march in itself was the definitive act of retribution against the South. Sherman's capture of Atlanta probably saved Lincoln the election. The very fact that he could march unharmed through the South eroded all support in the North for Democrats and Copperheads who advocated negotiated peace or surrender under the guise of settlement. Overseas there would be no further talk of recognizing the Confederacy.

Moreover, in purely strategic terms, Sherman was now three hundred miles closer to the last major source of Confederate resistance, Lee's army in Virginia. Until Sherman reached Savannah, Grant was holding Lee firmly in his grasp and waging, whether intended or not, a brutal and steady war of annihilation. When Sherman reached the Atlantic—as he had foreseen all along—the complexion of that death lock changed radically: Lee was faced with the prospect of a lethal force marching steadily northward at his rear, devouring the source of supply for his army, and ruining the homes of his soldiers in the trenches. Where as before, Lee had kept Grant out of Richmond and had the option either to threaten Washington or to just stay still, now he had to move either northward over Grant or southward through Sherman.

Had Sherman not torched a single Southern estate, his march would nevertheless have been strategically brilliant for its role in the coordination of the Union armies—and psychologically devastating to the Confederate cause. As the artillery officer Thomas Osborn wrote when Sherman and his men reached Savannah: "Thus the immediate object of the campaign is completed. This army has been transferred from the middle of the country to the sea coast, this city captured and the lines for supplies for General Lee's army south of here are destroyed. The Confederacy proper is now southern Virginia and North and South Carolina. It has no other territory now at its disposal for military operations and this campaign has shown there is not much more left to it, except General Lee's army and the small force in our front."

Damage, of course, Sherman did. Even by 1870 the assessed valuation of farms in Georgia was little more than a third what it had been ten years earlier. Unfortunately for the poor of the South, the ripples of Sherman's plunge into the Georgian countryside continued for decades; the result of his depredations against the plantations and state was to create years of general economic stagnation that would affect both the free black and white poor. Sherman's apologists—and in the years after the armistice they continued to shrink as the horror of frontal infantry assault was forgotten—would defend his actions on three grounds: First, better that Southerners be poor and alive in Georgia than rotting in the mud of northern Virginia—and the South's only apparent strategy of salvation was the doomed quest to crush Grant's Army of the Potomac; second, the poverty of a few hundred thousand citizens for decades was to be reckoned against the bondage of millions of slaves for centuries; and third, war cannot be "refined." Revolutionaries suffer inordinately when they precipitate war, lack the high moral ground, and turn out to be impotent. Sherman would come to be hated in a way Grant never would be because he humiliated and impoverished the South with ease and impunity, rather than kill Southern youth with difficulty and at great cost.

The march through Georgia made all subsequent campaigns by the Army of the West easier. Hundreds of thousands of Confederate civilians, once so critical in encouraging their men at the front, now would have precisely the opposite effect. When Sherman turned north into the Carolinas, Confederate soldiers wrote their

General Sherman blazed a path of destruction. Intending to "demonstrate the vulnerability of the South and make its inhabitants feel that war and individual ruin are synonymous terms," General William Tecumseh Sherman waged total war, systematically cutting a path of unprecedented destruction through Georgia and the Carolinas in late 1864 and early 1865.

governor: "It is not in the power of the Yankee Armies to cause us to wish ourselves at home. We can face them, and can hear their shot and shell without being moved; but, Sir, we cannot hear the cries of our little ones and stand."

This natural reaction had been foreseen by Sherman: "I attach more importance to these deep incisions into the enemy's country, because this war differs from European wars in this particular: we are not only fighting hostile armies, but a hostile people, and must make old and young, rich and poor, feel the hard hand of war, as well as their organized armies. I know that this recent movement of mine through Georgia has had a wonderful effect in this respect. Thousands who have been deceived by their lying newspapers to believe that we were being whipped all the time now realize the truth, and have no appetite for a repetition of the same experience."

Whereas much has been written of the destruction of Southern morale, too little has been devoted to the radically changed spirit in the North brought on by Sherman's march. Lincoln put it best as he summed up the Union effort in his annual message to Congress on December 6, 1864: "[We] have *more* men *now* than we had when the war *began*. . . . We are *gaining* strength, and may, if need be, maintain the contest indefinitely." Grant's army was a force vital to the preservation of the Union and the destruction of the best Confederate soldiers in the field, but neither Grant nor the Army of the Potomac—given the frightful casualties of summer 1864 and the absence of movement forward—could embolden the American populace to continue the war.

Americans might now sing "Marching Through Georgia" or read poems about "The March to the Sea"; they would never write hymns to celebrate Cold Harbor or read verses about "The Wilderness." Sherman—in light of his army's speed, his preservation of Union lives, his transection of the Confederacy, the sheer hatred he incurred from the South, and his gift for the language of doom—captured the mind of America. In a little more than thirty days he had redefined the entire Civil War as a death struggle between yeomen farmers and the privilege of aristocratic plantationists, and the verdict of that ideological contest was plain for all to see in the burning estates of central Georgia. Had Sherman not taken Atlanta, Lincoln might not have been re-elected President; had he lost his army in Georgia, a negotiated peace would have been a real possibility; and had he rested on his laurels in Savannah, Grant would have fought Lee for another six months to a year. It is true that Sherman redefined the American way of war, but his legacy was not Vietnam but rather the great liberating invasions of Europe during World War II, in which Americans marched right through the homelands of the Axis powers. Sherman, in short, invented the entire notion of American strategic doctrine, one that would appear so frequently in the century to follow: the ideal of a vast moral crusade on foreign soil to restructure a society through sheer force of arms.

We should keep in mind that the timing of the war's close in April 1865 was not fortuitous. The Confederacy collapsed at that particular moment not because of Thomas's smashing victory in Tennessee nearly six months earlier, or because Grant had finally obliterated Lee, but rather because Sherman's gigantic army of Union veterans was now rapidly approaching Lee's rear. The South itself acknowledged this. The obituary for Sherman in the Americus, Georgia, *Daily Times* conceded that he "was the victorious general who really subdued the Confederacy. By his devastations in Georgia the morale of Lee's army was so reduced and his ranks so thinned that Grant's success was possible, so that at last Sherman and not Grant was entitled to the credit of Appomattox."

Moreover, Sherman's marches precipitated the war's end at a great savings in lives on both sides. More Southerners deserted, gave up, or simply ceased fighting because of Sherman's march than were killed in Grant's attacks. "Of course I must fight when the time comes," Sherman wrote his daughter, "but wherever a result can be accomplished without Battle I prefer it."

Was he sometimes lax in recruiting slaves into his army on his march? Yes. Did it ultimately matter? No. It is true that Sherman did not welcome very young, female, or aged freed slaves to join his march. He was interested primarily in taking on fit young male ex-slaves to serve in his engineering and pioneering corps—the thousands of impressive black troopers who would later carve a path through the Carolinas and march so proudly in review in Washington at war's end.

As events turned out, Sherman still had thousands of blacks in his army when it was all over; he had freed thousands more during his march—best estimates put them at more than twenty-five thousand, or almost a third of the size of his own force—and his efforts at destroying the plantation culture of the South had accelerated the general emancipation in the mere six months left after he cut through Georgia. Later he would put it succinctly: "My aim then was, to whip the rebels, to humble their pride, to follow them to their inmost recesses, and make them fear and dread us. 'Fear of the Lord is the beginning of wisdom.' I did not want them to cast in our teeth what General Hood had once done in Atlanta, that we had to call on *their* slaves to help us to subdue them. But, as regards kindness to the race, encouraging them to patience and forbearance, procuring them food and clothing, and providing them with land whereon to labor, I assert that no army ever did more for that race than the one I commanded in Savannah."

Finally, and most important, did Sherman bring on the evils of total conflict so well known to the modern age? He did not. The best of the Union generals—Thomas and Grant in particular—were bulldogs, not greyhounds, and it was they, not Sherman, who turned war into an anonymous process of an industrial state, where cannon, rifle, and manpower were thrown promiscuously into the inferno, with little regard to past custom or protocol and even less chance that individual achievement or skill in arms in themselves might win the day.

However inexact the comparison, the difference between World War I and World War II sheds some light on the respective manner in which Grant and Sherman each fought the South, and the contrast is not, as might be expected, entirely to Sherman's detriment. From 1914 to 1918 the Allies, Grant-like, waged a horrific war of annihilation in the trenches against the armies of autocracy that ultimately ruined their entire military but left the populations of the Central Powers largely unscathed—and eager to find scapegoats. Another world war followed a mere two decades later. After World War II and the savage and systematic demolition of the German and Japanese landscapes—far in excess of what even Sherman might have imagined or condoned—neither society warred again, and there has been peace in Europe and Japan thus far not for twenty years but for half a century. No German or Japanese civilians after 1945 could ever underestimate the power of the British and American military, or think that their culture had been betrayed rather than conquered, or believe that their support for murderous regimes did not have personal consequences. Germans had far more respect for—and fear of—Patton in 1945 than they had had for Pershing in 1918.

For Sherman, then, the attack on property and infrastructure was permissible, if the war was an ideological one against anarchy, treason, and slavery and if it would lead to a permanent peace based on just principles. Terror, as a weapon to be employed in war by a democratic army, must be proportional, ideological, and rational: proportional—Southerners, who fought to preserve men as mere property, would have their property destroyed; ideological—those who would destroy property would do so as part of a larger effort of abolition that was not merely strategic but ethical as well; and rational—burning and looting would not be random, nor killing gratuitous, but rather ruin was to have a certain logic, as railways, public buildings, big plantations, all the visible and often official infrastructure of a slave society, would be torched, while the meager houses of the poor and the persons themselves of the Confederacy would be left relatively untouched.

The issues of age and property are also often forgotten in Sherman's march, but again they are decisive. Sherman constantly stressed his affection for "his boys" and the need to save his army; he showed a shocking lack of concern for those of adult age in the Confederacy who had carried through secession. Yet it seems to me a far more moral act to make the middle-aged and elderly, male and female alike, who fight wars for property pay for their folly with their possessions, than to exterminate those youngsters, without possessions, and with little real knowledge of the politics that put them in harm's way.

The historian B. H. Liddell Hart best summed up Sherman's view of what constituted real savagery: "It was logical, and due to reasoning that was purely logical, that he should first oppose war; then, conduct it with iron severity; and, finally, seize the first real opportunity to make a peace of complete absolution. He cared little that his name should be execrated by the people of the South if he could only cure them of a taste for war. And to cure them he deliberately aimed at the non-combatant foundation of the hostile war spirit instead of its combatant roof. He cared as little that this aim might violate a conventional code of war, for so long as war was regarded as a chivalrous pastime, and its baseness obscured by a punctilious code, so long would it be invested with a halo of romance. Such a code and such a halo had helped the duel to survive long after less polite forms of murder had grown offensive to civilized taste and gone out of fashion."

I am also surprised not at the contrasts drawn between Sherman and Grant—their differences in strategic thinking, their close friendship, and their shared responsibility for winning the war invite obvious and spirited comparisons that have merit on both sides—but rather at the absence of contrasts drawn between Sherman and Lee. Lee, who wrecked his army by sending thousands on frontal charges against an entrenched enemy and who himself owned slaves, enjoys the reputation of a reluctant, humane knight who battled for a cause—States' Rights and the sanctity of Southern soil—other than slavery. Sherman, who was careful to save his soldiers from annihilation and who freed thousands of slaves in Georgia, is too often seen as a murderous warrior who fought for a cause—federalism and the punishment of treason—other than freedom.

Lee, as Sherman noted, crafted the wrong offensive for an outmanned and outproduced South, which led to horrendous casualties; Sherman's marches drew naturally on the material and human surpluses of the North and so cracked the core of the Confederacy, with few killed on either side. Lee wrongly thought the Union soldier would not fight as well as the Confederate; Sherman rightly guessed that the destruction of Southern property would topple the entire Confederacy. The one ordered thousands to their deaths when the cause was clearly lost; the other destroyed millions of dollars of property to hasten the end of bloodshed. Yet Sherman, who fought on the winning side, who promised in the abstract death and terror, who was unkempt, garrulous, and blunt, is usually criticized; Lee, who embodies the Lost Cause, who wrote of honor and sacrifice, and who was dapper, genteel, and mannered, is canonized. Historians would do better to assess each on what he did, not on what he professed.

Sherman's most impressive statue, a forty-three-foot-high equestrian rendition of the general on the march, still towers in Washington, D.C., in a beautiful, small park at Fifteenth Street and Pennsylvania Avenue, between the Treasury Department and the Ellipse. Few Washingtonians know where the statue is, and fewer still of those who lunch in the park seem ever to approach the monument itself. If they did, they would discover, on the north side of the granite base, beneath the mounted general, Sherman's own declaration that the proper purpose of battle was to make society right: "War's Legitimate Object Is More Perfect Peace."

The South's Inner Civil War

Eric Foner

That the Civil War divided the nation is a commonplace, but it involved divisions far more complicated than the obvious split between North and South. In both the Union and the Confederacy, the people were far from unanimous in their support of the conflict. Opposition to the war in the North has been studied at length, but most people and indeed many historians have assumed that the Southerners, fighting to defend not only their way of life but their homes against northern "invaders," were united in support of the Confederacy. The decision of Colonel Robert E. Lee, who despite his devotion to the United States and his dislike of slavery resigned his commission and offered his services to the Confederacy when his state, Virginia, seceded, has been seen as typical.

That the South was in fact badly divided by the conflict is convincingly demonstrated in this essay by Professor Eric Foner of Columbia University. In addition to pointing out what should have been obvious, that black Southerners were overwhelmingly pro-Union, Foner shows that large elements in the white population also opposed first secession and then the vigorous conduction of the war. Professor Foner's book, *Reconstruction: America's Unfinished Revolution, 1863–1877*, won a Bancroft Prize and many other honors.

———————

Americans tend to think of the Civil War as a titanic struggle between two regions of the country, one united in commitment to the Union, the other equally devoted to its own nationhood. Yet neither North nor South was truly unified. Lincoln was constantly beset by draft resistance, peace sentiment, and resentment of the immense economic changes unleashed by the war. Internal dissent was, if anything, even more widespread in the wartime South. Not only did the four million slaves identify with the Union cause, but large numbers of white Southerners came to believe that they had more to lose from a continuation of the war than from a Northern victory. Indeed, scholars today consider the erosion of the will to fight as important a cause of Confederate defeat as the South's inferiority in manpower and industrial resources. Even as it waged a desperate struggle for independence, the Confederacy was increasingly divided against itself.

This was a matter of conflict more than simple warweariness. The South's inner civil war reflected how wartime events and Confederate policies eventually reacted upon the region's distinctive social and political structure. Like a massive earthquake, the Civil War and the destruction of slavery permanently altered the landscape of Southern life, exposing and widening fault lines that had lain barely visible just beneath the surface. The most profound revolution, of course, was the destruction of slavery. But white society after the war was transformed no less fully than black.

From the earliest days of settlement, there had never been a single white South. In 1860 a majority of white Southerners lived not in the plantation belt but in the upcountry, an area of small farmers and herdsmen who owned few slaves or none at all. Self-sufficiency remained the primary goal of these farm families, a large majority of whom owned their land. Henry Warren, a Northerner who settled in Leake County in Mississippi's hill country after the war, recalled white families attending church "dressed in homespun cloth, the product of the spinning wheel and hand loom, with which so many of the log cabins of that section were at that time equipped." This economic order, far removed from the lavish world of the great planters, gave rise to a distinctive subculture that celebrated mutuality, egalitarianism (for whites), and proud independence. But so long as slavery and planter rule did not interfere with the yeomanry's self-sufficient agriculture and local independence, the latent class conflict among whites failed to find coherent expression.

It was in the secession crisis and subsequent Civil War that upcountry yeomen discovered themselves as a political class. The elections for delegates to secession conventions in the winter of 1860–61 produced massive repudiations of disunion in yeoman areas. Once the war had begun, most of the South's white population rallied to the Confederate cause. But from the outset disloyalty was rife in the Southern mountains. Virginia's western counties seceded from the Old Dominion in 1861 and two years later reentered the Union as a separate state.

In East Tennessee, long conscious of its remoteness from the rest of the state, supporters of the Confederacy formed a small minority. This mountainous area contained a quarter of the state's population but had long been overshadowed economically and politically by the wealthier, slave-owning counties to the west. A majority of Tennessee's white opposed secession, although once war had begun a popular referendum supported joining the Confederacy. But East Tennessee still voted, by a two-to-one margin, to remain within the Union. Indeed, a convention of mountain Unionists declared the state's secession null and void and "not binding" on "loyal citizens." The delegates called for the region's secession from the state (an idea dating back to the proposed state of Franklin in the 1780s). Andrew Johnson, who had grown to manhood there, was the only United States senator from a seceding state to remain at his post in Washington once the war had begun, and in August 1861 East Tennessee voters elected three Unionists to represent them in the federal Congress.

Meanwhile, almost every county in the region saw Unionist military companies established to disrupt the Confederate war effort. In July 1861 the local political leader William B. Carter traveled to Washington, where he proposed to President Lincoln that Unionists try to cut East Tennessee off from the rest of the Confederacy by burning railroad bridges. Carter later claimed that Gen. George B. McClellan promised that once this had been done, a Federal army would liberate the area.

Carter's plan proved to be a disaster for East Tennessee Unionists. Four bridges were in fact burned, but others proved too heavily guarded. In one case Unionists overpowered the Confederate guards only to discover that they had misplaced their matches. And it was a Confederate army, not a Union one, that invaded East Tennessee in force after these incidents. Several men were seized and summarily executed, and hundreds of Unionists were thrown in jail. The result was a massive flight of male citizens from the region. Many who made their way through the mountains to safety subsequently returned as members of the Union army. Felix A. Reeve, for example, one of the earliest exiles, reentered East Tennessee in 1863 at the head of the 8th Regiment of Tennessee Infantry. All told, some thirty-one thousand white Tennesseans eventually joined the Union army. Tennessee was one of the few Southern states from which more whites than blacks enlisted to fight for the Union.

Throughout the war East Tennessee remained the most conspicuous example of discontent within the Confederacy. But other mountain counties also rejected secession from the outset. One citizen of Winston County in the northern Alabama hill country believed yeomen had no business fighting for a planter-dominated Confederacy: "all tha want is to git you . . . to fight for their infurnal negroes and after you do their fightin' you may kiss their hine parts for o tha care." On July 4, 1861, a convention of three thousand residents voted to take Winston out of the Confederacy; if a state could withdraw from the Union, they declared, a county had the same right to secede from a state. Unionists here carried local elections and formed volunteer military bands that resisted Confederate enlistment officers and sought to protect local families from harassment by secessionists.

Georgia's mountainous Rabun County was "almost a unit against secession." As one local resident recalled in 1865, "You cannot find a people who were more averse to secession than were the people of our county. . . . I canvassed the county in 1860–61 myself and I know that there were not exceeding twenty men in this county who were in favor of secession." Secret Union organizations also flourished in the Ozark Mountains of northern Arkansas. More than one hundred members of the Peace and Constitutional Society were arrested late in 1861 and given the choice of jail or enlisting in the Confederate army. As in East Tennessee, many residents fled, and more than eight thousand men eventually served in Union regiments.

Discontent developed more slowly outside the mountains. It was not simply devotion to the Union but the impact of the war and the consequences of Confederate policies that awakened peace sentiment and social conflict. In any society war demands sacrifice, and public support often rests on the conviction that sacrifice is equitably shared. But the Confederate government increasingly molded its policies in the interest of the planters.

Within the South the most crucial development of the early years of the war was the disintegration of slavery. War, it has been said, is the midwife of revolution, and whatever politicians and military commanders might decree, slaves saw the conflict as heralding the end of bondage. Three years into the conflict Gen. William T. Sherman encountered a black Georgian who summed up the slaves' understanding of the war from its outset: "He said . . . he had been looking for the 'angel of the Lord' ever since he was knee-high, and, though we professed to be fighting for the Union, he supposed that slavery was the cause, and that our success was to be his freedom." On the basis of this conviction, the slaves took actions that not only propelled the reluctant North down the road to emancipation but severely exacerbated the latent class conflict within the white South.

As the Union army occupied territory on the periphery of the Confederacy, first in Virginia, then in Tennessee, Louisiana, and elsewhere, slaves by the thousands headed for the Union lines. Long before the Emancipation Proclamation slaves grasped that the presence of occupying troops destroyed the coercive power of both the individual master and the slaveholding community. On Magnolia Plantation in Louisiana, for example, the arrival of the Union army in 1862 sparked a work stoppage and worse. "We have a terrible state of affairs here," reported one planter. "Negroes refusing to work. . . . The negroes have erected a gallows in the quarters and [say] they must drive their master . . . off the plantation hang their master etc. and that then they will be free."

Even in the heart of the Confederacy, far from Federal troops, the conflict undermined the South's "peculiar institution." Their "grapevine telegraph" kept many slaves remarkably well informed about the war's progress. And the drain of white men into military service left plantations under the control of planters' wives and elderly and infirm men, whose authority slaves increasingly felt able to challenge. Reports of "demoralized" and "insubordinate" behavior multiplied throughout the South. Slavery, Confederate Vice-President Alexander H. Stephens proudly affirmed, was the cornerstone of the Confederacy. Accordingly, slavery's disintegration compelled the Confederate government to take steps to save the institution, and these policies, in turn, sundered white society.

The impression that planters were not bearing their fair share of the war's burdens spread quickly in the upcountry. Committed to Southern independence, most planters were also devoted to the survival of plantation slavery, and when these goals clashed, the latter often took precedence. After a burst of Confederate patriotism in 1861, increasing numbers of planters resisted calls for a shift from cotton to food production, even as the course of the war and the drain of manpower undermined the subsistence economy of the upcountry, threatening soldiers' families with destitution. When Union forces occupied New Orleans in 1862 and extended their control of the Mississippi Valley in 1863, large numbers of planters, merchants, and factors salvaged their fortunes by engaging in cotton traffic with the Yankee occupiers. Few demonstrated such unalloyed self-interest as James L. Alcorn, Mississippi's future Republican governor, who, after a brief stint in the Southern army, retired to his plantation, smuggled contraband cotton into Northern hands, and invested the profits in land and Union currency. But it was widely resented that, as a Richmond newspaper put it, many "rampant cotton and sugar planters, who were so early and furiously in the field of secession," quickly took oaths of allegiance during the war and resumed raising cotton "in partnership with their Yankee *protectors.*" Other planters resisted the impressment of their slaves to build military fortifications and, to the end, opposed calls for the enlistment of blacks in the Confederate army, afraid, an Alabama newspaper later explained, "to risk the loss of their property."

Even more devastating for upcountry morale, however, were policies of the Confederate government. The upcountry became convinced that it bore an unfair share of taxation; it particularly resented the tax in kind and the policy of impressment that authorized military officers to appropriate farm goods to feed the army. Planters, to be sure, now paid a higher proportion of their own income in taxes than before the war, but they suffered far less severely from such seizures, which undermined the yeomanry's subsistence agriculture. By the middle of the war, Lee's army was relying almost entirely upon food impressed from farms and plantations in Georgia and South Carolina.

The North Georgia hill counties suffered the most severely. "These impressments," Georgia's governor Joseph E. Brown lamented in 1863, "have been ruinous to the people of the northeastern part of the State, where . . . probably not half a supply of provisions [is] made for the support of the women and children. One man in fifty may have a surplus, and forty out of the fifty may not have half enough. . . . Every pound of meat and every bushel of grain, carried out of that part of the State by impressing officers, must be replaced by the State at public expense or the wives and children of soldiers in the army must starve for food." The impressment of horses and oxen for the army proved equally disastrous, for it made it almost impossible for some farm families to plow their fields or transport their produce to market. These problems were exacerbated by the South's rampant inflation.

During the war poverty descended upon thousands of upcountry families, especially those with men in the army. Food riots broke out in Virginia and North Carolina. In 1864 a group of farmers in Randolph County, Alabama, sent a poignant petition to Confederate President Jefferson Davis describing conditions in their "poor and mountainous" county: "There are now on the rolls of the Probate court, 1600 indigent families to be Supported; they average 5 to each family; making a grand total of 8000 persons. Deaths from Starvation have absolutely occurred. . . . Women riots have taken place in Several parts of the County in which Govt wheat and corn has been seized to prevent Starvation of themselves and families. Where it will end unless relief is afforded we cannot tell."

But above all, it was the organization of conscription that convinced many yeomen the struggle for Southern independence had become "a rich man's war and a poor man's fight." Beginning in 1862, the Confederacy enacted the first conscription laws in American history, including provisions that a draftee could avoid service by producing a substitute and that one able-bodied white male would be exempted for every twenty slaves. This legislation was deeply resented in the upcountry, for the cost of a substitute quickly rose far beyond the means of most white families, while the "twenty Negro" provision—a direct response to the decline of discipline on the plantations—allowed many overseers and planters' sons to escape military service. Even though the provision was subsequently repealed, conscription still bore more heavily on the yeomanry, which depended on the labor of the entire family for subsistence, than on planter families supported by the labor of slaves.

In large areas of the Southern upcountry, disillusionment eventually led to outright resistance to Confederate authority—a civil war within the Civil War. Beginning in 1863, desertion became a "crying evil" for the Confederate army. By war's end more than one hundred thousand men had fled. "The deserters," reported one Confederate army officer, "belong almost entirely to the poorest class of nonslaveholders whose labor is indispensable to the daily support of their families. . . . When the father, husband or son is forced into the service, the suffering at home with them is inevitable. It is not in the nature of these men to remain quiet in the ranks under such circumstances."

Poverty, not disloyalty, this officer believed, produced most desertions. But in many parts of the upcountry, the two became intimately interrelated. In the hill counties and piney woods of Mississippi, bands of deserters hid from Confederate authorities, and organizations like Choctaw County's Loyal League worked, said one contemporary observer, to "break up the war by advising desertion, robbing the families of those who remained in the army, and keeping the Federal authorities advised" of Confederate military movements. Northern Alabama, generally enthusiastic about the Confederacy in 1861, was the scene two years later of widespread opposition to conscription and the war. "The condition of things in the mountain districts," wrote John A. Campbell, the South's assistant secretary of war, "menaces the existence of the Confederacy as fatally as . . . the armies of the United States."

Campbell's fears were amply justified by events in Jones County, Mississippi. Although later claims that Jones "seceded" from the Confederacy appear to be exaggerated, disaffection became endemic in this piney woods county. Newton Knight, a strongly pro-Union subsistence farmer, was drafted early in the war and chose to serve as a hospital orderly rather than go into combat against the Union. When his wife wrote him that Confederate cavalry had seized his horse under the impressment law and was mistreating their neighbors, Knight deserted, returned home, and organized Unionists and deserters to "fight for their rights and the freedom of Jones County." In response, Confederate troops seized and hanged one of Knight's brothers, but the irregular force of Unionists subsequently fought a successful battle against a Confederate cavalry unit.

Outside of East Tennessee the most extensive antiwar organizing took place in western and central North Carolina, whose residents had largely supported the Confederacy in 1861. Here the secret Heroes of America, numbering perhaps ten thousand men, established an "underground railroad" to enable Unionists to escape to Federal lines. The Heroes originated in North Carolina's Quaker Belt, a group of Piedmont counties whose Quaker and Moravian residents had long harbored pacifist and antislavery sentiments. Unionists in this region managed to elect "peace men" to the state legislature and a member of the Heroes as the local sheriff. By 1864 the organization had spread into the North Carolina mountains, had garnered considerable support among Raleigh artisans, and was even organizing in plantation areas (where there is some evidence of black involvement in its activities).

One of the Heroes' key organizers was Dr. John Lewis Johnson, a Philadelphia-born druggist and physician. After serving in the Confederate army early in the war and being captured—probably deliberately—he returned home to form bands of Union sympathizers. In 1864 he fled to the North, whereupon his wife was arrested and jailed in Richmond, resulting in the death of their infant son. For the remainder of the war, Johnson lived in Cincinnati with another son, who had deserted from the Confederate army.

North Carolina's Confederate governor Zebulon Vance dismissed the Heroes of America as "altogether a low and insignificant concern." But by 1864 the organization was engaged in espionage, promoting desertion, and helping escaped Federal prisoners reach Tennessee and Kentucky. It was also deeply involved in William W. Holden's 1864 race for governor as a peace candidate. Holden was decisively defeated, but in Heroes' strongholds like Raleigh he polled nearly half the vote.

Most of all, the Heroes of America helped galvanize the class resentments rising to the surface of Southern life. Alexander H. Jones, a Hendersonville newspaper editor and leader of the Heroes, pointedly expressed their views: "This great national strife originated with men and measures that were . . . opposed to a democratic form of government. . . . The fact is, these *bombastic, high-falutin* aristocratic fools have been in the habit of driving negroes and poor helpless white people until they think . . . that they themselves are superior; [and] hate, deride and suspicion the poor."

As early as 1862 Joshua B. Moore, a North Alabama slaveholder, predicted that Southerners without a direct stake in slavery "are not going to fight through a long war to save it—never. They will tire of it and quit." Moore was only half right. Non-slaveholding yeomen supplied the bulk of Confederate soldiers as well as the majority of deserters and draft resisters. But there is no question that the war was a disaster for the upcountry South. Lying at the war's strategic crossroads, portions of upcountry Tennessee, Alabama, and Mississippi were laid waste by the march of opposing armies. In other areas marauding bands of deserters plundered the farms and workshops of Confederate sympathizers, driving off livestock and destroying crops, while Confederate troops and vigilantes routed Union families from their homes. Kinship ties were shredded as brother fought brother and neighbor battled neighbor not only on Civil War battlefields but in what one contemporary called the South's "vulgar internecine warfare."

No one knows how many Southerners perished in this internal civil war. Atrocities were committed by both sides, but since the bulk of the upcountry remained within Confederate lines, Unionists suffered more severely. After April 1862, when President Davis declared martial law in East Tennessee and suspended the writ of habeas corpus, thousands of Unionists saw their property seized. In Shelton Laurel, a remote valley in Appalachian North Carolina, Confederate soldiers in January 1863 murdered thirteen Unionist prisoners in cold blood. Solomon Jones, the "Union patriarch" of the South Carolina mountains, was driven from his farm, forced to live in the woods, and eventually jailed by Confederate authorities. Throughout the upcountry Unionists abandoned their homes to hide from the conscription officers and Confederate sheriffs who hunted them, as they had once hunted runaway slaves, with bloodhounds; some found refuge in the very mountain caves that had once sheltered fugitives from bondage.

For Southerners loyal to the Union, the war left deep scars. Long after the end of fighting, bitter memories of persecution would remain, and tales would be told and retold of the fortitude and suffering of Union families. "We could fill a book with facts of wrongs done to our people. . . ," an Alabama Unionist told a congressional committee in 1866. "You have no idea of the strength of principle and devotion these people exhibited towards the national government." A Mississippi Unionist later recalled how the office of James M. Jones, editor of the Corinth *Republican,* "was surrounded by the infuriated rebels, his paper was suppressed, his person threatened with violence, he was broken up and ruined forever, all for advocating the Union of our fathers." Jones later fled the state and enlisted in the Union army (one of only five hundred white Mississippians to do so). A Tennessean told a similar story: "They were driven from their homes . . . persecuted like wild beasts by the

The Unionist William Brownlow became governor of Tennessee.

rebel authorities, and hunted down in the mountains; they were hanged on the gallows, shot down and robbed. . . . Perhaps no people on the face of the earth were ever more persecuted than were the loyal people of East Tennessee."

Thus the war permanently redrew the economic and political map of the white South. Military devastation and the Confederacy's economic policies plunged much of the upcountry into poverty, thereby threatening the yeomanry's economic independence and opening the door to the postwar spread of cotton cultivation and tenant farming. Yeoman disaffection shattered the political hegemony of the planters, separating "the lower and uneducated class," according to one Georgia planter, "from the more wealthy and more enlightened portion of our population."

The war ended the upcountry's isolation, weakened its localism, and awakened its political self-consciousness. Out of the Union opposition would come many of the most prominent white Republican leaders of Reconstruction. Edward Degener, a German-born San Antonio grocer who had seen his two sons executed for treason by the Confederacy, served as a Republican congressman after the war. The party's Reconstruction Southern governors would include Edmund J. Davis, who during the war raised the 1st Texas Cavalry for the Union Army; William W. Holden, the unsuccessful "peace" candidate of 1864; William H. Smith and David P. Lewis, organizers of a Peace Society in Confederate Alabama; and William G. Brownlow, a circuit-riding Methodist preacher and Knoxville, Tennessee, editor.

Perhaps more than any other individual, Brownlow personified the changes wrought by the Civil War and the bitter hatred of "rebels" so pervasive among Southern Unionists. Before 1860 he had been an avid defender of slavery. The peculiar institution, he declared, would not be abolished until "the angel Gabriel sounds the last loud trump of God." (His newspaper also called Harriet Beecher Stowe a "deliberate liar" for her portrayal of slavery in *Uncle Tom's Cabin,* adding that she was "as ugly as Original sin" to boot.)

With secession, Brownlow turned his caustic pen against the Confederacy. In October 1861 he was arrested and sent North, and his paper was closed. He returned to Knoxville two years later, when Gen. Ambrose E. Burnside occupied the city. Now he was a firm defender of emancipation and an advocate of reprisals against pro-Confederate Southerners. He would, Brownlow wrote in 1864, arm "every wolf, panther, catamount, and bear in the mountains of America . . . every rattlesnake and crocodile . . . every devil in Hell, and turn them loose upon the Confederacy" in order to win the war.

The South's inner civil war not only helped weaken the Confederate war effort but bequeathed to Reconstruction explosive political issues, unresolved questions, and broad opportunities for change. The disaffected regions would embrace the Republican party after the Civil War; some remained strongholds well into the twentieth century. The war experience goes a long way toward explaining the strength of Republican voting in parts of the Reconstruction upcountry. To these "scalawags" the party represented, first and foremost, the inheritor of wartime Unionism.

Their loyalty first to the Union and then to Republicanism did not, however, imply abolitionist sentiment during the war or a commitment to the rights of blacks thereafter, although they were perfectly willing to see slavery sacrificed to preserve the Union. Indeed, the black-white alliance within the Reconstruction Republican party was always fragile, especially as blacks aggressively pursued demands for a larger share of political offices and far-reaching civil rights legislation. Upcountry Unionism was essentially defensive, a response to the undermining of local autonomy and economic self-sufficiency rather than a coherent program for the social reconstruction of the South. Its basis, the Northern reporter Sidney Andrews discovered in the fall of 1865, was "hatred of those who went into the Rebellion" and of "a certain ruling class" that had brought upon the region the devastating impact of war.

Although recent writing has made Civil War scholars aware of the extent of disaffection in the Confederacy, the South's inner civil war remains largely unknown to most Americans. Perhaps this is because the story of Southern Unionism challenges two related popular mythologies that have helped shape how Americans think about that era: the portrait of the Confederacy as a heroic "lost cause" and of Reconstruction as an ignoble "tragic era."

For much of this century historians who sympathized with the Confederate struggle minimized the extent of Southern discontent and often castigated the region's Unionists as "Tories," traitors analogous to Americans who remained loyal to George III during the Revolution. And many Northern writers, while praising

Unionists' resolve, found it difficult to identify enthusiastically with men complicitous in the alleged horrors of Reconstruction. Yet as the smoke of these historiographical battles clears, and a more complex view of the war and Reconstruction emerges, it has become abundantly clear that no one can claim to fully understand the Civil War era without coming to terms with the South's Unionists, the persecution they suffered, and how they helped determine the outcome of our greatest national crisis.

Why They Impeached Andrew Johnson

David Herbert Donald

The story of presidential Reconstruction after Lincoln is told in this essay by David Herbert Donald, Charles Warren Professor of American History at Harvard University. Lincoln's approach to restoring the Union was cautious, practical, thoughtful—humane in every sense of the word. Because of his assassination, however, the evaluation of his policy has to be a study in the might-have-beens of history. The Reconstruction policy of his successor, Andrew Johnson, superficially similar to Lincoln's, was reckless, impractical, emotional, and politically absurd. While historians have differed in evaluating his purposes, they have agreed unanimously that his management of the problem was inept and that his policy was a total failure.

Professor Donald's essay provides an extended character study of Johnson, and it is not an attractive portrait. Donald believes that Johnson "threw away a magnificent opportunity" to smoothly and speedily return the Confederate states to a harmonious place in the Union. But he also shows how difficult Johnson's task was and to how great an extent Southern white opinion was set against the full acceptance of black equality. Donald is the author of many books, including a Pulitzer Prize–winning biography of the Massachusetts senator, Charles Sumner.

———————

Reconstruction after the Civil War posed some of the most discouraging problems that have ever faced American statesmen. The South was prostrate. Its defeated soldiers straggled homeward through a countryside desolated by war. Southern soil was untilled and exhausted; southern factories and railroads were worn out. The four billion dollars of southern capital invested in Negro slaves was wiped out by advancing Union armies, "the most stupendous act of sequestration in the history of Anglo-American jurisprudence." The white inhabitants of eleven states had somehow to be reclaimed from rebellion and restored to a firm loyalty to the United States. Their four million former slaves had simultaneously to be guided into a proper use of their newfound freedom.

For the victorious Union government there was no time for reflection. Immediate decisions had to be made. Thousands of destitute whites and Negroes had to be fed before long-range plans of rebuilding the southern economy could be drafted. Some kind of government had to be established in these former Confederate states, to preserve order and to direct the work of restoration.

A score of intricate questions must be answered: Should the defeated southerners be punished or pardoned? How should genuinely loyal southern Unionists be rewarded? What was to be the social, economic, and political status of the now free Negroes? What civil rights did they have? Ought they to have the ballot? Should they be given a freehold of property? Was Reconstruction to be controlled by the national government, or should the southern states work out their own salvation? If the federal government supervised the process, should the President or the Congress be in control?

Intricate as were the problems, in early April, 1865, they did not seem insuperable. President Abraham Lincoln was winning the peace as he had already won the war. He was careful to keep every detail of Reconstruction in his own hands; unwilling to be committed to any "exclusive, and inflexible plan," he was working out a pragmatic program of restoration not, perhaps, entirely satisfactory to any group, but reasonably acceptable to all sections. With his enormous prestige as commander of the victorious North and as victor in the 1864 election, he was able to promise freedom to the Negro, charity to the southern white, security to the North.

The blighting of these auspicious beginnings is one of the saddest stories in American history. The reconciliation of the sections, which seemed so imminent in 1865, was delayed for more than ten years. Northern magnanimity toward a fallen foe curdled into bitter distrust. Southern whites rejected moderate leaders, and inveterate racists spoke for the new South. The Negro, after serving as a political pawn for a decade, was relegated to a second-class citizenship, from which he is yet struggling to emerge. Rarely has democratic government so completely failed as during the Reconstruction decade.

The responsibility for this collapse of American statesmanship is, of course, complex. History is not a tale of deep-dyed villains or pure-as-snow heroes. Part of the blame must fall upon ex-Confederates who refused to recognize that the war was over; part upon freedmen who confused liberty with license and the ballot box with the lunch pail; part upon northern antislavery extremists who identified patriotism with loyalty to the Republican party; part upon the land speculators, treasury grafters, and railroad promoters who were unwilling to have a genuine peace lest it end their looting of the public till.

Yet these divisive forces were not bound to triumph. Their success was due to the failure of constructive statesmanship that could channel the magnanimous feelings shared by most Americans into a positive program of reconstruction. President Andrew Johnson was called upon for positive leadership, and he did not meet the challenge.

Andrew Johnson's greatest weakness was his insensitivity to public opinion. In contrast to Lincoln, who said, "Public opinion in this country is everything," Johnson made a career of battling the popular will. A poor white, a runaway tailor's apprentice, a self-educated Tennessee politician, Johnson was a living defiance to the dominant southern belief that leadership belonged to the plantation aristocracy.

As senator from Tennessee, he defied the sentiment of his section in 1861 and refused to join the secessionist movement. When Lincoln later appointed him military governor of occupied Tennessee, Johnson found Nashville "a furnace of treason," but he braved social ostracism and threats of assassination and discharged his duties with boldness and efficiency.

Such a man was temperamentally unable to understand the northern mood in 1865, much less to yield to it. For four years the northern people had been whipped into wartime frenzy by propaganda tales of Confederate atrocities. The assassination of Lincoln by a southern sympathizer confirmed their belief in southern brutality and heartlessness. Few northerners felt vindictive toward the South, but most felt that the rebellion they had crushed must never rise again. Johnson ignored this postwar psychosis gripping the North and plunged ahead with his program of rapidly restoring the southern states to the Union. In May, 1865, without any previous preparation of public opinion, he issued a proclamation of amnesty, granting forgiveness to nearly all the millions of former rebels and welcoming them back into peaceful fraternity. Some few Confederate leaders were excluded from his general amnesty, but even they could secure pardon by special petition. For weeks the White House corridors were thronged with ex-Confederate statesmen and former southern generals who daily received presidential forgiveness.

Ignoring public opinion by pardoning the former Confederates, Johnson actually entrusted the formation of new governments in the South to them. The provisional governments established by the President proceeded, with a good deal of reluctance, to rescind their secession ordinances, to abolish slavery, and to repudiate the Confederate debt. Then, with far more enthusiasm, they turned to electing governors, representatives, and senators. By December, 1865, the southern states had their delegations in Washington waiting for admission by Congress. Alexander H. Stephens, once vice president of the Confederacy, was chosen senator from Georgia; not one of the North Carolina delegation could take a loyalty oath; and all of South Carolina's congressmen had "either held office under the Confederate States, or been in the army, or countenanced in some way the Rebellion."

Johnson himself was appalled, "There seems in many of the elections something like defiance, which is all out of place at this time." Yet on December 5 he strongly urged the Congress to seat these southern representatives "and thereby complete the work of reconstruction." But the southern states were omitted from the roll call.

Such open defiance of northern opinion was dangerous under the best of circumstances, but in Johnson's case it was little more than suicidal. The President seemed not to realize the weakness of his position. He was the representative of no major interest and had no genuine political following. He had been considered for the vice presidency in 1864 because, as a southerner and a former slaveholder, he could lend plausibility to the Republican pretension that the old parties were dead and that Lincoln was the nominee of a new, nonsectional National Union party.

A political accident, the new Vice President did little to endear himself to his countrymen. At Lincoln's second inauguration Johnson appeared before the Senate in an obviously inebriated state and made a long, intemperate harangue about his plebeian origins and his hard-won success. President, Cabinet, and senators were humiliated by the shameful display, and Charles Sumner felt that "the Senate should call upon him to resign." Historians now know that Andrew Johnson was not a heavy drinker. At the time of his inaugural display, he was just recovering from a severe attack of typhoid fever. Feeling ill just before he entered the Senate chamber, he asked for some liquor to steady his nerves, and either his weakened condition or abnormal sensitivity to alcohol betrayed him.

Lincoln reassured Republicans who were worried over the affair: "I have known Andy for many years; he made a bad slip the other day, but you need not be scared. Andy ain't a drunkard." Never again was Andrew Johnson seen under the influence of alcohol, but his reformation came too late. His performance on March 4, 1865, seriously undermined his political usefulness and permitted his opponents to discredit him as a pothouse politician. Johnson was catapulted into the presidency by John Wilkes Booth's bullet. From the outset his position was weak, but it was not necessarily untenable. The President's chronic lack of discretion made it so. Where common sense dictated that a chief executive in so disadvantageous a position should act with great caution, Johnson proceeded to imitate Old Hickory, Andrew Jackson, his political idol. If Congress crossed his will, he did not hesitate to defy it. Was he not "the Tribune of the People"?

Sure of his rectitude, Johnson was indifferent to prudence. He never learned that the President of the United States cannot afford to be a quarreler. Apprenticed in the rough-and-tumble politics of frontier Tennessee, where orators exchanged violent personalities, crude humor, and bitter denunciations, Johnson continued to make stump speeches from the White House. All too often he spoke extemporaneously, and he permitted hecklers in his audience to draw from him angry charges against his critics.

On Washington's birthday in 1866, against the advice of his more sober advisers, the President made an impromptu address to justify his Reconstruction policy. "I fought traitors and treason in the South," he told the crowd; "now when I turn around, and at the other end of the line find men—I care not by what name you call them—who will stand opposed to the restoration of the Union of these States, I am free to say to you that I am still in the field."

During the "great applause" which followed, a nameless voice shouted, "Give us the names at the other end. . . . Who are they?"

"You ask me who they are," Johnson retorted. "I say Thaddeus Stevens of Pennsylvania is one; I say Mr. Sumner is another; and Wendell Phillips is another." Applause urged him to continue. "Are those who want to destroy our institutions . . . not satisfied with the blood that has been shed? . . . Does not the blood of Lincoln appease the vengeance and wrath of the opponents of this government?"

The President's remarks were as untrue as they were impolitic. Not only was it manifestly false to assert that the leading Republican in the House and the most conspicuous Republican in the Senate were opposed to "the fundamental principles of this government" or that they had been responsible for Lincoln's assassination; it was incredible political folly to impute such actions to men with whom the President had to work daily. But Andrew Johnson never learned that the President of the United States must function as a party leader.

There was a temperamental coldness about this plain-featured, grave man that kept him from easy, intimate relations with even his political supporters. His massive head, dark, luxuriant hair, deep-set and piercing eyes, and cleft square chin seemed to Charles Dickens to indicate "courage, watchfulness, and certainly strength of purpose," but his was a grim face, with "no genial sunlight in it." The coldness and reserve that marked Johnson's public associations doubtless stemmed from a deep-seated feeling of insecurity; this self-educated tailor whose wife had taught him how to write could never expose himself by letting down his guard and relaxing.

Johnson knew none of the arts of managing men, and he seemed unaware that face-saving is important for a politician. When he became President, Johnson was

A Harper's Weekly *cartoon depicts Johnson (left) and Thaddeus Stevens (right) as engineers committed to a collision course.*

besieged by advisers of all political complexions. To each he listened gravely and non-committally, raising no questions and by his silence seeming to give consent. With Radical Senator Sumner, already intent upon giving the freedmen both homesteads and the ballot, he had repeated interviews during the first month of his presidency. "His manner has been excellent, & even sympathetic," Sumner reported triumphantly. With Chief Justice Salmon P. Chase, Sumner urged Johnson to support immediate Negro suffrage and found the President was "welldisposed, & sees the rights & necessities of the case." In the middle of May, 1865, Sumner reassured a Republican caucus that the President was a true Radical; he had listened repeatedly to the Senator and had told him "there is no difference between us." Before the end of the month the rug was pulled from under Sumner's feet. Johnson issued his proclamation for the reconstruction of North Carolina, making no provisions for Negro suffrage. Sumner first learned about it through the newspapers.

While he was making up his mind, Johnson appeared silently receptive to all ideas; when he had made a decision, his mind was immovably closed, and he defended his course with all the obstinacy of a weak man. In December, alarmed by Johnson's Reconstruction proclamations, Sumner again sought an interview with the President. "No longer sympathetic, or even kindly," Sumner found, "he was harsh, petulant, and unreasonable." The Senator was depressed by Johnson's "prejudice, ignorance, and perversity" on the Negro suffrage issue. Far from listening amiably to Sumner's argument that the South was still torn by violence and not yet ready for readmission, Johnson attacked him with cheap analogies. "Are there no murders in Massachusetts?" the President asked.

"Unhappily yes," Sumner replied, "sometimes."

"Are there no assaults in Boston? Do not men there sometimes knock each other down, so that the police is obliged to interfere?"

"Unhappily yes."

"Would you consent that Massachusetts, on this account, should be excluded from Congress?" Johnson triumphantly queried. In the excitement the President unconsciously used Sumner's hat, which the Senator had placed on the floor beside his chair, as a spittoon!

Had Johnson been as resolute in action as he was in argument, he might conceivably have carried much of his party with him on his Reconstruction program. Promptness, publicity, and persuasion could have created a presidential following. Instead Johnson boggled. Though he talked boastfully of "kicking out" officers who failed to support his plan, he was slow to act. His own Cabinet, from the very beginning, contained members who disagreed with him, and his secretary of war, Edwin M. Stanton, was openly in league with the Republican elements most hostile to the President. For more than two years he impotently hoped that Stanton would resign; then in 1867, after Congress had passed the Tenure of Office Act, he tried to oust the Secretary. This belated firmness, against the letter of the law, led directly to Johnson's impeachment trial.

Instead of working with his party leaders and building up political support among Republicans, Johnson in 1866 undertook to organize his friends into a new party. In August a convention of white southerners, northern Democrats, moderate Republicans, and presidential appointees assembled in Philadelphia to endorse Johnson's policy. Union General Darius Couch of Massachusetts marched arm in arm down the convention aisle with Governor James L. Orr of South Carolina, to symbolize the states reunited under Johnson's rule. The convention produced fervid oratory, a dignified statement of principles—but not much else. Like most third-party reformist movements it lacked local support and grass-roots organization.

Johnson himself was unable to breathe life into his stillborn third party. Deciding to take his case to the people, he accepted an invitation to speak at a great Chicago memorial honoring Stephen A. Douglas. When his special train left Washington on August 28 for a "swing around the circle," the President was accompanied by a few Cabinet members who shared his views and by the war heroes Grant and Farragut.

At first all went well. There were some calculated political snubs to the President, but he managed at Philadelphia, New York, and Albany to present his ideas soberly and cogently to the people. But Johnson's friends were worried lest his tongue again get out of control. "In all frankness," a senator wrote him, do not "allow the excitement of the moment to draw from you any *extemporaneous speeches.*"

At St. Louis, when a Radical voice shouted that Johnson was a "Judas," the President flamed up in rage. "There was a Judas and he was one of the twelve apostles," he retorted. ". . . The twelve apostles had a Christ. . . . If I have played the Judas, who has been my Christ that I have played the Judas with? Was it Thad Stevens? Was it Wendell Phillips? Was it Charles Sumner?" Over mingled hisses and applause, he shouted, "These are the men that stop and compare themselves with the Saviour; and everybody that differs with them . . . is to be denounced as a Judas."

Johnson had played into his enemies' hands. His Radical foes denounced him as a "trickster," a "culprit," a man "touched with insanity, corrupted with lust, stimulated with drink." More serious in consequence was the reaction of northern moderates, such as James Russell Lowell, who wrote, "What an anti-Johnson lecturer we have in Johnson! Sumner has been right about the *cuss* from the first. . . ." The fall elections were an overwhelming repudiation of the President and his Reconstruction policy.

Johnson's want of political sagacity strengthened the very elements in the Republican party which he most feared. In 1865 the Republicans had no clearly defined attitude toward Reconstruction. Moderates like Gideon Welles and Orville Browning wanted to see the southern states restored with a minimum of restrictions; Radicals like Sumner and Stevens demanded that the entire southern social system be revolutionized. Some Republicans were passionately concerned with the plight of the freedmen; others were more interested in maintaining the high tariff and land grant legislation enacted during the war. Many thought mostly of keeping themselves in office, and many genuinely believed, with Sumner, that "the Republican party, in its objects, is identical with country and with mankind." These diverse elements came slowly to adopt the idea of harsh Reconstruction, but Johnson's stubborn persistency in his policy left them no alternative. Every step the President took seemed to provide "a new encouragement to (1) the rebels at the South, (2) the Democrats at the North and (3) the discontented elements everywhere." Not many Republicans would agree with Sumner that Johnson's program was "a defiance to God and Truth," but there was genuine concern that the victory won by the war was being frittered away.

The provisional governments established by the President in the South seemed to be dubiously loyal. They were reluctant to rescind their secession ordinances and to repudiate the Confederate debt, and they chose high-ranking ex-Confederates to represent them in Congress. Northerners were even more alarmed when these southern governments began to legislate upon the Negro's civil rights. Some laws were necessary—in order to give former slaves the right to marry, to hold property, to sue and be sued, and the like—but the Johnson legislatures went far beyond these immediate needs. South Carolina, for example, enacted that no Negro could pursue the trade "of an artisan, mechanic, or shopkeeper, or any other trade or employment besides that of husbandry" without a special license. Alabama provided that "any stubborn or refractory servants" or "servants who loiter away their time" should be fined $50 and, if they could not pay, be hired out for six months' labor. Mississippi ordered that every Negro under eighteen years of age who was an orphan or not supported by his parents must be apprenticed to some white person, preferably the former owner of the slave. Such southern laws indicated a determination to keep the Negro in a state of peonage.

It was impossible to expect a newly emancipated race to be content with such a limping freedom. The thousands of Negroes who had served in the Union armies and had helped conquer their former Confederate masters were not willing to abandon their new-found liberty. In rural areas southern whites kept these Negroes under control through the Ku Klux Klan. But in southern cities white hegemony was less secure, and racial friction erupted in mob violence. In May, 1866, a quarrel between a Memphis Negro and a white teamster led to a riot in which the city police and the poor whites raided the Negro quarters and burned and killed promiscuously. Far more serious was the disturbance in New Orleans two months later. The Republican party in Louisiana was split into pro-Johnson conservatives and Negro suffrage advocates. The latter group determined to hold a constitutional convention, of dubious legality, in New Orleans, in order to secure the ballot for the freedmen and the offices for themselves. Through imbecility in the War Department, the Federal troops occupying the city were left without orders, and the mayor of New Orleans, strongly opposed to Negro equality, had the responsibility for preserving order. There were acts of provocation on both sides, and finally, on July 30, a procession of Negroes marching toward the convention hall was attacked.

"A shot was fired . . . by a policeman, or some colored man in the procession," General Philip Sheridan reported. "This led to other shots, and a rush after the procession. On arrival at the front of the Institute [where the convention met], there was some throwing of brick-bats by both sides. The police . . . were vigorously marched to the scene of disorder. The procession entered the Institute with the flag, about six or eight remaining outside. A row occurred between a policeman and one of these colored men, and a shot was again fired by one of the parties, which led to an indiscriminate firing on the building, through the windows, by the policemen."

"This had been going on for a short time, when a white flag was displayed from the windows of the Institute, whereupon the firing ceased and the police rushed into the building. . . . The policemen opened an indiscriminate fire upon the audience until they had emptied their revolvers, when they retired, and those inside barricaded the doors. The door was broken in, and the firing again commenced when many of the colored and white people either escaped out of the door, or were passed out by the policemen inside, but as they came out, the policemen who formed the circle nearest the building fired upon them, and they were again fired upon by the citizens that formed the outer circle."

Thirty-seven Negroes and three of their white friends were killed; 119 Negroes and seventeen of their white sympathizers were wounded. Of their assailants, ten were wounded and but one killed. President Johnson was, of course, horrified by these outbreaks, but the Memphis and New Orleans riots, together with the Black Codes, afforded a devastating illustration of how the President's policy actually operated. The southern states, it was clear, were not going to protect the Negroes' basic rights. They were only grudgingly going to accept the results of the war. Yet, with

Johnson's blessing, these same states were expecting a stronger voice in Congress than ever. Before 1860, southern representation in Congress had been based upon the white population plus three fifths of the slaves; now the Negroes, though not permitted to vote, were to be counted like all other citizens, and southern states would be entitled to at least nine additional congressmen. Joining with the northern Copperheads, the southerners could easily regain at the next presidential election all that had been lost on the Civil War battlefield.

It was this political exigency, not misguided sentimentality nor vindictiveness, which united Republicans in opposition to the President.

Johnson's defenders have pictured Radical Reconstruction as the work of a fanatical minority, led by Summer and Stevens, who drove their reluctant colleagues into adopting coercive measures against the South. In fact, every major piece of Radical legislation was adopted by the nearly unanimous vote of the entire Republican membership of Congress. Andrew Johnson had left them no other choice. Because he insisted upon rushing Confederate-dominated states back into the Union, Republicans moved to disqualify Confederate leaders under the Fourteenth Amendment. When, through Johnson's urging, the southern states rejected that amendment, the Republicans in Congress unwillingly came to see Negro suffrage as the only counterweight against Democratic majorities in the South. With the Reconstruction Acts of 1867 the way was open for a true Radical program toward the South, harsh and thorough.

Andrew Johnson became a cipher in the White House, futilely disapproving bills which were promptly passed over his veto. Through his failure to reckon with public opinion, his unwillingness to recognize his weak position, his inability to function as a party leader, he had sacrificed all influence with the party which had elected him and had turned over its control to Radicals vindictively opposed to his policies. In March, 1868, Andrew Johnson was summoned before the Senate of the United States to be tried on eleven accusations of high crimes and misdemeanors. By a narrow margin the Senate failed to convict him, and historians have dismissed the charges as flimsy and false. Yet perhaps before the bar of history itself Andrew Johnson must be impeached with an even graver charge—that through political ineptitude he threw away a magnificent opportunity.

Ride-In: A Century of Protest Begins

Alan F. Westin

The last quarter of the nineteenth century—after the federal government relaxed its pressure on the southern states to deal fairly with their black citizens—has been called "the nadir" of the history of black Americans after emancipation. Some historians argue that the low point came somewhat later, during the early twentieth century, but few would disagree with the thesis that the period in question was indeed disastrous for American blacks. Although never really treated decently (in the North as well as in the South), they had made important gains during Reconstruction; the Fourteenth and Fifteenth amendments "guaranteed" their political and civil rights, and Congress passed stiff laws protecting these rights, including the Civil Rights Act of 1875, which outlawed discrimination in places of public accommodation.

After the so-called Compromise of 1877, however, these gains were gradually stripped away by a combination of southern pressure, northern indifference, and a series of crippling legal interpretations by the Supreme Court. In this essay Professor Alan F. Westin of Columbia University, an expert on constitutional history, describes one of the first and most significant of the Supreme Court decisions of the era, one that emasculated the Civil Rights Act of 1875. His story reads in some ways like an account of the civil rights struggles of the 1950s and 1960s, but with the terrible difference that freedom and justice were in this instance the losers, not the winners, of the fight.

It began one day early in January when a Negro named Robert Fox stepped aboard a streetcar in Louisville, Kentucky, dropped his coin into the fare box, and sat down in the white section of the car. Ordered to move, he refused, and the driver threw him off the car. Shortly after, Fox filed a charge of assault and battery against the streetcar company in the federal district court, claiming that separate seating policies were illegal and the driver's actions were therefore improper. The district judge instructed the jury that under federal law common carriers must serve all passengers equally without regard to race. So instructed, the jury found the company rules to be invalid and awarded damages of fifteen dollars (plus $72.80 in legal costs) to Mr. Fox.

Immediately there was sharp criticism of the Fox decision from the city and state administrations, both Democratic; the company defied the court's ruling and continued segregated seating. After several meetings with local federal officials and white attorneys co-operating with them, Louisville Negro leaders decided to launch a full-scale "ride-in." At 7 P.M. on May 12, a young Negro boy boarded a streetcar near the Willard Hotel, walked past the driver, and took a seat among the white passengers. The driver, under new company regulations, did not attempt to throw him off but simply stopped the car, lit a cigar, and refused to proceed until the Negro moved to "his place." While the governor, the Louisville chief of police, and other prominent citizens looked on from the sidewalks, a large crowd which included an increasingly noisy mob of jeering white teen-agers gathered around the streetcar.

Before long, there were shouts of "Put him out!" "Hit him!" "Kick him!" "Hang him!" Several white youths climbed into the car and began yelling insults in the face of the young Negro rider. He refused to answer—or to move. The youths dragged him from his seat, pulled him off the car, and began to beat him. Only when the Negro started to defend himself did the city police intervene: they arrested him for disturbing the peace and took him to jail.

This time the trial was held in Louisville city court, not the federal court. The magistrate ruled that streetcar companies were not under any obligation to treat Negroes exactly as they treated whites, and that any federal measures purporting to create such obligations would be "clearly invalid" under the constitutions of Kentucky and the United States. The defendant was fined, and the judge delivered a warning to Louisville Negroes that further ride-ins would be punished.

But the ride-in campaign was not halted that easily. In the following days, streetcar after streetcar was entered by Negroes who took seats in the white section. Now the drivers got off the cars entirely. On several occasions, the Negro riders drove the cars themselves, to the sound of cheers from Negro spectators. Then violence erupted. Bands of white youths and men began to throw Negro riders off the cars: windows were broken, cars were overturned, and for a time a general race riot threatened. Moderate Kentucky newspapers and many community leaders deplored the fighting; the Republican candidate for governor denounced the streetcar company's segregation policies and blamed the violence on Democratic encouragement of white extremists.

By this time, newspapers across the country were carrying reports of the conflict, and many editorials denounced the seating regulations. In Louisville, federal marshals and the United States attorney backed the rights of the Negro riders and stated that federal court action would be taken if necessary. There were even rumors that the President might send troops.

Under these threats, the streetcar company capitulated. Soon, all the city transit companies declared that "it was useless to try to resist or evade the enforcement by the United States authorities of the claim of Negroes to ride in the cars." To "avoid serious collisions," the company would thereafter allow all passengers to sit where they chose. Although a few disturbances took place in the following months, and some white intransigents boycotted the streetcars, mixed seating became a common practice. The Kentucky press soon pointed with pride to the spirit of conciliation and harmony which prevailed in travel facilities within the city, calling it a model for good race relations. Never again would Louisville streetcars be segregated.

The event may have a familiar ring, but it should not, for it occurred almost one hundred years ago, in 1871. The streetcars were horse-drawn. The President who considered ordering troops to Louisville was ex-General Grant, not ex-General Eisenhower. The Republican gubernatorial candidate who supported the Negro riders, John Marshall Harlan, was not a post–World War II leader of the G.O.P. but a former slaveholder from one of Kentucky's oldest and most famous political families. And the "new" Negroes who waged this ride-in were not members of the Congress of Racial Equality and the National Association for the Advancement of Colored People, or followers of Dr. Martin Luther King, but former slaves who were fighting for civil rights in their own time, and with widespread success.

And yet these dramatic sit-ins, ride-ins, and walk-ins of the 1870s are almost unknown to the American public today. The standard American histories do not mention them, providing only thumbnail references to "bayonet-enforced" racial contacts during Reconstruction. Most commentators view the Negro's resort to direct action as an invention of the last decade. Clearly, then, it is time that the civil-rights struggle of the 1870s and 1880s was rescued from newspaper files and court archives, not only because it is historically important but also because it has compelling relevance for our own era.

Contrary to common assumptions today, no state in the Union during the 1870s, including those south of the Mason-Dixon line, required separation of whites and Negroes in places of public accommodation. Admission and arrangement policies were up to individual owners. In the North and West, many theatres, hotels, restaurants, and public carriers served Negro patrons without hesitation or discrimination. Some accepted Negroes only in second-class accommodations, such as smoking cars on railroads or balconies in theatres, where they sat among whites who did not have first-class tickets. Other northern and western establishments, especially the more exclusive ones, refused Negro patronage entirely.

The situation was similar in the large cities of the southern and border states. Many establishments admitted Negroes to second-class facilities. Some gave first-class service to those of privileged social status—government officials, army officers, newspapermen, and clergymen. On the other hand, many places of public accommodation, particularly in the rural areas and smaller cities of the South, were closed to Negroes whatever their wealth or status.

From 1865 through the early 1880s, the general trend in the nation was toward wider acceptance of Negro patronage. The federal Civil Rights Act of 1866, with its guarantee to Negroes of "equal benefit of the laws," had set off a flurry of enforcement suits—for denying berths to Negroes on a Washington-New York train; for refusing to sell theatre tickets to Negroes in Boston; and for barring Negro women from the waiting rooms and parlor cars of railroads in Virginia, Illinois, and California. Ratification of the Fourteenth Amendment in 1868 had spurred more challenges. Three northern states, and two southern states under Reconstruction regimes, passed laws making it a crime for owners of public-accommodation businesses to discriminate. Most state and federal court rulings on these laws between 1865 and 1880 held in favor of Negro rights, and the rulings built up a steady pressure on owners to relax racial bars.

Nevertheless, instances of exclusion and segregation continued throughout the 1870s. To settle the issue once and for all (thereby reaping the lasting appreciation of the Negro voters), congressional Republicans led by Senator Charles Sumner pressed for a federal statute making discrimination in public accommodations

Cartoonist Thomas Nast mocked the provision of the Civil Rights Act of 1875 that allowed blacks to colect $500 from those who barred them from places of public accommodation.

a crime. Democrats and conservative Republicans warned in the congressional debates that such a law would trespass on the reserved powers of the states and reminded the Sumner supporters that recent Supreme Court decisions had taken a narrow view of federal power under the Civil War amendments.

After a series of legislative compromises, however, Sumner's forces were able to enact the statute; on March 1, 1875, "An Act to Protect all Citizens in their Civil and Legal Rights" went into effect. "It is essential to just government," the preamble stated, that the nation "recognize the equality of all men before the law, and . . . it is the duty of government in its dealings with the people to mete out equal and exact justice to all, of whatever nativity, race, color, or persuasion, religious or political . . . "

Section 1 of the act declared that "All persons within the jurisdiction of the United States shall be entitled to the full and equal enjoyment of the accommodations . . . of inns, public conveyances on land or water, theaters and other places of public amusement; subject only to the conditions and limitations established by law, and applicable alike to citizens of every race or color. . . ." Section 2 provided that any person violating the act could be sued in federal district court for a penalty of $500, could be fined $500 to $1,000, or could be imprisoned from thirty days to one year. (A separate section forbade racial discrimination in the selection of juries.)

Reaction to the law was swift. Two Negro men were admitted to the dress circle of Macauley's Theatre in Louisville and sat through the performance without incident. In Washington, Negroes were served for the first time at the bar of the Willard Hotel, and a Negro broke the color line when he was seated at McVicker's Theatre in Chicago. But in other instances, Negroes were rejected despite "Sumner's law." Several hotels in Chattanooga turned in their licenses, became private boardinghouses, and accepted whites only. Restaurants and barber shops in Richmond turned away Negro customers.

Suits challenging refusals were filed en masse throughout the country. Perhaps a hundred were decided in the federal district courts during the late 1870s and early 1880s. Federal judges in Pennsylvania, Texas, Maryland, and Kentucky, among others, held the law to be constitutional and ruled in favor of Negro complainants. In North Carolina, New Jersey, and California, however, district judges held the law invalid. And when other courts in New York, Tennessee, Missouri, and Kansas put the issue to the federal circuit judges, the judges divided on the question, and the matter was certified to the United States Supreme Court.

But the Supreme Court did not exactly rush to make its ruling. Though two cases testing the 1875 act reached it in 1876 and a third in 1877, the Justices simply held them on their docket. In 1879, the Attorney General filed a brief defending the constitutionality of the law, but still the Court reached no decisions. In 1880, three additional cases were filed, but two years elapsed before the Solicitor General presented a fresh brief supporting the statute. It was not until late in 1883 that the Supreme Court passed upon the 1875 act, in what became famous as the *Civil Rights Cases* ruling. True, the Court was badly behind in its work in this period, but clearly the Justices chose to let the civil-rights cases "ripen" for almost eight years.

When they finally came to grips with the issue, six separate test suits were involved. The most celebrated had arisen in New York City in November of 1879. Edwin Booth, the famous tragedian and brother of John Wilkes Booth, had opened a special Thanksgiving week engagement at the Grand Opera House. After playing *Hamlet, Othello,* and *Richelieu* to packed houses, he was scheduled to perform Victor Hugo's *Ruy Blas* at the Saturday matinee on November 22.

One person who had decided to see Booth that Saturday was William R. Davis, Jr., who was later described in the press as a tall, handsome, and well-spoken Negro of twenty-six. He was the business agent of the *Progressive-American,* a Negro weekly published in New York City. At 10 o'clock Saturday morning, Davis' girl friend ("a bright octoroon, almost white," as the press put it), purchased two reserved seats at the box office of the Grand Opera House. At 1:30 P.M., Davis and his lady presented themselves at the theatre, only to be told by the doorkeeper, Samuel Singleton, that "these tickets are no good." If he would step out to the box office, Singleton told Davis, his money would be refunded.

It is unlikely that Davis was surprised by Singleton's action, for this was not the first time he had encountered such difficulties. Shortly after the passage of the 1875 act, Davis had been refused a ticket to the dress circle of Booth's Theatre in New York. He had sworn out a warrant against the ticket seller, but the failure of his witnesses to appear at the grand jury proceedings had led to a dismissal of the complaint. This earlier episode, as well as Davis' activity as a Negro journalist, made it probable that this appearance at the Opera House in 1879 was a deliberate test of the management's discriminatory policies.

Though Davis walked out of the lobby at Singleton's request, he did not turn in his tickets for a refund. Instead, he summoned a young white boy standing near the theatre, gave him a dollar (plus a dime for his trouble), and had him purchase two more tickets. When Davis and his companion presented these to Singleton, only the lady was allowed to pass. Again Davis was told that his ticket was "no good." When he now refused to move out of the doorway, Singleton called a policeman and asked that Davis be escorted off the theatre property. The officer told Davis that the Messrs. Poole and Donnelly, the managers of the Opera House, did not admit colored persons. "Perhaps the managers do not," Davis retorted, "but the laws of the country [do]."

The following Monday, November 24, Davis filed a criminal complaint; on December 9, this time with witnesses in abundance, Singleton was indicted in what the press described as the first criminal proceeding under the 1875 act to go to trial in New York. When the case opened on January 14, 1880, Singleton's counsel argued that the 1875 law was unconstitutional. "It interferes," he said, "with the right of the State of New York to provide the means under which citizens of the State have the power to control and protect their rights in respect to their private property." The assistant United States attorney replied that such a conception of states' rights had been "exploded and superseded long ago." It was unthinkable, he declared, that "the United States could not extend to one citizen of New York a right which the State itself gave to others of its citizens—the right of admission to places of public amusement."

The presiding judge decided to take the constitutional challenge under advisement and referred it to the circuit court, for consideration at its February term. This left the decision up to Justice Samuel Blatchford of the Supreme Court, who was assigned to the circuit court for New York, and District Judge William Choate. The two judges reached opposite conclusions and certified the question to the United States Supreme Court.

Davis' case, under the title of *United States* v. *Singleton*, reached the Supreme Court in 1880. Already lodged on the Court's docket were four similar criminal prosecutions under the act of 1875. *U.S.* v. *Stanley* involved the refusal of Murray Stanley in 1875 to serve a meal at his hotel in Topeka, Kansas, to a Negro, Bird Gee. *U.S.* v. *Nichols* presented the refusal in 1876 of Samuel Nichols, owner of the Nichols House in Jefferson City, Missouri, to accept a Negro named W. H. R. Agee as a guest. *U.S.* v. *Ryan* involved the conduct of Michael Ryan, door-keeper of Maguire's Theatre in San Francisco, in denying a Negro named George M. Tyler entry to the dress circle on January 4, 1876. In *U.S.* v. *Hamilton,* James Hamilton, a conductor on the Nashville, Chattanooga, and St. Louis Railroad, had on April 21, 1879, denied a Negro woman with a first-class ticket access to the ladies' car.

There was a fifth case, with a somewhat different setting. On the evening of May 22, 1879, Mrs. Sallie J. Robinson, a twenty-eight-year-old Negro, purchased two first-class tickets at Grand Junction, Tennessee, for a trip to Lynchburg, Virginia, on the Memphis and Charleston Railroad. Shortly after midnight she and her nephew, Joseph C. Robinson, described as a young Negro "of light complexion, light hair, and light blue eyes," boarded the train and started into the parlor car. The conductor, C. W. Reagin, held Mrs. Robinson back ("bruising her arm and jerking her roughly around," she alleged) and pushed her into the smoker.

A few minutes later, when Joseph informed the conductor that he was Mrs. Robinson's nephew and was a Negro, the conductor looked surprised. In that case, he said, they could go into the parlor car at the next stop. The Robinsons finished the ride in the parlor car but filed complaints with the railroad about their treatment and then sued for $500 under the 1875 act. At the trial, Reagin testified that he had thought Joseph to be a white man with a colored woman, and his experience was that such associations were "for illicit purposes."

Counsel for the Robinsons objected to Reagin's testimony, on the ground that his actions were based on race and constituted no defense. Admitting the constitutionality of the 1875 law for purposes of the trial, the railroad contended that the action of its conductor did not fall within the statute. The district judge ruled that the motive for excluding persons was the decisive issue under the act: if the jury believed that the conductor had acted because he thought Mrs. Robinson "a prostitute travelling with her paramour," whether "well or ill-founded" in that assumption, the exclusion was not because of race and the railroad was not liable. The jury found for the railroad, and the Robinsons appealed.

These, with William Davis' suit against the doorkeeper of New York's Grand Opera House, were the six cases to which the Supreme Court finally turned in 1882. The Justices were presented with a learned and eloquent brief for the United States submitted by Solicitor General Samuel F. Phillips, who reviewed the leading cases, described the history of the Civil War amendments to the Constitution, and stressed the importance to the rights of citizens of equal access to public accommodation. Four times since 1865, Phillips noted, civil-rights legislation had been enacted by a Congress filled with men who had fought in the Civil War and had written the war amendments. These men understood that "every rootlet of slavery has an individual vitality, and, to its minutest hair, should be anxiously followed and plucked up. . . ." They also knew that if the federal government allowed Negroes to be denied accommodation "by persons who notably were sensitive registers of local public opinion," then "what upon yesterday was only 'fact' will become 'doctrine' tomorrow."

The Supreme Court Justices who considered Phillips' brief and the six test cases were uncommonly talented, among them being Chief Justice Morrison R. Waite, a man underrated today; Joseph P. Bradley, that Court's most powerful intellect; and Stephen J. Field, a *laissez-faire* interpreter of American constitutional law. John Marshall Harlan, the youngest man on the Court, had already started on the course which was to mark him as the most frequent and passionate dissenter in the Gilded Age.

As a whole, the Court might have appeared to be one which would have looked favorably on the 1875 act. All were Republicans except Justice Field, and he was a Democrat appointed by Abraham Lincoln. All except Justice Harlan, who was the Court's only southerner, had made their careers primarily in the northern and western states. Without exception, all had supported the northern cause in the war, and none had any hostility toward Negroes as a class.

Yet on the afternoon of October 15, 1883, Justice Bradley announced that the Court found Sections 1 and 2 of the Civil Rights Act of 1875 to be unconstitutional.

(This disposed of five of the cases; the sixth, *U.S.* v. *Hamilton,* was denied review on a procedural point.) There was added irony in the fact that Bradley delivered the majority opinion for eight of the Justices. A one-time Whig, Bradley had struggled for a North-South compromise in the darkening months of 1860–61, then had swung to a strong Unionist position after the firing on Fort Sumter. He had run for Congress on the Lincoln ticket in 1862 and in 1868 headed the New Jersey electors for Grant. When the Thirteenth and Fourteenth Amendments were adopted, he had given them firm support, and his appointment to the Supreme Court by Grant in 1870 had drawn no criticism from friends of the Negro, as had the appointment of John Marshall Harlan seven years later.

Bradley's opinion had a tightly reasoned simplicity. The Thirteenth Amendment forbade slavery and involuntary servitude, he noted, but protection against the restoration of bondage could not be stretched to cover federal regulation of "social" discriminations such as those dealt with in the 1875 statute. As for the Fourteenth Amendment, that was addressed only to deprivations of rights by the *states;* it did not encompass *private* acts of discrimination. Thus there was no source of constitutional authority for "Sumner's law"; it had to be regarded as an unwarranted invasion of an area under state jurisdiction. Even as a matter of policy, Bradley argued, the intention of the war amendments to aid the newly freed Negro had to have some limits. At some point, the Negro must cease to be "the special favorite of the law" and take on "the rank of a mere citizen."

At the Atlanta Opera House on the evening of the Court's decision, the end man of Haverly's Minstrels interrupted the performance to announce the ruling. The entire orchestra and dress circle audience rose and cheered. Negroes sitting in the balcony kept their seats, "stunned," according to one newspaper account. A short time earlier, a Negro denied entrance to the dress circle had filed charges against the Opera House management under the 1875 act. Now his case—their case—was dead.

Of all the nine Justices, only John Marshall Harlan, a Kentuckian and a former slaveholder, announced that he dissented from the ruling. He promised to give a full opinion soon.

Justice Harlan's progress from a supporter of slavery to a civil-rights dissenter makes a fascinating chronicle. Like Bradley, he had entered politics as a Whig and had tried to find a middle road between secessionist Democrats and antislavery Republicans. Like Bradley, he became a Unionist after the firing on Fort Sumter. But there the parallels ended. Although Harlan entered the Union Army, he was totally opposed to freeing the slaves, and his distaste for Lincoln and the Radicals was complete. Between 1863 and 1868, he led the Conservative party in Kentucky, a third-party movement which supported the war but opposed pro-Negro and civil-rights measures as "flagrant invasions of property rights and local government."

By 1868, however, Harlan had become a Republican. The resounding defeat of the Conservatives in the 1867 state elections convinced him that a third party had no future in Kentucky. His antimonopoly views and his general ideas about economic progress conflicted directly with state Democratic policies, and when the Republicans nominated his former field commander, Ulysses S. Grant, for President, in 1868, Harlan was one of the substantial number of Conservatives who joined the G.O.P.

His views on Negro rights also changed at this time. The wave of vigilante activities against white Republicans and Negroes that swept Kentucky in 1868–70, with whippings and murders by the scores, convinced Harlan that federal guarantees were essential. He watched Negroes in Kentucky moving with dignity and skill toward useful citizenship, and his devout Presbyterianism led him to adopt a "brotherhood-of-man" outlook in keeping with his church's national position. Perhaps he may have been influenced by his wife, Mallie, whose parents were New England abolitionists. As a realistic Republican politician, he was also aware that 60,000 Kentucky Negroes would become voters in 1870.

Thus a "new" John Harlan took the stump as Republican gubernatorial candidate in 1871, the year of the Louisville streetcar ride-ins. He opened his rallies by confessing that he had formerly been anti-Negro. But "I have lived long enough," he said, "to feel that the most perfect despotism that ever existed on this earth was the institution of African slavery." The war amendments were necessary "to place it beyond the power of any State to interfere with . . . the results of the war. . . ." The South should stop agitating the race issue, and should turn to rebuilding itself on progressive lines. When the Democrats laughed at "Harlan the Chameleon" and read quotations from his earlier anti-Negro speeches, Harlan replied: "Let it be said that I am right rather than consistent."

Harlan soon became an influential figure in the Republican party and, when President Rutherford B. Hayes decided to appoint a southern Republican to the Supreme Court in 1877, he was a logical choice. Even then, the Negro issue rose to shake Harlan's life again. His confirmation was held up because of doubts by some senators as to his "real" civil-rights views. Only after Harlan produced his speeches between 1871 and 1877 and party leaders supported his firmness on the question was he approved.

Once on the Supreme Court, Harlan could have swung back to a conservative position on civil rights. Instead, he became one of his generation's most intense and uncompromising defenders of the Negro. Perhaps his was the psychology of the convert who defends his new faith more passionately, even more combatively, than the born believer. Harlan liked to think that he had changed because he knew the South and realized that any relaxation of federal protection of the rights of Negroes would encourage the "white irreconcilables" first to acts of discrimination and then to violence, which would destroy all hope of accommodation between the races.

When Harlan sat down in October of 1883 to write his dissent in the *Civil Rights Cases,* he hoped to set off a cannon of protest. But he simply could not get his thoughts on paper. He worked late into the night, and even rose from half-sleep to write down ideas that he was afraid would elude him in the morning. "It was a trying time for him," his wife observed. "In point of years, he was much the youngest man on the Bench; and standing alone, as he did in regard to a decision which the whole nation was anxiously awaiting, he felt that . . . he must speak not only forcibly but wisely." After weeks of drafting and discarding, Harlan seemed to reach a dead end. The dissent would not "write." It was at this point that Mrs. Harlan contributed a dramatic touch to the history of the *Civil Rights Cases*.

When the Harlans had moved to Washington in 1877, the Justice had acquired from a collector the inkstand which Chief Justice Roger Taney had used in writing all his opinions. Harlan was fond of showing this to guests and remarking that "it was the very inkstand from which the infamous *Dred Scott* opinion was written." Early in the 1880s, however, a niece of Taney's, who was engaged in collecting her uncle's effects, visited the Harlans. When she saw the inkstand she asked Harlan for it, and the Justice agreed. The next morning Mrs. Harlan, noting her husband's reluctance to part with his most prized possession, quietly arranged to have the inkstand "lost." She hid it away, and Harlan was forced to make an embarrassed excuse to Taney's niece.

Now, on a Sunday morning, probably early in November of 1883, after Harlan had spent a sleepless night working on his dissent, Mallie Harlan remembered the inkstand. While the Justice was at church, she retrieved it from its hiding place, filled it with a fresh supply of ink and pen points, and placed it on the blotter of his desk. When her husband returned from church, she told him, with an air of mystery, that he would find something special in his study. Harlan was overjoyed to recover his symbolic antique. Mrs. Harlan's gesture was successful, for as she relates:

> The memory of the historic part that Taney's inkstand had played in the Dred Scott decision, in temporarily tightening the shackles of slavery upon the negro race in those ante-bellum days, seemed, that morning, to act like magic in clarifying my husband's thoughts in regard to the law . . . intended by Sumner to protect the recently emancipated slaves in the enjoyment of equal 'civil rights.' His pen fairly flew on that day and, with the running start he then got, he soon finished his dissent.

How directly the recollection of Dred Scott pervaded Harlan's dissent is apparent to anyone who reads the opinion. He began by noting that the pre–Civil War Supreme Court had upheld congressional laws forbidding individuals to interfere with recovery of fugitive slaves. To strike down the act of 1875 meant that "the rights of freedom and American citizenship cannot receive from the Nation that efficient protection which heretofore was unhesitatingly accorded to slavery and the rights of masters."

Harlan argued that the Civil Rights Act of 1875 was constitutional on any one of several grounds. The Thirteenth Amendment had already been held to guarantee "universal civil freedom"; Harlan stated that barring Negroes from facilities licensed by the state and under legal obligation to serve all persons without discrimination restored a major disability of slavery days and violated that civil freedom. As for the Fourteenth Amendment, its central purpose had been to extend national citizenship to the Negro, reversing the precedent upheld in the Dred Scott decision; its final section gave Congress power to pass appropriate legislation to enforce that affirmative grant as well as to enforce the section barring any state action which might deny liberty or equality. Now, the Supreme Court was deciding what legislation was appropriate and necessary for those purposes, although that decision properly belonged to Congress.

Even under the "State action" clause of the Fourteenth Amendment, Harlan continued, the 1875 act was constitutional; it was well established that "railroad corporations, keepers of inns and managers of places of public accommodation are agents or instrumentalities of the State." Finally, Harlan attacked the unwillingness of the Court's majority to uphold the public-carrier section of the act under Congress' power to regulate interstate trips. That was exactly what was involved in Mrs. Robinson's case against the Memphis and Charleston Railroad, he reminded his colleagues; it had not been true before that Congress had had to cite the section of the Constitution on which it relied.

In his peroration, Harlan replied to Bradley's comment that Negroes had been made "a special favorite of the law." The war amendments had been passed not to "favor" the Negro, he declared, but to include him as "part of the people for whose welfare and happiness government is ordained."

> Today, it is the colored race which is denied, by corporations and individuals wielding public authority, rights fundamental in their freedom and citizenship. At some future time, it may be that some other race will fall under the ban of race discrimination. If the constitutional amendments be enforced, according to the intent with which, as I conceive, they were adopted, there cannot be in this republic, any class of human beings in practical subjection to another class. . . .

The *Civil Rights Cases* ruling did two things. First, it destroyed the delicate balance of federal guarantee, Negro protest, and private enlightenment which was producing a steadily widening area of peacefully integrated public facilities in the North and South during the 1870s and early 1880s. Second, it had an immediate and profound effect on national and state politics as they related to the Negro. By denying Congress power to protect the Negro's rights to equal treatment, the Supreme Court wiped the issue of civil rights from the Republican party's agenda of national responsibility. At the same time, those southern political leaders who saw anti-Negro politics as the most promising avenue to power could now rally the "poor whites" to the banner of segregation.

If the Supreme Court had stopped with the *Civil Rights Cases* of 1883, the situation of Negroes would have been bad but not impossible. Even in the South, there was no immediate imposition of segregation in public facilities. During the late 1880s, Negroes could be found sharing places with whites in many southern restaurants, streetcars, and theatres. But increasingly, Democratic and Populist politicians found the Negro an irresistible target. As Solicitor General Phillips had warned the Supreme Court, what had been tolerated as the "fact" of discrimination was now being translated into "doctrine": between 1887 and 1891, eight southern states passed laws requiring railroads to separate all white and Negro passengers. The Supreme Court upheld these laws in the 1896 case of *Plessy* v. *Ferguson*. Then in the Berea College case of 1906, it upheld laws forbidding private schools to educate Negro and white children together. Both decisions aroused Harlan's bitter dissent.

In the next fifteen or twenty years, the chalk line of Jim Crow was drawn across virtually every area of public contact in the South.

Today, as this line is slowly and painfully being erased, we may do well to reflect on what might have been in the South if the Civil Rights Act of 1875 had been upheld, in whole or in part. Perhaps everything would have been the same. Perhaps forces at work between 1883 and 1940 were too powerful for a Supreme Court to hold in check. Perhaps "Sumner's law" was greatly premature. Yet it is difficult to believe that total, state-enforced segregation was inevitable in the South after the 1880s. If in these decades the Supreme Court had taken the same *laissez-faire* attitude toward race relations as it took toward economic affairs, voluntary integration would have survived as a countertradition to Jim Crow and might have made the transition of the 1950s less painful than it was. At the very least, one cannot help thinking that Harlan was a better sociologist than his colleagues and a better southerner than the "irreconcilables." American constitutional history has a richer ring to it because of the protest that John Marshall Harlan finally put down on paper from Roger Taney's inkwell in 1883.

TEXT CREDITS

ILLUSTRATION CREDITS

240   Photograph Copyright B. A. Cohen, Photographer

245   Library of Congress

249   *Departure of Seventh Regiment from New York,* M. and M. Karolik Collection of American Watercolors and Drawings, 1800–1875, Courtesy, Museum of Fine Arts, Boston

260   *John Brown Going to His Hanging* by Horace Pippin, 1942. Oil on canvas, 24⅛ × 30¼ in. Acc. no.: 1943.11. Courtesy of the Pennsylvania Academy of the Fine Arts, Philadelphia. John Lambert Fund

269   Stone Mountain Park, Georgia

276   Library of Congress

287   Culver Pictures, Inc.

294   Library of Congress